Russia's Frozen Frontier

Russia's Frozen Frontier

A History of Siberia and the Russian Far East 1581–1991

Alan Wood

BLOOMSBURY ACADEMIC

First published in 2011 by:

Bloomsbury Academic

An imprint of Bloomsbury Publishing Plc
36 Soho Square, London W1D 3QY, UK
and
175 Fifth Avenue, New York, NY 10010, USA

Copyright © Alan Wood 2011

CIP records for this book are available from the British Library
and the Library of Congress.

ISBN 978-0-34097-124-6 (hardback)
ISBN 978-1-84966-025-9 (ebook)

This book is produced using paper that is made from wood grown in
managed, sustainable forests. It is natural, renewable and recyclable.
The logging and manufacturing processes conform to the
environmental regulations of the country of origin.

Printed and bound in Great Britain by the MPG Books Group, Bodmin, Cornwall.

www.bloomsburyacademic.com

To the memory of my late parents,
Tom and Doris

Contents

Illustrations

Maps

Preface

In 1985, the late Stuart Kirby, veteran British scholar of what he liked to call 'SIBFE' (Siberia and the Far East) wrote: 'The Russian literature specifically on Siberia would fill a large modern library, the non-Russian at most a few shelves.'[1] Since he wrote those words 25 years ago, the situation regarding western studies of Siberia has changed considerably. There has been published a range of erudite monographs and anthologies analysing various aspects of Siberia's history, exploration, economic resources, environment and indigenous peoples (see 'Suggestions for Further Reading'). In 1981, a unique, multidisciplinary academic journal entitled *Sibirica*, devoted to research on all aspects of Siberia's rich history and culture, was founded, first edited by the present author and now taken over by a team of experts based at the University of Aberdeen in Scotland. However, despite the increased number of specialized investigations of 'Russia's Frozen Frontier', much of them connected with its crucial role as a colony exploited for its natural resources, there still exists an alarming amount of public ignorance about what is one of the world's most enormous territorial-administrative regions, and the source and depository of boundless subterranean and surface wealth. At the risk of making an overgeneralization, when one speaks to people either in a university senior common room or in the local village pub, Siberia – its location, its size, its global significance – is as much known about or understood as life in Tiruchirapalli, Tierra del Fuego or Timbuktu. As far as I know at the time of writing, not a single undergraduate university course specifically on the history and culture of Siberia exists anywhere in the Western world.

This book seeks to dispel something of that miasma of ignorance and misconception surrounding this vast expanse of the planet's land-surface, its fascinating history, its natural environment and – most importantly – the peoples who live, or have lived and died, there. The methodology and approach I have adopted here is very much influenced by the great nineteenth-century Siberian regionalist writer and scholar, Nikolai Mikhailovich Yadrintsev, whose work and that of his fellow *oblastniki* (regionalists) is discussed in Chapter Four. The core of Yadrintsev's thesis was that right from the 'conquest' of Siberia by Russian cossacks in the late sixteenth century the territory, its natural reserves and its indigenous peoples were ruthlessly and recklessly exploited for the benefit of the autocratic, tsarist government located in European Russia. The whole political, social and economic history of Russia has been marked, like that of other nations, by what was defined by Karl Marx and Friedrich Engels as 'the history of class struggles'.[2] In the case of relations between the European-based metropolitan centre of the Russian Empire and its north Asian provinces of Siberia, the peripheral yet fabulously profitable possessions over the Urals, the notion – and the actuality – of social struggle between the lower and the ruling classes, known in Russian as the *nizy* and the *verkhi*, were overlaid by a continuing conflict between the Kremlin or the Winter Palace on the one hand, and the increasingly resentful inhabitants, both native and immigrant, of the continent beyond the Urals. Indeed, the very term 'beyond the Urals' to describe Siberia betokens an obviously Eurocentric view of the place. After all, if one looks at it from the Siberian, i.e. Eastern, perspective, 'beyond the Urals' signifies not Asiatic, but European Russia. Over the centuries since the original Russian conquest and subsequent colonization of the territory, the Siberians (*sibiryaki*), including both the aboriginal peoples and the Slavic incomers who later became known as the *starozhily* (old inhabitants), gradually developed a sense of their own specific regional identity, and even nationality, with their own specific interests that challenged those of Muscovite and Imperial Russia. (The situation is very similar to that of European refugees, migrants and intruders who crossed the Atlantic and began to call themselves 'Americans'.) It is hoped that the contents and arguments of this book will substantiate Yadrintsev's hypothesis of 'Siberia as a Colony' – the title of his magisterial work published in 1881.

A mixture of chronological and thematic approaches has been adopted, starting with a description of the geophysical environment of Siberia and the Far East, and moving on through an analysis of Slavonic incursions – military, mercenary and scientific expeditions – across the Urals from the late sixteenth century up to the dying decades of the Russian Empire. Two separate chapters are devoted to the plight of the Siberian aboriginal peoples, and to the history of the notorious Siberian exile system. A whole section deals with the building of the great Trans-Siberian Railroad. The final chapters address the revolutions of 1917 and the ensuing Civil War, of which Siberia and the Far East were the major theatre, the development of Siberia during the period of Stalin's dictatorship, including the infamous labour-camp operation – the GULag – and the years following his death in 1953 until the collapse of the Soviet Union in 1991. A brief afterword follows, indicating the role of Siberia and the Russian Far East in the early twenty-first century, and possible future political and economic developments in this gigantic and important area of 'Russia's Frozen Frontier'.

Acknowledgements

The number of people who have supported, advised and encouraged me in my study of Russian and Siberian history and culture over the years is legion. Some have been passing, though valuable, acquaintances. Others are long-standing and very dear friends and close colleagues. In particular, I still remain much indebted to my tutors at Oxford University in the early 1960s and at Moscow and Leningrad State Universities in the late 1960s, and to a whole range of scholars in the UK, the USA, Canada, France and, of course, the old USSR and the Russian Federation ever since. Sadly, many of these – John Fennell, Eugene Lampert, Anne Pennington, A.P. Okladnikov, S.F. Koval – are now deceased, but their inspiration still remains. I would also like to acknowledge the contribution made to the study of Siberia by the members of the British Universities Siberian Studies Seminar, the first conference of which was held at Lancaster University, UK, in 1981, and the latest at the Far Eastern Division of the Russian Academy of Sciences in Vladivostok in 2006. In Russia I have benefited from the warm comradeship and outstanding scholarship of Sergei Savoskul, Albina Girfanova, Nikolai Sukhachev, the late Leonid Goryushkin, Vladimir Shishkin and a whole gallery of historians, librarians, archivists and writers in Moscow, St Petersburg, Novosibirsk, Barnaul, Irkutsk, Bratsk, Khabarovsk, Krasnoyarsk, Tura and Vladivostok. To all of you – *bol'shoe spasibo*.

On the editorial staff at Hodder Arnold, which first commissioned this work, Tamsin Smith and Liz Wilson were unswervingly supportive; and at Bloomsbury, which has now taken over publication, Emily Salz, Emily Gibson, Fiona Cairns and Lacey Decker have been magnificent in their assistance, encouragement and patience when my writing schedule was interrupted by recurring illness. Many thanks to Howard Watson for his copy-editing.

Several distinguished scholars and friends have been kind enough to read through either individual chapters or in some cases the whole text of the book while it was in preparation. To Professors Victor Mote, David Shotter, Mike Kirkwood and John Walton, and to Doctors John Swift, Michael Perrins, Sarah Badcock and Jenny Brine (*bibliothécaire extraordinaire*), to my sister, Sylvia Bosworth, and, of course, to my wife, Iris, I am extremely grateful for their thoughtful comments, suggestions, criticisms and queries. I share with them responsibility for any remaining errors or infelicities.

Finally, this book is dedicated to the memory of my late parents, Tom and Doris Wood, who followed my school, university and early academic career with a judicious medley of encouragement, puzzlement and intelligent neglect.

Alan Wood

Notes on the Text

(1) Transliteration of Russian technical terms and names of people and places is according to the Library of Congress system, with some emendations. Cyrillic initial letters Е, Ю and Я are rendered as Ye, Yu and Ya. The character й is transliterated as i. The 'soft sign' has been omitted, except in italicized transliterations of various institutions, technical terms, titles of books, etc.

(2) All Russian forenames and patronymics are given in the system noted above (e.g. Aleksandr, Mikhail and Yekaterina), except in the case where anglicized forms are more familiar (e.g. Tsar Nicholas II, Peter the Great, Empress Elizabeth).

(3) The stressed phoneme 'ye', pronounced 'yo', is represented throughout with a diaeresis – 'ё'; thus Dezhnёv, pronounced Dezhnyov.

(4) Dates. From January 1700 until February 1918, Russia used the Julian calendar, which in the eighteenth century was 11 days, in the nineteenth century 12 days, and in the early twentieth century 13 days behind the Gregorian calendar used in the West. Dates given before February 1918 are according to the Julian calendar (Old Style, O.S.) and thereafter the Gregorian (New Style, N.S.).

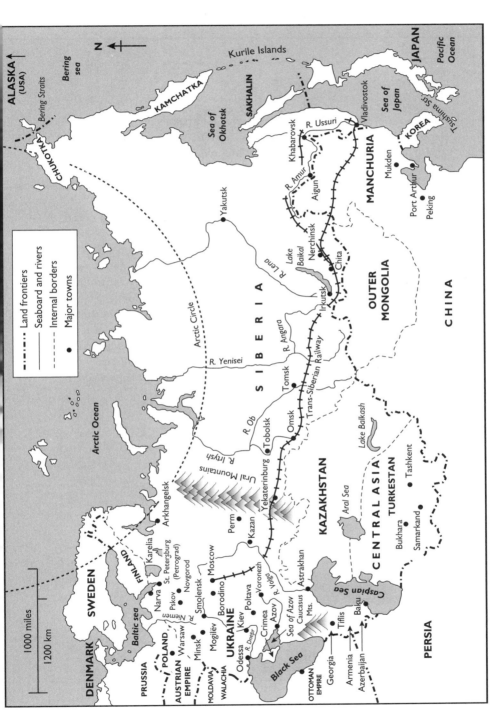

Map 1 The Russian Empire and Siberia: late nineteenth and early twentieth centuries.

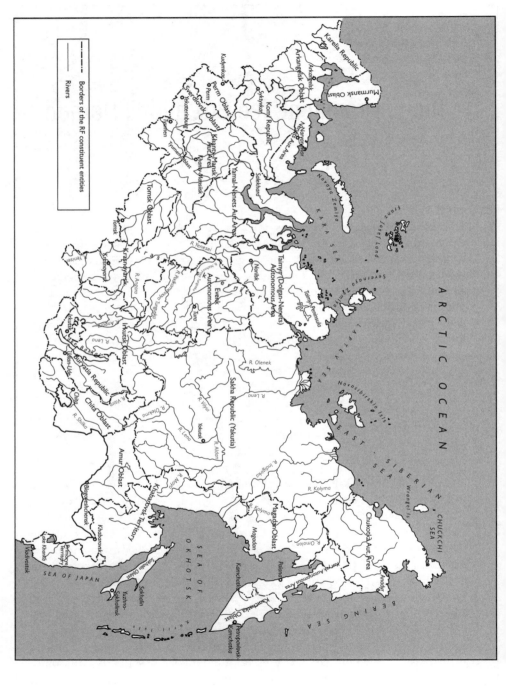

Map 2   Territorial-administrative divisions of Siberia, the Russian north and the Far East, with major towns, as of 2005.

1

The Environment: Ice-Box and El Dorado

Siberia is a word that conjures up a number of stereotypical images in the minds of Russians and non-Russians alike. And the images are seldom complimentary. It is almost invariably conceived of, and perceived as, a vast wilderness of ice and snow, a land of perpetual winter, sub-zero temperatures and blinding blizzards set on a gigantic, continent-sized subterranean iceberg of permanently frozen ground – the permafrost or, in Russian, *merzlota*. For a majority of people it is equally notorious as a place of banishment, exile, forced labour and imprisonment, a forbidding, barren land dotted with prison camps denizened by millions of the wretched victims of Russian central authoritarianism – convicts, criminals, enemies of the state, enemies of the people, forced labourers and *zeks* (prison slang for *zaklyuchënnyi*, a prisoner). Siberia has become a byword, an almost proverbial touchstone, for extremes of cold, incarceration and sheer human suffering. In the evocative words of an early twentieth-century British traveller, John Foster Fraser: 'The very word Siberia is one to make the blood run chill. It smells of fetters in the snow.'[1] This grim mental picture is sometimes supplemented by vague notions of dense interminable forests, salt mines, the Trans-Siberian Railroad, big, brown bears, woolly mammoths, reindeer, mystic shamans and a few Eskimos.

In fact, most of these hackneyed images are pretty well justified, but they are only part – if a significant part – of the total picture. Siberia does contain some of the coldest spots on planet earth; it does have long, cruel and bitter winters; and since the end of the sixteenth century right until the present day it has been used by Russia's rulers as a place of punishment and exile. The frozen mammoths, bears, reindeer, shamans, Eskimos and the Trans-Siberian Railroad are all real – though the salt mines are a bit of a myth.

It is also a land which possesses literally immeasurable natural resources – animal, vegetable and especially mineral – which has earned it such epithets as 'a treasure trove on ice' and 'Russia's El Dorado'. From early Muscovite times, that is, during the sixteenth and seventeenth centuries, when a substantial portion the state's economy was dependent on the Siberian fur trade, right through to the twenty-first century when a considerable amount of the Russian Federation's income now relies on the export of huge quantities of oil and natural gas to other parts of the world, Siberia has been consistently exploited as a resource-rich frontier on which the metropolitan powers have always depended. Indeed, the great eighteenth-century Russian polymath, Mikhail Vasilevich Lomonosov (1711–65) – among his other talents a student of Russia's Arctic north – accurately predicted that: 'Through Siberia and the Northern Ocean shall the might (*moguchestvo*) of Russia grow.'[2] This observation became something of a mantra adorning the walls of Soviet science schoolrooms until the 1980s. However, the vast distances, the often vicious climate and the harsh terrain have posed – and still pose – tremendous problems in the acquisition, extraction and exploitation of these fabulous riches, as will be seen.

In contrast to the punitive image of Siberia as 'a land of damnation and chains' or 'a vast roofless prison' (see Chapter Six), it has at the same time also been regarded paradoxically as a land of freedom and opportunity for those wishing to escape centralized officialdom, religious persecution or serfdom, or simply seek their fortune. Over the centuries literally millions of voluntary settlers or fugitives flocked to take advantage of Siberia's boundless vistas, comparatively free from the stifling bureaucratism and oppression of Moscow or St Petersburg. Apart from the fur hunters, merchants, religious dissidents, service personnel (both civil and military) and others in the early decades of Muscovy's penetration of Siberia – whose story will be addressed in the following chapters – in more recent times, the tsarist government, under the Prime Ministership of Pëtr Arkadeevich Stolypin (1862–1911; Prime Minister 1906–11) offered massive financial and other incentives for Russian and Ukrainian peasants to migrate beyond the Urals. This turned southern Siberia into one of the empire's most productive and lucrative agricultural regions (see Chapter Seven). Moving on, in the post-Second World War period, Siberia became a major focus for scientific exploration and development as new, prestigious research centres – such as Akademgorodok near Novosibirsk – were established. These young academic institutions attracted hundreds of the country's leading scientists and scholars to Siberia, where they contributed enthusiastically to the further investigation, discovery and exploitation of the territory's vast resources, in particular oil and natural gas, which are still today such a crucial factor in the whole nation's economy.[3] This process, along with other cultural and industrial developments, has been described as the 'Third Discovery of Siberia'.[4]

Also, during the 1960s, 1970s and 1980s, thousands of young Soviet men and women from European Russia were lured to live and work in the booming economic development of Siberia, attracted by various inducements such as the so-called 'northern increment', which guaranteed them far higher wages and both vocational and vacational perks in comparison with employment in their original localities to the west of the Urals. However, as will be argued in Chapter Ten, the huge costs of building the required infrastructure – transport, housing, heating, utilities, social amenities, etc. – for the new generation of mainly youthful immigrants meant in fact that attempts to develop Siberia's industrial base (in both the extractive and manufacturing sectors) to the benefit of the entire USSR proved to be an overall burden on the total Soviet economy, and have left a somewhat negative legacy to the Soviet Union's successor state.[5]

All of these themes will be investigated in the following pages, but this initial chapter concerns itself with Siberia's physical, geographical environment, beginning with a discussion of its size and its notorious climate.

SIZE

Siberia is the name historically given to the huge territory of northern Asia stretching from the low-lying Ural Mountains in the west (the conventional dividing line between European and Asiatic Russia) to the Pacific littoral in the east, and from the Arctic Ocean in the north to the borders of Central Asia, Mongolia and China in the south. In the Arctic seas (the Kara, Laptev, East-Siberian and Chukotka) it includes the islands of Novaya Zemlya (New Land), Novosibirskie (New Siberian) and Wrangel Island; and in the Far East, the island of Sakhalin lying north of Japan, and the Aleutian and Kurile archipelagos. During the centuries of Moscow's and St Petersburg's dominance over the territory, it has undergone a number of different administrative appellations and designations.

Unfortunately, in recent times the traditional historical, geographical and political boundaries of Siberia have been bureaucratically muddled by a redefinition of the region's sub-units which took place in the year 2000. These changes – including the amalgamation of some of the most westerly areas of Siberia into what is nowadays classified as the Urals Federal District – rather complicates the issue of just what actually constitutes Siberia. Boundaries have shifted, names have been changed and the governance of the so-called 'federal subjects' (i.e. political-administrative sub-units of the Russian Federation) has altered. Since May 2000, the whole territory (now including the Urals) has been divided into the three administrative entities officially known as the Urals Federal District (*Ural'skii federal'nyi okrug*), the Siberian Federal District (*Sibirskii federal'nyi okrug*) and the Far Eastern Federal District (*Dal'nevostochnyi federal'nyi okrug*). However, for the purposes of the present study, in strictly geographical terms what follows throughout this chapter adheres to the administrative boundaries of what – pre-2000 – were called West Siberia, East Siberia and the Far East, as described in the 22-volume geographical encyclopaedia of the Soviet Union published between 1969 and 1971.[6]

Excluding the Urals provinces, historical Siberia is one-and-a-half times larger than the United States of America and one-and-a-third times larger than Canada. It covers an area of over 13 million square kilometres (5 million square miles) and accounts for more than one-twelfth of the planet's entire land surface. The Russian Far Eastern District alone is bigger than the continent of Australia, and all three territories sprawl over eight different time zones. From Moscow to Vladivostok via the Trans-Siberian Railroad is a distance of 9,000 kilometres (5,592 miles) and takes more than a week to travel even when the trains are running on time.[7] North-south, the distance between the Arctic coastline to the borderlands of Kazakhstan and Mongolia is over 3,000 kilometres (c.1,860 miles).

These enormous distances over difficult terrain, and the consequent problems of transport, communication and supply, have naturally had palpable effects on the human settlement and economic exploitation of the region, and still cause problems which, despite the development of air transport, fuel pipelines and other modern technological advances, have not been fully overcome to the present day. These topics will be returned to in later chapters. As recently as the 1940s, enclaves of tiny communities of religious schismatics (Old Believers) were discovered living in the remote depths of the Siberian forests – the mighty *taiga* (forest – see below) – people whose existence was previously unknown, and who had dwelt there since the seventeenth century in a kind of time-warp, and in total ignorance of events in the wider world. (It is not recorded whether the Soviet authorities extracted from them any tax arrears.) Extensive forest-fires – not infrequent occurrences – which can destroy huge areas of timberland as large as, say, Wales or Belgium, though obviously massively destructive, do not necessarily have a terminally disastrous impact on the total woodland ecology. Such is the sheer enormousness of this vast landmass that it has been estimated that a detailed aerial photographic survey of the territory covering 1,500 square kilometres (580 square miles) a day would take 15 years to complete.[8] East Siberia also boasts the world's deepest and – in liquid volume – largest lake, Baikal, which has a unique ecosystem and contains no less than one-fifth of the planet's fresh water supply (around 23,000 cubic kilometres/5,500 cubic miles). It is fed by over 300 rivers and streams, but emptied by only one outlet, the great Angara river at the lake's southern tip, near the city of Irkutsk. In a fanciful, hypothetical calculation, it has been estimated that, if all current water supplies dried up or were cut off, and the Angara continued to empty at its present hourly volume, to drain the entire lake would take over 300 years. These are no hyperborean hyperboles: simply statistical facts of the geography of Russia's huge frozen frontier. Further information on Baikal is given in the section on East Siberia, below.

Apart from its size, the other two major distinguishing features of the Siberian physical environment are its extremes of climate and the great diversity of its landscape and natural features. Despite the fact that large areas of tundra, swampland or seemingly endless forests are marked by a monotonous uniformity, it is inconceivable that such a large slice of the earth's land surface should display any kind of topographical homogeneity. The subject of regional geographical, geological and vegetational variety will be dealt with below. But first, the climate.

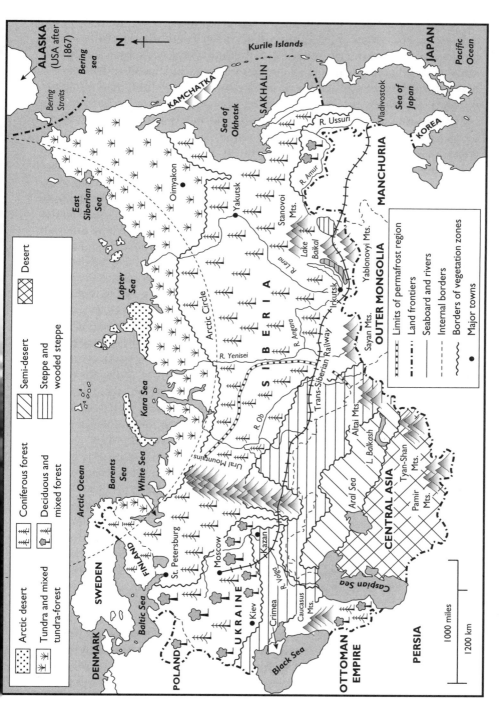

Map 3 Russia and Siberia: climatic and vegetational zones.

CLIMATE

All three geographical regions of Siberia, as defined above, are marked by extreme continentality of climate, of which the most notorious features are the long, harsh winters and the intense cold.[9] The two obvious reasons for this are Siberia's location in the high northern latitudes – much of it beyond 60 degrees north, including a huge portion above the Arctic Circle – and the vastness of its landmass, which means that many regions are too remote to benefit from the moderating influences of the oceans to the west, east and south. Strong, icy gales blowing along and inland from the almost permanently ice-bound Arctic coast also increase the wind-chill factor, and in the south high mountain ranges prevent warm air flowing in from the Indian Ocean and adjacent seas. On the other hand, large parts of Siberia's southern regions lie on the same degree of latitude as more temperate European cities. Irkutsk, for instance, near the southern end of Lake Baikal, lies roughly on the same latitude as Birmingham, UK, while the Far Eastern port city of Vladivostok is approximately on that of Marseille, on the Mediterranean coast of France, and Rome.

In general, the degree of continentality and the severity of the climate increase the further east and north one travels. Indeed, there are meteorological data that demonstrate that eastwards progression is as important in accounting for temperature reduction as northwards. For instance, journeying east along a line from Yekaterinburg in the Urals to the Sea of Okhotsk, without deviating to the north, one would pass through a series of isotherms (longitudinal belts of equal temperature) representing a progressive drop in temperature of around 20°C.[10] In Yakutia (now known as Sakha) in the far north-east, for instance, winter regularly lasts for up to eight months a year, with an average January temperature of −43°C and over 205 days of annual snow cover. Further north, beyond the Arctic Circle, the town of Verkhoyansk records a mean (a *really* mean) January temperature of almost −50°C, with an annual snow cover of 223 days, and only 69 frost-free days per year. But the prize for extreme frigidity must go to the small settlement of Oimyakon, situated in a depression on the Indigirka river, many kilometres *south* of the Arctic Circle, where temperatures of below −70°C are not uncommon, even without taking the wind-chill factor into account, hence its designation as the northern hemisphere's 'pole of cold'. In other words, outside Antarctica, it is the coldest spot on earth. However, if one does take in the wind-chill element, around the far northern coastal areas, where air conditions are less stable than deep inland, the freezing Arctic winds can produce temperature equivalents of as low as −130°C in the eastern parts. Even in western Siberia, where actual temperatures are significantly higher (Surgut, for example, centre of the oil and gas industry, has an average January temperature of a balmy −22°C), the added-on effects of wind-chill make working and living conditions extremely unpleasant and perilous. Also multiplying the climatic hazards of life in Siberia are such natural phenomena as freezing fog, monsoons on the Pacific coast, ferocious blizzards (*purgi*), gale-force winds and airborne ice crystals caused by rising moisture from inhabited localities meeting the extremely cold air layers. Breath freezes, eyelids gelate, frostbite attacks the extremities, and, not surprisingly, urinating and defecating in the open can be quite a nasty experience. In the words of the Afghani novelist, Khaled Hosseini: 'if you fling snot in Siberia, it's a green icicle before it hits the ground'.[11]

Things are rather different during the short, hot summers, and the range in differences between winter and summer temperatures is often quite dramatic. Even Verkhoyansk, at a latitude way north of the Arctic Circle and almost a thousand kilometres (620 miles) due north-east of Yakutsk, has a median July temperature of around 16°C, and in the southern steppelands of west Siberia, summer temperatures average out at 23°C. On the borders of south-west Siberia and Kazakhstan, periods of severe aridity and drought are not uncommon. The greatest extremes are to be found in the Far East, where the climate differs according to elevation, latitude and the effects of the Pacific Ocean air currents. Rates of annual precipitation in its coastal regions are far higher than elsewhere in the Russian Federation, mainly as a result of the heavy monsoon rains, which offset the clemency of the relatively mild summers. In this most easterly region of Russia, temperatures vary from the freezing winter colds of Yakutia/Sakha to the congenial summer and even autumnal warmth of the seaside resorts of the southern maritime region, where people regularly swim and sunbathe in the sea and on the sands close to Vladivostok as late as September and early October, and where even grapevines grow. Indeed, such are the climatic attractions of the region that since the collapse of the Soviet Union the increased costs of long-haul internal travel has led to a boom in so-called 'rogue tourism' in the Primorskii district – i.e. campers and picnickers from the local population spending their weekends and holidays around the nearby beaches with a significantly deleterious effect on the environment. For example, the number of local holidaymakers visiting Vostok Bay (a secondary bay of Peter the Great Bay in the Sea of Japan) rose from 20,000 in the summer of 2001 to 45,000 in 2003, with a consequent growth in the incidence of pollution in the temperate coastal waters due to the effects on the marine ecology of non-disposed rubbish, non-biodegradable waste and human sewage.[12] Elsewhere, the high temperatures of the brief Siberian summers – particularly around rivers, swamps and waterfalls – also bring their own particular torments in the shape of plagues of mosquitoes, midges and other morbific flying insects and arachnids, including the often deadly tick (kleshch).

Both ice and snow are obviously major features of Siberia's winter climate and landscape. From the Arctic Ocean down to Lake Baikal and along the territory's mighty river system, the water surfaces are frozen for most of the year. It is only in the last half-century or so that the Northern Sea Route from north European Russia, say, Murmansk or Arkhangelsk, eastwards along the coastline and through the Bering Strait to the ports of the Far East, has been kept open throughout the year by powerful ice-breakers, some of them nuclear-powered, such as the prototype Lenin, commissioned in 1959.[13]

Siberia's great rivers, such as the Ob, the Yenisei and the Lena are ice-bound for six or seven months per year, and longer in their lower, northern reaches than the upper. The lower Ob, for instance, which together with its tributary, the Irtysh, is the fifth longest river system in the world and the longest in Russia, freezes over in mid-October and stays frozen for an average of 220 days. On the upper stretches the period is around 150 days – the consequent two-month time-lag causing the melt waters of the southern Ob to flood the adjacent lowlands. A largely similar pattern of freeze and thaw applies to the other Siberian rivers, which during the winter are turned into long ice-roads which can support heavy motorized vehicles, and form an important part of the internal transport and communication system.

Lake Baikal, in south-eastern Siberia, does not freeze over until mid-December, but remains so until May in the southern parts, and June in the north. The thickness of the ice varies from 0.7 metres to almost 2 metres (27 to 79 inches), and, like the rivers, can carry heavy vehicles. In fact, during the Russo-Japanese War (1904–5), in order to expedite the transportation of military equipment to the battlefronts, a railway track was built across the ice, as the lake was not navigable, even using ice-breakers, and the road around Baikal's southern tip was too treacherous to negotiate.

The track was 42 versts (44.5 kilometres; 1 *versta* = 1.06 kilometres) in length, had telegraph wires and electric lights running parallel to it, and was even served by a station half-way across, appropriately named 'Seredina' (Middle), with first-, second-, and third-class buffet bars! During the brief period of its operation, five trains per day with carriages containing in total 16,000 passengers and 500,000 puds (8,190,000 kilograms; 1 *pud* = 16.38 kilograms or 36.1 pounds) of freight were hauled across the frozen waters of Baikal by teams of horses numbering 3,000 in all.[14] The reason for the use of draft horsepower was that the ice had shattered under the weight of the first locomotive engine to be tested on the frozen surface. Other engines were thereafter dismantled and transported in pieces to the other side on the horse-drawn wagons and then reassembled to continue the journey to the front. As the American scholar, Victor Mote – one of the West's leading experts on Siberia – has remarked: 'What a way to win a war! (Needless to say, they did not.)'[15] In fact Russia's enormous hinterland has worked both to the country's advantage and disadvantage in times of war. Both Napoleon in 1812 and Hitler in Russia's 'Great Fatherland War' between 1941 and 1945 were defeated as much by insurmountable problems of climate and distance as by the dogged fighting power of the country's armed forces. On the other hand, a major contributing factor to Russia's defeat in both the Crimean War (1853–5) and the Russo-Japanese War (1904–5) was the logistical difficulty of transporting men and military equipment to the scene of battle over such huge distances and daunting terrain of their *own* territory.

Almost all of Siberia is covered in snow from around October to April or May, though the depth and length of cover varies from region to region. The greatest depths (over 80 centimetres/32 inches) are found in the central Yenisei valley, and the longest cover (around 280 days per year) is along the Arctic coast. By contrast, Vladivostok in the south averages only about

80 days of snow a year. While facilitating limited travel by sledge, dog-sleigh or motorized 'snowmobile', very deep drifts can seriously impede mobility, totally cut off communities for weeks on end, and even add to mortality rates with people dying after losing their way, being 'marooned' and succumbing to hypothermia, their frozen bodies being buried beneath further snowfalls, only to emerge during the spring thaws. These emerging cadavers are engagingly known locally as 'snowdrops' (*podsnezhniki*).

It really goes without saying that the sub-zero temperatures and Siberia's legendary extremes of cold create a very inhospitable, fierce, debilitating and dangerous environment in which to attempt to live, settle and survive. Indeed, one may speculate why anyone would want to go there in the first place. This thought is articulated by Victor Mote who, in an article enumerating 'the geographic extent of problematic environments [and] the physical constraints to the development of Siberia', concludes that: 'The obstacles are so great that one wonders why Siberia should be developed for any permanent settlement at all.' Among the obstacles described by Professor Mote are the literally steel-shattering effects on machinery, engines and vehicles; frozen fuel; the greatly reduced efficiency and productivity of the human body and its capacity – or incapacity – to work under such atrocious conditions; the enormous costs of maintaining and repairing equipment; the difficulties in obtaining spares; the necessity of using special building materials; loss of working time due to illness, inebriation and the need to take regular breaks in order to warm up; and the greatly enhanced prices of even subsistence living. Mote calculates that: 'In an average year, total losses to cold comprise 33 per cent of all possible working time in the Soviet North.'[16] Of course, it is not only the desperately low temperatures, but also the effects of snowstorms and freezing gale-force winds that make outdoor, manual work almost impossible at times. Readers familiar with Alexander Solzhenitsyn's celebrated, but overrated, novella, *One Day in the Life of Ivan Denisovich*, will remember the harrowing description of a brigade of convict labourers struggling against the elements to build a power-station in sub-zero temperatures with frozen sand, frozen water and frozen mortar.[17]

In the final analysis, because of the use of differing indices, the application of complex, algebraic calculating aids such as the 'temperature per capita' (TPC) factor, regional variations and fluctuating government policies, it is almost impossible to arrive at any kind of accurate, sustainable, overall estimate of the total 'cost of cold' to Siberia's economy and society – indeed to that of Russia as a whole.[18] What is certain is that the stark, icy, awesome reality of Siberia's winter climate lives up to its infamous, bone-chilling reputation.

THE REGIONS OF SIBERIA

West Siberia

The most westerly former administrative unit of Siberia, though the smallest of the three, nevertheless covers an area of 2.5 million square kilometres, or

1 million square miles, from the Yamal Peninsula in the north to the mountain-ous Altai in the south, and from the Urals in the west to the river Yenisei at its eastern edge. Around 80 per cent of the region is taken up by the Great West Siberian Plain, one of the largest flatland expanses in the world, which drains into the Arctic Ocean via the great Ob-Irtysh river system. In the far north, the tundra zone stretches for hundreds of kilometres south from the Kara Sea. Vegetation here is confined to primitive lichens and mosses, and sparsely scat-tered dwarf bushes. Agricultural production is virtually impossible. Reindeer husbandry, hunting and fishing were, and for some still are, the traditional pursuits of the indigenous peoples of this region – predominantly the Khanty, Mansi and Nentsy (formerly known by Russians as the Ostyaks, Voguls and Samoeds – see Chapter Five). The discovery and exploitation of huge natural gas and oil deposits since the 1950s and 1960s has transformed north-western Siberia into one of the most important economic areas of the former Soviet Union and has led to a massive influx of population, the growth of new urban settlements, and the construction of communications and delivery networks. The town of Surgut, one of the first Russian settlements in western Siberia, founded in 1594 as a fortress close to the banks of the Ob, is now the virtual capital of the local oil industry with a population in 2002 of 285,000.

The oil and gas fields reach further south into the immense swamp-and-forest zone of the taiga, which covers roughly two-thirds of western Siberia. Here, thin top-soil, geological concavity caused by pre-historic glacial move-ment and poor drainage have created huge areas of bogland, such as the great Vasyugan swamp in the Ob basin, where the establishment of drilling stations, transport and pipeline networks – not to mention living and working conditions – are fraught with major difficulties. Apart from the principal waterways, the basin is criss-crossed by thousands of small rivers and streams, and drenched with the waters of around 50,000 lakes. Needless to say, it suf-fers from severe annual flooding. In the 1950s and 1960s the Soviet planning authorities came up with ambitious, futuristic schemes to divert some of west Siberia's superabundance of water southwards in order to irrigate the arid regions of Central Asia. These plans were eventually abandoned for practical and ecological reasons, though the idea occasionally resurfaces in the press and technical literature.

The southern half of the West Siberian Plain is covered by three extensive areas of fertile lowland known as the Ishim, the Baraba and the Kulunda steppes. In contrast to the grimmer northern climes, the rich black-earth soil (*chernozem*) makes this an extremely productive agricultural area. Livestock production, dairying and arable farming account for the bulk of Siberia's home-grown agricultural output. In the early years of the twentieth century it was the major destination for the millions of peasant migrants who settled beyond the Urals, turning it very rapidly into one of the empire's most pro-ductive agricultural regions (see Chapter Seven). Nowadays, it contains the bulk of western Siberia's population, most of it concentrated in the cities and major industrial centres of Novosibirsk (population in 2005, *c.*1.5 million),

Omsk (1.2 million), Barnaul (631,221), Novokuznetsk (563,260), Kemerovo (523,000) and Tyumen (510,000), all of them lying along or within easy access to the Trans-Siberian Railroad. Kemerovo is also the centre of the famous Kuzbass (Kuznets Basin) coal industry, which played such a major role in the Soviet five-year plans and is still an important, though reduced, factor in the region's economy (see below).

Finally, at the south-easternmost tip of western Siberia, occupying about 10 per cent of the whole territory, is the region of the Altai, sometimes described as Siberia's 'little Switzerland'. The use of the epithet 'little' is rather odd, considering the fact that the Altai administrative district stretches over an area of 262,000 square kilometres (101 square miles), in comparison with Switzerland's 41,228 (15,918 square miles). However, in terms of its breath-taking mountain scenery in the south and the relatively verdant pasturelands in the northern half of the territory, the comparison is perhaps not so far-fetched. The northern, non-mountainous, sector, with its capital at Barnaul – now administratively part of the Siberian Federal District – has a diverse, mixed agricultural/industrial economy which includes machine-building, chemical, textile and food industries along with cereal production, horticul-ture (fruit and vegetables) animal husbandry and the cultivation of industrial crops (sunflowers, sugar-beet, flax, hemp, etc.). It also produces superb vodka. The mountain ranges in the south – the Gornyi Altai (highest point, Mount Belukha, at 4,506 metres/14,783 feet) – now a semi-autonomous republic, boast a fair variety of extractable minerals, including gold, mercury, iron and manganese. Although in the past the discovery of these deposits led to the appellation of Altai's mountains as 'a mineralogical museum', they are not found in sufficient quantities to make them commercially or industrially significant, although in tsarist times, the personal coffers of the Romanovs benefited considerably from the gold- and silver-workings on the so-called 'Cabinet Lands', i.e. territory owned directly by the royal family, or, more exactly, by the emperor himself and administered on his behalf by the 'Cabinet of his Imperial Majesty'. They were, quite properly, nationalized in 1917.

East Siberia

Before 1963, when the Yakut Autonomous Soviet Republic was incorporated into the Russian Far East, East Siberia was the largest administrative-territorial unit in the USSR. That prime position in the present Russian Federation is now held by the Far Eastern Federal District (see below).

The geographical area comprising eastern Siberia lies between the Yenisei and Lena rivers and stretches eastwards in the south beyond Lake Baikal, covering a landmass of some 4.2 million square kilometres (1.6 million square miles). It is marked by a much more rugged terrain, with more permafrost (underlying around 90 per cent of the region), tundra, forest and mountain areas than western Siberia. Its central feature is the great Central Siberian Plateau, a vast irregular upland averaging some 600 metres (1,968 feet) in height and rising in the north to 1,700 metres (5,577 feet). It is traversed, both north-south and east-west, by many rivers rushing through deep, steep-sided gorges and covered by the seemingly limitless, mostly coniferous, taiga. The most ubiquitous tree is the larch, which because of its shallow root system is well adapted to growing over permafrost. This gigantic central massif with its dense forest cover occupies over three-quarters of the entire territory of eastern Siberia and supports very little human population (averaging less than 1 person per square kilometre). It is, however, the home of a wide variety of fur-bearing mammals, e.g. brown bear, glutton, lynx, elk, fox, polecat, squirrel, badger, various species of deer and, of course, the fabled sable. The pursuit of these animals' valuable pelts was the major lure attracting the early Russian pioneers across Siberia in the sixteenth and seventeenth centuries (see Chapter Two).

To the north, beyond the Arctic Circle, the North Siberian Lowland presents a landscape of mixed forest and tundra that forms a broad intermontane east-west corridor between the northern slopes of the Central Siberian Plateau and the Byrranga mountain range, which dominates the Taimyr Peninsula, the northernmost part of the Siberian landmass, thrusting out into the Arctic Ocean and spreading over an area of c.400,000 square kilometres (150,000 square miles). In addition to the fauna mentioned above, the sea waters here are inhabited by seals, walruses and white whales, while the frozen littoral zones, islands and glaciers are roamed by the polar bear. The acclimatized musk-ox also grazes on the sparse vegetation. The traditional, largely nomadic, occupations of the aboriginal Samoed peoples inhabiting these northern zones were hunting, fishing and reindeer herding. These activities are still continued by the present-day population of the numerically 'small peoples (*malye narody*) of the north' – the Dolgany, Nentsy and Nganasany (see Chapter Five) – though now augmented by silver-fox farming and small-scale milk and meat production.

Since the 1930s, the area's economy has also been supplemented – to both good and bad effect – by industrial developments connected with the intensive mining of nickel, cobalt and platinum-group metals in the region of Norilsk, a settlement founded by geologists in 1921 and elevated to town status in 1953. It is still one of the five most northerly urban centres in the world, but has gained an ugly reputation over the years as one of the most deadly locations of the Stalinist forced labour camp system, the notorious GULag (see Chapter Nine). The number of prisoners – both common criminal and political – working in literally lethal conditions in what was known as 'Noril'lag' rose from c.1,250 in 1936 to 72,500 in 1951. According to Noril'lag's archives, during the period of the camp's existence (1935–56) around 17,000 forced labourers died of cold, exhaustion and starvation. Ironically, one of the thousands of inmates at one time was Nikolai Nikolaevich Urvantsev (1893–1985), honoured geographer, geologist and explorer, who first discovered the rich strata of copper-nickel-platinum ores in the Norilsk region.[19] Today the city of Norilsk has a population of 142,500, and is still a thriving industrial centre, but also has one of the most heavily polluted local atmospheres in the world. In 2007, the New York-based Blacksmith Institute calculated that the mineral processing industries in the Norilsk region belch out 4 million tons of cadmium, copper, lead, nickel, arsenic, selenium and zinc particles into the atmosphere every year, and an article in the British newspaper *The Guardian* earlier reported that: 'This is the most polluted place in Russia – where the snow is black, the air tastes of sulphur and the life expectancy for factory workers is 10 years below the Russian average.'[20]

Other research estimates that toxic emissions from the largest industrial plant in the Taimyr region, the Norilsk Nickel Mining and Metallurgical Combine (NNMMC), were responsible for such widespread devastation of the surrounding tundra and taiga that: 'there was not a single living tree within 48 km of the nickel smelter'.[21] The knock-on effects of this include a massive reduction of the grazing lands for the local reindeer herds and a significant loss of stock and weight reduction in the surviving animals. Also, the level of chemical pollutants in Taimyr's rivers and lakes has led specialist environmentalists to advise people not to eat fish caught in lakes Lama, Glubokoe and Pyasino.[22] These two facts obviously create a very serious problem, given the importance of venison and fish in the local diet. In February 2008 the Russian Federation's environmental watchdog, *Rosprirodnadzor*, filed a lawsuit against NNMMC claiming 4.35 billion rubles (US$178 million) compensation for the company's pollution of the region's waterways. This is only one of a number of legal actions – for instance in Sakhalin and in the Kemerovo Region – against multibillion dollar industrial companies for the devastating effects of their activities on the Siberian environment.

Around 2,000 kilometres (1,240 miles) to the south, Lake Baikal – the famed 'pearl of Siberia' – was the scene of another environmental battle between conservationists and industrialists during the 1960s and 1970s. Brief mention of this limnological wonder has already been made above, but such is its marvellous uniqueness that it is worth devoting a few extra words to it. It is without challenge the most outstanding geophysical feature of south-eastern Siberia, indeed, some might say, of the entire Russian Federation. This huge inland sea – first described in vivid literary terms by the great seventeenth-century rebel priest and exile, Archpriest Avvakum (see Chapter Two) – has a surface area in excess of 31,500 square kilometres (12,162 square miles) and is the deepest and one of the oldest lakes in the world. A few more statistics are in order at this point: length – 636 kilometres (395 miles); width – 79.5 kilometres (49.4 miles) at its widest, 25 kilometres (15.5 miles) at its narrowest; shoreline – over 2,000 kilometres (1,243 miles); average depth – 730 metres (2,395 feet), plunging to 1,637 metres (5,370 feet) at its lowest point; liquid volume – 23,000 cubic kilometres (5,518 cubic miles), that is 80 per cent of the total fresh-water supply in Russia, and 20 per cent of the entire planet earth. However, Baikal's impressive dimensions and geographical data are constantly changing, as it lies in a region of high seismic activity. Sub-aquatic earthquakes measuring as much as 10 to 11 on the Richter scale are not uncommon. In August 1959 the underwater epicentre of a quake registering 9 on the Richter scale caused a rift making the lake 20 metres (66 feet) deeper.

The lake is also renowned for the purity and clarity of its water, and even when the surface is frozen to a thickness of 1 to 2 metres (3.2 to 6.5 feet) it is possible to gaze through the crystal-clear ice and plainly identify saucer-sized objects at a depth of around 50 metres (164 feet). One of the reasons for the lake's remarkable limpidity is to be found in the voracious eating habits of the almost microscopic, shrimp-like *Epischura baikalensis*, a tiny crustacean unique to Baikal, trillions upon trillions of which permanently sweep, scour, filter and devour algae, bacteria and other living, or dead, animal matter in Baikal's waters. As one writer has put it: 'During a year, the armada of insatiable crustaceans can purify the upper fifty-metre-deep layer of water three times over ... These little scavengers toil away, safeguarding the purity of their legendary lake.'[23] These and other slightly larger endemic crustaceans can strip to the bare bones the flesh of a drowned man in a matter of hours. Another contributing factor to the lake-water's purity is that most of the rivers feeding Baikal flow over hard, impermeable rock, thus creating what in limnological terms is technically known as an 'oligotrophic' lake, i.e. one having low levels of mineral content and dissolved salts, a high oxygen level and low organic content.

It was in fact partly due to the purity of Baikal water that it became the centre of a public campaign against industrial pollution during the mid- and late 1960s, a campaign in large part orchestrated by the celebrated Siberian writer and environmentalist, Valentin Rasputin (b.1937). The problem was caused by the central Soviet economic planning authorities' decision to construct a large cellulose processing plant near the town of Baikalsk at the extreme southern tip of the lake. The Baikalsk Pulp and Paper Mill, completed in 1966, was responsible for discharging thousands of gallons of waste-water contaminated with pollutants from the industrial process. A much publicized campaign from scientists, scholars, writers, journalists and others was unsuccessful in having the factory closed down, but more stringent controls over the levels of effluents were introduced, and constant scientific monitoring of the water's quality continues, as does the debate between ecologists and industrial developers.

However, it is not just the paper mill itself that causes the problem. Other human activities have also had an impact on Baikal's environment, including intensive logging along the rivers and the floating of huge rafts of logs across the lake to feed the plant. Industrial and civil construction projects have spread, the human population has expanded, and there has been an increased use of chemicals in agricultural production in the surrounding area, residues of which ultimately seep into the lake. The rapid growth of tourism and the building of ski resorts have also impacted on the lakeside environment. Finally, the building of the Baikal-Amur Mainline (BAM), a railroad running parallel to – and hundreds of kilometres north of – the Trans-Siberian, starting from Taishet at the northern end of the lake and terminating at the Pacific coast, has created a wide range of negative environmental consequences. (The whole controversial issue of the BAM is dealt with in Chapter Ten.)

It is impossible to leave Baikal without mention of the fantastic diversity and uniqueness of its flora and fauna, hundreds of species of which are not to be found anywhere else on earth. For instance, there are over 1,500 different species of animal life, two-thirds of which are exclusively endemic to the lake and its shores. Of these, perhaps the most celebrated is the famous fresh-water seal (*nerpa*) – only to be found in Baikal. Today there is an estimated seal population of c.70,000. These enchanting creatures share the waters of the lake with – and feed on – the large variety and huge quantity of fish. Of the 52 varieties of fish, the most abundant, and the biggest in body weight, is the *golomyanka* (*Comephorus baicalensis*), while Arctic *omul*, a type of salmon, is the most commercially important. The high fat content of Baikal's sturgeon was even remarked on in the writings of the seventeenth-century Archpriest Avvakum, mentioned above. In his famous autobiography he comments on Baikal's abundant fowl and fish as follows:

> Great multitudes of birds live there as well, geese and swans which cover the lake like snow. And the lake is full of fish – sturgeon, salmon, sterlet and trout and many other kinds. The water is fresh, but there are huge seals and sea-lions, bigger than anything I saw in the great ocean-sea when I was living on the Mezen. And the fish are very fatty, especially the great sturgeon and the salmon – impossible to fry them, there would be nothing but grease.[24]

The geographical area of eastern Siberia, now part of the central Siberian Federal District, also contains the Buryat Republic lying to the east of Lake Baikal, and further south the tiny Tyva (formerly Tuva) Republic bordering on the north-west corner of Mongolia. In Kyzyl, the capital of this little-known country, there stands an obelisk marking the putative geographical centre of Asia. The Buryat people living around Baikal engage in extensive sheep-farming on the relatively lush grasslands.[25]

As the BAM moves steadily eastwards from its starting point at Taishet, it leaves eastern Siberia and enters the vast territory of the Russian Far East, to which we now turn.

The Russian Far East

Now administratively known as the Far Eastern Federal District (FEFD), this is the largest of the federal districts of Russia, covering an area of 6,215,900 square kilometres (2,400,000 square miles). Though it is the largest in area, with a population of 6.7 million it is the least densely populated federal district of Russia, averaging roughly 1 person per square kilometre. It is divided into 8 administrative areas – republics, regions and territories (*respublika*, *oblast'*, *krai*) – each of which enjoys a good deal of autonomy on local issues and policies.

In geophysical terms, despite the fact that 80 per cent of its territory lies on permafrost (some of it 1.5 kilometres/0.9 miles deep), and 75 per cent of it is covered by mountains and forest, its topography nevertheless offers great diversity and contrast. From the frozen Bering Strait in the extreme Arctic north it stretches roughly 4,500 kilometres (2,800 miles) south to the paddy fields on the Korean border; at its widest point it is 4,000 kilometres (2,485 miles). Including Sakha/Yakutia, which was incorporated into the Far East in the 1960s, it sprawls in total over more than a quarter of the Russian Federation's landmass, but contains less than 3 per cent of its population. Its landscape includes low, swampy marshland and extensive forests, where, in the south, the magnificent, but endangered, Siberian tiger prowls, On the Kamchatka Peninsula sits the highest volcano in Eurasia, Mount Klyuchevskaya. From its peak at 4,750 metres (15,580 feet) above sea-level to the bottom of the Kurilo-Kamchatka ravine in the Pacific Ocean is a vertical distance of 15 kilometres (9.3 miles). Its last major eruption was in 1972–4. Apart from Klyuchevskaya itself, the peninsula is highly volcanic and also contains an abundance of hot-water geysers and thermal pools. In 2007 a huge, spectacular hot mudslide in the Kronotskii national park, a UNESCO world heritage site lying about 200 kilometres (124 miles) north of Kamchatka's capital, Petropavlovsk, destroyed a whole valleyful of geysers and springs. About two-thirds of the valley was buried under millions of cubic tons of rock and mud in a matter of minutes.[26]

The northernmost part of Russia's Far East is a mixture of high mountainous terrain (the Verkhoyansk and Cherskii fold mountains and the peaks of the Chukotskii Peninsula) and the flat lowland tundra plains of the Kolyma-Indigirka basin and coastline. Much further south, the Aldan, Stanovoi and Dzhugdzhur ranges give way to the Amur River valley, which, together with the Zeya-Bureya lowland and the region around Lake Khanka, are the only areas in which any successful agricultural activity is possible. Traditional cereals as well as vegetables, soya beans and rice are cultivated, but despite fertile soils and a relatively long growing season, yields are often reduced by the effects of monsoon rains and widespread flooding. Despite measures to alleviate this situation, it seems that for the foreseeable future the region's position as a net importer of foodstuffs will not alter significantly. On the other hand, the Far East is the Russian Federation's largest producer of fish and other seafood. The region has a 27,000-kilometre (16,777-mile) coastline with direct access to five seas and the Pacific Ocean. The great port-city of Vladivostok, capital of Primorskii administrative territory, is the centre of the Russian Far East's fishing industry, and the region as whole supplies 30 to 40 per cent of the entire country's fish and other marine and aquatic food products, including the Amur salmon, the world-famous Kamchatka crab and huge quantities of edible, highly nutritious kelp (*morskaya kapusta*).

The Far East's agricultural deficiency is offset by its great mineral wealth and other natural resources. A whole alphabetic gamut of valuable deposits – from antimony to zinc – is hidden beneath its formidable terrain, including gold, diamond, mercury, tungsten, tin, copper, boron, other non-ferrous metals, and also oil and natural gas. The coalfields of Sakha are among the largest in the Russian Federation, while diamond mining at Myrnyi and Udachnyi has turned the republic into one of the world's most prolific diamond producers. Indeed, according to recent estimates, diamonds are considered to be Russia's third-largest earner of foreign exchange after oil and natural gas. It was, in fact, the desire to improve the extraction, exploitation and transportation of the natural mineral resources that was one of the major driving forces behind the building of the Baikal-Amur Mainline and the formation of the so-called Territorial-Industrial Complexes (TPKs) along its route.

Further information concerning the natural resources and mineral wealth of Siberia as a whole is given in the following section.

NATURAL RESOURCES

Throughout Siberia's history – at least since Russia's original conquest and assimilation of the territory in the sixteenth and seventeenth centuries – its natural resources have always been exploited by the central, metropolitan authorities, whether Muscovite, imperial, Soviet or post-Soviet, as what is usually described as a 'resource frontier'. That is to say, from the trapping of the first sable to the sinking of the latest oil-well, the territory's great natural resources – animal, vegetable and mineral – have been hunted, mined, extracted, despoiled, transported west or exported on world markets to the advantage of the central exchequer, and often to the degradation, detriment and destruction not only of the natural environment, but also of the original human inhabitants of the territory. (The impact of Russia's subjugation of the indigenous peoples of Siberia is discussed at length in Chapter Five.) Historically this has caused a clash of interests, a tension and often a good deal of resentment in what can be described as a perpetual 'core-periphery' conflict: the 'core' in this case being the heartland of 'European' Russia with its capital in either Moscow or St Petersburg; the 'periphery' being the lands and riches of Siberia – over which Russian military, political and commercial control marched inexorably eastwards, steadily expanding the limits of Russia's 'frozen frontier'. It was a typically 'colonial' situation. That is, in the same way as the great maritime empires of Europe invaded and penetrated overseas territories in Africa, Asia, Australasia and the Americas – exploiting the labour of the native peoples, sometimes exterminating them, and pillaging the local lands and resources in order to enrich the economies of the metropolitan power – so did successive Russian governments occupy, subdue and despoil the lands, forests, rivers and subterranean and sub-glacial wealth of Siberia. One of the most cogently articulated indictments of Russia's colonial policies and ruthless exploitation of its northern empire still remains the seminal work of the great nineteenth-century Siberian regionalist scholar and activist, Nikolai Mikhailovich Yadrintsev (1842–94), *Siberia as a Colony*.[27] This splendid book, at the same time erudite and passionate, but unfortunately not available in English translation, will be referred to often in the following chapters.

The fact of the matter is that, whereas most of what eventually became the Russian Empire's resources lay east of the Urals, the majority of the population lived to the west, in the central European part of the country. This led to a situation whereby the successive Muscovite, imperial and Soviet authorities exercised what they believed to be their right to batten on the natural wealth of the northern lands that they had invaded, occupied and settled, regardless of the interests of the indigenous peoples or the impact on the natural environment. So, what exactly were, and are, the much sought-after treasures of Russia's 'ice-box and El Dorado'? This book is not intended to be a treatise in economic geography, of which a good number are available (see 'Suggestions for Further Reading'). What follows in the rest of this chapter, therefore, is merely a brief thumbnail indication, unburdened by too much statistical data, of the diversity, richness, past, present and potential value of Russia's vast 'resource frontier'.

The Soviet Union was, and the Russian Federation still is, the world's largest producer of all three major fossil fuels – coal, oil and natural gas – and it has been estimated that as much as 80 per cent of its potential oil reserves, 90 per cent of its gas and 90 per cent of its coal lies within Siberia and the Far East. Much of this is located in extremely remote and barely accessible parts of the country and its provable and probable deposits have yet to be exploited to their full potential. That fact notwithstanding, Siberia and the Far East still continue to provide the lion's share of the entire country's domestic fuel needs and her export revenue.

The largest centre of coal production is the Kuznetsk Basin (Kuzbass), which as early as the 1930s was fuelling the iron and steel industry and local electric power stations in the Urals. This led to the formation of the huge Urals-Kuznetsk Coal and Metallurgical Combine, a major enterprise in the pre-Second World War and postwar Soviet five-year economic plans. Since the collapse of the Soviet Union and the consequent loss to Russia of the equally productive Donbass coalfields in now independent Ukraine, the Kuznetsk coal basin has taken on a renewed significance. Another major centre of the coal industry is the Kansk-Achinsk basin further east, but because of the lower-grade lignite coal's propensity to spontaneous combustion during transportation, most of the output is used for purely local needs. However, the overall energy output derived from Kansk-Achinsk brown coal ultimately feeds into the national electricity grid by virtue of its use in fuelling coal-fired electric power stations built during the 1980s and 1990s, the electricity generated being transmitted westward along high-voltage power lines. Another major coalfield has more recently been developed at the new town (founded in 1975) of Nerungri in southern Sakha/Yakutia. This coal town is linked to the BAM by a northern spur (the 'little BAM') to facilitate transportation and export of Siberian coal to China and Japan.

Russia's major oil reserves are concentrated in the northern regions of Siberia which in 2002 accounted for three-quarters of the country's total oil and gas condensate production.[28] Of these, the vast bulk is situated in the Tyumen region in western Siberia – in particular the giant Samotlor field near Nizhnevartovsk, now part of the Urals Federal District. During the 1980s, some American commentators suggested that the Soviet oil boom was over and that an energy crisis was in the offing. However, these (arguably) politically motivated prognostications were soon shown to have been misplaced; in the 1990s output began to soar and new world records in barrel-per-day production were established.[29] New fields further north on the Yamal Peninsula and in the Kara Sea region, in addition to recent developments in eastern Siberia and the Far East, including the exploitation of huge deposits in the Sakha Republic and off the coast of Sakhalin, will ensure Siberia's predominant role in Russia's oil production for the foreseeable future.

Natural gas was discovered in western Siberia during the 1960s. Major developments during the next two decades at the Medvezhe and Urengoi fields boosted total Soviet production of natural gas from 194 billion cubic metres (6,850 cubic feet) in 1970 to almost 900 billion (31,783 cubic feet) in 1990. With an area of almost 6,000 square kilometres (2,320 square miles) by far the largest of the gas fields is at Urengoi, which prompted the construction of the new town of Novyi Urengoi, founded in 1980 and with a population in 2002 of around 95,000. While production here still continues on a massive scale, attention shifted during the late Soviet period to the Taz and Yamal Peninsulas.

At the beginning of the twenty-first century, north-west Siberian gas accounted for around 75 per cent of the former USSR's total. Recent estimates suggest that total natural gas production throughout the northern area of western Siberia will increase from 524 billion cubic metres (18,500 cubic feet) in 2002 to 550 billion (19,400 cubic feet) in 2010. Moving further eastwards, discovery and development of gas fields in north-eastern Siberia, Sakha and the Sakhalin shelf has underpinned Russia's (or rather Siberia's and the Russian Far East's) role as the world's leading producer of this important energy resource, over one-third of which is annually exported via giant pipeline networks to customers outside the Russian Federation, both to the 'near abroad' (i.e. former republics of the USSR) and to countries in eastern and western Europe. This continuing outflow of the territory's valuable resources reinforces the notion of Siberia as a colony or resource frontier of the 'motherland', since on the whole the Russian north consumes only about 9 per cent of Siberian gas utilized for the economic needs of the entire country. This can obviously be explained with reference to low population density in the north and east, but, ironically, some areas – and their residents – of the gas-producing regions are not even connected to the supply network!

As already mentioned above, apart from its highly lucrative subterranean energy resources, Siberia is also lavishly endowed with a whole variety of mineral deposits. Iron is an ore with which Siberia is not overly provisioned, but in the production of non-ferrous metals, Siberia and the Far East still play a pre-eminent role in Russia's economy. The former USSR was, for instance, the largest producer of gold after South Africa, though its global output position fell from second to fifth place during Russia's economic crisis of the 1990s. Three-quarters of the Russian Federation's gold reserves, however, still lie within Siberia and the Far East, and, given the high cost of the metal on the world's commodity markets (US$1,000 an ounce at the time of writing) it goes without saying that Siberian gold is still a significant factor in not only the Russian but also the global economy.

In addition to gold, Siberia also has a monopoly in the production of tin within the Russian Federation, and during the 1960s became the world's number two producer after Malaysia. Much of this was concentrated at the Solnechnyi tin mines in the Far East, which also produced – and still produces – a wide range of other materials including tungsten, copper, lead and zinc. Nickel production at Norilsk has already been mentioned above, and this region maintains its position as one of the world's major suppliers, despite the appalling effects on the local environment. Siberia also makes a significant contribution to Russia's output of non-metallic minerals such as boron, lithium, fluorspar, mica, asbestos, apatite and, of course, the precious diamonds. Other geologically proven, but hitherto untapped, natural resources of enormous size and potential locked within Siberia's frozen ground suggest that the territory will maintain and even enhance its position as one of the world's principal mineral storehouses for a considerable time to come. Indeed, the still hidden riches of perhaps as much as 85 per cent of the territory of Siberia and the Russian Far East remain to be fully established by professional geologists and mineralogists.

Two other traditional Siberian resources also make a contribution, though less than in the past, to the Russian economy – namely, timber and fur. Russia contains the world's most extensive forestlands and timber stands, most of which are located east of the Urals. It has been argued that the woods, forests and the taiga are the Russians' natural habitat. From wooden cradle to wooden cross, Russia's arboreal expanses have for centuries provided fuel, building material, shelter, the source of food and fur, and other essentials of human existence in these northern climes. Unfortunately, and despite references made above about the seeming inexhaustibility of Siberia's forest resources, recent developments in both legal and, more worryingly, illegal logging activities have created grave cause for concern among both Russian and foreign environmentalists. Since the break-up of the Soviet Union, domestic demand for timber has declined at the same time as foreign, particularly Asian, demand has increased. The Siberian and Russian Far East's timber industry is now almost entirely export-driven and therefore at the mercy, according to a recent report, of the fluctuating largely Chinese and Japanese markets. In May 2000, Russia's new president, Vladimir Putin, signed a decree abolishing the country's Environmental Protection Committee including the Russian Federal Forest Service (*Rosleskhoz*) which until then had kept a watching brief over the whole country's huge woodland and forest areas.

The result has been a significant growth in criminal lumbering activities, which were in any case thriving with the connivance of corrupt local officials, and the decidedly dodgy activities of illegal Chinese entrepreneurs greedy to exploit Siberia's timber resources for their own constantly expanding construction programmes. Russian law enforcement agencies have proved ineffectual in combating small private and illegal Russian and Chinese logging gangs from despoiling the Far East's taiga of its riches.[30]

On the other hand, and on the 'right side' of the law, more diversified and more or less efficient use of forest resources has been made over the last few decades with the establishment of wood-processing industrial plants and pulp mills, such as the huge Bratsk Wood Production Complex (BLPK) fuelled by the Bratsk hydroelectrical station, producing paper, cellulose, plywood, chipboard and a range of chemical byproducts.[31] However, the legality of its operations does not prevent the BLPK from creating a huge pall of stinking chemical pollutants hovering over the environs of Bratsk for many kilometres in all directions.

Finally, a few words should be said about the fur trade, which was, after all, the major imperative in medieval Muscovy's original conquest of Siberia. Whereas in earlier times Siberian peltry was the largest trading commodity in Russia's internal and external marketing, today it plays a minimal role in the country's overall economy. However, fur hunting and, increasingly, fur-farming, is still widespread in Russia's northern regions. In the tundra zone the principal quarry is the arctic fox, while further south in the taiga regions the main objects of the chase are squirrel (between 5 and 10 million pelts per year), sable (1 to 2 million), red fox, ermine, marten and hare. Although a pair of rampant sables surrounded by crossed arrows was one of Siberia's traditional heraldic emblems, it is today no more than a metaphor for the region's fabulously rich natural resources. In the modern world, Siberia's illustrious 'soft gold' (as pelts came to be known) has been replaced by harder – or, in terms of national revenue, oleaginous and gaseous – exploitable and exportable commodities.

CONCLUSION

It should be clear from the preceding sections of this introductory chapter that both historical and modern Siberia – including the Far East – have played a pivotal, though often under-appreciated, role in the Russian nation's economic and social development, despite the tremendous climatic, communications and geophysical problems posed by its intimidating natural features. However, it is equally clear that this frozen colonial frontier, both 'ice-box and El Dorado', has suffered in both human and ecological terms for the benefit and fluctuating prosperity of Russia's rulers in the Winter Palace or the Kremlin from the sixteenth century to the present day. How the early Muscovite tsars originally established their military, political and commercial authority over their gigantic northern empire is the subject of the following chapter.

2

The Russian Conquest:
Invasion and Assimilation

An old English mnemonic ditty reminds us that, 'In fourteen hundred and ninety-two, Columbus sailed the ocean blue' – thus 'discovering' what from Europe's perspective was the 'New World' of the Caribbean and the Americas. Of course, this later had global historical consequences for both good and ill (devastatingly more ill than good, as far as the fate of the aboriginal inhabitants was concerned). What is less well known in the West is that in fifteen hundred and eighty-two, just 90 years after the celebrated Genoese navigator sailed westwards across the Atlantic, a rough, Russian cossak adventurer and *ataman* (chieftain), by the name of Yermak Timofeevich (c.1537–85), plied eastwards by river through the Urals to 'discover' what was to become Russia's own new world of Siberia, with similarly portentous repercussions. Both expeditions were driven by mercenary, military and monarchical considerations, Columbus being sponsored by the Spanish rulers, Ferdinand of Aragon (1452–1516) and Isabella of Castile (1451–1504), and Yermak's crew by Tsar Ivan IV of Moscow and All Russia (1530–84).

Over the next century, 'All Russia' was to include the whole continent of northern Asia, as described in geophysical terms in the previous chapter. In the second half of the twentieth century, after the defeat in the Second World War of Nazi Germany and imperial Japan, both the United States of America and Russia became the world's only two 'superpowers', dangerously antagonistic during the years of the Cold War, but each ultimately tracing their modern origins to daring feats of exploration, and dreadful feats of conquest of non-European lands and oppression of non-European peoples in the sixteenth and seventeenth centuries. So what were the principal purposes and imperatives of medieval Muscovy's *Drang nach Osten*, and just how did this land-locked, troubled, east-European Slavonic tsardom establish its hegemony over the enormous, cryogenic wastes of the forbidding *terra incognita* of Siberia?[1]

For the purposes of this book, the story of Siberia's 'pre-Russian' antiquity is largely irrelevant, though not without its own intrinsic importance. It is, however, more the preserve of the anthropologist and archaeologist than of the modern historian. What is clear from the scholarly literature is that many indigenous tribes, civilizations and peoples, both nomadic and sedentary, which inhabited Siberia in earlier centuries from the Palaeolithic era to early modern times, had developed a rich pattern of independent cultures which were neither European nor wholly Far Eastern in their provenance.[2] Emphasizing the uniqueness and specificity of pre-modern Siberian civilizations, the late academician A.P. Okladnikov, one of the great Russian luminaries of Siberian antiquarian studies, dismissed both the 'Eurocentric' and the 'Asiacentric' approaches to the study of Siberian culture as 'reactionary'. He quoted with enthusiasm the conclusions of the nineteenth-century Siberian regionalist writer, N.M. Yadrintsev, that 'it is indisputable that in these regions there developed a distinctive, original culture'.[3]

At the beginning of the thirteenth century, the whole vast swathe of the southern Siberian steppes was overrun, or overridden, by the fierce warrior Mongol and Tatar horsemen of Chenghiz Khan (c.1162–1227) and his descendants. Under the leadership of Chenghiz's grandson, Baty Khan (1208–55), the Mongols swept westwards across the southern Urals, and penetrated and defeated the autonomous petty princedoms of Kievan Russia. From his tented capital at Sarai on the river Volga, Baty lorded it over the conquered lands and tribute-paying vassal peoples of the most westerly part of the Mongol Empire, the 'Golden Horde'.[4] Towards the end of the fifteenth century, two significant developments took place which would determine the history of Eurasia for the following centuries down to the present day. First was the rapid disintegration and collapse of the Mongol Empire and the Golden Horde – the reasons for which need not detain us here – and the second was the establishment of the Grand Principality of Moscow as the virtual capital of a reunified, embryonic and more or less centralized Russian state. The prime mover in the latter process was Grand Prince Ivan III ('Ivan the Great', ruled 1462–1505), continued by his successor, Vasilii III (ruled 1505–33), and dramatically consolidated and expanded by his grandson, Ivan IV (ruled 1533–84), better known to history by his sobriquet 'the Terrible'. Ivan the Terrible is renowned for many things, including his violence, his cruelty, his furious, filicidal temper, his ambiguous domestic reforms, his unsuccessful military attempts to gain access to the Baltic, his fulminatory literary activities, his psychotic eccentricities, and the perverse mixture of sanctimony and sadism that was the hallmark of his controversial reign.[5]

Rather less well known, in contrast to his military and diplomatic failures in the west (including his forlorn overtures to Queen Elizabeth I of England to bed an English bride) are his exploits in the east, including the capture of the Tatar khanate of Kazan – the gateway to the Urals – in 1552, and then Astrakhan, lower down the Volga, in 1556. (It was the victory over Kazan that inspired Ivan to commission the building of the magnificent St Vasilii cathedral on Moscow's Red Square by the Kremlin. Topped by its seven glittering cupolas, it is a polychromatic, architectural *pièce de résistance* which is still one of Russia's most famous, iconic landmarks, and also – along with the Kremlin – a national symbol of the power of Moscow.) With the disintegration of the Golden Horde in the late fifteenth century, a number of independent Tatar khanates had been established, including those of Kazan and Astrakhan, but more significantly for present purposes, Sibir, otherwise known as Isker, beyond the Urals on the banks of the river Irtysh. It was this relatively tiny realm, under its ruler, Kuchum Khan (?–1598), which was destined to bequeath its name to a territory covering two-thirds of the Russian Empire and one-twelfth of the world. After the fall of Kazan and Astrakhan in the 1550s, for the time being Sibir itself remained relatively unmolested, partly because its chieftains prudently decided to carry on the practice of paying annual tribute to the more powerful Russian tsar, whose superior military might and more advanced fire-power had been amply demonstrated before the walls of Kazan. It was also partly because at that time the Muscovite government had in all probability no specific plans for the invasion or further expansion into what was still regarded as a remote, inhospitable and unknown land. In some ways, the prospect of traversing the dark, seemingly interminable forests and labyrinthine waterways of Siberia were just as awesome as the perils of crossing the Atlantic.

This is not to suggest that the lands lying east of 'The Rock' (*Kamen'* – an ancient, demotic Russian term for the Urals) were totally virgin territory as far as Russian penetration was concerned. As early as the eleventh century, merchants and hunters from the rich independent trading city of Novgorod had moved in a northern arc into the upper parts of western Siberia – then known as the 'Yugrian land' (*Yugorskaya zemlya*) – in quest of valuable peltry either through direct hunting, trading or the enforced imposition of fur tribute (*yasak*) on the local natives, mainly the Uralic-speaking Voguls and Ostyaks (present-day Mansi and Khanty). (The reasons for the economic value and importance of the fur trade for medieval Russia are explained below.)

During the 1470s the inter-city rivalry between the Grand Principality of Moscow and the republic of Novgorod ended in the brutal annexation of the latter by the former and the confiscation of thousands of square kilometres of Novogorodian territories, including its Yugrian colonies. Thus, Moscow's 'pacification' of Novgorod and the sequestration of her sizeable northern properties and their attendant fur trade meant that she already had a valuable trans-Uralian entrepôt well before the dramatic thrust against the khanate of Sibir in 1581 (or 1582, according to some historians, see below), from which Moscow's conquest and settlement of Siberia is traditionally dated. Accordingly, and ironically, Moscow's earliest commercial interest in Siberia was geographically located in the very same region, i.e. north-west Siberia and the lower Ob, from which most of Russia's present-day wealth in oil and natural gas has recently flowed (see Chapters One and Ten).

YERMAK

In 1571, Kuchum, leader of the khanate of Sibir – after a series of bloody internal dynastic conflicts – finally made the fateful decision to cease paying tribute to Moscow, and was probably involved in instigating a series of rebellions and raids into Muscovite territory at about the same time. Soon afterwards, the powerful Russian merchant family of the Stroganovs, which owned enormous territorial and commercial interests throughout the Urals, was authorized by a series of royal charters to fortify their eastern boundaries and mount military expeditions against the uppity Siberian tribes.

The Stroganovs had originally accumulated their considerable fortune in the mid-fifteenth century by the exploitation of a large salt lake near the small town of Solvychegodsk (*sol'* is the Russian word for salt) on what was then Muscovy's north-eastern frontier. By the middle of the reign of Ivan the Terrible, the clan's patriarch, Anikei Stroganov (1497–1570) had established himself as Moscow's equivalent of Croesus. By that time the Stroganovs had, so to speak, beefed up their interests beyond the panning and purveying of sodium chloride, and expanded into other lucrative enterprises, including the fur trade. (Legend has it that the surname Stroganov derives from the Russian verb *strogat'*, meaning to strip, plane or peel off the surface of something with a sharp instrument – alluding to the fate of one of the family's ancestors whose living skin and flesh were said to have been sliced off in strips as punishment for some act of treachery against the Mongols. The implications of this in the culinary preparation of Russia's famous dish need no further elaboration.) The tsar had also granted the Stroganovs vast territories in Perm region and the Urals which brought them face to face with Kuchum's khanate of Sibir, key to the treasure chest of the Siberian forests' fabulous hoard of pelts.

It was in this context that the celebrated cossak chieftain and freebooter, Yermak Timofeevich – sometimes extravagantly described as the Russian Cortés or the Russian Pizarro – made his portentous appearance in the annals of Russia's conquest of Siberia. In fact, for all his formidable reputation, not a lot is known about 'the conqueror of Siberia' that has any degree of sound historical authenticity. His origins, his provenance, his early career, his status, the chronology of his expedition, the manner of his death, his relationship with both the tsar and the Stroganovs – even his actual name – are surrounded by legend, conflicting chronicle accounts, myth and folklore, a confusion made even more disputatious by the differing interpretations of respectable eighteenth-century, nineteenth-century and more recent historians both in Russia and the West.[6] There is no doubt, of course, that such a character did exist, but the story of his exploits is often made up of the same stuff as the fables of Robin Hood or King Arthur and the Knights of the Round Table, or, for that matter, other famous semi-mythical and biblical figures.

The intricacies of the historiographical controversies surrounding the exact dates, the provenance of the instructions and the motives for his campaign need not detain us long. Suffice to say that the distinguished Russian historian, R.G. Skrynnikov, has, on the basis of meticulous textological research, persuasively argued that Yermak and his band of cossaks – probably acting as agents for the Stroganovs with the tsar's blessing – launched their initial onslaught against Kuchum's Siberian khanate in 1582, and not, as traditionally thought in 1581.[7] The same author also demolishes a number of other misconceptions. The number of Yermak's men, not all of them Russian, as the cossaks were a motley crew in general, is usually given as 540 (though some scholars reckon more) setting out to take on a much larger Tatar force, but with the advantage of superior weaponry. It is often mistakenly stated that Yermak's success was the result of the fact that his men's muskets, arquebuses and cannon outgunned their opponents who could only respond with primitive swords, spears, bows and arrows. In the State Russian Museum in Moscow there hangs the famous painting by the celebrated Siberian-born artist, V.I. Surikov (1848–1916), *Yermak's Subjugation of Siberia* (1895), which dramatically illustrates this particular misconception. On the huge canvas, on the left are portrayed Yermak's fierce, grim-faced warriors on their boats, bearing icons and the flag of St George slaying the dragon, with blazing muskets and cannon fire tearing into the panic-stricken infidel hordes in their fragile skiffs on the opposite side of the river. The Tatars' faces are contorted with fear and horror as their arrows fall harmlessly into the water before the Russian boats. Not a Tatar gun in sight, while on the high bank Kuchum's cavalry looks ineffectually on at the carnage below. This iconic image celebrating the conqueror of Siberia's great feat of arms is almost pure pictorial mythology. In Skrynnikov's words: 'No more erroneous view exists than the one which holds the Siberian Tatars were unfamiliar with firearms. The roar of the cossacks' cannons did not cause them to panic... Ermak disposed of little more firepower than was available to Kuchum in his forts, but all the cossacks had rifles [sic], which were formidable weapons in their hands.'[8]

In fact, Kuchum was well apprised of the coming of the cossaks and had his defences prepared with an infantry and cavalry force that has been estimated as between five and ten times greater in number than that of Yermak. However, Skrynnikov's speculation about the effectiveness of the Russians' firearms may well have been a crucial factor in scaring off the Tatars, as well as the ferocity and courage of the battle-hardened warrior cossaks. At any rate, against all the odds, within two months of launching their attack, Yermak's men had taken Kuchum's capital, and the Siberian khan was forced to make his escape. However, the victory was not an unqualified success. Although Kuchum had abandoned his capital, the cossaks soon lost control, and the Tatars returned. Lacking reinforcements from Moscow, the much depleted cossaks still continued battling across Sibir for another two or three years until Yermak himself was finally drowned during a skirmish on the river Irtysh in 1585. Here another legend still persists: that Yermak drowned because the weight of the suit of chainmail armour he was wearing dragged him down below the waters of the Irtysh – armour which had been a personal gift from the tsar. Again, the ever- sceptical Skrynnikov adduces plenty of evidence and sound historical reasons to explode this particular piece of folklore, but it is still good story.[9]

The widely differing posthumous evaluations of Yermak as either a heroic pioneer of Russia's manifest destiny, a mercenary agent of the wealthy Stroganovs, a faithful soldier in the service of the tsar, or merely a marauding bandit bent on plunder – which was the cossaks' preferred recreational activity – nicely reflect the later and broader historical debates over the very nature and quality of Russia's conquest, or assimilation, of Siberia as a whole, an issue to be discussed below.

Kuchum for his part continued a courageous guerrilla campaign against fresh Russian occupying forces sent by Moscow following in Yermak's wake. The lack of unity and internal squabbling among rival Tatar princelings and leaders of other Siberian tribes weakened their resistance to the renewed Russian incursions, and eventually Kuchum Khan was killed following a defeat in battle in 1598. His descendants continued the struggle well into the seventeenth century, but they were now no match for the steadily advancing Muscovites with their greater firepower, and aided by the construction of a series of interconnecting fortified, garrisoned strongholds (*ostrogi*) and settlements.

By the turn of the seventeenth century Russia's military, political and commercial presence was firmly established and vigorously enforced. Not only the minor khanate of Sibir, but now the whole vast continent of northern Asia was there for the taking. They took it. What had begun as the audacious enterprise of cossak conquistadores – 'a typical cossack raid, impetuous and irresistible'[10] – and merchant adventurers now had the full and determined backing of the Muscovite state.

THE RUSSIAN ADVANCE

Russia's steady eastward advances were remarkably swift and her new domains were easily consolidated. By the 1640s, after a period when European Russia had been in a state of acute domestic turmoil during the 'Time of Troubles' (c.1598–1613) and the turbulent reign of the first Romanov tsar, Mikhail Fëdorovich (ruled 1613–45), Russian trailblazers and troops had already reached the Pacific littoral and founded the garrison of Okhotsk, from where the maritime route to Kamchatka lay open. The astonishing speed of this transcontinental anabasis was facilitated by a number of important factors. The terrain and climate (see Chapter One) were not wholly dissimilar from that of European Russia and by the skilful use of Siberia's river systems and interfluvial portages – i.e. dry land over which vessels could be dragged between two rivers – a steady eastwards progression was maintained by constructing and consolidating the interlacement of defensive stockades. These strongholds formed the basis of future towns, and served initially as the military-administrative and commercial centres from which the Russians imposed their

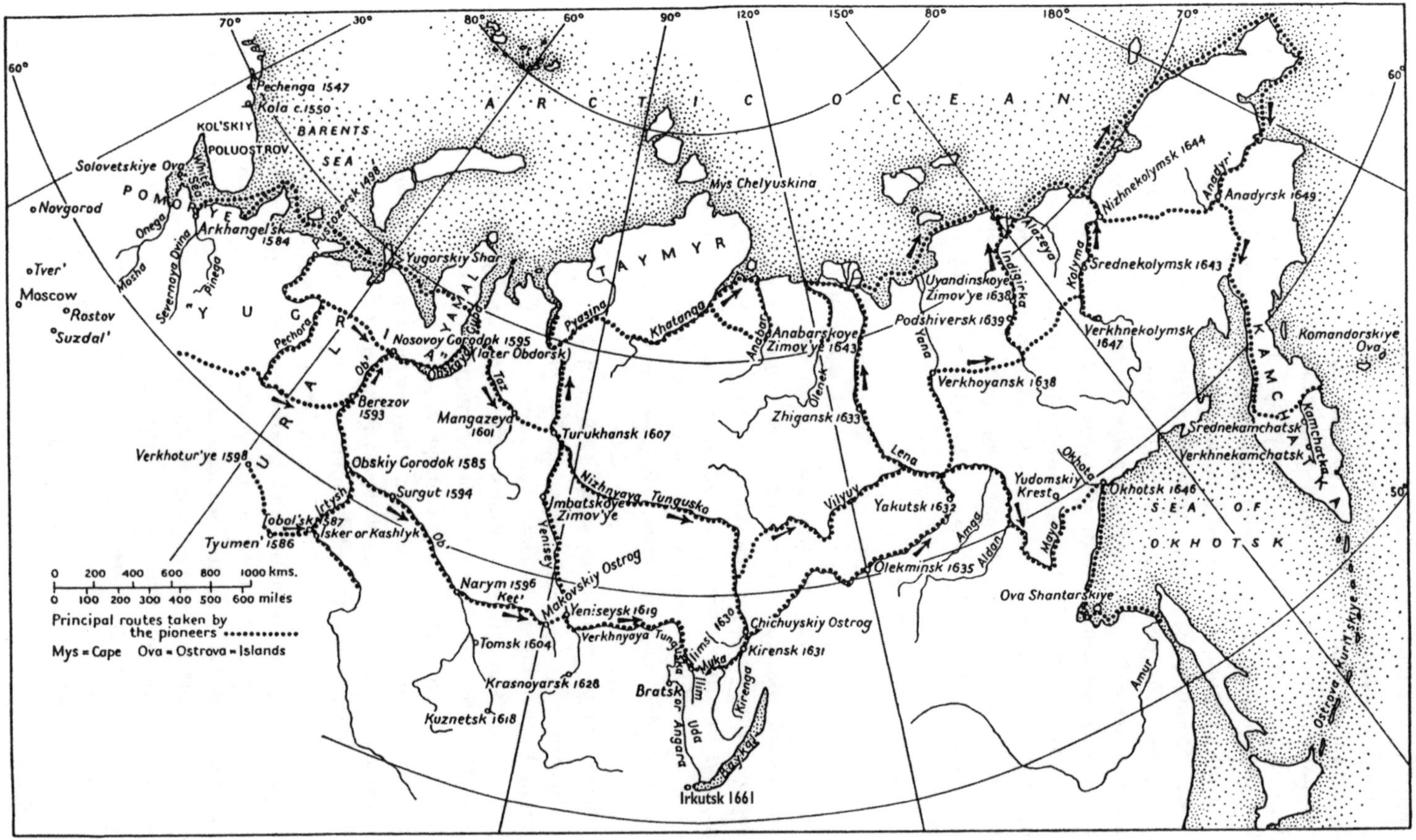

Map 4 The Russian advance across Siberia: major routes and settlements with date of foundation.

Tver'
Moscow
Rostov
Suzdal'

Novgorod

Solovetskiye Ova
P O M O R Y E
Severnaya Dvina
Pinega
Onega
Mezen'
Arkhangel'sk 1584
Onega 1547

KOL'SKIY POLUOSTROV
Kola c.1550

BARENTS SEA

Vaigach
Yugorskiy Shar
Y A M A L

Pechora
Usa
U G R A
U R A L

Verkhotur'ye 1598
Tyumen' 1586
Tobol'sk 1587
Isker or Kashlyk
Irtysh

Berezov 1593
Obdorsk
Ob'
Nadym
Nosovoy Gorodok
Novaya Gorodok (later Obdorsk) 1595
Mangazeya 1601
Taz

Obskiy Gorodok 1585
Surgut 1594
Ob'

Ket'
Narym 1596
Tomsk 1604
Kuznetsk 1618
Krasnoyarsk 1628

Yenisey
Makovskiy Ostrog
Yeniseysk 1619
Podkamennaya Tunguska
Turukhansk 1607

Pyasina

TAYMYR
Mys Chelyuskina

Khatanga
Anabar
Anabarskoye Zimov'ye 1643

Olenek
Zhigansk 1633

A R C T I C   O C E A N

Tunguska
Ilim
Bratsk or Angara
Uda
Kirenga
Irkutsk 1661
Kirensk 1631
Chichuyskiy Ostrog
Ilimsk 1630
Lena

Vilyuy
Yakutsk 1632
Olekminsk 1635
Aldan
Amga
Maya
Yudomskiy Krest
Okhota
Ova Shantarskiye
Amur

Olenek
Lena

Verkhoyansk 1638
Yana
Yandinskoye Zimov'ye 1630
Indigirka
Alazeya
Verkhoyansk 1638

Poddniversk 1639

Srednekolymsk 1643
Kolyma 1647
Verkhnekolymsk 1643
Nizhnekolymsk 1644

S E A   O F   O K H O T S K
Okhotsk 1648
Srednekamchatsk
Verkhnekamchatsk
K A M C H A T K A
Komandorskiye Ova

Anadyr'
Anadyrsk 1649

O C E A N

Ostrova Kuril'skiye

0   200   400   600   800   1000 kms.
0   100 200 300 400 500 600 miles

Principal routes taken by
the pioneers ....
Mys = Cape   Ova = Ostrova = Islands

authority on the indigenous Siberian peoples whom they encountered along their route.

A few words need to be said at this point about the construction and function of these wooden, fortified outposts, which both facilitated and defended the Russians' rapid advance. It is obvious that, once having subdued the local tribes and asserted control over a particular area, the incomers needed to establish some kind of base from which to consolidate their gains, provide shelter and security, and act as a launching pad for further expeditions. Originally, the *ostrogi* consisted of small, crude, palisaded enclosures of vertically emplaced timbers, the so-called 'upright fort' (*stoyachii ostrog*), and contained within their walls simple buildings providing rudimentary accommodation, store houses, kitchens and other facilities to provide for the day-to-day existence of both resident and passing personnel. Later, larger, more elaborate fortifications were built on a quadrangular, or sometimes hexagonal or octagonal plan, the outer walls consisting of courses of horizontal logs rising to a height of between 5 and 6.5 metres (16 and 21 feet). The average length of each wall was typically around 500 metres (1,640 feet). At intervals along the walls were towers – usually four, six or eight of them, depending on the size and layout of the fort – about twice as high as the actual walls, which were punctuated between the towers with gated entrances. The towers were topped by a sloping, tent roof with lookout posts. One of the towers, furnished with a solid gate, would act as the main entrance into the fortress. The towers were also sometimes embellished with balconies, carved motifs, two-headed eagles and, at the pinnacle, the seven-pointed Orthodox cross. Apart from dwelling places, the main, official buildings inside the walls comprised the headquarters of the local commander (*voevoda*), a customs house, warehouses, a church, a trading centre (*gostinyi dvor*) and a prison – the last for the confinement of both offenders and native hostages (see Fig. 1).[11] (A surviving seventeenth-century tower from the Bratsk fortress may be seen today in the grounds of the old Kolomenskaya palace in Moscow. One also remains at Bratsk itself.)

Once one of these strongholds was established and secured, it was safe to venture out further through the forests and along the rivers to continue the business of acquiring more territory, subjugating more peoples, exploiting more of Siberia's resources and, of course, building more fortresses. Facilitating this seemingly inexorable process was the superiority of the Russian pioneers' weaponry. The indigenous tribesmen's knives, bows and arrows were no match for Russian gunpowder and shot, and in any case the resistance of the native tribes was minimal, inured as they were to vassal status under Mongol control. It was little hardship for them to switch their payment of the *yasak* from the Mongol khan to the Russian tsar. 'In this sense it may be said', according to George Vernadsky, 'that the Russians inherited their Empire from Chingis-Khan.'[12] In addition, it was the invaders' standard practice to take hostage tribal leaders, elders and shamans in order to guarantee their clansmen's docility and ensure that fur tribute and other impositions continued to be paid.

Figure 1   Manuscript sketch of *yasak* (fur tribute) gathering at Tyumen *ostrog* (stronghold), *c.*1586. Note the upright palisades, and horizontally laid logs in the construction of the towers. Already in the late sixteenth century the *ostrog* contains within its walls not only the central official building and dwelling houses but also an Orthodox church.

Source: Seventeenth-century Remezov chronicle, reproduced on the cover of Okladnikov, A.P. (ed.), *Istoriya Sibiri s drevneishikh vremen do nashikh dnei*, vol. 2, *Sibir' v sostave feodal'noi Rossii* (Leningrad, 1968).

Despite what has just been said about 'minimal resistance', that is not to say that there was no opposition to the occupying Russians, particularly in the more northern territories that had not suffered under Mongol control. The archives contain many reports to Moscow from local commanders of instances of plots, conspiracies and insurgencies, both planned and attempted. Orders back from Moscow were unequivocal that these acts of what were described as 'treason' should be ruthlessly put down and their leaders rooted out and severely punished. Just to give one example: a *gramota* (order, instruction) dated 28 October 1607 was sent from Tsar Vasilii Ivanovich Shuiskii (Vasilii IV, ruled 1606–10) to the commander of Berëzov, Prince Pëtr Cherkaskii, concerning an uprising of Ostyaks, Voguls and Samoeds. This was in response to a report of the planned uprising sent to the tsar on 5 September, containing information, originally supplied by an Ostyak woman, about secret plans for a general insurgency and the plundering of the fortress settlement of Berëzov, founded in 1593. Names were named, and when tracked down, the leaders confessed under torture that: 'all the Ostyaks of the Berëzov and Surgut region were involved in the plot to raid the warehouses, attack the town and ostrog, and kill the servitors [Russian civilian and military personnel]'.

This led to more arrests, and the tsar sternly ordered that the chief conspirators, including one of their wives, should be hanged, 'so that by witnessing this, other potential criminals will be dissuaded from committing like crimes. Other traitors to be knouted [i.e. flogged with the *knut*, a fearsome and often lethal instrument of flagellation].'[13] Under interrogation the rebels stated that the reason for their revolt was the excessive imposition of the *yasak*.

In his *gramota*, the tsar acknowledged that: 'This has impoverished them and put them so deep in debt that they have to sell their wives and children to pay the *yasak*. Many have starved to death.' In recognition of these allegations, the tsar further ordered that 'two or three' of the complainants should be allowed to come to Moscow to petition the tsar for redress of their grievances. Further, Cherkaskii was commanded to conduct a census of all the *yasak*-paying people in the area together with details of how much each paid, and to cease collection of the fur tribute until 'We have issued an *ukaz* [decree] about this.'[14]

Thus, swift and ruthless punishment of those involved in the planned revolt was to some extent tempered by the tsar's apparent willingness to listen to the people's complaints about the excessive taxes placed upon them. The whole business of the fur trade and treatment of the indigenous peoples is discussed below and in Chapter Five.

Just how quickly and systematically Moscow established its hegemony and control over the territory once the thrust beyond the Urals had begun in earnest can be demonstrated by plotting the foundation dates of some of the major fortresses and future towns. Moving west to east in chronological order are, for example: Tyumen (1586), Tobolsk (1587), Mangazeya (1601), Tomsk (1604), Yeniseisk (1619), Krasnoyarsk (1628), Bratsk (1631), Yakutsk (1632), Okhotsk (1647), and – moving back westwards – Irkutsk in 1661.[15] If one accepts the date of Yermak's original foray as 1582, then Russia's early pioneers had traversed the entire continent from the Urals to the Pacific in the space of only 65 years. When one considers the harshness of the terrain, the rigours of the climate, the lack of maps, charts and modern navigational equipment, the primitiveness of the transport and the logistical difficulties of supply, it was a truly outstanding feat of exploration and settlement. Native guides, pressed or bribed into Russian service, no doubt played an important role as pathfinders and sources of local knowledge, but nevertheless this does not detract from the achievement of the early pioneers. (By comparison, it is worth noting that, whereas the Russians established Okhotsk on the Pacific coast in 1647, after a similar pioneering movement westwards across North America, the first fur-trading post in what became the 'Beaver State' of Oregon on the American Pacific coast was set up only in 1811.) The major motive behind this determined rapid push further and further east – as behind many another imperial venture – was an economic one, in this case primarily the quest for fur.

FUR AND FURTHER SETTLEMENT

It was above all the lure of fur, in particular that of the coveted and luxurious sable, which drew the Russian trappers and traders, closely followed or accompanied by military and administrative personnel (collectively known in Russian as *sluzhilye lyudi* – literally 'serving people', hereafter referred to as 'servitors'), deeper and deeper into the taiga, initially teeming with the unfortunate fauna whose pelts for many decades provided the principal trading commodity for Muscovy's internal and external markets. Just how valuable was this 'soft gold' of Siberia is illustrated by the following calculation quoted by Raymond Fisher. In 1623, two black fox skins were valued at 110 rubles. For this sum, the owner, 'could have purchased more than fifty acres of land, erected a good cabin, bought five horses, ten head of cattle, twenty sheep, several dozen fowl, and still have had almost half his capital left over'.[16]

If the game was profitable for individual huntsmen and traders, so it was for the state exchequer. Again, Fisher estimates that in the seventeenth century, i.e. before the fiscal reforms of Tsar, later Emperor, Peter the Great (ruled 1696–1725), the fur business accounted for as much as 10 per cent of total state revenue – not an inconsiderable proportion, which more than justified the administrative energies and expenditures devoted to its promotion.[17]

That is not to say, however, that the commercial – and political – value of the fur trade was only appreciated following the 'discovery' of Siberia. In her book, *Treasure of the Land of Darkness*, the American historian, Janet Martin, persuasively argues for the paramountcy of fur from the ninth to the early sixteenth centuries in the economies and political power of, successively, Bulgar-on-the-Volga, Kiev, Novgorod, Kazan and, finally, Moscow. There is nothing especially novel in the idea that commercial and political power go hand-in-hand, but the sheer volume and importance of fur as a preponderant item on the international exchange market suggests that a monopoly in the procurement, supply and delivery of this particular commodity was a decisive factor in the political experience of successively dominant Russian principalities for over half a millennium.

Well before Moscow's drive through Siberia, the most treasured furs sought and bought by the rich and powerful throughout the medieval world – in Europe, Byzantium, Central Asia and the Far East – originated in the dense forests of central and northern Russia, 'the land of darkness' that gives Professor Martin's book its somewhat romantic title. Over the centuries, squirrel, fox, marten, beaver, sable and other furry fauna were slaughtered in their millions to satisfy the physical needs, vanity, greed and political ambition of the whole of Eurasia from Iberia to India, from Scandinavia to the Seljuk Turks. The figures are staggering: a single merchant ship would carry as many as a quarter of a million pelts in one voyage; the tyrant king, Henry VIII of England, had a single satin gown embellished with the fur of 350 sables; even the European lower classes' almighty craving for squirrel had to be curbed by legislation. In Russia, rents were paid to boyar landlords (*boyar* – member of the hereditary landowning nobility) in fur, direct taxes were extracted by government agencies in fur, peasants hunted and sold pelts direct to merchants for profit, and, as we have seen, fur tribute – the *yasak* – was imposed on vassal tribes. With such a voracious demand, it is hardly surprising that those who controlled the supply networks were – albeit impermanently – so powerful.[18] As domestic and international demand continued to increase, the gradually declining reserves of the 'land of darkness' began to be replenished by the wildlife of the vast, newly appropriated lands beyond 'the Rock'.

Given the impressive figures adduced by Fisher, it is small wonder that the 'fur fever' impelled so many private entrepreneurs (*promyshlenniki*) and state officials to seek and exploit these new sources of wealth. Nor is it surprising that over-hunting and the lack of modern conservation awareness led to the rapid depletion of natural stocks and the more extensive search for fresh killing fields. This ever-widening and repeated pattern of exploration, exploitation and exhaustion of resources – leading to further exploration, etc. – is, according to Fisher, the basic factor that, more than any other, explains the rapidity of Russia's advance across Siberia. The spirit of adventure, scientific curiosity, territorial imperatives, the 'urge to the sea', the quest for other natural riches and sheer imperial prestige may have all contributed in their own way to the process, but the major motivating factor was unquestionably the economic determinant represented by animal fur. In later centuries, too, as indeed in the present day, the physical discomforts and disincentives to voluntary settlement in Siberia would hardly have been overcome had they not been offset by the prospect of considerable material and economic reward both for the state and the individual.

Some idea of how the combined, state-sponsored extortion racket of crushing the natives and looting the forests of their fur operated may be gained by examining a report to Tsar Mikhail Fëdorovich from Pëtr Ivanovich Beketov (*c.*1610–60), a celebrated cossak leader who played a prominent role in the exploration and settlement of large tracts of eastern Siberia from the 1630s to the 1650s, even navigating the whole length of the river Amur. Dated 6 September 1633, the report from Beketov, then holding the rank of a *streletskii sotnik* (a 'centurion' in charge of a hundred soldiers; the term *strelets* literally means a 'shooter', or musketeer), described his exploits along the Lena river region, browbeating the local Tungus (modern Evenki) and Yakuts into submission, establishing Russian military control over their lands and exacting the *yasak*. Setting off from his base at the fortress of Yeniseisk, and commissioned by the local commander on instructions from the tsar, Beketov spent two-and-a-half years marauding throughout the Tungus and Yakut territories on his oppressive colonial mission.

The report describes the events of around 20 expeditions and encounters with various local tribes, all following roughly the same pattern of initial approach to the chiefs demanding submission and 'allegiance to "the Great Sovereign"' and payment of the *yasak*; refusal on the part of the native leaders, sometimes involving armed resistance; followed by unevenly matched combat between the Russians and the natives, always resulting in the victory of the former, the slaughter of many of the latter, and the taking of hostages. Thus cowed, the indigenous Siberian tribesmen would finally see the futility of further resistance, swear fealty 'for all time to His Sovereign Majesty', and deliver up the required fur tribute. During his campaign, Beketov also established more *ostrogi*, including the new fortress of Yakutsk, winter shelters (*zimov'e*) and collection points. He sums up his achievements in the tsar's service as follows:

> Sovereign, in two and a half years of service on the Lena River I, your humble servant, with the servitors and *promyshlenniki* [independent entrepreneurs, mercenaries etc.] collected a total of 61 forties and 31 sables,[19] 25 Yakut shubas [coats or cloaks made of furs], 10 sable *plastinas* [pelts sewn together], 2 beavers, 7 red fox, and one red fox pup ... Moreover, my men and I have brought under your mighty Tsarist hand many of your previously rebellious subjects [sic] who defied your Sovereign Majesty during these two and a half years ... Merciful Sovereign Tsar of All Russia, reward us, your humble servants ... For you, Great Sovereign, we have shed our blood, suffered every privation, starved, eaten every unclean thing, and defiled our souls during those two and a half years. Tsar, Sovereign, have mercy.[20]

As further evidence of the tsar's determination to keep these remote peoples in fearful and trembling obedience to Moscow, and to ensure their eternal subservience, it is worth quoting from an official address given in 1646 by the commander (*voevoda*) of Yakutsk, one Pëtr Golovin, to a pair of prominent hostages taken after acts of violent insubordination by the people of Bratsk, including the killing of several Russian state servitors. Having finally suppressed the disturbances, Golovin informed his prisoners that, although they deserved to be hanged for their 'many acts of treason and destruction', the Sovereign Tsar had exercised clemency for the time being and was holding them in close confinement on condition that they swear an oath pledging that:

> all your people will be under his Sovereign Tsarist mighty hand in direct servitude, for ever, loyally, undeviatingly, and that you will pay *yasak* in full, without shortages, every year, for yourself and all your people ... But if you rebel against the Sovereign again and do not pay *yasak* in full each year, or if you attack agricultural peasants near the *ostrozhek* [a small *ostrog*], then, in accordance with the Sovereign's *ukaz* [decree], you will be punished for this treason. The *voevoda* and his

men will send many government troops with guns against you and your *ulus* [settlement]. These men will be instructed that not only you and your wives and children and *ulus* people be killed because of your treason, but your livestock are to be destroyed, and your iurts [or yurts, tent-like dwellings made from felt or skins] are to be burned relentlessly. These men will be ordered not to take any of you prisoner to be held for ransom, and that if they should capture any of you, they are to put you to death by hanging, just as was done to the Yakut traitors. And you will have brought this destruction upon yourselves.[21]

Elsewhere in the archive materials are many accounts of the atrocities committed by the conquering Russians in their efforts to bring the Siberian peoples into state of abject vassalage while pillaging their traditional homelands. The savagery of the process of subjugation, whether threatened or perpetrated, goes some way to explaining why, despite the pockets of resistance, the Russian advance was so swift. This subject will be returned to in Chapter Five.

Despite the overwhelming importance of the fur business, it was by necessity complemented by other important economic activities. Indeed the steady growth in Siberia's population figures during the early period of Russia's expansion can hardly be explained with reference to the number of personnel engaged in the fur trade alone. At first, the Russian pioneers brought with them the material necessities of everyday life in terms of equipment, clothing, tools and all the other paraphernalia of day-to-day frontier existence. But as time went on, as the incomers advanced further from their home base, and as their supplies dwindled, their continuing needs were to some extent met by utilizing the artefacts, raw materials and products of the indigenous population – for example hides, leather and fur for clothing, footwear, gloves etc., small boats and fishing tackle, and metalware produced by primitive local manufactories. This was, however, insufficient, both in terms of quantity and quality, to satisfy the requirements of the incoming and expanding population. Consequently, more goods and consumables were imported from European Russian to feed and provide for the demands of the new colony, amply compensated for, obviously, by the rich rewards torn from the taiga flowing in the reverse direction into Moscow's coffers.

In general, government agencies were responsible for the export of much needed cereal grains to Siberia, while other commodities were the preserve of private traders and merchants. Among the imported goods were such essentials as textiles and finished items of clothing and footwear, simple domestic utensils (frying pans, bowls, cutlery, plates, tankards and even salt cellars), metal tools (ploughshares, spades, saws, axes, augers, hammers and sickles, and nails), and even in those harsh conditions such luxury items as haberdashery, perfumes, spices and fruits – obviously destined for the most wealthy classes or eminent members of Siberia's fledgling society. The lion's share of these goods came from centres of trade and industry in European Russia, not only Moscow but also such places as Velikii Ustyug, Kholmogory, Yaroslavl, Vyatka, Kostroma and Kazan. These were referred to in Siberia as

'Russian goods' (*russkie tovary*). A small proportion of the merchandise also came from western Europe and from Central Asia and China. In an unpublished doctoral dissertation on this trade, concentrating on the provisioning of the west Siberian town of Tobolsk, the Soviet historian, O.N. Vilkov, came to the conclusion that: 'At the end of the sixteenth and beginning of the seventeenth centuries Siberia was in a position of total and absolute economic dependence on the metropolis.'[22] But Vilkov's conclusion is questionable, given that 'the metropolis' relied so heavily on the commercial profitability of the products of Siberia itself, from which Moscow undoubtedly benefited.

However, this supposed 'total' dependence was soon offset by the development of local trades, crafts and small and medium-sized manufacturing enterprises producing goods 'on the spot'. In this way a Siberia-based diverse economy began to develop with many essential branches of production, using local raw materials, local skills, manpower and expertise. For instance, the discovery of mineral resources with which Siberia is so richly endowed, such as iron, gold, silver, lead, copper and mica, led to the early establishment of industrial enterprises, mines and foundries with their attendant workforces. The metallurgical industries were not only important in the manufacture of ordnance and other military materiel, but also in the output of everyday items forged and beaten out of metal (see Chapter Three). The fabled Siberian salt-workings, too, performed a crucial function in the territory's early economy, particularly high-quality deposits found on the upper Irtysh at the beginning of the seventeenth century. There in 1626, according to P.P. Yepifanov: 'six hundred *sluzhilie lyudi*, cossacks, Tatars and Ostyaks extracted around 40,000 *pud*s of salt and delivered it to Tobolsk in boats'. By the end of the century similar workings of the precious commodity had been developed throughout Siberia, even as far as Okhotsk, the substance being used not only in the preservation of foodstuffs, but also as a medium of exchange and remuneration.[23]

The importance of an extensive and efficient transport and communications system cannot be overstated in any examination of Russia's colonization of Siberia. Central to this was water transport along Siberia's great rivers, which led very early on to the development of a thriving boat-building industry and the founding of sizeable fleets based on most of Siberia's major waterways: thus there came into existence, for example, the Ob, the Yenisei, the Angara and the Lena fleets. The craft ranged in size from small, swift skiffs to great barges and heavy transport vessels, their construction obviously requiring a large force of skilled workmen – carpenters, shipwrights, rope-makers and sail-makers. In some of the major boat-building yards, often anything from 70 to 100 vessels were built per year, and the huge demand for flax and hemp for the production of stout ships' cables and sails provided a stimulus for the growth of local agriculture. The large haulage vessels were not dragged overland across the portages, the cargo being shifted from one river system to the next usually by packhorse or wagon.

This brings us to the land transport network. By the mid-seventeenth century many towns and settlements had their own 'transport workers' quarter' (*yamskaya sloboda*) inhabited by hundreds of coachmen, drivers, farriers, ostlers, wheelwrights, stable hands, wagon-builders and their families who were responsible for keeping Siberia's provisioning, merchandise and human traffic in motion across the region's enormous expanses in all weathers.

More figures and examples could be adduced to demonstrate quite clearly that during the course of the seventeenth century there developed a variegated, vigorous and viable local Siberian economy that both complemented and supplemented the fur trade, and also corresponded to the needs of the new immigrant population.

POPULATION AND COLONIZATION

Among the various groups of people moving into Siberia from European Russia – cossaks, free traders and tradesmen, merchants, government officials, priests, vagrants, fugitives, religious dissidents, artisans, exiles and military servitors (*voennosluzhilie lyudi*) – the Soviet historian, N.I. Nikitin, reckons that by far the largest category of the Russian population of Siberia during the period of its early settlement was composed of military servitors. He calculates that it was not until the early eighteenth century that the Russian peasant population of Siberia was equal to that of the military men – and the vast majority of the former was concentrated in the relatively small Verkhoture-Tobolsk agricultural region. Elsewhere, particularly in the far north, in the south-west, Transbaikal and in the major towns – Tobolsk, Tyumen, Tomsk, Irkutsk, Nerchinsk, Yakutsk – military service personnel far outnumbered the rest of the population groups, despite the fact that military commanders constantly complained of insufficient troop numbers (*malolyudstvo*). The vast majority of the *voennosluzhilie lyudi* were made up of common cossaks originating from European Russia, particularly those provinces closest to the Urals.

So, who, exactly, were the Siberian cossaks? The term cossak – *kazak* in Russian – derives from a Turkic word meaning something like a 'free man', a 'bold fellow', perhaps with connotations of the 'desperado', or according to others, a light horseman. This is not the place to trace the history of 'cossakdom' (*kazachestvo*), but suffice it to say that the early cossak communities (usually referred to as 'hosts') appeared around the end of the thirteenth century in the so-called 'Wild Field' (*dikoe pole*) on the southern frontiers, steppelands and rivers of present-day Ukraine. They comprised a motley conglomeration of runaway peasants, brigands, deserting soldiers, disaffected petty nobles, religious schismatics, some Tatars and other 'self-made' outlaws from Russian society. They lived their swashbuckling lives in free democratic communities through a mixture of banditry, farming, piracy and mercenary military activities in the service of the Russian tsar, the Polish king or the Turkish sultan – generally of the highest bidder. It was from among the Volga cossaks that Yermak and his band hailed when they entered the service of Ivan the Terrible and the Stroganovs at the start of the Siberian campaign (see above).

Thereafter, the Siberian cossaks took on a special identity, different from the buccaneering cossak hosts in the south. They were officially classed as being in government service and received payment from the state, though their income was much augmented by their own lawless pillaging activities. Because of the difficulties of the terrain, much of it frozen tundra or dense forest, the majority of the Siberian cossaks, unlike the cossaks of the steppes, did not ride horseback, but travelled and fought on land as infantrymen. Their main duties were those of acquiring new territories, crushing the natives, helping to man the *ostrogi*, and collecting the *yasak*, if necessary by brute force. They were also employed on garrison duty in the forts, and by the mid-seventeenth century there were companies of cossaks in all the major towns and fortresses, from Tobolsk in the west to Yakutsk in the north and Irkutsk in the east. In addition, they engaged in fishing, building work, escorting prisoners and supervising transport of merchandise. Their numbers were increased throughout the seventeenth century by the dispatch of other government troops from European Russia seconded permanently to Siberia, foreign prisoners of war from the Baltic region – collectively referred to as *Litva* – some exiled criminals and other disparate groups, and also, of course, by natural procreation. By the beginning of the eighteenth century, it is estimated that there were between 5,000 and 6,000 cossaks in Siberia, nearly one-third of them in and around Tobolsk, which by then had come to be regarded of the unofficial 'capital' of Siberia – at least of western Siberia.

Apart from the duties mentioned above, the cossaks also engaged in agriculture and a variety of trades and crafts. Military records reveal that among the civilian occupations of the Siberian cossaks were millers, leather-, silver-, gun- and blacksmiths, carpenters, soap-makers, tailors and glaziers, not to mention the butchers, the bakers and candlestick makers. In this way the 'rude soldiery' of Siberia contributed much to the civic development and economic diversity of the territory – as well as committing some of the worst atrocities in their treatment of the aboriginals and, because of their unruly, coarse and often savage behaviour, constituting a permanently unpredictable and undisciplined segment of Siberian society.[24]

According to P.A. Slovtsov, in 1662 the Russian and other immigrant population of Siberia stood at 105,000 out of an overall total of 393,000. One century later (1762), the Russian population heavily outnumbered the native peoples (420,000 and 26,000 respectively), and by the time of the major census of 1897, Russian Siberians numbered almost 5 million, in comparison to only 870,000 natives. Even more spectacularly, by 1911, barely a decade-and-a-half later, the Russian element had nearly doubled to 8.4 million, while the indigenous peoples only marginally increased to 973,000. In both pre-revolutionary (i.e. pre-1917) and later Soviet historiography there have been many attempts to analyse the population dynamics of Siberian settlement from European Russia, some of them muddied by ideological presuppositions dictated by the prevailing political climate. Western scholars, too, notably Armstrong, Coquin and Treadgold,[25] have made valuable contributions to the debate. The basic question seems to boil down to this: was Russia's penetration and colonization of Siberia the result of state-sponsored and government-directed initiatives, or did it owe more to the spontaneous movement of the Russian people migrating freely and voluntarily to fill up the huge vacuum across the Urals in search of wealth, land or freedom from an oppressive central government? Allied to this is the crucial question of the nature and quality of the Russian conquest in its effects on the Siberian aboriginal peoples, a topic to be examined in detail in Chapter Five.

On the matter of migration and settlement, what is perfectly clear is that this complex phenomenon is not reducible to a single, all-embracing formula which will satisfactorily explain the process completely. Different factors operated in different times and in different places. In an excellent survey published in 1982, David Collins has drawn together the results of the Russian historiography to demonstrate convincingly that what might hold good for north-west Siberia does not necessarily apply to the more fertile south, while in Yakutia and the Far East the picture changes yet again. In one case the major attraction was fur, in another, land and in yet another the chief deter-minant was the need to establish fortified (and hence populated) defence lines to protect important trade and communication routes against the encroach-ment of hostile neighbours. Despite the variety of circumstances, Collins is persuaded that there is much in the thesis that a leading role was played in the colonization process by the fortress towns, the establishment of which in most cases *preceded* the wider settlement of a particular region by incoming free migrants. Indeed, it is sensible to suppose that people would be more inclined to settle in a region that was already pacified, garrisoned and pro-tected than one in which the situation was still volatile, uncertain and dangerous.

Contrary to the spontaneous, mass peasant-migration theory favoured by nineteenth-century regionalist historians and subscribed to by some eminent Soviet Marxist scholars, notably V.I. Shunkov – for whom the prime moving force of history is the common people – this view suggests that, fur-hunters apart, it was the *sluzhilie lyudi*, state servitors both military and civilian, who arrived first in any large numbers, established military control and then engaged in non-military activities which created conditions favourable for further civilian settlement.[26] This is certainly consistent with the case put forward by Nikitin (above).

However, in the final analysis the argument over 'who came first, the *muzhik* or the militia?'[27] becomes a circular one, and it is not simply a matter of avoiding the issue by agreeing with the conclusion of N.V. Ustyugov that, 'government-directed and "free" colonization [of Siberia] are two parallel, mutually dependent and closely connected processes which are impossible to understand one without the other ... [There is] a distinct, organic connec-tion between both directions [in the history] of Russian colonization'.[28]

What is certainly indisputable is that, contrary to popular misconceptions connected with Siberia's reputation as a vast penal colony, the compulsory settlement of Siberia by common criminals and political offenders exiled by judicial or administrative order played a very minor and almost wholly negative role in the history of Siberian colonization (see Chapter Six). The major factor was always a symbiotic combination of state service, voluntary migration and – despite problems of gross sexual imbalance – the process of natural procreation.[29]

ARCHPRIEST AVVAKUM: RUSSIA'S 'TURBULENT PRIEST'

Most of our historical knowledge of the first century of Russia's conquest of Siberia is based on the contents of various archives, government decrees, local officials' reports, inventories, ledgers, statistical information, chronicles and family histories, some of it of unreliable quality and often contradictory. Much of this material is couched in the spare, bureaucratic language of officialdom, the so-called *prikaznyi yazyk* (literally 'chancery language', or the 'language of the bureaux'). We are fortunate, however, in addition and stark contrast to these bare, official documents, to have for our further enlightenment a remarkable piece of medieval literature that gives us a unique and fascinating firsthand account of an exceptional individual who experienced the sufferings, privations and torments of frontier existence in seventeenth-century Siberia, which, besides being a passionate, pyrotechnic literary tour de force, is also a treasure trove of closely observed historical detail. This particular gem is the riveting life-story of the cantankerous rebel cleric, defender of the 'Old Belief', exile and autobiographer extraordinaire, Archpriest Avvakum Petrovich (c.1620–82), briefly mentioned in Chapter One.[30]

It is unnecessary for present purposes to go into the historical and religious background of the Great Schism (*raskol*) that sundered the Russian Orthodox Church in the mid-seventeenth century.[31] Put very simply, Avvakum, along with a significant section of the lower clergy, refused to accept a range of ecclesiastical and liturgical reforms in the ceremonial practices and worship of the official Russian Church, which had been introduced with the full support of Tsar Aleksei Mikhailovich (ruled 1645–76) and the powerful Patriarch Nikon. With Avvakum as one the most outspoken, refractory and vociferous of the dissidents – known because of their defence of the traditional rituals as the 'Old Believers' – they launched a campaign of public denunciation, defiance and condemnation of the innovations, for which they were duly persecuted and subjected to a variety of degrading and often brutal punishments. In August 1653, Avvakum was arrested, beaten, abused, imprisoned and finally sentenced by patriarchal decree to banishment in Siberia, already a standard form of punishment as well as a convenient way of ridding Muscovy of criminals and other socially undesirable elements (see Chapter Six). Originally condemned to be banished to the remote outpost of Yakutsk in north-east Siberia, Avvakum had his sentence commuted on the tsar's intervention to exile in the less distant Tobolsk, the most important town in west Siberia. Moreover, rather than being unfrocked, he was allowed to retain his ecclesiastical status as archpriest, and orders were sent to Archbishop Simeon of Tobolsk that he should be appointed to a position in a church either there or somewhere else in the diocese. After all the necessary preparations had been made by the *Sibirskii prikaz* (Bureau for Siberian Affairs), on 27 September 1653, Avvakum (then aged 32), his wife, Anastasiya, their four young children (including a week-old baby) and his niece left Moscow under armed military guard on the first stage of their gruelling, 11-year odyssey.

After a 13-week journey they arrived at their destination. All things considered, Avvakum had so far got off rather lightly in comparison with some of the other schismatics. He had not been tortured, physically mutilated or permanently incarcerated; he had not had his hair shorn or been unfrocked; he was still united with his family and he was destined for a senior clerical post in Siberia's most important town under the jurisdiction of an archbishop who was already an old acquaintance.

Despite its status as virtual capital, Tobolsk was still very much a wild frontier town bustling with a heterogeneous, polyglot population of soldiers, cossaks, exiles, artisans, native tribesmen, and both Russian and foreign merchants lured to Siberia by avarice, adventure or impatience with the constraints of Muscovite officialdom and serfdom. Standards of social and moral behaviour were rough and ready, and the archbishop complained in his reports to Moscow of widespread drunkenness, debauchery, abandoned children and the regular traffic in native women among Siberian officials. There were also insufficient numbers of clergy, at any rate of a sufficiently high standard of literacy or morality to discharge their religious duties effectively. In fact, before Avvakum's arrival the archbishop had already petitioned Moscow to send him more priests who were 'neither drunkards nor lechers'. It was, therefore, probably with some enthusiasm, or at any rate with relief, that Archbishop Simeon welcomed the stalwart, sober and seemingly incorruptible Avvakum, and immediately installed him in the newly approved post of archpriest of the town's second cathedral, the Voznessenskii.

However, despite the benefits of his position, Avvakum's stubborn, self-righteous – almost arrogant, belligerent and puritanical temperament did not make for easy relations with the townsfolk of Tobolsk, and in his later autobiography he honestly recounts a number of unfortunate, even bizarre, incidents and run-ins with members of his flock, which point to a strong mixture of over-zealous piety and punitive vengeance. On one occasion, a lunatic who had supposedly been afflicted with madness after having sexual intercourse – albeit with his wife – on Easter Sunday (an activity rather meanly forbidden by canon law) was flogged on Avvakum's orders and chained to the church wall. The frenzied soul managed to break from his chains, fled from the church, broke into the *voevoda*'s house, ransacked his possessions and finished his rampage by parading about dressed in the commander's wife's clothes! According to Avvakum, the crazy transvestite was eventually cured of his mania after the archpriest had appeared to him in a dream and blessed him. Maybe he should have tried that trick in the first place.

Avvakum's propensity to physical violence is illustrated by other incidents, in one of which a drunken monk was forced to perform 150 prostrations while the church sexton whipped him with a lash. Later, the monk returned, confessed his sins and was granted absolution. The archpriest also ordered a similar flogging of an unrepentant prostitute who had been caught *in flagrante*, but had shown no remorse even after being locked in Avvakum's cellar for three days without food. This time, Avvakum's chosen methods did not have the desired effect, for he tells us how 'the vessel of Satan soon reverted to her old trade'.

It is no wonder that Avvakum's high-handed, brutal and overly intrusive treatment of his congregation made him so unpopular among the good, and the bad, citizens of Tobolsk, but his open, honest description of these and other incidents do give us some insight into the atmosphere, the violence and the lawlessness of existence in a Siberian frontier town. It was eventually after a protracted and complex affair concerning Avvakum's relationship with a clerk in the archiepiscopal chancellery, one Ivan Struna, that the decision was taken to remove Avvakum and send him further east. During the Struna affair, Avvakum had accused the clerk of embezzlement, personally thrashed him in the church, and later indicted him for taking a bribe from a man accused of incest with his daughter. Before that, Struna had incited the townspeople to raid Avvakum's house, seize him and drown him in the river Irtysh. Avvakum survived and went into hiding, and was later seemingly exonerated from his dubious role in the whole murky business. However, Avvakum's time in Tobolsk was drawing to a close. Following further formal investigations into his conduct and abuse of his position, about 27 June 1655, he and his family once more set sail for distant Yakutsk, thousands of kilometres to the east.

While wintering en route in Yeniseisk, further orders arrived from Moscow, assigning Avvakum as chaplain to a military expedition under the command of one Afanasii Filipovich Pashkov (c.1600–64). The object of the expedition was to conquer and explore the territory between Lake Baikal and the Chinese border, then known as the kingdom of Dauria. In Dauria, Pashkov was to gather intelligence of the region, impose the *yasak* on the local peoples, build fortifications and a church, prospect for minerals, cultivate the land, and establish relations with China and other adjacent lands. Pashkov had a reputation as an energetic commander, a fierce warrior, a sound administrator and a tough disciplinarian. A former *voevoda* of Yeniseisk, he was also stamped with the same degree of cupidity, cruelty and corruptibility that seemed to be the hallmark of most of the tsar's Siberian provincial governors. Having received his new commission and Avvakum his new orders, it was at this point that that the lives and fortunes of the brutal and pitiless commander, and the truculent and intractable archpriest became inextricably intertwined for the next seven years.

On 18 July 1656, the expeditionary force of 400 men, including Avvakum and his family, set off in a flotilla of 40 boats along the Angara river to Lake Baikal and beyond. The journey was an extremely perilous one, fraught with difficulties and dangers, the boats struggling against the current through fearsome rapids, portages and mountainous terrain, all of which Avvakum vividly describes in his autobiography with a keen eye for the landscape through which they passed, together with detail of the local flora and fauna. Apart from the physical difficulties of the journey, Avvakum was also to suffer the terrible wrath of Pashkov on more than one occasion during the first leg of their travels. At one point, for instance, Avvakum rather rashly compared Pashkov to the Devil and showed him such insolent disrespect that the furious chief knocked him to the ground, clubbed him where he lay and had him scourged with 72 blows of the knout, the dreaded whip. Amazingly, Avvakum survived this ordeal and the next stage of the journey where he was dragged in chains through the icy waters and jagged rocks of the great Padun Rapids – testimony to the man's enormous physical and mental stamina. Having arrived finally at the fortress of Bratsk, he was imprisoned half-naked in a freezing wooden tower, his back a mess of suppurating lacerations, his cell overrun with vermin and his body tormented by lice and fleas. Starved, frozen, flogged and fettered in a filthy dungeon, it is astonishing that he survived. But worse was still to come.

As Pashkov's cossacks pushed on into Dauria, they were decimated by famine, disease, sub-zero temperatures and sporadic warfare with superior Mongol forces. On one occasion a detachment of troops, led by Pashkov's own son, Yeremei, was slaughtered almost to a man. Only Yeremei survived to return, just in time to intercede with his father on behalf of Avvakum, for whom Pashkov had prepared a torture chamber and fires, intending to torment the priest for his suspected influence on the disastrous outcome of the foray. This is the point in Avvakum's autobiography where he provides a dramatic portrayal of the frenzied cavortings and divination rituals carried out by a local Tungus shaman – undoubtedly the first-ever literary eyewitness account of Siberian shamanism in practice (see Chapter Five). The writer also describes in harrowing detail the extremities to which the starving Russians were driven to obtain food while waiting in vain for fresh supplies and reinforcements from Yeniseisk. Barefoot and half-naked, they foraged and scrabbled for roots, grasses, bark, carrion and even an unborn foal ripped from the dead mare's belly to fend off starvation in the teeth of the bitter Siberian winter. Avvakum's sensitive observations and graphic descriptions of their awful predicament and Pashkov's further cruelties still make his own life-story a capital source for the history of this grim chapter in the annals of Russia's conquest of Siberia.

Eventually, in the summer of 1662, Avvakum was recalled to Moscow, which he reached in May 1664 after a hazardous two-year journey, travelling alone with his family, and experiencing more adventures, which – apart from two encounters with suspicious hostile natives – he passes over in uncharacteristic silence, vouchsafing only that 'there's plenty more to tell about that'. The rest of Avvakum's continuingly eventful life after his return from exile is not strictly germane to the history of Siberia itself, but nevertheless deserves of a brief, valedictory mention. Unsurprisingly, his Siberian ordeal had failed to chasten or silence him, and, although he initially received a warm welcome back in the capital, he still continued with his unrelenting and explosive denunciations of the Nikonian reforms and of the civil and religious establishment. Even formal excommunication from the Church in 1666, followed by imprisonment in a frozen, subterranean dungeon at Pustozersk, far beyond the Arctic Circle, failed to halt his vituperative outpourings. Finally driven to exasperation, the Muscovite authorities condemned him to death, and on 14 April 1682 Avvakum and three fellow prisoners were led from their icy cells to an elaborate pyre of pinewood billets and there burned alive. The tsar had finally rid himself of 'this turbulent priest'.[32]

It is a curious historical coincidence that the year of Avvakum's execution, 1682, also saw the enthronement – initially with his half-brother as joint tsar – of Pëtr Alekseevich Romanov, better known as Peter the Great, the future emperor who dragged Russia, sometimes kicking and screaming, from the side-wings of medieval Muscovy on to the centre stage of European, and eventually world, history. Although the eyes of Peter and his immediate successors were more firmly fixed on the west, significant developments also took place within Russia's massive Asiatic domains east of the Urals. It is to those developments in the eighteenth century that we now turn.

3

The Eighteenth Century:
Exploration and Exploitation

The Muscovite tsardom, including all the conquered lands from the Urals to the Pacific and inherited by Peter I as sole ruler in 1696, was already an empire in all but name before it was given that official status in 1721. In that year, Peter was re-crowned with the title of Emperor, and his realm was renamed as the Russian Empire (*Rossiiskaya Imperiya*). And so it remained until the revolutions of 1917. Peter the Great is justly famous, as alluded to earlier, for placing his realm fairly and squarely on the map of European and world history. By dint of relentless energy, grandiose visions, charismatic personality and ferocious brutality in pursuit of his aims and ambitions, he had managed by the end of his reign to transform medieval Muscovy, regarded by Western visitors as 'a rude and barbarous kingdom', into an embryonic, modern world power. Among his many achievements he had defeated Sweden in the 'Great Northern War' (1701–21), gained a maritime exit on the Baltic Sea, built Russia's first navy, founded the new capital city of St Petersburg (his 'window on Europe'), reformed the calendar, numerical system and the alphabet, personally engaged in the bloody slaughter of his rivals and opponents (including his own son), and introduced an astonishing range of military, fiscal, administrative, institutional, educational, cultural, sartorial and ecclesiastical reforms. These were aimed at driving out the semi-barbarism of medieval Muscovy, albeit by the prodigal use of barbaric, bullying and draconian methods, which his dreadful predecessor, Ivan the Terrible, would no doubt have relished with sadistic delight.[1]

For all the unsavoury aspects of Peter's personality and policies, he did display a genuine infatuation with the science, learning and technology of the West, and invited hundreds of foreign scholars, technicians, military officers, engineers, astronomers, scientists and other qualified experts to serve in the process of Russia's 'modernization'. In the field of knowledge, education and learning, Peter founded a number of so-called 'cipher schools' and academies for the advancement of engineering, medical, artillery and naval studies. But his greatest achievement in this respect was his establishment of the Imperial Academy of Sciences in 1724, opened shortly after his death by his illiterate widow and successor, Empress Catherine I (ruled 1725–30), thereby laying the foundation-stone for the edifice of what is still Russia's most prestigious and world-famous institution of scientific research. But for all his obsessive preoccupation with the West, Peter did not neglect his vast possessions in the East. It was in the same year as the Academy officially opened, 1725, that the emperor, ever hungry for the acquisition of further knowledge – always in the interests of the state – shortly before his death authorized the launching of an ambitious scientific and naval expedition, under the command of the Danish seafarer, Vitus Jonassen Bering (1681–1741), to explore the northern ocean and the coastline around Kamchatka, and ascertain whether a land-bridge existed linking north-east Siberia with the American continent. The so-called First Kamchatka Expedition (1725–30) set the pattern for further great journeys of exploration throughout the eighteenth century.

VOYAGES OF DISCOVERY AND THE FIRST KAMCHATKA EXPEDITION

Bering was not, in fact, the first to pass through the straits which still bear his name. Exactly 80 years before he did so, in 1648 a Yakutsk-based cossak ataman (chieftain), Semën Ivanovich Dezhnëv (c.1605–73), sailed eastwards from the mouth of the river Kolyma which empties in to the Arctic Ocean, circumnavigating the Chukotka peninsula, through the straits separating Asia and America, down to a point just south of where the river Anadyr flows into the northern Pacific. Although some later historians were sceptical as to whether the voyage actually took place, information gathered by Bering himself, later reinforced by the researches and publications of Gerhard Friedrich Müller (see below), and corroborated by modern scholarship, proves that Dezhnëv and his fellow mariners were unquestionably the first Europeans to sail through what came to be called, not the Dezhnëv, but the Bering Strait, thereby demonstrating the fact of north-eastern Asia's separation from the continent of northwestern America.[2] In the same way as they had opened up the land route into Siberia, it was again the intrepid cossaks who were in the vanguard of exploring its Arctic shores and discovering the north-east passage to the Pacific. However, the reality of Dezhnëv's 'discovery' was not itself 'discovered' until long after the event, which explains Peter's later orders to Bering and others to determine the precise maritime geography of the region.

While the circumstances of Russia's original penetration of Siberia in the late sixteenth and the seventeenth centuries, and her further exploration and expansion in the eighteenth century, bear many similarities – such as the type of terrain, the climate, the atrocious conditions, the dangers, the physical and human toll, the quest for fur and the oppressive treatment of the natives – there are also significant differences. First, of course, is that

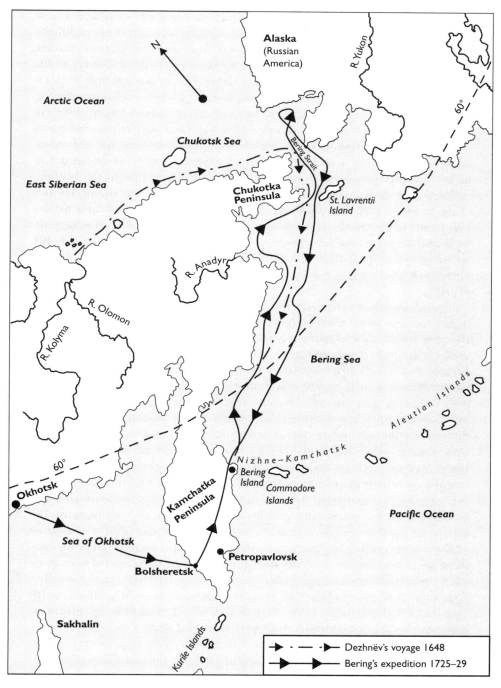

Map 5   North-east Siberia, Kamchatka and the Bering Strait with routes of Dezhnëv's and Bering's voyages.

while the early explorers travelled on foot, horse, sled or river boat, for their eighteenth-century successors it was more a matter of maritime expeditions, with sea-going vessels plying the treacherous waters of the Arctic and north Pacific oceans and the Okhotsk and Bering seas, establishing control of the islands in the Bering Strait and the Aleutian and Kurile archipelagos.

Also, while there was obviously a good deal of government involvement in the earlier movement – particularly in the construction and garrisoning of the fortified strongholds, the *ostrogi*, and the appointment of governing and administrative personnel, as described in the previous chapter, the major achievements in the seventeenth century owed as much to the initiative of private entrepreneurs (*promyshlenniki*), independent merchants, fugitive political and religious dissenters, vagabonds, runaway serfs, outlaws and other itinerant social outcasts who sought refuge in the forests and lived a precarious existence through whatever stratagems they could employ, both legal and illegal. These peripatetic misfits were generically described as the 'wandering folk' (*gulyashchie lyudi*), and comprised a not insignificant, unruly element in Siberia's tough frontier society right through until the revolutions of 1917.

Beginning, characteristically, during the reign of Peter the Great – a pathological 'control freak' whose efforts to force all his subjects into the service of the state foreshadowed modern totalitarianism – the amount of central government control of economic and social matters in the exploration of Siberia became much more marked. Although the private entrepreneurs, merchant adventurers and independent individuals still continued to play an important role, it was the government, above all, which ordered the direction, management, sponsorship, commissioning and supply of all the major expeditions of discovery, conquest and eastwards expansion throughout the eighteenth century. Indeed, while it was one thing to proceed relatively cheaply by land, the enormous sums required to finance the new maritime ventures half the world away – including first and foremost, of course, the building, provisioning, arming and manning of vessels of sufficient size, sturdiness and seaworthiness to withstand the prodigious distances and poundings of the uncharted northern oceans – could only realistically be met from the resources of the central exchequer. The same consideration also applied to the recruitment and commissioning of the necessary technical personnel required for such ambitious undertakings.

Captain Bering was not the first to receive his marching – or sailing – orders from Peter. On 2 January 1719, the tsar had issued the following curt command to two young geodesists, Ivan Yevreinov and Fëdor Luzhin:

> You are to proceed to Tobolsk and obtain guides, then go to Kamchatka and *beyond* [emphasis added] in accordance with your instructions and make a description of the area. Are America and Asia joined? This assignment is to be carried out very thoroughly, not only south and north, but also east and west. Make an accurate map of everything. An *ukaz* [decree] has been sent to the governor of Siberia and other

administrative officials concerning your departure from Tobolsk, and ordering that you be furnished with transports and guides.[3]

Armed with their instructions, the two scientists and their team duly set off for Tobolsk, Kamchatka 'and beyond', but were thwarted in their endeavours to carry out their assignment in full, mainly because of the dreadful weather, raging storms and heavy seas. They were, however, successful in sailing as far as the northern Kurile Islands, and in gathering intelligence from old cossaks and other Russian inhabitants of Kamchatka about conditions on the peninsula and adjacent territories and islands. They also managed to make a map of the region, as Peter had ordered, which they presented to the tsar on their return to St Petersburg in 1722.

Peter, by then having secured victory over Sweden in the Great Northern War, and newly crowned with the title of Emperor, was obviously disappointed with the meagre results of Yevreinov's and Luzhin's incomplete enterprise, and, possibly acting on the earlier advice of the German philosopher and polymath, Gottfried Leibniz (1646–1716), determined to fund and organize a more ambitious, systematic and better-equipped expedition of scientific discovery, which soon materialized as Vitus Bering's First Kamchatka Expedition. Again, it is worthwhile reproducing the emperor's terse, though somewhat vague, instructions to his Danish mariner in full (his orders were dictated three weeks before his death on 28 January 1725, and given to Bering by his successor, Catherine I, on 25 February):

1. In Kamchatka or some other place build one or two boats with decks.
2. On those boats sail close to the land that goes to the north which (since no one knows where it ends) seems to be part of America.
3. Discover where it is joined to America, and proceed as far as some town belonging to a European power; or, if you encounter a European ship, ascertain what that coast is called, write it down and go ashore yourself, gather genuine information, set it down on a map, and come back here.[4]

Earlier, Peter had also sent a message to the Governor of Siberia, Prince V.L. Dolgorukii, informing him of Bering's impending arrival and ordering him 'to render to him [Bering] every possible assistance to enable him to carry out [his] instructions'.

After setting out from St Petersburg in February 1725, Bering and his huge entourage travelled overland, encountering severe difficulties and setbacks en route, and arrived at Okhotsk more than a year-and-a-half later in October 1726. There he was joined in the following year by his second-in-command, Aleksei Chirikov (1703–48) and his fellow Dane, Martyn Spanberg (c.1700–61). In Okhotsk, they built a seaworthy boat called the *Fortuna*, on which they set sail for Kamchatka, where they built a second one, the *St Gavriil*. On 13 or 14 July 1728 Bering, Chirikov, Spanberg and their 44-man crew set a north-easterly course on the *St Gavriil*. Their voyage took them along the coast, discovering the island later named St Lavrentii, and ultimately around the Chukotka peninsula, arriving in the Arctic Ocean at a point approximately 67 degrees north latitude and 162 degrees west longitude on 15 August. Unfortunately, so dense was the fog as they rounded the Chukotka peninsula that they were not yet aware that they had successfully navigated the strait. And, both on the outward voyage and on their return to Kamchatka, they certainly did not espy the coast of America. Bering made one more effort to reach the coast of what was to become Alaska, but was forced by severe storms to abandon the attempt. He finally decided to depart for St Petersburg in July 1729, arriving back in the capital in January 1730, after a round trip lasting almost exactly five years.

Although the First Kamchatka Expedition was not an unqualified success, it nevertheless set an important precedent and, through its discovery of unknown islands, the charting of the waters washing the north-eastern coastline of Siberia, drawing up tables of geographical co-ordination points along their route and gathering ethnographical information about the indigenous peoples, played an important role in the further exploration of the far northeast. Perhaps dissatisfied with his own performance, almost immediately after his return Bering petitioned the government to launch a second, much bigger, more costly and better-equipped expedition to complete unfinished work. It took two years of determined lobbying, canvassing, arguing and politicking before the Ruling Senate, under Empress Anna (ruled 1730–41), finally approved Bering's new commission. But before examining the achievements of Bering's second Siberian venture, mention should be made of other important expeditions of scientific enquiry that were made at the time.

MESSERSCHMIDT AND KRASHENINNIKOV

Apart from a rather limited and fatal mission in 1729–30 led by Afanasii Shestakov and Dmitrii Pavlutskii, during which Shestakov was killed by hostile Chukchi tribesmen, two other prominent scholars played an outstanding role in the further scientific exploration of Siberia: the German, Daniel Gottlieb Messerschmidt (1685–1735), and a bright young Russian student, Stepan Petrovich Krasheninnikov (1711–55). Messerschmidt was born in Danzig, graduated in medicine at the university of Halle, entered Russian service and was invited by Peter in 1716 to carry out a thorough scientific survey of western and central Siberia. There he investigated, recorded and collected examples of a botanical, zoological and geological nature, and mapped and catalogued his discoveries. He left St Petersburg in 1719, and spent the next three years travelling through the Urals, Barabinsk Steppe, the Kuznetsk Basin and Khakasia, whence he journeyed up the river Irtysh, and eventually proceeded to Tomsk where he discovered the skeleton of a giant mammoth by the banks of the river Tom. Constantly logging his finds and adding to his collection of samples of rocks, plants and animal life, in 1723 he floated down the Yenisei and Lower Tunguska rivers, where he found deposits of graphite and coal. Extending his itinerary into Yakutia, Messerschmidt – who mostly travelled alone – discovered and described silver and lead ore deposits, salt lakes and springs. He finally returned westwards via the rivers Angara, Yenisei, Ket and Ob, correcting previous maps of the Ob as he journeyed, and ended up in the settlement of Samarovo, the present-day town of Khanty-Mansiisk near the confluence of the Ob and the Irtysh.

As well as his studies of the animal, vegetable and mineral world of Siberia, the lone German scholar also made important observations of an ethnographical and archaeological nature, and produced a quantity of maps of hitherto unexplored territories. He returned to St Petersburg in 1727 where he set about writing up his notes and findings, which he prepared in Latin manuscript form in ten volumes. Unfortunately, the tale of Messerschmidt's prodigious scientific exertions has a rather sorry ending. His works were never published during his lifetime, and he died – ignored, forgotten and penniless – in 1735. Twelve years later most of his writings and collections were destroyed in a fire. Some of the surviving fragments were much later published in German by the Berlin Academy of Sciences, but despite the tragic loss of the bulk of his work, Messerschmidt's investigations still deserve more than a footnote in the annals of Siberia's exploration.

An altogether different character was Stepan Krasheninnikov. Born and educated in Moscow, Krasheninnikov was a brilliant young student of natural history who joined Bering's second Kamchatka expedition as assistant to Johann Georg Gmelin (1709–55), one of three foreign scholars assigned by the Academy of Sciences to lead the scientific detachment of Bering's expedition, the other two being Gerhard Freidrich Müller (1705–83) and Louis de l'Isle de la Croyère (?–1741). The story of that gigantic enterprise is told in the following section, but, such was the outstanding nature of Krasheninnikov's individual researches and discoveries when he became separated from the main contingent, that his personal role merits special attention. After an eventful and gruelling three-year journey, the Academic division of the expedition finally reached Yakutsk in September 1736. There they found no supplies, no provisions and no support – all the available stocks having been requisitioned by an earlier advance party on its way to Kamchatka, the expedition's immediate destination. Müller, moreover, had fallen ill, and decided to retreat westwards to more salubrious quarters. Gmelin chose to accompany him. It was therefore left to the 25-year-old Krasheninnikov to push on to Kamchatka alone in order to investigate the huge northern peninsula by himself.

Kamchatka had a special interest for both the Russian government and for the newly settled inhabitants of eastern Siberia. One of the major difficulties for Russia's early explorers was the chronic shortage of food, most areas of eastern and northern Siberia being unsuitable for agricultural development. In the previous century, Russian pioneers had been unsuccessful in their attempts to conquer and colonize the more temperate, fertile regions along the Amur river, which were conducive to cultivation, having been balked in their endeavours by the powerful Manchu Empire in northern China. After

40 years of bloody warfare with the Manchus and other tribes of the Amur Basin, during which the Russian commander, Yerofei Pavlovich Khabarov (c.1606–71) had played a particularly cruel, ruthless and sadistic role, looting, pillaging, raping and roasting his victims at will, Russia and China finally agreed to negotiate a settlement, which resulted in the signing of the Treaty of Nerchinsk (a trading settlement near the Manchurian border) in 1689. Under its terms Russia was compelled to evacuate all its forces from the region and destroy its fortifications, in return for being granted limited trading concessions with China.

Not until the mid-nineteenth century was Russia to venture again into the Amur-Ussuri lands (see Chapter Four). So, having failed to acquire grain-growing territories in the south, the government now turned its attention north to Kamchatka, which despite its northern location, had a more temperate climate than the 'mainland', and held out the prospect of developing the cultivation of cereal crops and other foodstuffs. Kamchatka also offered fresh hunting grounds for those engaged in the fur trade, which, though still lucrative, was suffering from a severe depletion of stocks.

Krasheninnikov set out on his lone mission with a set of precise instructions from Müller and Gmelin on 8 July 1737. His journey nearly ended in tragedy when his boat (Bering's old and leaky *Fortuna*) was wrecked on the Kamchatka coast during a powerful earthquake. He and his crew survived the catastrophe, but in the wreck Krasheninnikov lost all his personal possessions, including his instructions and the two-year supply of food. Undaunted by this inauspicious start, the young scholar spent the next three years, travelling – like Messerschmidt – mostly alone throughout the length and breadth of Kamchatka, an area covering 370,000 square kilometres (143,000 square miles), roughly the same size as Japan and considerably larger than the Italian peninsula.

In the words of Elizabeth Crownhart-Vaughan, translator of Krasheninnikov's later account of his experiences, 'For three years ... In that distant, primitive land of mountains, avalanches, earthquakes, quagmires and volcanoes, besieged by hostile natives, mosquitoes and lack of food, Krasheninnikov observed, collected, noted.'[5] Among the astonishingly rich variety of things which he 'observed, collected and noted' were specimens of animal and plant life, details of the spectacular Kamchatka landscape and terrain – sometimes tramping over miles of treacherous ground to investigate some 'new' natural wonder, such as hot mud-baths, a geyser or volcano – and observations of the movement of the tides around Kamchatka's shores. Little escaped his scrutiny – birds, reptiles, insects, fish, land and marine mammals, metals, minerals and semi-precious stones, flowers, plants, trees, rivers, lakes – in fact almost the entire gamut of Kamchatka's natural wealth.

Krasheninnikov also made close and detailed ethnographical researches into the lifestyle, customs, habitation, diet, dress, languages, beliefs and rituals of the native inhabitants of Kamchatka, in particular the Kamchadals, even sometimes staying in what he described as their filthy subterranean dwellings and sharing their unappetizing, often literally nauseating, food such as putrescent graveolent fish, great, greasy gobbets of walrus blubber and raw, rancid offal. Perhaps over-fastidious, however, he refrained from indulging in other delicacies, like the fistfuls of lice which the Kamchadals scraped from their own infested locks, crunched into a pulp and gobbled up. On the other hand, he did conduct experiments with the raising of crops, planting seeds of barley and rye in order to ascertain whether Kamchatka had the potential to become a viable area of cereal cultivation. He also provides fascinating detail of primitive medicines, herbal nostrums, disposal of the dead (literally a dog's breakfast), contraceptive infusions, violent courtship and marriage ceremonies, polygamy, concubinage and sundry sexual taboos. Here, for instance is what he has to say, dead-pan, about the eligibility of widows for re-marriage:

> No-one may lie with a widow until she has been purified of her sins. For this it is necessary that she have intercourse with a man other than the one who is to marry her; but it will only be a stranger, or someone beyond the prejudice of shame and infamy, who will perform this service for widows, this action being considered dishonourable by the Kamchadals. Thus it was formerly only with great difficulty and expense that widows could find men to purify them, and they were sometimes obliged to remain widows all their lives.

However, rescue was at hand as the incoming Russians gallantly did what they could to help the bereaved Kamchadal ladies out of their frustrating predicament. Krasheninnikov explains: 'But since our Cossacks have settled in Kamchatka, widows no longer have this trouble; they can find as many men as they wish to absolve them of their sins.'[6]

Without any exaggeration, it can safely be said that Krasheninnikov's accumulated knowledge of Kamchatka was truly encyclopaedic. It can just as safely be surmised that he himself did not offer his own services in the process of rescuing Kamchatka's unfortunate dowagers from a life of dismal celibacy.

In September 1740, Krasheninnikov's isolation was broken by the appearance on Kamchatka of Georg Wilhelm Steller (1709–46), a clever, youngish, German associate professor of natural history who was invited by the Academy to join Bering's expedition. His presence on Kamchatka was not entirely welcome to Krasheninnikov, for the newcomer from the outset displayed an arrogant and overbearing attitude to the younger man (who was also his academic junior), often treating him as a mere clerical assistant. Fearing that for some reason Krasheninnikov might stand in his way to joining Bering in his quest for North America, Steller managed to engineer his subordinate's recall to St Petersburg, a prospect not altogether unattractive to Krasheninnikov. He consequently rejoined Müller and Gmelin in Siberia, and then travelled on to St Petersburg, reaching the capital in 1741, where, in recognition of his achievements, he was appointed to a junior post at the

Academy, later being promoted to the status of full Academician in 1750. He spent his last years writing up his voluminous notes (supplemented by those of Steller, who had died in Tyumen from the ravages of alcoholism while returning home in 1746), which resulted in his magnificent *Description of the Land of Kamchatka*, published under the imprimatur of the Academy of Sciences in 1755. Sadly, he did not survive to see its publication. Despite the fact that Krasheninnikov never actually joined up with the main part of Bering's expedition, his long, solitary scientific labours on Kamchatka still mark him out as one of the most distinguished scholars of early modern Siberia.

There were many other journeys of exploration and discovery in the mid-eighteenth century undertaken by Russians and foreigners alike, some of them private enterprises, others still state-financed. Among the foreign contributors to our knowledge of eighteenth-century Siberia are the German, Peter Simon Pallas (1705–83), whose account of his extensive travels and researches in Siberia was published in three volumes in St Petersburg (1771–6), entitled *A Journey through Various Provinces of the Russian Empire*; the famous English navigator Captain James Cook (1728–79);[7] and his compatriot, clergyman, writer and traveller, William Cox (1747–1828) whose popular travelogue with the wonderfully prolix title, *Account of the Russian Discoveries between Asia and America to which are Added the Conquest of Siberia, and the History of the Transactions and Commerce between Russian and China*, appeared in 1782. Because it presented the English reading public with much new first-hand information about Siberia, this came to be regarded as a classic of its kind. But, for all the intrinsic interest of these and other journeys of discovery, undoubtedly by far the most important and the most celebrated is Vitus Bering's Second Kamchatka Expedition (1733–43), otherwise known as the Great Northern Expedition. Some historians regard the first and second Kamchatka expeditions as actually two stages of a single process, considering the first as a kind of preliminary 'recce' for the second, and describe them jointly as the 'Siberian-Pacific Expedition' (*Sibirsko-Tikhookeanskaya ekspeditsiya*), which is how the enterprise will be referred to in the following section.

THE SIBERIAN-PACIFIC EXPEDITION

What follows in this section falls into two halves, reflecting the dual nature and purpose of the expedition, which came under the combined auspices of the Admiralty and the Academy of Sciences. On the one hand the government was greedily bent on extending its possessions and control over their economic resources, and by dint of territorial aggrandizement on enhancing the international prestige of the Russian Empire, already the largest land empire in the world, if not in human history. On the other hand, there was a genuine desire, at least on the part of the good Academicians, to gain more detailed and accurate knowledge of the physical geography, climate, animal and plant life of Siberia, as well as of its mineral, pedological and other natural resources — which also had a practical, economic motive especially in the discovery of new metal ore deposits (see below).

The organization of the nautical side of the operation was under the direct control of Bering, who divided his personnel and resources into seven separate, though related, commands, each with responsibility for exploring and charting different sections of the oceans and coastlines. The whole entourage included over 500 soldiers, sailors and officers, a technical corps of hydrologists, topographers, surveyors and geologists, and thousands of support staff (cooks, grooms, carpenters, scribes, interpreters, porters, wagoners, couriers and general dogsbodies). It was not just the far north-east that was the object of their attention but the whole of Russia's Arctic coastline from the mouth of the river Dvina on the White Sea, eastwards and along the entire length of Siberia's northern littoral, past the deltas of the Ob, the Yenisei and the Lena, round the Yamal, Taimyr and Chukotka peninsulas, and southwards as far as the estuary of the river Anadyr on the far-eastern coast. Some units of the expedition even sailed as far south as the northern shores of Japan and as far east (from the Russian perspective) as the coast of north-west America, where the German scientist Georg Steller, who had finally realized his ambition in joining Bering's squadron (see above), was almost certainly the first European, the first white man, to set foot on Alaskan soil, or snow, albeit on an offshore island rather than the mainland.

For present purposes it is unnecessary to give a sea-mile by sea-mile account of Bering's and his deputy commanders' voyages, and the navigational and cartographical achievements. The story has been well rehearsed.[8] It is sufficient to note that the various naval contingents set off at staggered intervals from St Petersburg during the spring and early summer of 1733, and when they arrived at their allotted destination, they began the long, hard process of carrying out their comprehensive instructions and fulfilling their daunting tasks of maritime exploration in those forbidding Arctic waters. Conditions from the outset were horrendous, and the courageous polar explorers had to struggle against permanently sub-zero temperatures, crushing floes and icebergs, howling gales and blizzards, snow-blindness, frostbite, scurvy, near famine and, because of the unforested landscape, an absence of timber with which to build onshore wintering shelters when the frozen seas were impassable. Hundreds of ordinary seamen and a fair number of their officers and commanders perished in the icy wastes, including the leader of the Taimyr group, Lieutenant Vasilii Vasilevich Pronchishchev (1702–36) and his wife, Tatyana Fëdorovna, née Kondyrova (1710–36), Russia's first woman Arctic explorer, after whom Pronchishcheva Bay on the Taimyr peninsula is still named.

Further east, Bering and his companions, Aleksei Chirikov and Martyn Spanberg, continued their quest finally and conclusively to confirm the existence of the north-east passage, and, ultimately, to make landfall on the coast of North America, an objective which they failed to achieve, though some of the company, including Steller, disembarked on Kayak Island. How the Russians finally established their primitive colony of 'Russian America' on the American mainland is dealt with in the following chapter. According to Steller, Bering did not seem as elated with the sighting of Alaska as Steller himself, and, already suffering badly from scurvy, the commander of the great Siberian-Pacific Expedition ordered his crew to set sail back to base in Kamchatka. Ferocious weather conditions as well as the physical debilitation of the seamen, however, forced them to land on a small island in the Commander archipelago before they could make harbour at Petropavlovsk. There, after a few days, Bering died, and was buried on the island which now bears his name, and where his tomb was discovered by a Russian-Danish expedition in 1991.

Though not every one of the objectives of Bering's final mission had been achieved, nevertheless, almost the whole of Eurasia's northern coastline had now been charted, the depths of Siberian rivers' Arctic reaches had been accurately plumbed, successful voyages had been made to North America and the coast of Japan, and numerous new islands in the Arctic Ocean and in the Aleutian and Kurile chains had been discovered.

Also, deep in the heartland of central Siberia, the expedition's two leading academic specialists, Müller and Gmelin, had carried out superlative feats of scientific discovery, as described below. In the words of the American historian, W. Bruce Lincoln: 'While men in fragile ships had been fighting to make headway against the fog, ice and cold of Siberia's northern coast, others had been at work in its interior in the largest scholarly venture to be undertaken by any group of scientists before the nineteenth century.'[9] Others have described it as the greatest scientific expedition in the history of mankind. While one may quibble with the hyperbole, there is little doubt that, for its time, and given the formidable obstacles and the fantastic achievements, Müller, Gmelin and their helpers succeeded in writing a new chapter – indeed, new volumes – in the natural and human history of Siberia.

With the two German scholars at its head, the Academy's contingent of the Siberian-Pacific Expedition numbering around 600 men and comprising surveyors, instrument-makers, translators, draughtsmen, a physician, research assistants, grooms, guards and other support personnel had set forth from St Petersburg in August 1733. Larry Black, one of the West's leading experts on the Müller/Gmelin mission, tells us they took along with them 'nine wagonloads of instruments, a library of more than 200 books, writing paper, paints, drafting materials and other items necessary for scientific study'.[10] They also took along 40 pack-horses and numerous barrels of Rhineland wine, for which Gmelin in particular had a well-developed taste. According to their brief, Gmelin was to conduct research into Siberia's natural life, recording in as much detail as possible its flora and fauna, mineral deposits, physical geography and, in short, just about everything he could gather about the region's entire environment. Müller was cast in the role of historian, ethnographer, archivist, economist, demographer, philologist, archaeologist and, in fact, investigator of anything touching on the sum total of the activities of the species *Homo sapiens* across Siberia's huge expanses. They spent the next ten years – 1733 to 1743 – accomplishing their tasks in the teeth of extremities of 'cold and heat, sickness, mosquitoes, raging storms, dangers from brigands, mutual dislike and indifference from Bering and his associates, bureaucratic obstinacy, and even hostility from Siberian officials, and a variety of other hardships'.[11]

In the same article, Professor Black maintains that: 'During their decade in Siberia, Gmelin and Müller were rarely separated.' While this may be the case in the sense that they followed roughly the same itinerary – visiting the Altai, the Kuznetsk Basin, along the Yenisei to Krasnoyarsk, thence to Irkutsk and Transbaikalia, northwards to Yakutia, covering roughly 34,000 kilometres (21,100 miles) by foot, sledge, carriage and boat – their tasks (and their temperaments) were so different and their researches so diverse, that it is difficult to think of theirs as a co-operative, companionable and cosy joint venture. While Gmelin was busy pressing his flowers, chipping his rocks and hunting his bugs, Müller was otherwise occupied searching the archives, checking his sources and pursuing his various contacts in order to compile an authentic record of humankind's history, experience of and interaction with that huge chunk of planet earth now known as Siberia. Among his other myriad discoveries, Müller managed to disinter Dezhnëv's mouldering message about his voyage of 1648 through the Bering Strait, a document which had lain forgotten in a dusty Yakutsk archive for almost a century. Meanwhile, out in the field, Gmelin continued his botanical researches, collecting over 1,200 species of flower and plant life which he was later to collate in his four-volume *Flora Sibirica*, published between 1747 and 1769. Also published in four volumes, after his return to his native Germany, was his description of his personal experiences in Siberia – *Journey through Siberia, 1733–43*.[12] Müller for his part did not pen a complete personal memoir as such, but, through his journalistic and other literary activities, including his monumental, 22-part history of Siberia, *Description of the Siberian Tsardom*, and collected articles only published over a century after his death, he established himself as the real father of Siberian historiography.[13]

However, a comparative perusal of the two German scholars' accounts and reminiscences of their time in Siberia reveals some remarkably different memories and interpretations of what they each observed and experienced there. To quote Larry Black once more: 'It remains to illustrate why it was that Müller wondered aloud, after reading Gmelin's account, if they had really been together on the same expedition.'[14] Their subsequent accounts did actually have much in common, as is to be expected after what was a shared – if disparately diagnosed – experience. But there are also significant differences in tone, detail and approach. Gmelin is much more critical in his assessment of both Russians' and native Siberians' attitudes, mores and general behaviour, relishing his own descriptions of bawdiness, drunkenness, brigandage and widespread lawlessness, including an incident where renegade cossaks and Tatars attacked a village, tortured and massacred all the men, raped the women, and abducted them and all the children. Moreover, he states that local administrators and troops were totally ineffectual in preventing such atrocities, despite the horrific nature of such punishments as were inflicted on convicted wrongdoers. He recounts in gruesome detail, for instance, how two women, charged with murdering their husbands, were buried up to their neck until they died slowly of thirst, starvation, and the attacks of vermin and plagues of stinging insects. (Actually, this barbaric practice was not peculiar to Siberia: it was a standard punishment for husband-killers and adulteresses in eighteenth-century Russia.) Not surprisingly, central government was not well-pleased with Gmelin's scarifying revelations of the crudeness, cruelty and coercive practices which he described as routine in the lands beyond the Urals. Perhaps because Müller, unlike his former colleague, continued to live and work in Russia, he was more cautious about disclosing the seamier side of life in Siberia, and his accounts of social habits, official practices and local customs are much less sensational and more muted than Gmelin's occasionally lurid narrative.

But whatever their personal and academic differences, Müller, Gmelin and, indeed, the entire membership of Bering's redoubtable Siberian-Pacific Expedition produced results which stand comparison with the world's most famous journeys of discovery. Let Professor Black have the last word:

> The consequences of Bering's second expedition to Kamchatka and its myriad byproducts ... are almost beyond counting. The expedition may have been the largest of all time, for it consisted of over 3,000 men during the ten years of its existence. It set forces in motion which accelerated and made more efficient state and entrepreneurial investment in trade, mining, agriculture and administration ... Surveys of the Arctic coast, new maps of, and information about, Japan, the official discovery of the northern coast of America, and a final proof of the existence of a strait between Asia and America, all presented new knowledge of far-reaching significance ... [Q]uestions of the value of Russian colonization of Siberia by free peasants were raised and new expeditions were organized – all on the basis of new information and ideas provided by participants in Bering's *tour de force*.[15]

Müller's extensive publications in particular provided 'an invaluable wellspring for the consolidation of the notion of Siberia as the most vital part of the "Russian Lands"'.[16]

BLACK METAL AND SOLID GOLD

Beneath Siberia's frozen land surface are buried loads and lodes of precious, semi-precious and malleable metals. During the course of the eighteenth century, partly owing to the discoveries of the determined explorers and investigators described above, the minerals and metallic ores of Siberia began to outstrip fur as the region's most profitable, exploitable and employable commodity. Victor Mote has used 'gold' as a generic metaphor for the succeeding waves of Siberia's wealth: 'When someone writes the ultimate economic history of Siberia, "gold" will hold a prominent place – that is soft gold (furs), solid gold (metals), dry gold (grain), creamery gold (butter), and black and blue gold (oil and gas).' He continues, 'As the fur trade diminished, the relative importance of metals ascended.'[17]

Indeed, very soon after Muscovites first began their progress through Siberia in the sixteenth century, they were under orders to report any serendipitous sightings of deposits of ores such as gold, silver, copper, lead and ferrous metal (known in Russian as 'black metal' – *chërnyi metall*). A leading position in the 'metallurgical boom' in eighteenth-century Siberia was held by the wealthy family of the Demidovs, who played a not altogether dissimilar economic role from that of the merchant Stroganovs in the sixteenth century (see Chapter Two).

The patriarch and founder (in both senses of the word) of the Demidov dynasty was Nikita Demidovich Antufev (1656–1725), better known under the surname, Demidov. He learned his craft in the town which was the centre of the Russian metal-working industry, Tula, and soon came to the attention of Peter the Great, who – already in the early throes of the Great Northern War, and smarting from his defeat by Charles XII of Sweden at the battle of Narva (1700) – was in desperate need of great quantities of good-quality, home-produced artillery, ordnance and other military materiel. Before the meeting of the ironsmith and the tsar, Russia had needed to rely on small deposits of low quality ore smelted and forged in cottage foundries. For higher grade stuff, it was necessary to import iron and steel from Sweden, with which Russia was now at war. Demidov had established his own ironworks – the Demidov-Tula Factory (*Demidovykh-Tul'skii zavod*) in 1695, and soon became recognized for the quality and craftsmanship of his products. Suitably impressed, Peter granted Demidov possession of recently discovered good quality ferrous ores at Nevyansk in the Urals, right on Siberia's western frontier. State-run efforts to exploit Nevyansk's riches had proved unsuccessful, and Peter decided to see what the master from Tula could do, giving him unlimited freedom to build new foundries and smithies, hire labourers and founders and utilize the forests for fuel. He even bestowed on Demidov – a peasant and commoner by origin – the unique privilege of purchasing serfs to supplement the manpower necessary to service his new metallurgical empire, which stretched over an area of around 26,000 square kilometres (10,000 square miles).

When Peter had finally avenged himself for his humiliation by the Swedes at Narva through victory at the battle of Poltava in 1709, Demidov had made himself virtually the 'iron tsar' of his own industrial empire. In doing so – by massive recruitment of workers in the mining and manufacturing sides of his huge and lucrative business – he created for the first time in Russia something which in Marxist terms could be called an industrial proletariat, as Soviet historians were fond of pointing out. Later in the eighteenth century, the labourers in the Urals and west Siberian mines and factories were to play a significant role in the popular uprisings that took place during the reign of Catherine the Great (ruled 1762–96), particularly the colossal cossak-led rebellion headed by the doughty, but doomed, Emelyan Pugachëv between 1773 and 1775.

By the time that both Peter the Great and Nikita Demidov died in 1725 their synergetic relationship had fuelled each other's achievements to that extent that Peter's Russia was now a major European military power, and his continuous wars that had brought this about had created the voracious demand for the arms, which Demidov's vast metallurgical enterprises on the edge of Siberia had been able to satisfy, thereby ensuring the enormous fortunes of the Demidov industrial dynasty. At the beginning of Peter's reign, Russia had been a net importer of iron and other metals. By its end, his country was the largest producer and supplier of iron in the whole of Europe, and over 60 per cent of these ferrous exports came from the Demidovs' Siberian mines, forges and foundries. Nikita's son and heir, Ankifii Nikitich (1678–1745), expanded his father's inheritance many times over, founded new factories of his own, including copper-smelteries in the Altai, and built what was then the world's biggest blast-furnace. At the time of his death, just 20 years after that of his father and largely through Ankifii's own efforts and acumen, he had increased the Demidov family fortune to almost 1,000 times its 1701 value, and owned 25 industrial enterprises in the Urals, western Siberia and the Altai, employing 38,000 serfs.[18]

Of course, the Demidovs, while almost certainly the most successful, were not the only metallurgical industrialists in eighteenth-century Russia. The state itself held large holdings throughout Russia under the direct control and management of the College of Mines (*Berg-kollegiya*) one of the new 'ministries' established by Peter the Great as part of his central government reforms of 1719 to 1722. The fact that the country now had its own 'Ministry of Mines', exclusively dedicated to the extractive industries, demonstrates the same level of priority to this branch of the national economy as that of the special 'Sable Treasury' (*Sobolinaya kazna*) – secure behind the crenellated walls of the Moscow Kremlin – which handled all the fur pelts flowing from Siberia into the central exchequer in the seventeenth century.

The proximity of the Urals/west-Siberian ironworks to European Russia obviously meant that they played a greater role in the nation's industrial economy than those further east, but there, too, in eastern Siberia and the Far East, the metallurgical industries had a not inconsiderable role to play in the economic development of that vast area.[19] As mentioned in Chapter Two, while Russians penetrated even further and further east, and as the population of the region expanded as a result of continuing migration and natural growth, increased distances precluded the continuing import of essential tools, etc., from the metropolis at the same time as the demands of a growing population increased. It therefore became essential to discover local ore deposits and develop a regional iron industry. The early Russian prospectors were greatly helped in this quest by the indigenous peoples – particularly the

Yakuts, the Buryats and the Tungus — who had been mining ore and producing metal artefacts on a small scale for over two-and-a-half centuries before the Russian arrival. With native help and the skills of immigrant Russian specialists and craftsmen, over time the foundations of a local iron industry were laid, but, in comparison with the huge Demidov enterprises, at the turn of the seventeenth and eighteenth centuries the achievements in the east were relatively modest. Logistical, financial and technical problems were compounded by scarcity of sufficiently skilled personnel, which together at first impeded large-scale production. Most forges, foundries and workshops were of the cottage-industry type, using primitive smelting, processing and production methods. There was some success, however, and fairly large workings were finally established, with central government finance and management, at Ilimsk. One obvious factor that added to Ilimsk's productivity was the sensible decision to group together the extracting, forging and manufacturing processes in one location, rather than — as was often the case — the site of the ore deposits being at a distance from the manufacturing centre. It was said that the quality of the iron and metal products of Ilimsk were not inferior to those produced in Tula. Despite this limited success, another factor which prevented greater development in eastern Siberia was that production was essentially for the local commercial market. In other words what were lacking were the huge government procurement orders for military and naval equipment enjoyed by the Demidovs, for example.

However, in the second quarter of the eighteenth century a major boost was given to the eastern Siberian iron industry as a direct consequence of Vitus Bering's great expeditions and voyages of exploration described above. At the beginning of the century, there had been some increase in demand as a result of the development of other forms of economic activity. The spread of salt-, mica-, lead-, silver-, brewing- and textile-works all required the equipment to operate them, which increased the demand for more iron. However, the cottage industries, smithies and domestic-size forges were unable to meet even the modest surge in demand, which meant that already the need existed for reorganization and the establishment of large-scale factories such as existed in European Russia (e.g. Tula) and the Demidov lands in west Siberia. The first of these larger enterprises to be established in eastern Siberia were the Telminskii in the Irkutsk region, and the Tamginskii in Yakutia, but although they were bigger in capacity and output than the cottage foundries and village blacksmiths' shops, they still used fairly primitive techniques of smelting and hand forging. The situation was to change significantly with the arrival in eastern Siberia of Bering and his expeditions.

After his first expedition, Bering himself had already informed the government in St Petersburg of the existence of large, good-quality metal ore deposits in eastern Siberia, and in 1732 the Ruling Senate and the College of Commerce (*Kommerts-kollegiya*) issued a decree for the building of the Telminskii factory, mentioned above. Sited near the settlement of Telma, north of Irkutsk, and financed by the central exchequer, the management of the new ironworks was given a specific directive to produce sufficient quantities of metal and metal products to fit out Bering's boats (with anchors, fastenings, chains and other nautical equipment), as well as satisfying local needs with the manufacture of axes, scythes, sickles, knives, shovels, etc.[20] To some extent the factory was able to fulfil these production requirements, but the daunting problems of transporting the finished heavy equipment so far north to Yakutsk led to a further decree establishing a second factory close to Yakutsk on the banks of the river Tamga, the force of the waters of which could be harnessed in the production process. In 1753 the Tamginskii ironworks employed 75 workers including master founders, forgers and smiths, as well 5 cossaks, 24 apprentices and 34 exiles sentenced to hard labour.[21]

As it turned out, neither the Telminskii nor the Tamginskii works stayed in production for long, but a major development took place towards the end of the century, which led to a great surge in ferrous metal production in Siberia centred on the much larger Yezagashkii works near Krasnoyarsk, and the huge Petrovskii iron-smelting and metalworking factory to the west of Lake Baikal. The major development was the invention and employment of steam-powered machinery used for a variety of functions. The man most responsible for designing this mechanical equipment was one F.P. Borzov, who, although a brilliant engineer, bore the modest title of 'apprentice mechanic' (*mashinnyi uchenik*), but who, because of his independent and obstreperous attitude to the authorities, finally found himself arrested 'under heavy guard' for 'insolent words against the tsar'. However, despite his personal fate, Borzov had already provided the wherewithal for a massive increase in the productivity of the iron industry, and it quickly became obvious – as in any branch of industrial production – that larger-scale mechanized plants far outstripped small-time cottage industries or even medium-sized mills in productivity. For instance, the Yezagashkii steam-powered factory turned out the same quantity of iron and iron-based products in three or four days as the older Tamginskii works produced in a whole year.[22] In the words of P.G. Lyubimov, '[By the end of the eighteenth century] the blast furnace and the steam hammer had triumphed over the manual forge.'[23] (See Fig. 2)

Ferrous metals apart, developments also took place throughout the eighteenth century in the exploitation of other metals – precious, semi-precious and non-precious. Of these, the two most important were, of course, gold and silver, about which a few words must be said. Silver was more successfully produced in the eighteenth century than gold, the heyday of which was to occur in the nineteenth and early twentieth centuries. The major deposits were in the Altai and in the Nerchinsk region of Transbaikalia near the Chinese border (the ancient Dauria). Working of these lodes began in the early years of the century and continued throughout the tsarist period. Of the two, the Altai mines were by far the more productive. According to official government figures, whereas the Nerchinsk fields produced 10,000 puds of silver between 1701 and 1870, over a rather shorter period (1745–1860) the Altai managed to turn out over 123,000.[24] Both of these important mining

Figure 2 Drawing of a late seventeenth-/early eighteenth-century Siberian iron foundry with blast furnace. Note (a) the mountains in the background (almost certainly the Urals); (b) the large bellows on the left, serving the blast furnace; (c) the ingenious Heath Robinson apparatus of cogs, wheels and pulleys operating the power-hammers.

Source: Okladnikov, A.P. (ed.), *Istoriya Sibiri s drevneishikh vremen do nashikh dnei*, vol. 2, *Sibir' v sostave feodal'noi Rossii* (Leningrad, 1968)

regions, including all their mineral deposits – and profits therefrom (as mentioned in Chapter One) – belonged to and were administered by 'The Cabinet of His Imperial Majesty', which meant that they were the personal property of the tsar. For all its own intrinsic value, silver took second place to gold, but it was actually as a byproduct of the silver-smelting process that gold was first detected by Russian operators of the Nerchinsk silver mines.

According to V.V. Danilevskii, author of a scholarly history of the Russian gold industry,[25] Russians working the newly discovered silver deposits near Nerchinsk 'found that every ton of smelted metal from these new mines would yield about a hundred ounces of gold as part of the refining process'.[26] But as yet no actual veins of gold itself had been discovered, though folk wisdom, legend and archaeological discoveries of golden artefacts from ancient times all pointed to the existence of such a 'pot'. It was, however, only towards the middle of the century that rich gold deposits were found by geologists prospecting in north-west Siberia near the township of Berëzov. Important as this discovery was, the subterranean mineshafts of Berëzov, where gold-diggers toiled in appalling, often deadly, conditions, only yielded up about one-quarter of the gold that resulted from the silver smelting process in the Altai. By the end of the century, although the basis had been laid down for the vast surge – particularly in gold-mining – during the nineteenth century, Russia, despite its huge as yet undiscovered and unexploited precious metal resources, only accounted for a tiny proportion (around 1 per cent) of total world production.[27] It was not until the application of large-scale panning and washing of gold particles found in the auriferous gravel of Siberian riverbeds in the nineteenth century that Siberia really did became in fact Russia's 'El Dorado' (see Chapter Seven).

Much of the workforce in the silver mines, and later the gold mines, in Siberia was made up of convict labourers and exiled criminals. The full story of exile and forced labour in Siberia will be addressed in Chapter Six, but before we leave the eighteenth century, it is worthwhile to say something about the exile system as it operated during that period.

SSYLKA, KATORGA AND COLONIAL SETTLEMENT[28]

By the end of the seventeenth century, exile to Siberia had already become well established as the central feature of the Russian penal system. Not only common criminals, but also political and religious dissidents and other social outcasts were condemned to undergo various forms of corporal punishment and physical mutilation, and then marched across the Urals to carry out a variety of enforced service to the state, thereby, it was hoped, fulfilling the combined objectives of punishment and colonization. Numerous terms were used to describe the different sorts and conditions of banishment, but the most commonly used Russian word for exile is *ssylka*. It is impossible to arrive at any reliable estimate of the numbers of people so banished, but the Soviet historian, F.G. Safronov, reckons that between 1640 and 1700, around 1,150 convicts were exiled to eastern Siberia alone, a figure which can easily be doubled if accompanying family members are included (remember that the banished Archpriest Avvakum took with him his wife, his four children and a niece during his exile), and the numbers in western Siberia were even higher.[29]

A government report of 1698 complains that, 'Siberian towns, suburbs and villages are everywhere filled with so many exiled people.'[30]

During the reign of Peter the Great, two new, though intimately connected, factors affected the pattern of Siberian exile. First was a significant reduction in the flow of exiles entering Siberia, and second was the introduction of a new category of punishment, called *katorga*, i.e. forced labour. The reason for the relationship between these two factors is that Peter's main preoccupation, as we know, was with his military ambitions in the west and his efforts to 'Europeanize' his realm. His priority lay more with the defence, reorganization and fortification of the European heartland and its new maritime frontiers in the west. There was an insatiable demand for conscript labour on his gigantic military and civilian construction projects, as well as for recruits and conscripts into his expanded army and newly founded navy. The soaring demand for workers meant that the settlement of Siberia took second place to the tsar's occidental projects, and each convicted criminal was looked on not as a potential colonist, but as a slave labourer for the building of new fortresses, the construction of St Petersburg or the manning of the galleys. In fact, it was the creation and deployment of the new galley fleet, propelled by the collective muscle power of its conscript oarsmen, that was to introduce the new word, *katorga*, into Russia's penal vocabulary. The word was borrowed from the medieval Greek word for a galley – κατεργον. Peter's decree of 1699, ordering that people convicted of certain customs and excise offences should, in place of execution, 'be knouted without mercy and sent to exile in Azov, there to work in the galleys (*byt im na katorgakh v rabote*)',[31] introduced a draconian punitive practice that was to remain at the core of the Russian penal system until, and beyond, the revolutions of 1917. The word soon lost its nautical exclusivity and came to be applied to other types of forced hard labour. From the 1760s, the mine workings in the Urals and Nerchinsk in eastern Siberia became the most common destination for *katorzhane* (those condemned to *katorga*), though factories, mines, fortresses and salt-works in other places were also used in Siberia and elsewhere.

After the end of the Great Northern War, the near-completion of the western fortifications and harbour construction, and Peter's own death, the stream of exiles to Siberia resumed, though during this period no formal distinction existed between exile and hard labour, i.e. between *ssylka* and *katorga*. The *katorzhane* were regarded simply as convict labourers, and not as exiles (*ssyl'nye*). The link between *ssylka* and *katorga* really dates from laws passed by the Empress Elizabeth (ruled 1741–61), daughter of Peter the Great, which in effect abolished the death penalty for criminal offences in Russia. Without going into all the legal technicalities, the empress, whose tender, delicate sensibilities recoiled against the horrors of capital punishment, compassionately decreed that, instead of immediate execution, those convicted of capital crimes were now to be publicly displayed on the scaffold, scourged with the knout, have their nostrils ripped out with pincers, their forehead and cheeks branded with the letters VOR (*vor* – a 'malefactor'), and sent in chains into 'eternal exile' (*vechnaya ssylka*). For a while, a common destination for the 'reprieved', flogged, disfigured, fettered and branded *katorzhane* was Rogervik, a port on the Baltic coast, the construction of which was now nearing completion. When it was finished in 1767, the newly opened silver mines at Nerchinsk in east Siberia became the most favoured location (at least from the government's point of view) for the convict labourers, and it was from this time that *katorga* and exile to Siberia became notionally and practically linked. In the nineteenth century, the conjunction was formally recognized with the introduction of the judicial sentence officially designated as 'exile to penal servitude in Siberia' (*ssylka na katorgu v Sibir'*), which remained the most severe punishment for common criminal offences in the civil penal code until it was abolished after the February 1917 revolution.

If, under Peter and his immediate successors, the rate of enforced settlement of common criminals declined, the same period was also marked by an increase in the use of Siberia as a place of banishment for once highly placed opponents and rivals of those in power. In other words, Siberia now resumed its role as a place of political exile, one that it had already played in the previous century. During Peter's reign and the period of 'palace revolutions' which followed – when between 1725 and 1762 the throne of the Romanovs changed posteriors seven times – Siberia became the temporary or permanent abode of scores of disgraced officials, fallen favourites, ex-admirals, senators, counts, courtiers, lapsed lovers and others who had fallen foul of this, that or the other monarch, faction, palace clique or cabal. Lack of space precludes a detailed account of the fate of the many once prominent, but now dishonoured, personalities who suffered the indignities, disgrace and distress of Siberian exile during these years, but for more information the interested reader is referred elsewhere.[32] The names of some of the most illustrious, or notorious, however, merit a brief mention.

Among them are: Andrei Voinarovskii, nephew of the Ukrainian commander Ivan Mazepa, who supported Sweden against Russia in the Great Northern War – exiled to Yakutsk, where he was interviewed by G.F. Müller (see above); Major-General G.G. Skornyakov-Pisarev, one-time close confidant of Peter the Great and Over-Procurator of the Ruling Senate – knouted and exiled to Zhigansk in Yakutia for plotting the overthrow of Catherine I; Lieutenant-General A.E. Devier, a Portuguese Jew who rose to become Chief of Police in St Petersburg – also knouted and sent to Yakutia; Prince Aleksandr Menshikov, after Peter himself the most powerful man in Russia, the emperor's closest friend and advisor, Empress Catherine's (and also probably Peter's) lover – disgraced and exiled with his family to Berëzov;[33] members the largely Germanic entourage of Empress Anna (ruled 1730–40) – Bühren, Osterman, Münnich, Löwenwalde, Timiryazev, Golovkin, all originally sentenced to various gruesome forms of execution but reprieved and exiled to different parts of Siberia; Vice-President of the Admiralty F.I. Soimonov (who later became Governor of Siberia); and even Abraham Petrovich Gannibal (Hannibal), Peter the Great's black Ethiopian former slave and godson, and the poet Aleksandr Pushkin's great-grandfather – the celebrated 'Negro of Peter the Great' – whose melanin-enriched pigmentation no doubt made him a unique sight in eighteenth-century Siberia.[34]

There were many others whose fascinating tales could be told, but one of them deserves a special word, and that is the remarkable Heinrich von Füch (Fik), not a grandee but a trusted civil servant from Holstein who helped draft many of Peter's government reforms. Accused of complicity in a plot to prevent the accession of Empress Anna, he was exiled to various locations in both western and eastern Siberia, where he spent over a decade. On his eventual pardon and recall to St Petersburg by Empress Elizabeth in 1743, he provided a number of detailed memoranda on the parlous, corrupt state of the Siberian administration that he had witnessed, in particular the cruelties and privations inflicted on the local natives by the imperial tax and *yasak* gatherers. 'In eleven years [in Siberia],' wrote Füch, 'I saw only one honest official.'[35] Although the rampant corruption of St Petersburg's 'Siberian satraps' was well known (the first Governor-General of Siberia, M.P. Gagarin, was publicly hanged for malfeasance in office in 1721), nevertheless Füch's depositions were to influence later legislation in the interests of the Siberian aborigines.

All the people mentioned in the previous paragraph were only political criminals in the sense that they opposed, challenged or conspired against the person of a particular emperor or empress, rather than against the whole political or social system as such. They were all of them simply 'palace plotters', rather than revolutionary enemies of the autocratic state. The first 'real' political exile to Siberia, banished by Catherine the Great (ruled 1762–96) for his sweeping literary critique of the political, social and moral turpitude of the Russian Empire and his apocalyptic warnings of violent revolutionary change to come was Aleksandr Nikolaevich Radishchev (1749–1802), author of *A Journey from St Petersburg to Moscow* (1790), seemingly an innocuous travelogue, but in realty a mordant indictment of the whole rotten and oppressive feudal-autocratic system. This not the place to discuss the Radishchev affair in detail, but Catherine's shocking and gratuitously severe punishment of this highly educated, unassuming nobleman for merely enunciating the humanitarian principles of the European Enlightenment, to which the empress herself professed to subscribe, condemned him to a sentence of death by decapitation, subsequently commuted to ten years' exile in eastern Siberia. Radishchev thus became the first in the long distinguished line of critics, ideological opponents, political activists, liberals, free thinkers, radicals and revolutionaries who throughout the nineteenth century followed in his footsteps, both intellectual and itinerary. A self-respecting Russian revolutionary who had not done time in Siberia was, it appeared, not worth his salt.

What contribution did the exile system make towards the population increase and colonization of Siberia in the eighteenth century? In the case of political exiles, almost none at all. However, several pieces of legislation under empresses Elizabeth and Catherine II did have a significant impact on the rate of enforced migration. During the autumn of 1760 the Ruling Senate spent five full days debating how best to secure the manpower required to work the state-owned silver mines in Nerchinsk. Drafting of peasants from the local population was rejected, and on 13 December, an official decree was promulgated: 'On the reception for settlement in Siberia of *pomeshchik* [i.e. landowners'], synodal, monastic, merchants' and state peasants in lieu of military recruits ...' This and other similarly worded decrees over the next two years confirmed the right of serf-owners in European Russia to divest themselves of their unwanted peasants in return for a military recruit quittance; that is to say that for every serf handed over for exile to Siberia, the owner would be given a receipt that would be set against the number of peasants he was obliged by law to supply to the army as military recruits. The wording of the original decree was extremely vague as to the reasons for which a serf might be so banished, including 'unseemly' or 'impudent' behaviour, or 'causing a disturbance' – which obviously gave the serf-owners a good deal of leeway in the law's interpretation. Much more precise were the details of the regulations defining the age and suitability of those who could be so exiled. Only healthy male peasants under the age of 45 could be sent, and married men were to be accompanied by their wives and their children at their owners' discretion. Financial compensation was given to the serf-owner for the loss of the women and children.

The emphasis on the exile of whole family units underlines the colonizing aspects of the legislation, as do the provisions concerning the peasants' physical fitness and ability to work. Moreover, a law of 16 March 1761 thoughtfully stated that even serfs whose misdemeanours had earned them a public flogging before their departure should not be beaten so severely as to render them unfit for work – a fine example of tsarist health and safety regulations in operation. But despite these provisos, serf-owners were reluctant to deprive themselves of their most energetic and virile workers, and therefore regularly abused the legislation to get rid of peasants who were elderly, infirm, lame or otherwise decrepit and unable to work. Indeed, reports from the exile administration frequently complained about the large numbers of physically disabled, senile, feeble and frankly moribund members of the exile convoys, many of whom, of course, never made it to their destination.

Despite the high morbidity and mortality rates, large numbers did manage to survive the exile journey, and in the two decades between the third and fourth censuses (1762–82), the number of landowners' serfs exiled for settlement in the Tobolsk, Irkutsk and Kolyvan provinces of Siberia alone increased fourfold from 2,573 to 10,016 males. (This despite a temporary interruption between 1773 and 1775 as a result of the Pugachëv rebellion's cutting off the route across the Urals). These figures need to be multiplied by a factor of three or four to account for accompanying family members, as well as thousands of soldiers either retired or undergoing punishment who were also regularly deported to Siberia at this time. Overall, the number of exiled serfs in the three named provinces between 1762 and 1782 rose from 0.66 per cent to 3.84 per cent of the total population. These may not seem to be high proportions, but the figures do not include the number of exiles sent directly to work in the Nerchinsk mines, nor the thousands of common criminals exiled by judicial procedure.

In the final analysis it is virtually impossible to arrive at anywhere near a precise figure of the exile population of Siberia in the eighteenth century. Attempts were made to keep proper files, records and statistics, but many of these were destroyed in a fire at Tobolsk in 1788, and in any case the process of maintaining accurate information was bedevilled by such things as shifting nomenclature, administrative incompetence, overlapping identification, and the huge incidence of flight and abscondence. However, after a judicious balancing of all the available archival evidence, the distinguished Soviet demographic historian, A.D. Kolesnikov, comes to the conclusion that between 1761 and 1781 no fewer than 35,000 male souls of all categories were exiled to Siberia (a 'soul' – *dusha* – was the standard unit of computation in old Russian census taking). If wives and children are factored in, then the figure rises to around 70,000.[36]

If Kolesnikov's calculations are accepted, then it would appear that, despite the negative effects and debilitating social and criminal problems caused by thousands of escaped convicts and recidivist fugitive villains, exile in the latter half of the eighteenth century did manage to make a definite, identifiable and statistically significant contribution to the colonization and settlement of Siberia. It was, however, a double-edged sword. A conglomeration of convicted murderers, rapists, arsonists, poisoners, pederasts, bandits and burglars does not necessarily provide sound, industrious, virtuous or procreative pioneering stock. Neither did the crippled or wilfully disobedient human flotsam and jetsam discarded by the serf-owning nobility. The increased rate of exile settlement indicated by Kolesnikov's figures does not therefore point automatically to a successful policy of enforced colonization. Once in Siberia, the exiles caused more social problems and public mayhem than their economic manpower solved. At any rate, when Count Mikhail Speranskii (1772–1839) became Governor-General of Siberia in 1819, he found the administration of the entire territory, including its exile system, in such a state of chaos, corruption, criminal mismanagement and universal disarray that he felt compelled to overhaul the whole operation from top to bottom.

Speranskii's sweeping reforms are dealt with in the following chapter, but before examining their impact, another important episode in the history of Russia's expansion into Siberia and the far north must be dealt with, and that is the discovery, occupation and exploitation of what came to be called 'Russian America'.

4

The Nineteenth Century:
Russian America, Reform and Regionalism

'The history of Russia is the history of a land that is being colonized ...
Migrations, colonization of the country, constituted the fundamental fact of
our history.'[1] So wrote the great Russian historian, V.O. Klyuchevskii (1841–
1911). He might well have added that it was the European Russians, a branch
of the Eastern Slavs, who were responsible for the colonization process as a
result of their imperialist conquests of non-Russian lands already inhabited by
non-Russian peoples (see Chapters Two and Five). Before Klyuchevskii, the
Siberian regionalist scholar, N.M. Yadrintsev (referred to in Chapter One),
entitled his magnificent work on the past, present and future of Siberia as
Siberia as a Colony.[2] However, the admirable Canadian historical geographer,
James Gibson, has argued that before its 'discovery' of America, Russia was
not really a colonial power: 'to the extent that "colonial" implies overseas or
noncontiguous expansion. This situation did not, of course, apply to Siberia.
[But] with the acquisition of Alaska Russia joined the ranks of Great Britain,
France, Spain, Holland and other European colonial powers.'[3]

Pace Professor Gibson, despite the absence of any maritime disjunction
between Russia west of the Urals and Siberia, it is quite clear that the land
beyond 'the Rock', the whole continent of northern Asia, geographically *con-
tiguous* with Europe, was already in the seventeenth century regarded, and
plundered, by Moscow as a 'colony' in the classic sense of the word: i.e. an
alien land invaded and occupied by an imperial, expansionist power that
exploited the conquered country's natural resources, screwed the indigenous
inhabitants and settled her own people on the occupied territory, claiming it
as her own, imposing her own values, language and religion, and looting its
material products and human stock for the benefit of the metropolitan centre.

In that sense, by the beginning of the eighteenth century, Russia already
was a huge colonial empire that sprawled over two continents, Europe and
northern Asia. Towards its end, the government endeavoured to spread its

power into a third, America, the first time Russia had attempted to acquire overseas possessions. The following section narrates the story of how Russia 'discovered' north-west America, established settlements, forts and trading posts there, pushed south into California, even ventured as far as Hawaii in the mid-Pacific, and finally pulled out, selling the territory of Alaska to the United States of America in 1867.

RUSSIAN AMERICA

Vitus Bering's second northern expedition, described in the previous chapter, was ultimately unsuccessful in landing on the continent of America, but the voyage had important consequences, not least the opening up to further Russian exploration of the coastal waters of Kamchatka, the Commander Islands, and the Kurile and Aleutian archipelagos. But the new commercial treaty of Kyakhta, agreed with China in 1727, was signed at a time when Russia's chief oriental trading commodity – Siberian fur – was in precipitous decline, due mainly to mindless, rapacious overkilling. The question now was: with what merchandise were Russian traders to replace the soft gold of the sable, already slaughtered in their millions and both warming and adorning the bodies of Eurasia's wealthy ruling classes? The answer was the sea otter (*Enhydra lutris* – in Russian, *kalan*), with which the waters, coastlines and islands of the northern seas were teeming. The sea otter is covered in rich, dark brown, deep velvety fur, highlighted with silvery hairs, which insulates it from the icy-cold waters in which it lives. Though its fur is thicker, softer and more lustrous than that of the sable, it gives less warmth than that of the land mammal, due to its stiffer, less pliable skin when dried and cured. However, it was still greatly prized on the markets of China in particular, where it was used mainly for ostentatious trimming and sartorial embellishment, and commanded fabulously high prices – in some trading posts fetching as much as 40 times that of a sable pelt.[4] Just as the quest for the sable, marten and fox had drawn men through the Siberian mainland's forests, so did the sea otter lure them, though not in such quantities, into the icy deeps of the northern Pacific and the Arctic coasts.

While the journey to the hunting grounds was extremely perilous – through treacherous waters in flimsy boats, pegged, woven and stitched together without metal braces and fastenings – the killing process, at least on dry land, was safe, easy and totally lacking in the skill, stealth and finesse of the stalking hunter. Slow-moving on land, the lumbering, helpless creatures were simply clubbed to death, often with a single, crushing blow to the head. The fact that the female sea otter whelps only once every two years made the knock-on effect even more disastrous. Not satisfied with the onshore harvest, the Russian entrepreneurs (*promyshlenniki*) coerced the native Aleuts, who were skilful at sea-hunting with harpoons and guns on their traditional kayaks and umiaks (an open boat made of wood and skin), to carry out the deadly cull on the Slavonic invaders' behalf. Over the years of Russia's presence in and around the northern seas, not only the sea otter, but also the larger fur seal (*Callorhinus ursinus*) with an equally luxuriant pelage, was hunted almost to extinction. The wretched Aleut sealers, too, suffered a similar fate at the hands of their Russian masters. It has been estimated that 'at least 80 per cent of the Aleut population perished during the first and second generations of Russian contact', making them the most ruthlessly exploited aboriginal group anywhere in Siberia and Russian Far East.[5]

The same pattern of over-hunting, over-killing and the near extermination of the wild livestock as had occurred on the mainland was now repeated to deadly effect in the northern seas, resulting in a further eastwards shift in search of yet more prey. But the further east from the home ports on the Siberian coast that the mammacidal predators ventured, the more precarious became their own chances of survival. It therefore became essential, in order to sustain their operation, to establish bases and initially temporary settlements on the Alaskan mainland. Russia's first pied-à-terre on American ground was planted by an independent merchant adventurer named Grigorii Ivanovich Shelikhov (1747–95), dubbed by the poet, Gavrila Derzhavin, as 'the Russian Columbus'.

Before the reign of Peter the Great, there had been many conflicting views, rumours, theories, reports, etc. concerning the conjunction or separation of north-east Siberia and north-west America, which are much too convoluted to unravel at this point. What is pretty certain is that Peter himself was aware of, first, the current ambiguities of the question, and second, the absolute necessity of resolving it. Hence his instructions to the various explorers discussed in the previous chapter. After Peter's death, the string of rather feeble and ineffectual monarchs who succeeded him evinced little, if any, of the vision and vigour, determination and drive of their formidable predecessor, which is one reason which may explain why the foundations of Russian America were delayed from the mid- to the late-eighteenth century. These selfish, sybaritic puppets on the throne were much too preoccupied with the frivolities and fandangles of court life in St Petersburg, and with the intricacies of their more urgent relationship with Europe, to be much bothered about what was happening amidst the icecaps and icebergs of the far northern Pacific. Another reason was that the exploitation of the plentiful sea otter around the Aleutian Islands was sufficiently lucrative to satisfy the greed of the hunter-traders, and temporarily dampened any desire to explore further east. Yet another explanation could be that St Petersburg was unwilling at that time to face a confrontation with other European powers, particularly Spain and Britain, who were becoming alarmed at what they saw as Russia's apparent interest in the Americas. Moreover, the whole enterprise was becoming far too expensive for the central exchequer to sustain. It was owing to this combination of possible explanations that concentration on tapping the rich reservoir of fur-bearing marine mammals around the Aleutians diverted the Russians' attention from the Alaskan mainland for over two decades.

It was only around 1760 that Russians on the Aleutians first heard of the existence of the 'forested Alakshak', from which the name Alaska is derived.[6] In fact, the term then designated, not the whole territory of present-day Alaska, but the narrow peninsula of the same name that juts outs out from the south-western mainland, pointing to the Aleutians. This was the home of the Russians' original informant, a captured Eskimo named Kashmak, and it was on the basis of his information and crude cartography that the polymath scholar, M.V. Lomonosov, later drafted a loxodromic map establishing conclusively that the peninsula of Alakshak was in fact a cape of the north American continent.[7] It was also following the Eskimo's additional information that later expeditions were dispatched further northwards, which by the early 1780s proved that the so-called 'Big Land' across the Bering Strait was indeed the extreme north-west tip of the continent of North America.

Although dubious legends and apocryphal rumours were afloat concerning earlier Russian presence in Alaska (including one which had it that merchants from Novgorod had landed there during the reign of Ivan the Terrible!), it is now accepted by most specialist scholars that, apart from the odd temporary quarters set up on various Aleutian islands, the first permanent Russian settlement on Alaskan territory was established on Kodiak Island by Grigorii Shelikhov in 1784. In a sense, Kodiak was the Russian Columbus's 'Hispaniola borealis'. The first few years of Russia's occupancy of North America was dominated by the formidable triumvirate of Shelikhov, Aleksandr Andreevich Baranov (1746–1819) and Nikolai Petrovich Rezanov (1764–1807). Shelikhov, described by Basil Dmytryshyn as 'the most energetic promoter of Russian colonial expansion in the North Pacific', and by the exiled dissident writer, Aleksandr Radishchev, as 'Little king Shelikhov',[8] was born into a merchant family in Kursk province, and in 1772, aged 25, moved to Irkutsk, which was then the relatively vibrant administrative and commercial centre of eastern Siberia. Three years later he married the young widow of a wealthy local merchant and formed a business alliance with a number of other ambitious entrepreneurs who soon made for themselves a small fortune in the fur trade around the Kurile and Aleutian Islands. In 1783, sponsored with cash from the Demidov iron empire (see Chapter Three), Shelikhov, his wife and an accompanying crew set sail from Okhotsk. After a stormy passage and sticky conflicts with hostile natives, they finally made landfall on Kodiak Island where they built a fortified outpost at what came to be called Three Saints Harbour, managed to establish fairly amicable relations with the aboriginal people – even converting some credulous souls to Christianity – and gathered considerable piles of fur.

Having, as it were, planted the Russian flag on Alaskan ground, Shelikhov, hardened by his adventure, enriched by its achievements, and convinced that Russia both should and could create a solid administrative, commercial and military network to govern and benefit from the region's rich resources, entreated the empress, Catherine II, to grant him exclusive rights to form a commercial company that would have total monopoly over the governance and economic exploitation of the region. Naturally, other businessmen who had their own interests to protect objected to Shelikhov's bold but selfish proposal, and ultimately the empress, while approving and rewarding his entrepreneurship and feats of exploration, turned him down in the interests of free trade and commercial competition, and also for fear of upsetting international relations with other foreign powers vying for control in America, while she had enough problems closer to home with Poland, Turkey and Sweden. However, she did grant Shelikhov certain concessions which strengthened his hand in expanding his commercial enterprises when, newly promoted to the ranks of the Russian nobility, he returned to the east in the early 1790s. There his position was even further enhanced by the recruitment as his senior business associate of Aleksandr Baranov, and by the marriage of his daughter with the ambitious courtier, Nikolai Rezanov, who not only had the empress's ear, but also shared his new father-in-law's imperial visions in America. Shelikhov himself died in 1795, but thereafter his widow, Natalya Shelikhova, his surviving partner, Baranov, and his son-in-law, Rezanov, administered his considerable legacy with the same tenaciousness, perspicacity and acumen as Shelikhov had displayed during his own lifetime.

Shelikhov was not only a successful businessman, but also a considerable scholar who collected a great deal of ethnographical material on the Kodiak Eskimos, the Indians of Alaska and the coastal islands. On his own initiative, he created Russian settlements in newly discovered territories, forced the local peoples to swear allegiance to the Russian monarch, and built Orthodox churches (some of which still survive), shipyards and small manufactories employing Russian and native workmen. He also drew up a plan for the economic development of the Kurile Islands and launched a scheme for the laying down of transport routes on the Siberian mainland that follow very closely the path of the modern Baikal-Amur Mainline (BAM) railway (see Chapter Ten). His efforts, and those of his relatives and successors, were finally rewarded by the Emperor Paul (ruled 1796–1801), son of Catherine the Great, with the granting of his royal assent to the foundation of the Russian-American Company (*Rossiisko-Amerikanskaya kompaniya*) on 8 July 1799, which in effect became the *de facto*, if not *de jure*, government of Russian America for the next seven decades.

Although the Russian-American Company had finally secured the trading monopoly originally sought by Shelikhov, that is not to say that its operations were totally independent of central government, though they have often been portrayed as such. Indeed, the headquarters of the company's main administration shifted in 1800 from Irkutsk to St Petersburg, and the emperor, other members of the royal family and government officials were major shareholders. Moreover, central government departments such as the Admiralty, the Ministries of Finance and Internal Affairs and the Holy Synod exercised control over the corresponding sectors of the company's activities, which – it was made clear in its various charters – were always to be in the interests of the entire nation. That said, the huge distances separating St Petersburg from

Alaska, the government's preoccupation with more pressing matters nearer home – the Napoleonic wars, for instance – and the domineering, determined and almost despotic personality of the company's chief administrator, Aleksandr Baranov, meant that in reality Russian operations on the continent of America were, although under the nominal aegis of the imperial government, pretty well self-determined, self-administered and self-regulated by the local officials. This situation was partly due to Baranov's bullying, battling and head-butting style (his surname is derived from the Russian word for a ram – *baran*), but things were to change after his 20-year near tyranny came to an end on his retirement in 1819. From then until the sale of Alaska to the United States of America in 1867, all his successors were high-ranking naval officers of the Russian Imperial Fleet, state employees of the Admiralty, subject to three-year (later five-year) fixed-term contracts, and with similar powers and duties to those of governors-general elsewhere in the empire. The chief administrator had under him an elaborate bureaucracy of officials, managers, clerks and clergymen whose responsibilities included the efficient and profitable running of the company, extending and consolidating Russian power on the islands and mainland, providing for the welfare of the territory's inhabitants, both settlers and natives, and supervising and recording intermarriages between the two. Native chieftains (*toyons*), and creoles (the issue of mixed marriages) were also incorporated into the lower ranks of the colonial administration.

However, despite well-intentioned official policies, the living and working conditions of all the company's lowest class employees, both Russian and indigenous, remained extremely harsh, exploitative, insanitary and brutal. Morbidity and mortality rates were high, the diet was minimal and in any case often uneatable, savage punishments were routinely inflicted for insubordination or infringement of company rules, and the workers – whether peasant settlers, native hunters or press-ganged sailors, to quote Dmytryshyn, 'In essence ... became Company slaves',[9] tied to their masters by financial indebtedness, physical debility, fear and the simple lack of anywhere else to escape to in those remote, forbidding climes.

But whatever the daunting difficulties, hardships and dangers of existence on the American-Russian frontier, for nearly 70 years the company managed to engage in a whole range of commercial and colonial enterprises: fur-hunting, fishing, whaling, shipbuilding, lumbering, trading and creating a chain of settlements and fortifications which for a short while, as mentioned above, stretched as far as Fort Ross near Bodega Bay in northern California (held from 1812 to 1841) and Hawaii (1815–17). All this occurred in spite of the ferocious climate, the vast distances, icy storms, near-famine, pestilential diseases and deadly attacks by hostile natives, in particular the fearsome and irrepressible Tlingit Indians, who remained a constant thorn in the Russians' flesh, on one occasion in 1802 even capturing the company's virtual capital, Novo-Arkhangelsk (now Sitka), on Baranov Island. For all its initial successes in the face of these extreme conditions, by the middle of the nineteenth century the company's mandate was beginning to run out of time and resources.

Several factors finally impelled the imperial government to terminate the company's charter and divest itself of its no-longer profitable nor sustainable overseas venture. Of these the most important were: (a) Russia's precarious international, political and financial situation following her humiliating defeat in the Crimean War (1853–6); (b) the government's equally urgent internal problems during what Soviet historians described as Russia's 'first revolutionary situation' (1856–64),[10] and also the not-unrelated, titanic legislative task of emancipating the Russian peasantry from serfdom – the statutes promulgating the terms of this major turning point in Russia's history being publicly announced on 5 March 1861;[11] (c) the fact that in the mid-1860s the Russian-American Company was teetering on the edge of bankruptcy (between 1842 and 1866 the value of its individual shares had plummeted from 224 silver rubles to 75, it was 1 million rubles in debt, and it was being subsidized by the government to the tune of 200,000 rubles per year); (d) the company's charter was in any case up for renewal and renegotiation in 1861, and not everyone was certain that it deserved refranchising; (e) despite the debilitating effects of the American Civil War, the United States was still a vigorous and ambitious power on its own continent and had its own territorial agenda; (f) in strategic terms Russia simply did not have sufficient military and naval power to protect its far-flung interests in the north Pacific in the case of any international conflict in the region; and (g) Russia's traditional paramountcy in the international fur trade was in a state of inexorable decline and challenged by such burgeoning firms as, for instance, the British Hudson's Bay Company. But in geopolitical terms, perhaps the major factor in Russia's decision to shed its north-American possessions was its shift of interest to the south, which materialized in its annexation and occupation of the Amur/Ussuri regions, peacefully appropriated – or expropriated – from China under the terms of the treaties of Aigun (1858) and Peking (1860) (a topic to be dealt with in the final section of this chapter).

In the event, after protracted, convoluted and often arcane political and financial negotiations, the Russian imperial government finally sold off its American colony, twice the size of Texas, to the United States of America for the grand sum of 7,200,000 gold dollars, which, James Gibson has helpfully calculated, works out in terms of contemporaneous real estate value at 2 cents an acre.[12] What subsequent Russian governments – tsarist, communist and post-Soviet – might have thought about the bargain-price land deal done by Alexander II's negotiators and their American purchaser is, in terms of contemporary international relations, a teasing question.

Although the heritage of Russia's historical presence still remains in present-day Alaska – in architecture, religious establishments and place names – overall, its seven decades of involvement on the American continent is a sad saga of unnecessary imperial aggrandizement, extermination of precious marine life, human suffering and misery, the gratuitous near-genocide of indigenous peoples and little practical gain except for the fur-lined pockets of a few ruthless and avaricious adventurers.

SIBERIA, SPERANSKII AND SUPEREROGATION

According to the *Shorter Oxford English Dictionary*, the word 'supererogation' in its transferred (rather than its theological) sense means: 'Performance of more than duty or circumstances require'. This definition can unequivocally be applied to the reforming legislative activities of Mikhail Mikhailovich Speranskii (1772–1839), close confidant and advisor to Emperor Alexander I (ruled 1801–25), brilliant bureaucrat, fallen favourite, exiled official, and Governor-General of Siberia from 1819 to 1821. Such was the man's impact on the administrative structure of Siberia in the nineteenth century that he well deserves special mention at this point. His humble origins, sparkling early career in the government apparatus, and the intrigues that led to his fall from favour and banishment to the provinces in 1812 – the year of Napoleon's invasion – need not detain us here.[13] What is important for present purposes is the way in which this complex, remarkable man succeeded in bringing about so radical a transformation of administrative practices and institutions in Siberia, which he found to be in such a sorry, dysfunctional and chaotic state on his arrival there in 1819 after his totally undeserved public disgrace in the capital, and five years spent in various administrative posts in remote towns and provinces of European Russia.

After more than a decade's outstanding service in various branches of the imperial government administration, which included the careful drafting of a 'liberal' constitutional project for Russia (ultimately unapproved of and shelved), the somewhat reclusive 40-year-old senior civil servant incurred the hostility of a clique of courtiers, Moscow-based aristocrats and jealous officials who ultimately engineered his banishment from St Petersburg and a ten-year spell of exile. This eventually landed him in Siberia where, despite the calumny which provoked his official ostracism, he was appointed Governor-General and began to apply his intellectual and managerial skills to a root-and-branch overhaul of the territory's administration, most especially in the treatment of Siberia's native peoples and in the operation of the exile system, of which he, in a sense, was an eminent victim.[14] There is no doubt that the tsar's domain east of the Ural Mountains when Speranskii arrived there was in need of drastic reorganization (as, indeed, was the rest of the empire). To put the problem into some kind of perspective: the emperor, and St Petersburg's *beau monde* in general, had little knowledge of, interest in, or concern for what was going on in the distant Siberian province. What happened between 1819 and 1822 was the fortuitous, but potentially fortunate, conjunction of a financially ruinous, administratively disreputable and socially catastrophic situation in Siberia with the presence of a distinguished, but now spuriously dishonoured high official, described by his biographer, Marc Raeff, as being 'considered as the most systematic, consistent and gifted advocate of the bureaucratic principle in government'.[15] The application of his gifted advocacy and bureaucratic skills while living in fairly comfortable exile had a palpable, though sometimes overrated, impact on the territory's governance for the next 90 years.

In many ways, Speranskii had always been a social and intellectual misfit, uncomfortable with his less intelligent village playmates, his dimmer seminary class fellows, and also in the company of his socially superior colleagues in government and court circles in St Petersburg, many of whom regarded him as a provincial, plebeian parvenu. It may be that this psychological condition of 'internal exile', emotionally compounded by the tragic death of his young wife in 1800, helped him to empathize with the pitiful lot of many of his temporary Siberian 'compatriots', and enthused him to apply his talents to ameliorate their situation during what Raeff rather oddly describes as his 'long years of lonely exile and enforced leisure'.[16] In Siberia Speranskii was neither lonely nor idle.

Although, to quote Raeff again, 'it is almost impossible to unravel the intricate and confused skein of intrigue which culminated in Speransky's exile',[17] it is nevertheless possible to argue that his prominent position in the political, governmental and bureaucratic life of the capital that contributed to his banishment was at least matched by his far-reaching, deeply influential and humanely conceived legislative reforms in Siberia, which were a direct result of his observations during his imposed sojourn in the vast, remote province. It is also the case that, compared with the stark, soul-destroying conditions in which most condemned or disgraced deportees made their involuntary journey to Siberia (see Chapter Six), Speranskii had not only a professionally productive, but also, in terms of his personal circumstances, a relatively cushy time while living there. Even during the seven years of his disgrace and banishment within Russia's European provinces, Speranskii had not been stripped of his rank of Privy Councillor and State Secretary, and – apart from experiencing some minor unpleasantness while in Nizhnii Novgorod, and a brief spell of public animosity and near penury in Perm – maintained a relatively civilized lifestyle and enjoyed a comfortable annual stipend personally granted by the tsar.

Despite his understandable resentment at not being recalled to St Petersburg, Speranskii, being Speranskii, applied himself to his new duties with the same kind of assiduous attention, perspicacity and liberal convictions as had marked his career before his downfall. As previous chapters in this book have demonstrated, in spite of some feeble attempts at the regional and administrative reorganization of Siberia in the late eighteenth and early nineteenth centuries, at the time of Speranskii's arrival the whole region was still in a largely ungovernable state, racked by corruption, venality, violence, and social and economic deprivation. It was virtually out of the control of St Petersburg, and its entire population – of whatever social class or ethnic origin – was almost totally at the mercy of ruthless and unaccountable governors and their equally corrupt and merciless minions.

One of the most vicious of these 'Siberian satraps' in the early nineteenth century was Ivan Borisovich Pestel (1765–1843, father of the future executed Decembrist leader – see Chapter Six), who together with his faithful lieutenant, Nikolai Ivanovich Treskin, Civil Governor of Irkutsk, ruled Siberia from 1805 to 1819 as their virtual personal fiefdom, with an arbitrariness, cruelty and level of oppression that became almost legendary. During their tenure of office, they combined what was probably a genuine attempt to bring some kind of order, discipline and efficiency into the governance of the territory, but with a degree of authoritarianism, brutality and tyrannical abuse of power that earned them the fear and loathing of the people over whom they exercised their dual despotism. This is not an unusual combination: many despots have sought to introduce administrative, economic and institutional reforms by the use of draconian, punitive methods (Peter the Great is an obvious example), but in the case of Pestel and Treskin their efforts did little to improve the administrative efficiency or social wellbeing of their province, and only added to the misery of its population. Even Siberia's powerful, wealthy merchant class suffered at their hands, a suffering for which they petitioned their emperor for redress.

Gradually learning of Pestel's depredations, the central government eventually realized that it was in the interests of the entire state to bring the affairs of its lands beyond the Urals into some kind of proper order. It took the decision to commission a person of proven integrity, incorruptibility, superior intelligence and legislative skills, first, to make a comprehensive investigation of the near-anarchical situation throughout Siberia, and then to put forward realistically implementable plans and projects for its transformation from a dangerous, daunting and socially shambolic frontierland into an integral, manageable and relatively law-abiding part of the empire. From the government's point of view, Speranskii was the obvious choice. In 1819, he accordingly replaced Pestel as the new Governor-General of Siberia with a wide-ranging brief to accomplish the tasks outlined above.

Roughly 100 years after Peter the Great gave his curt instructions to his explorers in the north (see Chapter Three), Alexander I was equally short, and equally woolly, in his orders to Speranskii. Endowing him with almost plenipotentiary powers in the region, the tsar instructed Speranskii as to his new duties in the following terms:

> You will correct everything that can be corrected, you will uncover the persons who are given to abuses, you will put on trial whomever necessary. But your most important occupation should be to determine on the spot the most useful principles for the organization and administration of this remote region. After you have put on paper a plan for such a reorganization, you will bring it to me personally, to St Petersburg, so that I have the means of learning from you orally the true condition of this important region and of basing on solid foundations its well-being for future times.[18]

This passage is a superb indication of the vacuum which occupied the heads of most of Russia's Romanov emperors and empresses.[19] Alexander – later known as 'the Blessed' – instructed Speranskii to write down his findings about Siberia 'on paper' (where-else would he write it?), and then scurry back to St Petersburg in order to report to his sovereign 'orally' what he had already written down. One might think that the crowned head of the world's largest state would have been sufficiently literate to read his esteemed Governor-General's report without having to be talked through the text verbatim. But maybe not. The ineptitude and intellectual shortcomings of the majority of Russia's Romanov rulers are well illustrated in their incompetent and inefficient governance of their north Asian colony, about which most of them knew not a tittle and cared not a jot, nor even deigned to visit – until the last of them, Nicholas II (ruled 1894–1917), and then only as heir-apparent (see Chapter Seven).

But this is the point where the new Siberian Governor-General's acts of supererogation come into play. In order to fulfil his emperor's fatuous order to 'correct everything that can be corrected', Speranskii had to draw up, on the basis of his personal experience and observations, his own list of corrigenda. To that end, he undertook an exhausting, two-year length-and-breadth travel survey of as much of the territory as was possible, observing, annotating, recording and filing all the information that he could assimilate about its economic, natural and human resources as the basis of his plans for 'reorganization'. It is unnecessary to go into the small-print and minutiae of Speranskii's Siberian reforms – which are expertly analysed elsewhere[20] – but it is necessary to underline the way in which his legislation affected the governance of the province, its administrative structure, its function as a penal colony and the lives of the aboriginal peoples.

Speranskii's first problem as Governor-General was to overcome the antipathy and suspicion of the population – both native and Russian – towards his office as a result of their experiences of the rapacious and tyrannical activities of Pestel, Treskin and their ilk in the past. However, by dint of his own essentially humanitarian and compassionate nature, his habit of cultivating social contacts and his genuine interest in the life and customs of the indigenous peoples, he soon established a rapport that was later to inform his future legislation for the region's benefit – at least as he envisaged it. Complicating the issue, however, was the fact that at the same time as trying to establish good relationships, one of his primary tasks – as commanded by the tsar – was to investigate and prosecute corrupt and over-oppressive officials. But despite the extensive gubernatorial powers granted to Speranskii, even his authority to dismiss and punish was ultimately limited by the central government in St Petersburg. Added to which was the difficulty in substituting such personnel as *were* thrown out of office or subject to judicial proceedings with sufficiently experienced, qualified and educated replacements. Educational standards in Siberia were desperately low – a problem which Speranskii sought to address (see below) – and there was a lack of anything which could be called a 'civil society' (which was actually true of the whole empire). In Siberia there was no hereditary nobility; recruiting illiterate peasants as state officials was obviously out of the question; the clergy was notoriously ignorant, inebriated and uncouth; and even the prosperous and influential merchant class was felt by Speranskii to be an unlikely recruiting ground for honest public servants, given the widely acknowledged dubious and dodgy nature of their grasping commercial activities.

Despite these drawbacks, Speranskii set about his tasks with his accustomed thoroughness, and devoted himself to acquainting himself as fully as possible with the social, administrative, economic and commercial needs of his territory and its population. Among his priorities was the organization of schools and other educational institutions in order to raise the level of enlightenment among the people of Siberia; encouraging further scientific exploration of its various regions in the tradition of the eighteenth-century expeditions, though not on such a grandiose scale; arguing for the potential economic and commercial value of its as yet unexploited mineral assets; developing trade with China and supporting the enterprises of the Russian-American Company (see above); and establishing more cordial relationships with the native peoples. He also turned his attention to the more humane and efficient operation of the Siberian exile system. The more he discovered, the more he became convinced that Siberia, if given a proper administrative structure, legal institutions and sound financial management – rather than the wild, dangerous, forbidding, bleak and uncivilized wilderness of his original expectations – could became a thriving, prosperous and integral part of the empire.

But to fulfil his aims, he first needed to establish a more business-like and effective administrative structure for the proper governance of the territory, replacing the old, personalized, capricious practice of the traditional *voevody* (local commanders) and governors with more modern, rational, bureaucratically controlled institutions. In his administrative reforms, Speranskii was motivated by two guiding principles: first, that they should be in keeping with and meet local conditions and requirements; and second, that the new structure of government in Siberia should be essentially bureaucratic in nature, i.e. government by appointed officials.

To make things somewhat more manageable, the vast territory was divided into two Governor-Generalships – West Siberia and East Siberia – each, naturally, with its own Governor-General, and each subdivided into smaller territorial-administrative units or provinces. The Governors-General were to be assisted in their duties by an appointed Administrative Council which, in conjunction with the Governor-General, had certain limited powers to formulate policy, to take executive decisions, and also to keep a watching brief over any potential abuse of power or malfeasance in office by the Governor-General himself. A complex, hierarchical system of administration was introduced from the top office of the Governor-General, down through the provinces right to the lowest level of the local township or rural district.

In this way it was hoped to combine the two guiding principles of reform mentioned above, but despite Speranskii's good intentions, although there was some improvement in official practices, in reality the reforms cannot be said to have had a profound impact on the everyday life, economic expectations and quotidian conditions of the Siberian population. It was an essentially bureaucratic system devised by a quintessentially bureaucratic mind. Both the formulation and implementation of various policies remained a purely executive process, there was no 'civil society' independent of government control, no popular assemblies, continuing low levels of enlightenment and culture, and nothing resembling the separation of the powers. This is hardly to be wondered at, given that Speranskii was operating within the context of the autocratic Russian state as a whole, and the criticisms levelled above obviously applied to the entire Russian Empire, not just to Siberia. Still, steps had been taken in the right direction, and Speranskii's reforms were enshrined in his legislation and Statutes of 1822, after his recall to St Petersburg. In contrast to the reception of his rejected 'constitutional project' of 1809, his Siberian reforms were accepted almost without demur, possibly because – as was the case pre-Speranskii – the legislators in St Petersburg still neither knew nor cared much about what went on in the distant lands across the Urals. However, in evaluating Speranskii's achievement, Marc Raeff concludes: 'the Statute of 1822 introduced to Siberia for the first time in its history something which we can call the rule of law, a *Rechtsstaat*. The basis for clear and orderly government procedure had at last been established, and even though the practice continued to fall short of the aim, progress was being made in the right direction.'[21]

Apart from his purely political-administrative reforms, Speranskii also addressed himself to other urgent matters including the state of the Siberian economy, in particular its agricultural development, the exile system and the condition of the native peoples. He made genuine attempts to loosen up trade barriers and restrictions, to introduce more vitality and competitiveness in commercial activities and to encourage measures to stimulate agricultural production. His endeavours in the latter case, however, were somewhat stymied by the shortage of agricultural labour, which was impossible to supplement on any significant scale by the encouragement of peasant settlers from European Russia so long as the medieval system of serf-ownership existed. It was not until the early twentieth century that the agrarian reforms of the Prime Minister, Pëtr Stolypin (1862–1911), produced and encouraged a massive wave of peasant migration from European Russia to Siberia (see Chapter Seven). Attempts to settle forced exiles on the land were also rather unsuccessful, given the criminal, uncooperative and stubbornly disobedient nature of the majority of the exile population. Speranskii did, however, apply his skills to a thorough overhaul of the way in which the exile system operated along what were intended to be enlightened and humane principles. To what extent he was successful in this area is discussed in detail in Chapter Six. The same enlightened and humane principles informed his legislation regarding the treatment of the aboriginal peoples of Siberia, but, again, a full examination of the 'native question' is the subject of the following chapter.

Tsar Nicholas I's Minister of Education, Count Uvarov (1756–1855), suggested that the whole history of Siberia could be split into two periods: pre-Speranskii and post-Speranskii; Marc Raeff makes the remarkable claim that: 'though on a smaller scale, Speranskii's role in reforming Siberia can be compared to Peter the Great's a century before in European Russia';[22] and Speranskii himself in a letter to his daughter in February 1820 likened himself, with uncharacteristic immodesty, to Yermak Timofeevich, the sixteenth-century 'discoverer' of Siberia. Each of these encomiastic accolades is inappropriate, exaggerated or misplaced. There is no doubt that Speranskii had a positive effect on the administration of the province, and his bureaucratic reforms remained more or less in place until and beyond the end of the century, but to compare their impact on Siberia with the sweeping revolutionary transformation of Russia during the brutal tyranny of Peter the Great is simply a piece of gratuitous and grotesque hyperbole. Speranskii's own boastful self-evaluation likewise evinces a surprising lack of historical perspective, and Uvarov's dichotomous periodization of Siberian history is inconsistent with the fact that Siberia after Speranskii still continued to suffer from bureaucratic abuses, the oppression of the indigenous tribes and ethnic minorities, the exploitation of her natural resources and the ravages of the exile system.[23] In other words, Siberia was still regarded, and treated, as a colony. This much was certainly recognized by those enlightened sons of Siberia who in the mid-nineteenth century developed a school of thought aimed at the greater autonomy, independence or even – at the extreme – the separation of Siberia from Russia. This small but vigorous movement of Siberian regionalism – in Russian, *oblastnichestvo* – is the subject of the following section.

SIBERIAN *OBLASTNICHESTVO*

In twentieth-century Britain, and elsewhere in Europe and America, the 'swinging sixties' was a decade of intense cultural, social, sexual, musical and political excitement and change, creating a pulsating, heady atmosphere in which such phenomena as militant feminism, the Beatles, anti-Vietnam war protests, support for the 'Prague Spring', 'flower power', Woodstock, gay liberation, CND, political scandals (e.g. Profumo), student sit-ins and neo-Marxian philosophies flourished. All this is obviously a far cry from mid-nineteenth-century Siberia. But 100 years before, the 1860s in Russia was also a defining, if less hedonistic, decade in the country's history, during which profound changes took place, new, challenging movements emerged, and the beginnings of determined revolutionary activity occurred. At the start of the decade Russia experienced, as mentioned in an earlier chapter, what Soviet historians described as the country's 'first revolutionary situation', a time of tense anticipation when the nation was literally – as in the title of Ivan Turgenev's novel – 'On the Eve' (*Nakanune*, 1860) of great events.

In 1861 the Russian serfs were finally emancipated, signalling the initial stages of the transition from a feudal to a primitive capitalist economy; the government inaugurated a wide-ranging programme of local government, judicial, educational, administrative and military reforms (the bulk of the last not until the 1870s); the emergence of a revolutionary organization calling itself Land and Liberty (*Zemlya i volya*) marked the first stage of Russian revolutionary populism (*narodnichestvo*); there were student protests, strikes and demonstrations and a flurry of inflammatory anti-government manifestos; in 1863 Poland rose in a revolt against Russian imperial rule that was bloodily suppressed and thousands of the rebels exiled to eastern Siberia; a school of extreme cultural negativism called 'nihilism' set a trend among some sections of the radical intelligentsia; and in 1866 the first assassination attempt was made on Alexander II, the 'tsar liberator', and the would-be regicide, Dmitrii Karakozov, hanged. The whole younger generation of radical activists and oppositionists, who in many ways set the tone for these years, earned itself the collective appellation of the *shestidesyatniki* – 'the men (and women) of the sixties'. While this period was not exactly Russia's equivalent of the twentieth-century 'swinging' sixties' (Karakozov was the only one to swing), the decade did constitute a period of feverish, radical intellectual activity which pointed the way to more dramatic revolutionary upheavals to come.

It was against this backdrop of rapid change, protest, alienation, embryonic revolutionary ideologies and great expectations within what still remained a rigidly autocratic system of government that there emerged in the early 1860s the movement of Siberian regionalism – *oblastnichestvo* (from the Russian word *oblast'* meaning a region). The regionalists (*oblastniki*) were authentic representatives of the contemporary mood of intellectual and political chal-lenge to the tsarist social and political order, though in their case, rather than just calling, like their comrades, for an end to autocracy and the transforma-tion of society in the interests of the Russian 'people' (*narod*), they had an extra item on their agenda, based upon their burning and yearning desire for the greater welfare, greater autonomy and greater appreciation of the specific and peculiar needs of their homeland – Siberia.

The movement originated in the activities of a number of expatriate Siberian students at the University of St Petersburg who had formed themselves into 'regional fraternities' (*zemlyachestva*) where they discussed radical ideas and ideologies in general, and the problems and specific needs of Siberia in par-ticular. Prior to their arrival in St Petersburg some of them had been in con-tact with well-known political exiles in Siberia, including the Decembrists and members of the 'Petrashevtsy' Circle. The Decembrists, most of them highly educated army officers and well-placed members of Russia's nobility, were participants in an unsuccessful military uprising against the regime on 14 December 1825. Their revolt was crushed and over a hundred of the arrested conspirators sentenced to various forms of exile and hard labour in Siberia. Five of the ringleaders were publicly hanged, including Pavel Pestel, son of the notoriously despotic Governor-General of Siberia mentioned earlier in this chapter. The 'Petrashevtsy', far from taking action against the regime, were merely members of a clandestine radical discussion group, organized by Mikhail Petrashevskii, who met regularly to discuss the ideas and political philosophies of contemporary European socialist thinkers such as Proudhon and Fourier. Although their activities were purely cerebral, they suffered the same fate as the Decembrists, and were exiled in 1849, among them the young writer, Fëdor Dostoevskii, who later drew on the experiences of his years in Siberian prison in writing his semi-autobiographical, semi-fictional *Notes from the House of the Dead*.[24] Both the Decembrists and the Petrashevtsy carried with them into Siberia the same intellectual attitudes and political aspirations that had led to their banishment, and which were to exercise a significant intellectual influence on the future *oblastniki*.

Another early influence was the work of Pëtr Andreevich Slovtsov (1767–1843), later dubbed by the regionalists as 'the first Siberian patriot' and the ideological father of their movement. Slovtsov was a complex and contradictory figure. He was very much an admirer of the European Enlightenment and the ideals of the French Revolution, but at the same time a supporter of autocracy and the Orthodox Church. At one point he even considered taking monastic orders. The son of a priest, he was educated at seminaries in Tobolsk and St Petersburg, and later arrested for giving three 'sermons' in which he praised the French Revolution. After his release from brief confinement in a monastery, he swore henceforth to abjure his 'rebellious spirit'. Thereafter, from 1809 until his death in 1843 he devoted himself entirely to the study of his beloved Siberia, writing many scholarly treatises and articles about the country's history and native culture, of which the most famous and influential was his seminal *Historical Review of Siberia* (*Istoricheskoe obozrenie Sibiri*), published in two volumes, 1838 and 1844. One of the leading lights of the regionalist movement, Grigorii Nikolaevich Potanin (1835–1920), was later to describe Slovtsov's magnum opus as the 'encyclopaedia of Siberia'. For all his 'Siberian patriotism', however, Slovtsov was not an adherent of the separation, or even the greater autonomy, of Siberia from the metropolis, but rather believed in the future greatness of his motherland as a result of its further integration as a fully developed constituent part of the Russian Empire.

Another major influence on the *oblastniki* was Afanasii Prokopevich Shchapov (1831–76), himself a man of the 1860s, whose theories on the paramountcy of the 'regional principle' (*oblastnost'*) in Russian history, culture and society, and his dedication to his native Siberia and its people were a great inspiration for the members of the Siberian regionalist movement, though, paradoxically, he himself, like Slovtsov, was not given to separatist tendencies. Shchapov was born the son of a drunken village sexton and a Buryat (some say Tungus) peasant woman in Irkutsk province. After attending the local *bursa* – a kind of junior seminary for the elementary training of future priests, best known for its draconian discipline, regimented rote-learning and regular public whippings – in 1846 Shchapov was enrolled as a student in the Irkutsk Theological Seminary from which he graduated in 1852 with a reputation for shyness, sobriety (drunkenness and debauchery were rife among his fellow seminarists) and assiduous dedication to his studies. Between 1852 and 1856 he continued his education at the Kazan Ecclesiastical Academy, distinguishing himself by his maintained application to his studies, his eccentric nature and gauche social manners. Increasingly, he became fascinated with two interrelated areas of research, the seventeenth-century Russian Church Schism (the *raskol* — see the section on Archpriest Avvakum in Chapter Two), and the life of the common Russian people, of which he considered himself one ('*Ya sam iz muzhikov*' — 'I myself am from the peasantry', he would often declare). His final thesis on *The Schism of the Old Believers* (*Raskol staroobryadchestva*, 1856) was based in large part on his investigation of the Old Believer archives that had been transferred from the Solovetskii monastery in the Arctic north during the British naval blockade in the Crimean War. When it appeared in print in 1858 it was heavily criticized in the progressive press for its 'clericalism', misunderstanding of the term 'democracy' (*demokratizm*) and lack of scientific methodology, which caused Shchapov to reconsider his views and led him to the conclusion that the *raskol* was not a purely religious phenomenon, but an expression of mass, popular opposition to the centralized autocratic state. Although he did not express it in such terms, Shchapov was in fact enunciating in quasi-Marxist phraseology the notion of the class struggle. To put it another way, his new realization concerning the social nature of the *raskol* adumbrated the words of the twentieth-century scholar, Eugene Lampert: 'The heavy artillery of obscurantism and rigid ritualism which the Old Believer directed against the mind concealed a plebeian revolt against a gentry-ridden state, and a state-ridden church.'[25]

In 1860 Shchapov was appointed to the chair of Russian history at the Kazan Academy. Not a lot was expected of the ex-seminarist, but his inaugural lecture caused something of a sensation, and is generally recognized as the first fully articulated statement of the principle of *oblastnost'*. He set out his intellectual stall in his opening words:

> Let me say from the start that I bring with me to the University chair of Russian history not the idea of the State, nor that of centralization, but the idea of the 'spirit of the people' (*narodnost'*) and of 'regionalism' (*oblastnost'*). It is now a well-established notion that the fundamental factor of history is the people (*narod*) itself, and that it is the spirit of the people which makes history … But there is another principle which is not yet firmly established in our researches: the principle — if you will allow the expression — of regionalism. Until now the prevailing idea has been that of centralization … the general theory of the development of the State… Yet the history of Russia is, more than anything, the history of differing local groups, of constant territorial change, of reciprocal action and reaction, of the various regions before *and after* centralization [emphasis added].[26]

Shchapov immediately became the idol of the radically minded students, but his popularity grew into notoriety after the Bezdna tragedy of April 1861. In the village of Bezdna in Kazan province, nearly 500 peasants were massacred by government troops after refusing to surrender to them one Ivan Petrov, a literate peasant who had been trying to explain to a mass gathering of his less-educated brethren the contents of the recently promulgated statutes governing the emancipation of the serfs. Petrov himself was publicly executed.

The students organized a requiem service for the slaughtered peasants at which Shchapov delivered a passionate eulogy praising the centuries-long rebellious spirit of the Russian people, declaring that the blood of the new martyrs would once more arouse the people to insurrection and freedom, and in his peroration calling for a democratic constitution. He was arrested and taken to St Petersburg for interrogation and condemned to be incarcerated in a monastery. However, he was pardoned by the tsar and even given work in a government ministry as advisor on schismatic sects. But his continued researches, pronouncements and publications drawing attention to the demo-cratic traditions of the Russian peasantry, in particular as exemplified in the rural commune (*obshchina*), and also suspicions concerning links with émigré revolutionaries, led to his enforced return to Siberia where he was allowed to live in Irkutsk. He died there and was buried nearby in 1876.

Shchapov's theories about the paramountcy of the regions – as opposed to the centre – and his emphasis on core-periphery antagonisms fuelled the enthusiasm of the young Siberian *oblastniki* in their calls for the greater free-dom of their homeland. But according to the Soviet scholar, P.I. Kabanov, author of a monograph on Shchapov's social, political and historical views: 'The Siberian *oblastniki* were totally wrong (*naprasno*) in considering Shchapov to be their "spiritual father".'[27] However, V.G. Mirzoev, writing in 1970, states that: 'If the *oblastniki* could take from Slovtsov only his thesis of Siberian patriotism, then from Shchapov they adopted in already prepared form all the basic elements of their conception.'[28] The two leading lights and most influential theorists of Siberian *oblastnichestvo* were undoubtedly the previously mentioned Nikolai Yadrintsev and Grigorii Potanin. Although they and the other prominent *oblastniki* had no fully developed and thor-oughly articulated policy or action programme, by the early 1860s 'the basic elements of their conception' were well established. From their body of writings – scholarly, journalistic and propagandistic – it is possible to identify five particular areas of concern in which they demanded radical reform.

Agenda for Radical Regional Reform

First, and perhaps most urgently, was Yadrintsev and Potanin's call for the abolition of the exile system. As will be explained in Chapter Six, the practice of annually dumping thousands of often violent criminals, murderers, misfits and other anti-social elements from European Russia in the 'vast roofless prison' of Siberia was both resented and feared by the free, settled population, whether the so-called 'old inhabitants' (*starozhily*), more recent voluntary immigrants or the native peoples. Not only did the *oblastniki*, along with other progressive sections of society, rightly regard it as inhumane and of little penological value, but it also imposed a terrible incubus on Siberia's innocent citizenry who were constantly menaced and in terror of the murderous activi-ties of marauding gangs of escaped prisoners, exiles and recidivists, many of them originally banished there for particularly horrific crimes. Other, less dangerous elements consisted of wastrels, drifters, ne'er-do-wells, whores and those expelled by their communities for repeated petty offences against customary law, who also had a debilitating effect on Siberia's inchoate society. The abolition of the exile system was seen, therefore, as an essential condition for the orderly civic development of Siberia, as was the emancipation of the serfs for European Russia.

Second, the regionalists drew attention to and laid great emphasis on the long established and continuing exploitation of Siberia's natural resources. In their view, even post-Speranskii, a classic colonial situation still existed, with the metropolitan power plundering its eastern provinces and using its raw materials for the benefit of the centralized state. In *Siberia as a Colony*, Yadrintsev describes, analyses and condemns three centuries of Moscow and St Petersburg's continual and unrelieved pillaging of the region's wealth – animal, vegetable and mineral – and produces an impressive range of statistics, many of them from official sources, to demonstrate the enormity, the rapaciousness and the lack of concern for the natural environment of the central authorities' economic and commercial colonial policies. In fact, successive Russian rulers and governments had come to regard Siberia simply as a bottomless 'goldmine' (*zolotoe dno*), at first in the figurative and later in the literal sense of the term, or as a 'treasure chest' (*zolotoe sunduk*) to be systematically dipped into, or robbed, with an avaricious, blinkered unconcern for the effects of their myopic greed on the land and peoples of their vast colony. Only by assuming much greater control of the disposal of its own wealth could Siberia's own future be properly and justly secured.[29]

Third, the educational and cultural infrastructure of Siberia was woefully inadequate for the region's needs. Literacy rates throughout the entire Russian Empire were abysmally low in comparison with even some of the more backward European nations, and the situation in Siberia was even worse. Even many of the wealthiest merchants lacked a rudimentary knowledge of the 'three Rs', and the clergy was well-known for its low level of education, its evangelical zeal and its lack of concern for the proper enlightenment of the people. After all, the original 'conquerors' and settlers of Siberia were simple cossaks who knew little beyond the art of war, hunters who read only the lore of the forest and its beasts, ill-lettered artisans, the 'rude soldiery', illiterate peasants, and a host of displaced, peripatetic pariahs and crooks. Even the egregious governors of Siberia and their maladroit bureaucratic minions were hardly distinguished by their sophisticated commitment to the humanities or science. Apart from a few isolated luminaries such as Slovtsov, it was certainly impossible to talk of anything that could be described as a 'Siberian intelligentsia' – that is until the arrival of enlightened political exiles from European Russia, like the Decembrists and the Petrashevtsy – many of whom did what they could by their pedagogical, literary and journalistic activities to educate at least some of the local population – and, of course, the emergence of the *oblastniki*. Speranskii, too, had done what he could to raise the standards of public enlightenment. On arrival in Siberia, he was totally appalled by the general backwardness, ignorance and the benighted vulgarity of the population, both Russian and native. Yadrintsev quotes him as writing: 'For two years to see around one not a single educated person, to hear not a single intelligent word – that is awful!'[30] This was an exaggeration of the new Governor-General's predicament. He was already well acquainted, for instance, with the erudite Slovtsov, with whom he had earlier studied at the St Petersburg Seminary, and who now helped Speranskii found a number of elementary schools in Irkutsk and elsewhere using the 'Lancaster method' of mutual instruction.[31] A rudimentary network of primitive educational institutions was created during his governorship, but after his recall to St Petersburg, matters went into general decline. As late as 1869 the whole of Siberia boasted only four high schools (*gimnaziya*),[32] but was finally endowed with its first institute of higher education on the founding of the University of Tomsk in 1888. All the activists and theorists of the regionalist school were convinced that wider educational opportunities and raising the cultural awareness of the Siberian people – including greater knowledge of science and technology – was essential for the country's further development.

Their fourth major demand was for the implementation of a fully funded and organized programme of migration and settlement in order to encourage the development of Siberia's rich agricultural potential. Farming, both arable and animal husbandry, had always played a role in the Siberia economy, but the rich, fertile lands of southern Siberia were in desperate need of peasant manpower to realize the region's promise of far greater agrarian productivity. As mentioned above, this demand for increased migration was finally met in ample measure under the terms of Stolypin's reforms following the revolutionary events of 1905 (see Chapter Seven). Also in the economic sphere, Siberian merchants had grown increasingly resentful of financial policies affecting the region dictated by St Petersburg, which manifestly favoured and protected European-Russian business interests at the expense of their eastern partners. Particular concern was expressed over the maintenance of a kind of internal customs barrier between European and Asiatic Russia that not only damaged Siberian mercantile interests, but also resulted in the Siberian consumer having to pay higher prices for centrally produced manufactured goods. Without going so far as to advocate a protectionist policy, the regionalists fully incorporated the demands of the Siberian merchantry to be treated on an equal footing with the centre, and thereby throw off 'the economic yoke of Moscow over Siberia'.[33]

Last, but not least, the *oblastniki* were acutely aware of the continuingly wretched plight of Siberia's aboriginal peoples. Central to the regionalists' view of Russia's conquest and colonization of Siberia – 'the litmus paper of Siberian historiography'[34] – was the conviction that the indigenous peoples of the country, far from having benefited from contact with a supposedly superior civilization, had been the object of mindless brutality and savage exploitation, which in some cases had taken on almost genocidal proportions. It was the *oblastniki*'s purpose not only to guarantee their residual rights and save them from possible extermination, but also to improve their material circumstances and integrate them fully into the future development of an autonomous Siberia.[35]

At the heart of the regionalists' philosophy, therefore, lay what they regarded as a fundamental dichotomy between the regions and the centre, between the colony and the metropolis, between Siberia and Russia. It was rather as if the classic antagonism between Westernizers and Slavophils in the 1840s, with the latter's insistence on an atavistic, almost spiritual divide between Russia and the West, had taken a giant stride eastwards across the Urals. Some writers (notably Shchapov and, following him, Yadrintsev) even developed questionable theories about the evolution of a distinctly Siberian national type. Hereditary determinants such as the historical miscegenation of the incoming European Slavs with the autochthonous Siberian peoples, together with the environmental factors of climate, diet and natural surroundings, had, in their view, produced an anthropologically and physiologically identifiable *Homo sibiricus*, who was also, of course, psychologically and behaviourally distinguishable from *Homo russicus*.[36] This quasi-racialist notion, although not shared by all the regionalists, provided an emotional colouring to the major issues with which they were preoccupied – outlined above – and without a solution of which the orderly, civic development of Siberia was impossible.

Reform or Revolution?

Although the approach to all of these issues was based on the premise that Siberia was merely a colony of European Russia, and while it was made explicit that the future lay in a far greater degree of regional autonomy, there was as yet no specific call for the *political* separation of Siberia from Russia. In other words, the minimalist programme of the *oblastniki* at this stage was reformist rather than revolutionary. This interpretation supports the view of those Soviet Marxist historians who see the regionalist movement as a reflection of the interests of the Siberian bourgeoisie and the minuscule urban intelligentsia, with no resonance among the Siberian masses and no understanding of the class struggle.[37] On the other hand, prominent *oblastniki* such as Yadrintsev and Potanin were certainly influenced in their anti-government attitudes by the political philosophy of contemporary revolutionary theorists, including Aleksandr Herzen (1812–70), Nikolai Dobrolyubov (1836–61) and, of course, Nikolai Chernyshevskii (1828–89), who himself was to languish in solitary exile at Vilyuisk in distant Yakutia for nearly 20 years.[38] In an article of 15 October 1862, Herzen, 'the true founder of Russian Populism',[39] wrote from his self-imposed London exile: 'If Siberia were to be separated from Russia tomorrow, we would be the first to welcome the new life. The unity of the State is quite incompatible with the welfare of the people.'[40] Proven links between the Siberian regionalists and Russian revolutionary activists both at home and abroad have led S.F. Koval to the conclusion that, 'There is every reason to consider the social movement in Siberia as a serious potential reserve for the all-Russian revolutionary-democratic movement.'[41]

The nearest they ever got, however, to a call for an all-out revolution was in the affair of the Siberian separatists in 1865. A number of events, such as the return home of Siberian students from St Petersburg following the university demonstrations in 1862, the Polish revolt of 1863 after which thousands of Polish insurrectionists were exiled to the Baikal region in eastern Siberia, the 'civil execution' and exile of Nikolai Chernyshevskii in 1864, along with many more radical activists, injected a new sense of revolutionary awareness into Siberian regionalist circles. Potanin coined the term 'red separatists' (*krasnye separatisty*) to distinguish the more militant tendency, which sought the total overthrow of autocracy and the establishment of a United States of Siberia, from those with more moderate calls simply for greater regional autonomy within the Russian Empire. Between 1864 and 1866, the authorities were alerted to the existence of various extremist plots and conspiracies which seemed to link the *oblastniki* to known revolutionaries, dissident émigrés and exiles and banished Polish insurgents. Added to this was the discovery in Omsk of revolutionary manifestos addressed 'To Siberian Patriots', and the hatching of a complex plan in 1866 for a combined insurgency of Polish and Russian exiles around Lake Baikal, which it was hoped would be joined by sympathetic elements of the local population and lead to the formation of an independent republic, to be symbolically named *Svobodoslavia* ('Free Slavia'), with the liberated Chernyshevskii as its president. In the event the insurrection, which lasted from 25 June to 25 July 1866, was bloodily suppressed, four of its ringleaders shot, and the majority of the other rebels flogged and sentenced to longer terms of *katorga* (forced labour).[42]

To what extent was Siberian *oblastnichestvo* a genuine expression of the political and intellectual radicalism of the 1860s? Both pre-revolutionary Russian and Soviet historiography on the subject is riddled with contradictory views and conflicting evaluations as to its ideological credentials and social, i.e. class, characterization. Some writers regard the *oblastniki* as 'revolutionary democrats', others as bourgeois reformists, and yet others as downright 'reactionaries' and precursors of the Siberian anti-Bolshevik counter-revolution of 1918–21 (see Chapter Eight).[43] Although more recent scholarship, both Russian and Western, has done much to illuminate the history of nineteenth-century Siberian regionalism, it is still the case that 'the precise relationship between the regionalists and the revolutionary circles is still hazy and awaits further investigation'.[44] What is certain, however, is that in its hey-day Siberian *oblastnichestvo* was genuinely symptomatic of the highly charged atmosphere of widespread anti-government feeling, social unease, intellectual ferment, emotional concern for the plight of the Russian *narod* (people) and developing revolutionary challenge to the regime, which was the hallmark of the 1860s and 1870s.

During the stultifying reign of Emperor Alexander III (1881–94), following his father's assassination, radical and revolutionary activity in Russia, including its Siberian dimension, went into a period of relative quiescence in the face of the government crackdown. This lasted until the workers' strikes, peasant revolts and hectic upheavals of the early twentieth century which were to shake the whole empire to its foundations, culminating in the all-Russian revolutionary situation of 1905. The Siberian *oblastniki* largely confined themselves during this period to low-profile journalistic, literary and cultural activities until re-emerging as a potent force during the post-revolutionary Civil War between 1918 and 1922 (see Chapter Eight).

However, before picking up the threads of those momentous events, it is necessary to pay some attention to the process by which the empire, before divesting itself of its American possessions, as outlined above, added to its Siberian and Far Eastern territories by its successful, and peaceful, annexation of the strategically and reputedly economically valuable Amur and Ussuri regions of northern China.

FROM ALASKA TO THE AMUR

As was briefly explained in the previous chapter, Muscovy's attempts to establish control over fertile territories east of Lake Baikal along the Amur river basin, then referred to as Dauria had proved unsuccessful. The area was inhabited by Manchus, Tungus and other peoples, and ruled by China. Under the terms of the Treaty of Nerchinsk (1689), which finally brought four decades of bloody hostilities to an end, Russia was forced to evacuate the territory and abandon its outposts in return for profitable trading rights with China.[45] On the whole, Moscow shed very few tears over its failure to secure the Amur-Ussuri lands – useful as their agricultural products would have been for the poorly provisioned Russian pioneers in the east. Peter the Great was by that time much more fixated on his plans and ambitions concerning his relations with Western Europe. There were only a few thousand Russian settlers and cossaks in the region, it was too far away to defend against local military forces, and in any case the original inhabitants possibly found Chinese rule relatively more congenial than that of the savage Slavs whose atrocities across the region, particularly under the ferocious leadership of the warrior-explorer, Yerofei Khabarov (1603–c.1671), were all too fresh in the popular mind. Attention, too, was deflected northwards, resulting in the great voyages of exploration and hunting expeditions described in Chapter Three.

Throughout the eighteenth century any further interest in the Amur region lay dormant, and only revived around the 1840s, gaining especial momentum during the governor-generalship of East Siberia of Nikolai Nikolaevich Muravëv (1809–81). His exploits during his tenure of office (1847–61), and his successful annexation of the Amur and Ussuri districts, were to earn him the honorific surname of Muravëv-Amurskii. He presented a curious mixture of authoritarianism, huge ambitions for further Russian imperial expansion in the Far East and progressive, liberal social attitudes. Surrounded by a coterie of like-minded military men, merchants, scientists and enlightened political exiles – including some of the Decembrists – these fellow-thinkers, because of their obsession with the Amur region, became known as the *amurtsy*. After his appointment in 1847 he set about realizing his ambitions – which were not wholly approved of by Tsar Nicholas I and some of his senior ministers – through an adroit combination of opportunism, stealthy incursions into Chinese territory, and the establishment of Russian outposts in China's northern marches and on the island of Sakhalin. The Manchu Qing dynasty in Peking could do little to halt these operations, even when it knew of them, debilitated and preoccupied as it was with its own domestic difficulties such as the effects of the Opium Wars (1839–42), the Taiping Rebellion (1850) and military hostilities with Britain and France (1856–58). The combination of the Russian government's apprehension as to what Muravëv was up to, and the internal difficulties inside China, encouraged him to act ever more boldly. As John Stephan neatly puts it: 'Deftly manoeuvring between St Petersburg's caution and Beijing's caducity, Muraviev correlated defense with expansion, strengthening Russia's periphery while preparing to breach China's.'[46]

Important first stepping stones along the road that led to the final incorporation of the region into the Russian Empire were: the founding of a trading post at the mouth of the Amur in 1850, initially called Nikolaevskii Post (after 1856, Nikolaevsk, now known as Nikolaevsk-na-Amure); in 1852–3, the occupation of Sakhalin led by a young naval captain (later admiral), Gennadii Nevelskoi (1813–76); and the establishment of Russia's first proper settlement on the island, called Ilinskii Post. (Russia's claims over Sakhalin were bitterly contested by neighbouring Japan, and after a temporary withdrawal of Russian personnel – not unconnected with strategic considerations during the Crimean War – a negotiated rapprochement was reached in 1855, whereby the island became a joint Russo-Japanese condominium, an arrangement which lasted until 1875.) During 1857–8, Muravëv took advantage of Chinese embroilment with Britain and France to exact *de facto* recognition of Russian control of the newly acquired territories, converting this into quasi *de jure* status on the signing of the Treaty of Aigun in 1858. Russian presence was further consolidated with the founding of a military post on the middle Amur, named Khabarovka (after 1893, Khabarovsk), after the bloodthirsty seventeenth-century pioneer-cum-pillager, Yerofei Khabarov. Under the terms of the treaty – not fully ratified by Peking until forced to do so in the face of deteriorating relations with just about all the other major powers – Russia gained all the territories on the left (i.e. northern) bank of the Amur, but there was some ambiguity in the wording of the text concerning ownership of the lands between the Ussuri and the coast of the Sea of Japan. Impatient of these textological obscurities, Muravëv brazenly – and typically – dispatched troops into the area (known as the Primorye), unceremoniously announced to the local natives that they were now subjects of the tsar, navigated the coastline southwards almost as far as the Korean border, and, in an effort to signal the permanence of Russia's presence, renamed recently introduced English place names in the area with Russian toponyms. Finally, in 1860 two events took place which set the seal on the incorporation of the Priamurye and the Primorye provinces into the Russian Empire. These were: the signing of the Treaty of Peking on 14 November, which clarified and formally ratified the Treaty of Aigun, including recognition of Muravëv's encroachments beyond the Ussuri; and the raising of the Russian flag over a scruffy coastal hamlet on the shores of the renamed Peter the Great Bay with the new, triumphalist name of Vladivostok, 'Lord of the East', later to become Russia's greatest commercial and naval base in the Far East and home of her Pacific fleet.

Although Muravëv's tactics were not exactly those of 'softly, softly – catchee monkey', the potent mixture of cool audacity, imperial purpose and crafty diplomacy in his venture had secured for the empire an area the size of France and Germany combined without a drop of blood being spilt. The successful expansion in the Far East was hailed as a triumph for Russia, as demonstrated in the symbolism of the name 'Vladivostok'. But despite the initial euphoria and the grandiose visions entertained by some Russian enthusiasts (including the doyen of the radical left, Aleksandr Herzen) who saw the Amur-Ussuri regions as a 'new America', and the river system as Russia's Mississippi,[47] the history of the territory's further development did not live up to the great expectations of the *amurtsy* and other hopefuls. It was not until the twentieth century that the significance of Russia's presence in the Far East and the Pacific – both for good and ill – took on a different dimension.

An important consequence, however, of Russia's territorial aggrandizement in the East was to bring under her suzerainty more non-Russian peoples and the aboriginal inhabitants of the Amur-Ussuri region. How the imperial government implemented its colonial policies in its treatment of the empire's indigenous minority peoples and ethnic groups is examined in the following chapter.

5

The Native Peoples: Vanquished and Victims

As mentioned in the previous chapter, the Soviet scholar, V.G. Mirzoev, described the question of the nature of the European, Christian Russians' conquest, assimilation and settlement of the north Asian landmass as the 'litmus paper of Siberian historiography'[1] – in other words, 'the acid test'. A crucial, if not *the* crucial, factor in evaluating the real character, purpose, ethical standards and demographic consequences of Moscow and St Petersburg's colonization of Siberia and the Far East lies not in its economic and commercial value to the imperialist government, not in the huge amount of territory annexed and occupied, nor even its impact on the natural environment. It lies, rather, in the dramatic – indeed tragic – manner in which the Slavonic incomers' raids, incursions and armed campaigns across the Urals impacted on the lives, culture, traditional rites and customs, personal relationships and sheer physical existence of the aboriginal peoples, clans, tribes and communities that had inhabited the Arctic wastes, tundra, taiga, river banks, pasturelands, lakesides and littoral of Siberia for centuries before the Russian onslaught. In the works of both pre-revolutionary and Soviet Russian academics, as well as of their Western counterparts, most writing on the history of Siberia has concentrated, for perfectly understandable reasons, on the four-and-a-half centuries following Yermak's original foray (see Chapter Two). However, as A.P. Okladnikov and his fellow scholars have demonstrated, the indigenous peoples of Siberia had already developed an aeons-long pattern and variety of specifically and quintessentially 'Siberian' cultures and civilizations that owed little or nothing to either European or Oriental exemplars.[2] The following section looks briefly at the nature of those cultures before they were so rudely and, indeed, brutally transmogrified by the rapacious invaders from the west.[3]

THE PRE-RUSSIAN PEOPLES OF SIBERIA

First, a word about nomenclature, ethnonyms and terminology. At the time of Yermak's 'expedition' in the late sixteenth century, the whole territory from the Urals to the Pacific, from the Arctic Ocean to the borders of Central Asia and China, was inhabited by myriad, though sparsely scattered, groups of indigenous peoples, all of whom, whatever their tribal distinctions, lived – according to their often shifting localities – by a mixture of hunting, fishing, herding and gathering. Most, though not all, were nomadic or semi-nomadic. Each of them had its own 'ethnonym', i.e. the name of the *ethnos*, or ethnic group – Buryat, Tungus, Yakut, Eskimo, Kamchadal, etc. – to which its members belonged, though some of the labels were invented, adopted or imposed by hostile neighbours (sometimes in a pejorative sense), alien rulers or administrative officials. Many tribes referred to themselves in their own language with terms that are linguistically very different from those by which they have become to be generally recognized. The whole business of ethnic onomatology is extremely complex and fraught with all kinds of linguistic, historical and cultural controversies that are too intricate to be explored in detail in the present context.[4] At any rate, under tsarist suzerainty, they were all – whatever their racial affiliation – generically lumped together in Russian parlance with the designation of *inorodtsy* (singular, *inorodets*), meaning literally 'people of different birth (or descent)', or *inozemtsy* – 'people of a different land'. The word *inorodtsy* had no derogatory connotations, as neither does the English term 'natives' (i.e. people born in and inhabiting the same particular country or locality), though some etymologically ignorant zealots of 'political correctness' nowadays deem otherwise, and it is certainly not synonymous with 'savages', although they were often savagely treated as such. In this chapter the various terms – *inorodtsy*, natives, aborigines, indigenous or autochthonous peoples, tribesmen etc. – are used more or less interchangeably, and unapologetically. Also without apology is the use of the term 'small peoples', as in 'small peoples of the north'. This is a straight translation of the Russian term *malye narody* (literally, 'little peoples'). Despite some objections to its use in English, the reference is quite obviously – as most readers will no doubt understand – to the demographic statistics, rather than the physical stature, of the peoples concerned.

As noted in Chapter Two, the history of Siberia's 'pre-Russian' antiquity is more the preserve of the anthropologist and the archaeologist than of the modern historian. However, it is worthwhile to say a few words about the culture and life pattern of the various native Siberian peoples encountered – and ultimately conquered – by the invading Russians during their inexorable eastwards march. As also noted above, at the time of Yermak's original attack on Kuchum's minor Tatar khanate of Sibir – a remnant of the Mongol Empire – the seemingly endless expanses which lay beyond it were, and had been for thousands of years, inhabited by a great gallimaufry of aboriginal peoples and tribes at various levels of cultural and social development. Just as it is impossible to calculate the actual size of the indigenous population (though demographic estimates can and have been made – see below), so one cannot be arithmetically precise about the total number of ethnic groupings into which the population was divided. The reasons for this are both various and obvious. First, in the uncertain and volatile conditions which prevailed in the early decades of the Russian conquest there were, of course, no proper, systematic demographic surveys or censuses made – that is, until the need for counting the number of tax- and tribute-paying vassals of the conquering Russians arose. Second, the shifting, migratory nature of those tribes that followed a nomadic lifestyle prevented the gathering of even approximate statistics. A roving, peripatetic Yukagir reindeer herdsman struggling across the Arctic tundra could hardly have supplied his personal details, place of residence and postal code to the agents of the Muscovite exchequer. Third, even when rudimentary censuses for fiscal purposes were eventually introduced, it was the practice to take account of only the male tribute-paying members of a community, and so, working from the recorded figures, it is necessary to factor in the wives, womenfolk and children of the adult males in order to arrive at an overall estimate. Most historical ethnographers work on the basis of a multiplier of four or five in this respect. Fourth, the actual designation, i.e. identification and naming, of a particular *ethnos* was based variously on linguistic criteria, consanguinity, geographical location or administrative convenience, which makes for substantial margins of error, confusion and considerable fuzziness.

Despite these difficulties, attempts have been made by a number of distinguished scholars to offer some plausible figures. In his seminal work, *The Clan and Tribal Composition of the Siberian Peoples in the Seventeenth Century*,[5] the celebrated Soviet ethnographer, B.O. Dolgikh, calculated, on the basis of taxation records, that there were in excess of 500 different tribal groupings in Siberia, though some of these were, seemingly, administrative constructs rather than being derived from strictly ethnic or linguistic relationships. The figures, therefore, need to be treated with some caution. On a loose map accompanying volume 2 of A.P. Okladnikov's edited five-tome *History of Siberia from Ancient Times to the Present Day*,[6] the cartographer identifies in meticulous detail the location, broad ethnic affiliation and named tribal subdivisions of over 400 communities, both large and small. Collating these two authoritative sets of figures, and bearing in mind the various caveats mentioned above, it is reasonable to conclude that at the time of the Russian conquest towards the end of the sixteenth century, there were anything between 450 and 500 different tribal groupings scattered throughout the Siberian landmass, most of them sharing certain cultural and social affinities, but each of the major ethnic 'blocs', so to speak, possessing its own individual characteristics, customs and practices. There were also a number of dissimilarities among the different tribes even within the same ethno-linguistic group – differences, for example of dialect, ritual practices, modes of transport, domicile, dress, gender relationships and so on.

For instance, the widely dispersed Tungus, the Yukagirs and the more concentrated Yakuts (if it is possible to talk of the concentration of a population numbering roughly 28,500 in the seventeenth century scattered over an area in excess of 3 million square kilometres/1.2 million square miles) were differentiated as being either 'reindeer peoples' (referred to in Russian sources as *olennye*), those southern Evenks around Lake Baikal as 'horse-mounted' (*konnye*) and others, mainly fishers and shore-dwellers, as 'settled' or 'sedentary' (*peshie* – literally 'pedestrian'), though they did travel by dog-sleigh and canoe. The languages, or dialects, of the various tribes, even when belonging to the same broad linguistic group, were often mutually incomprehensible – rather like, say, modern Greek and English, both of which belong to the Indo-European family. In the overwhelming majority of cases there was no written language, alphabetic or ideographic system, except among the Buryats who came under the influence of neighbouring Mongol and Tibetan Lamaist Buddhists, and islamicized Tatars, some of whom were familiar with religious texts in the Arabic script.

According to Slovtsov, the total number of the indigenous population of Siberia of all ethnic groups in 1662, almost 100 years after Yermak's campaign, was 288,000 (compared to the immigrant Russians' 105,000).[7] One can assume that figures for the mid-sixteenth century were rather lower, just over 200,000.[8]

Okladnikov's map referred to above identifies 12 major ethnic groupings as follows (see Map 6):

1. Ugrian
2. Samoed
3. Turkic
4. Mongol
5. Tungus
6. Manchzhur
7. Ket
8. Gilyak
9. Yukagir
10. North-east Palaeoasiatic
11. Eskimo
12. Ainu

Of these, the two largest were the Tungus and the Turkic, with around 100 and 120 tribal subdivisions respectively, and the smallest of them were the Eskimo, Gilyak, Ainu and Manchzhur, comprising only a dozen or so sub-groups in total. In geographical terms, the most widely scattered and broadly distributed clans and tribes belonged to the Tungus (present-day Evenks and Evens). Obviously, as with any people or nationality in the world, the Siberian natives' lifestyle, habitat, economic activities, clothing, diet, modes of transport, cosmology, sexual mores, rites of passage, weaponry and types of warfare were – and still are – conditioned by the physical and natural environment in which they exist. The surrounding species and genera of flora and fauna are also vital to an understanding of the human inhabitants' means of subsistence, daily practices, health and life-expectancy. Coastal peoples naturally depend on the fruits of the sea, on fishing and hunting marine mammals such as the whale,

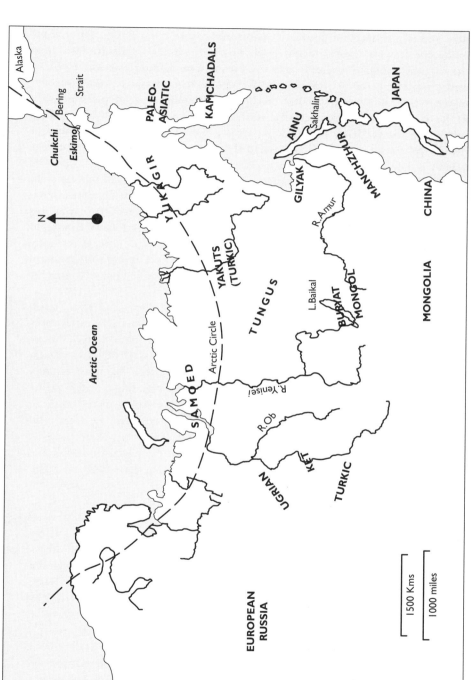

Map 6 Approximate distribution of the major Siberian native ethnic groups in the seventeenth century.

the seal and the walrus, whereas the woodland and forest dwellers, thousands of kilometres inland, rely on terrestrial fare – bear, elk, rabbit, hare, badger, deer and other ruminant ungulates, game birds and similar fowl – not only for food, but also for the skins and bones from which they skilfully fashioned their clothes, tents, tools and weapons. Fresh-water fishing was, and is, obviously important, too. Although in some regions leguminous or cereal supplements to their diet were available, on the whole the Siberian natives, especially in the far north, were, by necessity, almost totally carnivorous. Unlike peoples inhabiting the modern, so-called 'developed world' with a wider variety of readily produced and supplied foodstuffs, in which they have the spurious luxury of choosing to be omnivorous, vegetarian, vegan, anorexic, bulimic or pickers of a tasty smorgasbord, the tundra- and taiga-dwellers of Siberia were not only carnivorous, but positively all-devouring (see Krasheninnikov's description of the Kamchadals' grisly gourmandism referred to in Chapter Three). Without over-generalizing, most of the peoples listed above inhabited a common natural environment and experienced the same, or similar, climatic, vegetational and geographical features as described in Chapter One, though the Turkic tribes in the far south enjoyed a less frigid and inclement ambiance than their distant northern cousins.

Despite the linguistic and ethnic divisions which separated and distinguished the aboriginal Siberian clans, tribes and races from each other, there are a number of crucial phenomena which nearly all of them shared. At the risk of repetition, the common denominator is that they were all – to a greater or lesser extent – hunters, herders, fishers and gatherers, living essentially on the natural products of the seas, rivers, tundra and taiga, and battling with the harsh and unrelenting environment. Most of them were totally or partially nomadic, following their herds or hunting their prey on foot, reindeer or dog-sleigh according to the seasons, and living in portable, easily assembled and dismantled tepee-like dwellings made of animal skins, felt and wooden poles. Some, like the Kamchadals of Kamchatka, dwelt in semi-subterranean dugouts in which the atmosphere was at best warm and cosy, but was potentially pestilential and foul-smelling.

Among Soviet-era Russian historians and ethnographers, various debates used to take place concerning the precise level of socio-economic development of the Siberian natives, those arguments being fuelled by the arcane vagaries of Marxist cultural and historical taxonomy. Rather like medieval scholastics arguing about how many angels could dance on the head of a pin, their ideologically driven twentieth-century scions wasted thousands of words and pools of ink trying to establish whether this, that or the other Siberian tribe was, at the time of the Russian conquest (or assimilation), a matriarchal, post-matriarchal, patriarchal, clan, semi-feudal, transitional, primitive-communalist, property-owning, slave-based, hierarchical, socially stratified, class-ridden, pre-historic, Neolithic or whatever else type of society. To take just one example: at least three schools of thought existed about the level of social and economic development of the seventeenth-century

Turkic-speaking Yakut people of north-east Siberia. S.V. Bakhrushin and S.A. Tokarev argued that primitive-communalist relationships were already breaking down and that the Yakuts were in the early stages of transition to a wealth- and property-based form of feudalism, which was accelerated by the appearance of the Russian invaders. Okladnikov, on the other hand, was of the opinion that at the time of the Russian conquest there already existed sharp class contradictions within an essentially patriarchal social structure, which also retained vestiges of slavery, but a form of slavery which could not form the infrastructure of an animal-herding economy. Yet another position was adopted by Dolgikh, who stated quite definitely that Yakut society was totally patriarchal, but also pointed to the unequal distribution of wealth, the existence of an 'upper class' (*verkhushka*) and the early signs of emergent feudalism.[9] Readers are invited to make of this faux-Marxist mumbo-jumbo what they will.

What is certain is that all of the ethnic groupings referred to above were at a roughly equivalent stage of development, containing elements of both patriarchal-clan and embryonic feudal relationships, and all relied on an amalgam of hunting, herding, fishing and foraging for herbs, berries, fruit, roots and edible fungi. Some, especially the Buryats around Lake Baikal, also engaged in agriculture, sowing millet, buckwheat and barley, partly for their own consumption and partly for animal fodder – though it ultimately amounted to the same thing. Some were highly skilled at iron working – both smelting and forging – and produced their own tools, weapons, utensils and adornments for personal use and for barter with less technologically advanced neighbouring tribes. In sartorial terms, though there were many regional variations in style, custom and costume, the basic dress was composed of thick furs, pliable leathers and variously treated skins and pelts. Shoes, boots, leggings, moccasins and other foot- and leg-wear were cobbled together according to local conditions and raw materials, often embellished with elaborate and attractive embroidery. Woven textiles were rare, though woollen fabrics were produced in sheep-rearing communities. Coastal peoples also used fish skins to fashion their parkas, skirts, trousers and other items of apparel. Animal guts and sinews were universally used for sewing, stitching and threading purposes with bone or wooden needles.

In terms of clan, familial and sexual relationships, these varied from strictly exogamous matrimonial unions (i.e. marrying outside the clan), to group marriages with shared spouses, monogamy, polygamy and, of course, casual and temporary cohabitation, many of these intimacies often accompanied by sundry taboos concerning virginity, puberty, widowhood, incest, menstruation, perinatal practices, fertility and infertility. One of the most distressing effects of the Russians' voluntary or enforced social and sexual intercourse with the indigenous Siberians was the introduction of venereal diseases, especially syphilis, which was particularly virulent (see below).

Many Russian commentators, both past and recently present, justify their forebears' supposedly 'civilizing' mission among the aboriginal peoples of

Siberia with reference to the bloody, continuous and atavistic warfare among the various tribes – traditional conflicts which were both inter- and intra-tribal – which were allegedly brought to a peaceful end by the beneficent mediation of the incoming irenical Slavs. This, of course, is utter nonsense. Although it is true that the Siberian indigenes *did* regularly engage in mutual and mortal combat, albeit with rudimentary weapons, invading one another's ancestral homelands and indulging in routine bouts of slaughter, violent seizure of property, abduction of women and children, enslavement of prisoners-of-war and other standard accompaniments of warfare, these conflicts were no more or less brutal than those of other races all over the globe and throughout the centuries – indeed, possibly less so. As James Forsyth has succinctly put it:

> the scale of the slaughter, cruelty and destruction in European wars of the seventeenth and subsequent centuries was immeasurably greater than that of the tribal conflicts of the [Siberian] 'savages' ... They can scarcely be taken as a serious reason for the backwardness of the Siberian peoples, nor as a reason for their subjugation by the Russians.[10]

These were, after all, 'small peoples' engaging in small, localized, if lethal, embroilments, sometimes involving simply a one-to-one gladiatorial-type confrontation between two champions. In any case, these intestine battles were in no way commensurate with the horrific massacres perpetrated against the Siberian tribesmen and women by the invading cossaks and tsarist officials, both civil and military. Rather ironically, two seventeenth-century cossak documents describe the Siberian *inorodtsy* as 'bellicose people, ferocious in battle' and 'given to warfare and constantly attacking their neighbours'.[11] This really is rich coming from a report composed by the invading, marauding, iron-clad western warriors, renowned and feared for their own belligerence, brutality and barbaric treatment of their foes. The Russians' incursion and plunder of Siberia's human and natural resources can hardly be realistically portrayed as a pacific mission, and they were, over three centuries, responsible for more bloodshed, mayhem, butchery and, in some cases, genocide than the aboriginal peoples of Siberia ever inflicted on each other. Yadrintsev is particularly voluble and outraged in his own writings on this issue (see below).

In addition, the original Siberians did not all meekly submit to the Russians' superior military power. There were regular 'native uprisings', rebellions and resistance to the tsarist authorities, to the imposition of the *yasak* (fur tribute), hostage-holding, enforced miscegenation and concubinage, compulsory recruitment, despoliation of traditional hunting grounds, imposition of an alien and incomprehensible religion in the form of Russian Orthodox Christianity and other intrusions on their ancestral cultures. Needless to say, all these manifestations of anti-Russian, anti-tsarist and anti-Christian opposition were dealt with by bestial punitive reprisals. The more remote these insurgent tribes were from the central powers, however, the longer, fiercer and more indomitable was their recalcitrance. The Chukchis in particular succeeded in resisting Russian domination for three centuries, though the unfortunate neighbouring Yukagirs were virtually annihilated. Readers familiar with the history of western Europeans' deliberate extermination of the indigenous North and South American Indian populations need not delve too deeply into their fund of knowledge to imagine the atrocities inflicted on the original inhabitants of Russia's own 'new world'. White, Christian, European colonialists on both sides of the Atlantic and Pacific oceans have a lot, morally and historically, for which to answer.

Siberian Ethnic Groups

Before moving on to a consideration of the indigenous peoples' belief-systems, folklore, religious rituals and superstitions, it is appropriate at this point to provide a few brief notes, offer a selective general summation, and point out a few differences pertaining to some of the ethnic groups listed above.

(1) West-Siberian Tatars: hunters-fishers; some cattle and horse-rearing; primitive agriculture and cottage industry; mainly sedentary; hierarchical class structure; native 'upper classes' (*znat'*) recruited into Russian service for military, garrisoning and tax-gathering duties; lower classes forced to pay *yasak*.

(2) Ugrian (e.g. Khanty, Mansi, Selkups): hunting- and fishing-based economy; patriarchal clan structure consisting of a number of extended families; in some areas governed by a type of 'military democracy' (similar to that of the cossaks) with popular assemblies and elected commanders; prior to Russian conquest, Khanty and Mansi paid tribute and supplied troops to the Tatar khans; this practice supposedly ended with Yermak's defeat of Khan Kuchum, and the Ugrian tribes, according to one source, thereupon 'voluntarily transferred their allegiance to the Russians';[12] evidence of existence of slavery; fiercely resisted Russian attempts at forcible Christianization.

(3) Samoeds (e.g. Nentsy, Entsy, Nganasans): mainly tundra and northern taiga-dwellers, though some enclaves in the south, west of Irkutsk; reindeer hunters and herders; Arctic Nentsy also hunted marine mammals; practised common ownership of goods, produce and grazing lands; many forced to pay *yasak,* though those in more remote regions evaded it.

(4) Tungus (mainly modern Evenks, Evens and Negidals): widely distributed throughout central, southern and south-east Siberia; rough (though overlapping) division into sedentary fisher-folk and nomadic deer-hunters and herders; southern Evenks also practised horse- and cattle-breeding on a large scale; levels of technology differed between the northern and southern Tungus, the formers' tools and weapons being almost totally of stone and bone, whereas the latter had some knowledge of ironworking, though most metalware obtained through barter (for fur) with Buryats, Yakuts and Russians; clear class differentiation based on property-ownership, prowess in

battle, hereditary ties, etc.; also paid *yasak* to the Russian authorities, guaranteed by the widespread practice of hostage holding.

(5) Yakuts: most northerly located of the Mongoloid, Turkic-speaking peoples; main occupation horse- and cattle-breeding; also hunting and fishing; northern Yakuts culturally close to Evenks and Yukagirs; very skilled at metalworking, products of which were traded for fur with neighbouring Tungus in order to pay *yasak*; Yakut metalware also highly prized by incoming Russians; well-developed hierarchical clan and family system, organized into largely self-governing territorial-administrative regions (in Russian, *volosti*), in the internal affairs of which the Russians did not usually meddle; local chieftains (*toyons*) utilized by Russians for tax-gathering duties and maintaining civil peace; evidence of slavery and exploitation of the 'lower classes' of the free population known as 'settlement dwellers' (*ulusnye lyudi*); rich, vivid mythology and folklore (see next section); intermarried and assimilated freely with Russians.

(6) Yukagirs: once a relatively numerous people inhabiting the far northeast, west of the Chukotka peninsula, the Yukagirs spoke a language unrelated to any other, and even its two main dialects were almost mutually incomprehensible (a recent source states that nowadays only 50 people survive who speak the *taiga* Yukagir language);[13] main areas of settlement and peregrination around the Anadyr, Kolyma and Indigirka rivers; divided into 'settled' and 'reindeer' peoples; main occupations reindeer- and elk-hunting and fishing; from seventeenth century also engaged in reindeer herding, borrowed from the Tungus Evens; 'settled' Yukagirs travelled mainly by dogsleigh, while the 'reindeer folk' obviously used their own animals for transport; strong clan system with many marriage taboos; shamanism also very strong, with the shamans – apart from their spiritual and magical functions (see below) – often fulfilling role of clan chieftain; since the seventeenth century, the Yukagirs have been driven almost to extinction.[14]

(7) North-east Palaeoasiatic: (e.g. Chukchis, Kamchadals, Koryaks, Eskimos): inhabited Chukotka peninsula and northern Kamchatka; close similarity of cultural development and lifestyle; coastal Chukchis, Koryaks and Eskimos 'sedentary', living mainly by hunting sea mammals; the 'reindeer' Chukchis and Koryaks engaged chiefly in nomadic deer-herding, supplemented by fishing and gathering; level of cultural development generally reckoned to be far behind that of other Siberian peoples, early Russian sources describing them as living 'in the full sense of the term, in the Stone Age';[15] all tools and weapons made of stone and bone; still a matriarchal, rather than patriarchal, culture with group marriages, shared spouses, fire worship, etc.; Itelmens, Eskimos, coastal Chukchis and Koryaks lived in settled 'village' communities; nomadic Chukchis and Koryaks also had temporary encampments (*stoibishche*); individual territorial groupings would often unite into larger units, particularly if under military threat; shamanism deeply entrenched, and rich folklore.

(8) Nivkhs: formerly known as Gilyaks, closely related to the settled Palaeoasiatic peoples of the north-east, inhabiting the lower reaches of the

Amur river, eastern Sakhalin and the Okhotsk seaboard; lived by fishing and hunting marine mammals; language unrelated to that of any other Siberian peoples; according to L.I. Shrenk they were 'totally unique';[16] clothes made from fish skins; winter dwellings were semi-subterranean shelters (*zemlyanki*), in summer, huts built on piles; transport by dog-sleigh; some knowledge of metallurgy; system of patriarchal clans with elected leaders.

(9) Ainus: highly distinctive people originally inhabiting the Kurile Islands, southern Sakhalin, southern Kamchatka, the lower Amur region and parts of the Japanese archipelago; distinctive physical characteristics, including 'highly developed tertiary pelage',[17] i.e. thick, rich male body hair (Chinese sources call them *maozhen* – 'hairy people'); anthropologically originating in Late Palaeolithic Age, related in somatological terms to east Asian, northern Mongoloid, equatorial and 'Australoid' peoples: 'Thousands of years in isolation (mostly of island life) helped the Ainus conserve their ancient racial features and form idiosyncratic anthropological and cultural peculiarities';[18] fishing, hunting and animal rearing, including fox, raccoon, eagles and owls; dress made of tree-bark, fish skin and fur, often highly decorated; body-tattooing common, especially female facial tattoos; strong cult of the bear; most modern-day Ainus live on Hokkaido (Japan), where they still suffer racial discrimination.[19]

(10) Buryats: Mongoloid people inhabiting area around Lake Baikal; diversified economy; western (i.e. west of Baikal) Buryats semi-sedentary, semi-nomadic animal herders (cattle and sheep), some agriculture (sowing cereal crops for winter fodder); eastern (trans-Baikal) Buryats mainly nomadic pastoralists, similar to the related Mongols; both also hunters and fishers. Highly sophisticated system of social hierarchy, half-patriarchal, half-feudal with a form of land- and serf-ownership; tribes divided into clans headed by hereditary chieftain (*noion*); reputation for bellicosity and constant warfare against neighbours, which Russian sources claim was ended with their arrival; end of seventeenth century saw encroachment of Lamaist Buddhism from Mongolia and Tibet, opening of schools and lamaseries, and growth of literacy; some Christianization, and Russification through intermarriage quite common.

(11) Altaians: very complex ethnic mix of peoples in the Sayan-Altai mountain ranges and south Siberian steppelands; heavily influenced in their culture by neighbouring peoples such as Mongols, Teleuts, Yenisei Kirgiz, Tuvinians, etc; engaged in semi-nomadic animal husbandry – cattle, horses, sheep, goats and even camels; some simple forms of agriculture using mattocks and ploughs; metalworking was widespread, well developed and used extensively for trading purposes; highly hierarchical, part-patriarchal, part-feudal social structure with remnants of slavery; lower classes of society often forced to pay onerous 'double tribute' to their own feudal masters and to the invading Russians; the various native Altaic languages belong mostly to the Turkic group; religious beliefs and rituals mainly shamanistic, with widespread use of animal sacrifices; later attempts by Orthodox missionaries at enforced Christianization.[20]

From what has been said in the above notes, it should be clear that at the time of the Russian occupation of Siberia, the aboriginal peoples already had a pattern and style of life of their own that had developed over centuries, and which was peculiarly adapted to, and a product of, the harsh environment in which they lived and survived. However, the fact that many of them did not survive the coming of the western invaders and alien settlers is an indictment of the colonial regime imposed on them by military force and by the exploitative administrative, fiscal, sexual and punitive practices of their new Russian overlords. Before discussing the damning evidence on this compiled by the Siberian regionalist scholar, N.M. Yadrintsev, something needs to be said concerning the religious beliefs and practices, folk-culture, legends, rituals and superstitions of the primordial Siberian peoples.

ANIMISM, SHAMANISM AND SIBERIAN FOLK BELIEFS

All religions and faith systems are, by definition, based not on reason, logic or any process of rationality but on myth, superstition, wool-gathering, fairy tales, fantasy and credulity in the existence of various types of ghosts and gods, daemons and demons.[21] Unsurprisingly, given their lack of literacy and modern scientific knowledge, the various Siberian peoples developed their own entrenched religious beliefs and folklore.

The principal features of the Siberian natives' religious beliefs and practices were animism, shamanism, fetishism and totemism, which neither the Christian missionaries in the eighteenth and nineteenth centuries, nor the godless Marxist ideologues in the twentieth, managed to eradicate, even though many 'converts' paid convenient and salutary lip service to ecclesiological doctrine and political dogmata imposed by the Russian authorities. For instance, in the early eighteenth century a concerted attempt was made at the mass Christianization of the Mansi and Khanty in north-west Siberia under the leadership of the metropolitan of Tobolsk, Filofei Leshchinskii. Missionary expeditions were dispatched in 1704, 1707 and 1712, one of their chief participants being a certain G. Novitskii, responsible for enforcing the proper observation of the Orthodox rites in the *volost'* (region) of Kondinsk. He was murdered in an anti-Russian local uprising in 1717, and the vast majority of the native population continued with their old pagan practices, which were obviously much more fun.[22]

Almost all the Siberian indigenous peoples indulged in some kind of animistic worship, believing that various natural phenomena such as trees, mountains, rivers, lakes, the sea, as well as animals such as the elk, the bear, the deer and the tiger, possessed their own spirit or *anima*, to which reverence was due and which were celebrated in different kinds of rites, rituals, celebrations and festivals. Sun and moon worship was also common. These spirits (*dushi*) were referred to (in Russian) as 'masters' or 'lords' (*khozyaeva*) of the forest, river, or some other manifestation of nature. The most widely revered animal was the brown bear, often called the 'master of the taiga' (*khozyain taigi*), and the 'bear festival' was observed in most, though not all, Siberian cultures. The bear was hunted and killed, of course, for its rich meat and fur, but its spirit was placated with elaborate ceremonies designed to maintain the natural equilibrium between man and the rest of the animal, or at any rate ursine, kingdom. The ubiquitous 'bear feasts' featured not only consumption of the cooked meat, but also chanting, dancing, athletic contests, the ceremonial flaying, dismemberment and dispersal of the carcass, gathering of the bones, skull and muzzle, embellishment of the dwellings with the slaughtered beast's scattered remains, and often characterized by 'phallic and erotic pantomimes, immodest songs and dances, including those performed with wooden phalluses, free sexual relations and rites involving bear genitals'.[23] All this in solemn celebration of the great bear's sacred nature. In the folk-legends of some of the Siberian peoples, there are tales of sexual relations between bears and human girls, resulting in miraculous births and hybrid siblings, and children being raised by brown Bruins. (In comparison, Goldilocks got off pretty lightly.) Apart from the bear, other animals including the elk, the raven, the goose and the swan also featured as sacred creatures in the folklore of several tribes, in many cases the meat — especially of the raven — being regarded as forbidden food. The cult of the elk was particularly strong with the Yukagirs.

Among some peoples, for instance the Yakuts, the spirit world was divided into 'good' spirits and 'evil' spirits, the former inhabiting the 'upper world', and the latter the 'nether world'. This was part of the elaborate shamanistic cosmology that divided the universe into the celestial, the terrestrial and the underworld, all united by the mythological 'tree of life' — not unlike other religions' belief in earth, heaven and hell. But as well as the spirits, the Yakuts had also developed a primitive pantheon of gods, the two most important being D'yalga khan, the god of fate and destiny, and Ilbis — god of war. Among the Nentsy, there was also the belief in a supreme deity called Num, which in their language means 'sky', and the Itelmens also believed in a single creator of the world, called Kutkhe. The chief spirit or god of the coastal Chukchi was Keretkuna, 'master' of the seas and sea animals, which is unsurprising given their almost total dependence on the hunting of whale, walrus and seal. These examples do not add up to monotheism, though some sources suggest that belief in a paramount deity may in some cases have been influenced by Christian notions of a single god spread by Orthodox Russians. A special feature of the Eskimos' belief system was their reverence for female deities and spirits — 'mistress of the earth', 'mistress of the seas', 'mistress of the air', 'mistress of the animal kingdom' and so on — the greatest being Numichagau, 'mistress of the ocean depths' (in Russian, *podvodnaya vladychitsa*), who was worshipped and propitiated with festivals after the whale or walrus hunt. The importance of the harvest of the seas was also symbolized among some Arctic peoples with rough-hewn wooden totems carved in the shape of mermen, half-human, half-fish, which adorned their dwellings.

Apart from animism, the most common, widespread and distinctive feature of the Siberian peoples' faith system and religious practices was shamanism. A form of ancient, ritualistic polytheism, shamanism was once thought to be a phenomenon peculiar to Siberia, but most scholars now agree that different forms of shamanism have existed, and continue to exist, in many parts of the world. The word 'shaman' – meaning something like a mixture of witch-doctor, medicine man, priest, magician, mystic, spiritual healer, prophet and intermediary with the spirit world – is thought to be of Tungus origin, though each native Siberian language has its own word for it, e.g. Nenets *tadebya*, Selkup *tetypy*, Nganasan *nga*, Turkic *kam*, from which the term *kam-lanie* derives, meaning a shamanistic performance, ritual, or rite. During the *kamlanie*, the shaman, dressed in an elaborate costume and headgear made of animal skin and festooned with decorative and symbolic ornaments and trinkets made of metal or bone, often in the shape of various animals and birds, would perform an increasingly frenzied dance, chanting, whooping and whirling while waving rattles and banging on a skin-hide tambourine. This primitive percussion instrument was regarded with superstitious awe as the quintessential symbol of the shaman's power, even as the vehicle for his transportation to the spirit world (see Fig. 3). The performances usually ended in the shaman falling into a trance or epileptic-type fit, during which he would hallucinate and his soul would leave his body on a journey to communicate directly with the spirits. As noted earlier, the basic tenet of animistic belief is that everything in the universe – in the human, animal, plant, aquatic, mineral and celestial worlds – has its own spirit or *anima*, with whom it is the shaman's role to communicate and intercede, and act as intermediary between humans and the spirits or gods. The purposes of the 'journey' were manifold. It may be to plead for a successful hunt, to heal the sick, to encourage fertility, for victory in battle, to accompany the souls of the dead to the other world during funeral rites, or simply to foretell the future. The Nanai shaman even travelled regularly to the sun in order to gather the souls of children for barren women.

Probably the first ever literary description of frenzied shamanistic ritual was written by the seventeenth-century exile, Archpriest Avvakum, mentioned in Chapter Two. Wishing to ascertain the likely outcome of a military expedition in eastern Siberia, Avvakum's cossak commander, Pashkov, ordered a local tribesman to perform a shaman ritual (*shamanit'*) and prophesy what would happen.:

> That evening this sorcerer brought a live ram close to my hut and began to work his magic on it. First he spun the animal round and round, then wrenched its head and threw it aside. The he began to prance and leap about, summoning up evil demons. Shrieking and screaming, he threw himself on the ground and began to foam at the mouth. The demons overcame him and he asked them, 'Will the expedition succeed'? And the demons replied, 'You will return with great victory and great riches.'[24]

Figure 3 Tungus shamans. Note the three native dwellings (*yurta*) behind the crowd, each topped with a Russian flag; the Russian log cabin on the right; and also (far right), the two bemused-looking Russian Orthodox priests.

Source: Zhivopisnaya Rossiya, vol. 12, part 1, *Vostochnaya Sibir'* (St Petersburg and Moscow, 1895), p. 303.

Unfortunately, the demons, and the shaman, got it wrong, and Pashkov's troops were slaughtered, only his son surviving to tell the tale.

In some Siberian native cultures there were 'specialist' shamans, often identified as such in infancy and undergoing a process of spiritual maturation preparing them for their future roles (rather like Tibetan Buddhism's Dalai Lama). In others, for instance among the Itelmens, any clan-member could perform shamanistic rituals, though these were usually carried out by old women. Despite the fervent efforts of Orthodox proselytizers, Muslim imams, Buddhist lamas and Marxist commissars to eradicate it, shamanism still continues to thrive in the twenty-first century, and millions throughout the modern world still believe in its efficacy and power. In a recent BBC Radio 4 interview an Anglo-American author recounted his story of how his autistic son had been 'healed' (not 'cured') of his incontinence, fitting, and inability to communicate with his peers during a five-hour ritual conducted by nine Mongolian and Siberian shamans. A bizarre feature of the proceedings was the shamans' instruction that the boy's mother wash out her vagina with vodka, which seems rather a wasteful misuse of vodka.[25] Some of the far north-eastern Siberian peoples' shamans (e.g. Chukchis, Eskimos, Itelmens, Koryaks) also went in for transvestism, this taking the form most commonly of men not only adopting women's hairstyles and clothing, but also perceiving themselves as actually being of the opposite sex, even marrying another man. This practice was part of the tradition of integrating the male and female halves, or 'phratries', of the universe. Female-to-male gender change was rare, and physiologically rather more problematical.[26]

All the Siberian native peoples without exception had, and still have, a rich oral treasure house of folklore including legends, heroic epics, poetry, fairytales, songs, riddles and sagas passed down from generation to generation. These, like the famous Yakut *olonkho*, were recited at regular clan gatherings and festivals, chronicling and celebrating each individual people's history, ethnogenesis, military exploits and heroes, deities and daemons in a marvellous medley of fact, fiction and phantasmagorical creativity. Only in the twentieth century were many of these collated, translated and committed to print.[27]

SPERANSKII AND THE NATIVE SIBERIANS

In the previous chapter an account was given of Mikhail Speranskii's activities in his anomalous position as both exile and Governor-General of Siberia. One of the most important of the reforms that he introduced into the territory's governance concerned the administration of relationships between the ruling Russian authorities and the aboriginal Siberian peoples, as well as the territorial, political and judicial regulations within each of the different ethnic groups. This was brought about by the promulgation of the 'Statute on the administration of the native peoples' (*Ustav ob upravlenii inorodtsev*) in 1822, shortly after Speranskii's recall to the capital. What Speranskii sought to achieve was an amalgam of efficient, fair and – from the colonial government's point of view – peaceful and profitable running of native affairs, while at the same time preserving as much as possible of the indigenous peoples' own cultures, traditions and internal methods of organizing their own communities.

The plight of the Siberian natives had deteriorated significantly since the Russians' original incursions, and worsened during the eighteenth and early nineteenth centuries. To be fair, the central government had over the years issued many decrees which had as their stated objective the protection of the lives and livelihoods of the Siberian tribes and clans. However, these various injunctions emanating from far-off Moscow or St Petersburg had very little affect on the way in which the incoming rapacious merchants and hunters, conquering cossaks, greedy government officials and voracious *voevodas* actually treated the territory's original inhabitants. As will be described in the following section, the combination of fur-tribute exaction, hostage-taking, warfare, enslavement, introduction of virulent diseases, imposition of various labour, transport and custodial duties, and sequestration of lands all led to a sometimes gradual and at other times rapid destruction of traditional ways of life and of entire tribes. Speranskii's own investigations into the conditions of the indigenous Siberians led him to believe that their situation was in desperate need of improvement, but he drafted his legislation, to quote Marc Raeff, on 'the basic assumption that central government should not interfere any more than necessary with native life', and that as far as possible they (the aborigines) should be allowed to conduct their own internal affairs, disputes and arrangements according to traditional and local customs.[28]

However, despite the ex-Governor-General's apparently benign intentions, what he succeeded in doing was to introduce a bureaucratically inspired, arbitrary, Russian-colonial system of administration, tax-gathering, and tribal classification in which the people they directly affected had no voice, and which often totally ignored the very customs and practices they purported to protect. To put it bluntly, the Russian imperial government was arrogantly imposing Russian laws, Russian regulations, a Russian creed and a Russian modus operandi on non-Russian peoples whose lands they had invaded, usurped and occupied. In the process they behaved little differently from other European imperialist regimes in different parts of the world, but this in no way grants them any kind of historical or ethical exoneration from the consequences of their gratuitous, grasping depredations.

Some of the relatively more developed peoples, such as the Buryats and the Yakuts, did manage to thrive and indeed multiply under tsarist rule, their chieftains adopting Russian habits and entering into Russian military or civil service with appropriate incentives, awards, titles, honours and other perks. However, their privileged status often led to a situation in which they collaborated with the imperial authorities in exploiting and oppressing the lower classes of their own societies and kinsmen. On the other hand, many of the 'small peoples' became even smaller, in some cases to the point of near or total extinction (see below).

At the core of Speranskii's new legislation – passed by the St Petersburg government with hardly any debate or demur – was the arbitrary division of the Siberian natives into three administratively contrived groupings. These were designated as the 'settled' (*osedlye*), the 'nomadic' (*kochevye*), and the 'vagrant' or 'itinerant' (*brodyachie*). In fact, the so-called 'settled' or 'sedentary' native populations were in a minority, and their newly defined status actually placed them in an almost identical position in terms of administrative, judicial and fiscal liabilities as the immigrant Russian state peasants, including payment of the much hated poll tax introduced by Peter the Great. This placed an increased financial burden on the 'settled' natives, which reduced many communities to abject poverty. Often their response was to flee their settlements and take once more to the taiga and tundra in an effort to revert to a nomadic or vagrant status. Not that this helped matters, as the nomadic and vagrant tribes – the former migrating at the appropriate season from summer to winter locations, and the latter with no legally fixed territory, constantly roaming the forests and Arctic shores – were still obliged to pay the *yasak* (fur tribute), the amount of which was actually increased under Speranskii's new laws.

Apart from the more exacting fiscal arrangements, the actual administration and governance of the Siberian natives flew in the face of their own traditional practices. Lip service was superficially paid to these in the setting up of so-called 'Clan directorates' (*rodovye upravleniya*), 'Native administrations' (*inorodnye upravy*) and 'Steppe councils' (*stepnye dumy*). However, these were based, not on traditional clan structures (which had in any case often broken down as a result of Russian colonial operations), but on territorial or administrative convenience – that is, the convenience of the ruling authorities. Further, and even more iniquitous, was, as James Forsyth has pointed out, the arrogant assumption that the Siberian lands were the property of the Russian state, to be doled out and their indigenous inhabitants 'graciously' regulated and governed according to the *ukaz* (decree) of the Russian tsar.[29]

Speranskii was arguably full of good intentions, and approached his duties both as former Governor-General, senior bureaucrat, legislator and an enlightened man with genuine humanitarian concern for the condition of the Siberian *inorodtsy* (indigenous people or 'people of different birth)'. But precisely because he *was* a highly placed central government official, now returned to official favour, his 1822 administrative reforms in this area – which stayed in place until the revolutions of 1917 – were based primarily, firmly and unshakably on the interests of the imperial Russian state, and not on the interests of the indigenous Siberian peoples, who continued to exist (only just in many cases) in conditions of official discrimination, penury, exploitation and degradation. This situation was most graphically and persuasively described in the mid-nineteenth century by the passionate Siberian regionalist scholar and publicist, N.M. Yadrintsev. One of his central concerns was the plight, or 'question' of the Siberian natives – the *inorodcheskii vopros* (the native question).

YADRINTSEV AND THE *INORODCHESKII VOPROS*

Both Mikhail Speranskii and Nikolai Yadrintsev were in their own very different ways remarkable scholars and investigators of Siberian society, history and economic conditions. But whereas the former was a St Petersburg-based bureaucrat (apart from his years in exile), seeking to implement, supplement or initiate central government policy in the region, Yadrintsev's study of his homeland (he was born in Omsk, west Siberia) was fervently founded on the perspective of how the colonial, expansionist and imperialist activities of the metropolitan Russian state had impacted on the life, habitat, natural environment and culture of Siberia itself. He was a prolific writer, journalist and scholar, the leader of the mid- to late-nineteenth century *oblastniki* (Siberian regionalists, see Chapter Four), founder, co-editor of and contributor to the Siberian regionalist newspaper *Eastern Review* (*Vostochnoe obozrenie*), a political dissident exiled for five years *out* of Siberia to Arkhangelsk province (1868–73), and a lifelong, vociferous champion of the greater autonomy of Siberia in governing its own affairs. He wrote books on *The Russian Commune in Prison and Exile*[30] and *The Siberian Natives: Their Way of Life and Contemporary Situation*,[31] but his most comprehensive and damning indictment of the tsarist regime's despoliation of Siberia, its environment and its peoples is *Siberia as a Colony: The Contemporary Condition of Siberia. Her Needs and Demands. Her Past and Her Future*, first published in 1882 to mark the 300th jubilee of Russia's 'conquest' in 1582.[32] This seminal work contains a wealth of information on Siberia's geography, history, colonization, Russian settlement, ethnic complexion, exploitation of natural recourses, educational and cultural levels, social structure and penal system, as well as intelligent suggestions for the future development of the territory. Chapter III of the book, entitled 'Siberian natives and the native question', paints a devastating picture – with plenty of published statistics from official and semi-official sources – of the way in which the lives, and very survival, of the original Siberian peoples had been affected over the three centuries since the arrival of the Russian invaders.

At the time of writing his monograph (*c*.1880), Yadrintsev stated that the present *inorodcheskii vopros* in Siberia was different from that at the time of Yermak's and his successors' original incursion. In those days, to put it starkly, it was simply a matter of conquering and forcibly subduing those tribes which opposed or revolted against the Russians' presence and their own painful and humiliating subjugation. As described in Chapter Two, this was relatively easily accomplished by Moscow's military *force majeure*. In the late nineteenth century, with Russian superiority long established and the Russian population far outnumbering that of the depleted aboriginals, the 'native question' was not that of subjugation, but of administration, guardianship and placing their relationship on a new foundation, which is what Speranskii had attempted to do in 1822 with only limited success.

For Yadrintsev, the four main tasks were those of, first, simply trying to ensure the sheer physical survival of many of the peoples and saving them from the very real possibility of extinction; second, providing economic assistance and creating circumstances for their individual cultural development; third, building on Speranskii's initiative, to create a more equitable administrative and local government structure, while guaranteeing the natives' full civil rights; and, fourth, what the author rather ambiguously describes as assisting 'their spiritual development and enlightenment'.[33]

By far the most urgent of these was the question of preventing the further dying out and extinction of those peoples who had so far successfully managed to survive – though often in reduced numbers – the impact of Russia's colonial policies. Yadrintsev admits that it was difficult to collect and collate precise figures, there being no proper academic or comprehensive scientific investigation of the problem, and most available information relied on the early works of scholars such as Gerhard Friedrich Müller, Stepan Krasheninnikov (see Chapter Three) and, more recently, Pëtr Andreevich Slovtsov, together with accounts in a number of travellers' tales, and a scattering of such rudimentary local statistics as could be detected. Reliable evidence, however, does exist which bears witness to the total disappearance of such early Siberian tribes as the Omoks, Kotts, Khoidans, Shelags, Anyuits, Mators, Asans, Arintsy and several others. The populist and regionalist historian, Afanasii Shchapov (see Chapter Four), quoted by Yadrintsev, adduces a number of contributing factors to explain this human wastage: death through fighting the invading Slavs in battle, consequent reduction in virile male population capable of reproduction, general debilitation leading to greater vulnerability to other hostile neighbours such as the Mongols and Chinese, and recrudescence of pre-Russian intestine warfare in a struggle for land and survival.

As noted above, far from bringing peace and reconciliation among the warring Siberian peoples, the Russian conquest only served to exacerbate the situation. Yadrintsev produces a whole range of examples and statistics cataloguing the steady and seemingly inexorable numerical decline in numbers and depopulation of the Siberian heartlands caused by death, disease and internal migration from territories now occupied by Russian settlers. For instance, he presents figures from Slovtsov's published researches indicating that the Arintsy people in 1608 numbered 300 families; in 1753, according to Müller and Gmelin, only five individuals of that clan survived. In the Turukhansk district, between 1763 and 1816 three-quarters of the indigenous population had perished. Documents reveal that the Kamchadals of Kamchatka had been reduced from a population of 20,000 in 1744 to only 1,951 in 1850, literally a decimation of this nationality in one century.[34] One could go on regurgitating and reproducing Yadrintsev's and other scholars' figures relating to other tribes and clans, but the general picture is abundantly clear: that Russian policies and practices vis-à-vis the original Siberian peoples had led directly and indirectly to a massive reduction in the population through a variety of extraneous causes.

Of these the most distressing and destructive was the spread of epidemics of lethal diseases including smallpox, typhus, leprosy, syphilis and – one of the latter's accompaniments – widespread elephantiasis. Indeed, so widespread were the combined effects of 'the monstrous scourge' of small-pox, typhus and syphilis among the far northern peoples that one medical expert predicted their inevitable extermination.[35] Not all diseases were introduced by Russian incomers. Scurvy was endemic, and ophthalmic ailments, sometimes leading to total sightlessness, were common as a result of the gloomy, tenebrous conditions inside the *chum* (wigwam), alternating with the blinding brilliance of the snowy and icy wastes outside, and also the regular incidence of helminths (intestinal worms) caused by eating raw fish. This could also have led to the fact that in the mid-nineteenth century almost 20 per cent of deaths in the Surgut district were caused by dysentery and bloody flux. Various forms of dermatitis were also rife, simply as a result of lack of bodily hygiene. Leprosy was not uncommon.[36] None of this was helped by the almost complete absence of professional medical services in these remote regions. The northern township of Berëzov, for instance, had only one doctor serving the entire surrounding province measuring several thousands of square kilometres with a scattered population also of several thousands.

New economic circumstances as a direct result of the Russian presence also led to periodic famine during which, in some circumstances, instances of cannibalism were quite common. Again, Yadrintsev provides evidence of this practice, detailing the sorry tale of one family in the Turukhansk region in which the mother ordered the killing of one son after another for meat. When only two sons were left, refusing fastidiously to murder and eat their remaining sibling, they killed and ate their mother instead. Drowned and rotting human corpses were often fished out of rivers for food.

Apart from wartime slaughter, death through disease and starvation, and enforced migration from their traditional hunting grounds to more inhospitable and less productive lands, one of the most interesting aspects of Yadrintsev's analysis of the causes of the natives' dire predicament is his argument that they were the unwitting victims of economic, that is to say market or commercial, forces. Imposition of the *yasak* forced the Siberian natives to hunt and kill the forest animals, not simply for their own sustenance, as had been their custom, but to provide revenue for the imperial coffers, which seriously depleted the wild livestock on which their own lives depended. Beyond that, according to Yadrintsev's thesis, the mercenary minded, unscrupulous businessmen inveigled, seduced or by some means or other coerced the natives into trading their own products for alien imports, forcing them into trading-debts which they were increasingly unable to meet. Faced with the power, cunning and commercial chicanery of the foreign entrepreneurs, the naïve Siberian natives, says our author, 'like primitive peoples everywhere, were unable to escape their fate'. He continues: 'Having become acquainted with grain, vodka, tobacco, gun-powder and ironware, they kept up a never-ending demand for these goods, but at incredible costs, exhausting their own resources and re-selling their own products. Their demands, however, remained insatiable, and the result was them ending up in the position of the dying Tantalus.'[37]

Perhaps oddly, Yadrintsev goes on to suggest that the worst forms of impoverishment and debilitation came, not through alcohol or tobacco, but through an acquired addiction to grain, flour and bread. He presents evidence that the still nomadic northern tribes, living on their traditional diet of reindeer and other meat, were much healthier than the sedentarized, newly 'agrarianized' consumers of cereal products introduced by private and state-employed grain merchants.

Yadrintsev is adamant that the parlous condition and the rampant ills of the Siberian *inorodtsy* in the mid-nineteenth century – impoverishment, famine, contagious diseases and the threat of gradual extinction – were not the result of the fierce physical environment in which they lived, nor of any inherent racial characteristics, but of the deliberately exploitative economic practices introduced by the Russian colonialists. Faced with this problem, Yadrintsev suggests that the government must do everything in its power to protect the interest of the natives, but this could only be done on the basis of a properly informed study of their declared needs and cultural values. Moreover, they must be subject to the same civil rights (such as they were in autocratic Russia!) as the rest of the population, while preserving and respecting their own indigenous customs and beliefs. For example, returning to the point mentioned above, the authorities should actively encourage the nomadic herding and hunting way of life, rather than forcing the *inorodtsy* into settled, non-traditional agricultural pursuits. Tilling the soil and turning the sod maybe all right for the average Russian peasant, but not necessarily so for the naturally nomadic Siberian native.

So what conclusions can we draw? To summarize the 'litmus paper' question: was Russia the bearer of a superior civilization bringing with her the benefits of economic progress, advanced technology, agriculture and Christianity to a primitive patchwork of backward and mutually belligerent tribes; or was she merely a rapacious plunderer, viciously exploiting the natives, literally holding them hostage to a fortune in fur, and bringing only bad liquor and pathogenic bacilli which in some cases resulted in creeping genocide? Yadrintsev and his school certainly had no doubts as to the answer. Even where the state purported to safeguard the interests of the natives, this was, according to the Siberian regionalists, motivated purely by selfish fiscal considerations aimed at preventing any decrease in the tax- and tribute-paying capacities of the subjugated races. On the other hand, some Soviet scholars attempted to square the ideologically sound criticisms of tsarist colonial practices with what is regarded, from a Russian nationalist point of view, as the beneficial consequences flowing from the historically and dialectically predetermined 'fusion' or 'drawing together' (*sblizhenie*) of the Russian and Siberian peoples. In other words, to quote one typical Soviet view, Russia's 'assimilation' (*osvoenie*) of Siberia 'was not fortuitous, but governed by the laws of historical development' (*ne sluchainym, a istoricheski zakonomernym sobitiem*).[38] This was part of a process of what Raeff describes as 'organic Russification' following Speranskii's reforms of 1822.[39] However, as we have seen, enactments and government reforms passed in distant St Petersburg did little in real terms to alter or ameliorate the familiar calamitous pattern of Russo-aboriginal relations already established over the last three centuries. From all points of view Siberia still remained, as Yadrintsev persuasively demonstrated, unmistakably a colony, and its land and its peoples continued to be exploited as such.

Apart from the native question, the other burning issue for the proponents of Siberian regionalism was the continued practice of using Siberia as a place of punishment, exile and convict labour. This is the subject of the following chapter.

6

'Fetters in the Snow': The Siberian Exile System

The title of this chapter is taken from the words of the English traveller and writer, John Foster Fraser, already quoted in Chapter One of this book: 'The very word Siberia is enough to make the blood run chill. It smells of fetters in the snow.'[1] In two short sentences, Fraser neatly sums up two of the most notorious popular images of Siberia, that of a frozen land of perpetual ice and snow, and that of it as a benighted place of punishment, hard labour and exile. In both cases the word 'Siberia' has become almost proverbial, and indeed the centuries-old practice, used by both the tsarist authorities and their Soviet communist successors, of annually deporting thousands of their common criminals and political dissidents to exile, settlement or forced labour in Siberia and the Far East is one of the most distressing and controversial aspects of the country's social, judicial and penological history. In fact, as the writer Alexander Solzhenitsyn has pointed out: 'Mankind invented exile first and prison only later',[2] and the punitive use of banishment and exile does have a long historical pedigree going back at least to the time of classical antiquity. Indeed, if the book of Genesis is to be believed, the tradition goes back even further, and Adam and Eve may confidently be regarded as the world's very first exiles, cast out from the Garden of Eden by an irate God for committing the first earthly crime. Adam's punishment, more specifically, was to be banished to compulsory agricultural labour beyond the territorial limits of his original home. ('Therefore the Lord God sent him forth from the Garden of Eden to till the ground from whence he was taken.')[3] A sound biblical precedent had therefore been set for the use of exile and hard labour in later centuries. But more immediately, when Eve's son, Cain, slew his bother Abel, God dispatched him even further to dwell 'in the land of Nod, on the east of Eden', but when doing so omnisciently predicted the problem of vagrancy associated with the exile system by telling him: 'a fugitive and a vagabond shalt thou be in the earth'.[4] Adam and Eve's original sin, which had obvious sexual connotations, and Cain's fratricide and fugitive status prefigure the interrelated problems of sex, violence and vagrancy in Siberia, to be dealt with in later sections of this chapter.

Old Testament mythology apart, both ancient Greece and Rome practised various forms of exile, banishment, marooning on deserted islands, expulsion and ostracism. Only those enjoying full citizenship were so punished by excluding and physically removing them from their privileged position in society. There was, after all, no point in exiling a slave. For these, other forms of punishment were available, including crucifixion, the galleys or the gladiatorial arena. In more recent times, European nation states developed their different forms of exile as their overseas empires expanded. Earlier Anglo-Saxon law had permitted punitive banishment, outlawing individuals and forbidding them to reside within a given kingdom or territory, but it was really only from the sixteenth century that Portugal, Spain, France and Britain began to deport certain categories of criminals for forcible settlement overseas, mainly to different parts of the Americas. In Britain's case, the transportation business (for such it was) began during the reign of James I (ruled 1603–25) when shiploads of prostitutes were sold off to Virginian colonists for 100 pounds of tobacco a head. After the American War of Independence put an end to the traffic, and after casting about for other possible destinations (including Russia's Crimean peninsula!), Britain began the century-long operation of transportation to Australia and Tasmania, which ended only in 1870.[5]

In Brockhaus and Yefron's great *Encyclopaedia*, exile in all its historical forms is defined as: 'The forcible removal by the state authorities of its own citizens or aliens to remote regions on the periphery of the state or its colonies either for life or a limited period of residence.'[6] The aims of exile are usually to punish criminals (judicial exile); to populate under-inhabited or overseas possessions (enforced settlement); or to rid the metropolitan country of harmful or subversive elements (political or administrative exile); or there may be a combination of any of these. In Russia the system of exile developed independently from that of other nations and was not influenced by foreign examples. Over the centuries, almost from the time of the original conquest of Siberia, it gradually became the central and, alongside corporal punishment, the most characteristic feature of the tsarist penal system. Indeed, the prominent nineteenth-century penologist, I. Ya. Foinitskii, described it as follows: 'Exile (*ssylka*) represents one of the very few national institutions of our criminal law and has developed entirely on the basis of Russian needs and Russian conditions.'[7]

So, what were those unique 'needs and conditions'?

SIBERIAN EXILE: ORIGINS AND DEVELOPMENT

Despite Foinitskii's insistence on the exclusive nature of the Russian exile system, there is a common factor between Russian and other practices, and that is the distinction between *banishment* and *exile*. Banishment involves the expulsion of persons *from* a specific locality, to which they are forbidden, either permanently or temporarily, to return. Exile, on the other hand, consists of dispatching someone *to* a specific, designated location beyond the territorial limits of which he/she is forbidden to move. In the Russian context, the nineteenth-century writer, G. Feldstein, adds a further terminological refinement by drawing a distinction between expulsion, banishment and exile (in Russian, *izgnanie*, *vysylka* and *ssylka* respectively). In his definition, *vysylka* (which he translates into Latin as *deportatio*) is a kind of transition stage between simple *izganinie* (literally, 'driving out'), and *ssylka* proper. In other words, *vysylka* does represent banishment *to* a certain locality, but with no other restrictions imposed apart from those on movement, whereas *ssylka* in the narrowest sense involves 'the subjection of the criminal to a specific regimen incorporating measures which are designed to achieve certain desired objectives'.[8]

In the case of Siberia, the 'specific regimen' included severe curtailment of such personal rights as pertained to one's social status, and the imposition of an elaborate set of rules and procedures governing the everyday conduct, obligations, activities, movement, domicile, occupation, financial and even marital affairs of those exiled. In the earliest Russian law codes a whole series of penalties were prescribed for a wide assortment of criminal acts or minor offences. These ranged from various forms of capital punishment, either simple or 'aggravated', the latter involving more protracted and excruciating methods of execution such as impaling, quartering, eviscerating and roasting alive. Ivan the Terrible was particularly ingenious in devising gruesomely fiendish methods of inflicting a slow, agonizing death on his enemies. Next in order of severity came corporal punishment, which, according to Foinitskii, after its introduction by the Mongols turned Russia into 'the classical land of corporal punishment',[9] and which included ferocious floggings, beatings with a club and various forms of physical mutilation such as breaking or amputation of limbs, severing external organs and extremities, gouging out the eyes and castration. Deprivation of liberty or imprisonment were rarely used, except as a preventative, rather than a strictly punitive, measure. Finally, for lesser offences there was a system of fines and financial compensations payable either to the authorities or to the injured parties.

Although it was during the seventeenth century that punitive exile became fully established, there is evidence of its earlier use. The first unambiguous mention of *ssylka* occurs in a codicil to the Law Code (*Sudebnik*) of 1582, which specifies exile among the cossaks on the peripheries of Muscovy for certain crimes including perjury and sedition. However, it is known that the practice of expulsion, banishment and forcible relocation took place even earlier. After Moscow's defeat of Novgorod at the end of the fifteenth century, both Ivan III (ruled 1462–1505) and Ivan IV ('The Terrible', ruled 1533–84) brutally evacuated many of its prominent citizens, compelling them to settle elsewhere. Another mass deportation took place in 1591, when the townsfolk of Uglich were exiled to the fortress of Tobolsk in western Siberia as punishment for their suspected complicity in the murder of Tsarevich Dmitrii. One bizarre aspect of this exercise was the decision to exile the town's bell for ringing the tocsin on Dmitrii's death. In fact, the bell remained in the Tobolsk kremlin until 1892, when, according to S.V. Maksimov, it was finally 'repatriated' to the civic museum at Uglich.[10]

During the course of the seventeenth century, three interrelated factors served to foster and finally establish Siberian exile as a major component of Russian penal procedure. These were: first, the conquest of Siberia itself; and, next, the implementation of the two separate, but complementary, concepts of clemency and conscription. The Muscovite authorities simply needed the manpower necessary to populate the vast, thinly inhabited territories now under their control, to exploit their resources and consolidate Moscow's rule. In order, therefore, to supplement the limited flow of voluntary migration, the government was encouraged by both economic and political imperatives to conscript the necessary labour force and service personnel they required by the expedient of commuting sentence of death to exile in Siberia. Before formal exile regulations were established, the sentence was usually passed on the personal instructions of the tsar. A common formula found in royal decrees at the time was: 'The Great Sovereign has ordered that his life be spared; instead of death, send him to Siberia' (*Velikii gosudar' velel zhivot' dat'; vmesto smerti soslat' v Sibir'*). Those so sentenced were usually dispatched not to one regular location, but to 'wheresoever the tsar directed' (*kuda gosudar' ukazhet*). Tsar Aleksei's comprehensive Law Code of 1649 contains ten explicit references to exile as the penalty for a variety of offences ranging from homicide to hooliganism, though Siberia as the specific destination is mentioned only once.[11] In most cases the period of exile began only after the victim had already been subjected to a flogging with the knout, or suffered some form of physical mutilation, such as an ear sliced off, fingers severed or, in the cases of snuff-takers, the septum ripped from between their nostrils (probably the first clear government warning that the use of tobacco can seriously damage your health).

However, these barbaric preliminaries apart, there was, if not an enlightened, then a utilitarian side of the early exile system, at least from the colonial government's point of view, in that the seventeenth-century Muscovite authorities attempted as far as possible to accommodate the individual expertise of the exiled person to the particular needs of the region to which he was sent. To this end, three basic types of exile emerged: exile to the land (*ssylka na pashnyu*), exile for urban settlement (*ssylka v posad*) and exile for service (*ssylka v sluzhbu*). Accordingly, exiled peasants were settled on the land; exiled clergymen – such as Archpriest Avvakum (see Chapter Two) – were expected to carry on with their clerical duties; and others were assigned to whatever form of military or civil service for which they were suited or trained. The newly conquered territories were in fact in such great need of every type of personnel – manual workers, artisans, military and administrative staff, etc. – that they and the embryonic Siberian society very easily absorbed both the voluntary and compulsory colonists to their own, and the government's, advantage. Thus, rather than Siberia being regarded simply as a convenient dumping ground for Muscovy's flayed and disfigured criminal outcasts, exile beyond the Urals was deliberately and purposefully used as an instrument of the state's colonial policies. At the end of the nineteenth century a comprehensive government report on the whole question of Siberian exile summed up its conclusions on the implementation of the system in the seventeenth century as follows:

> It is impossible to deny the fact that exile [to Siberia] in the Muscovite period had a great and beneficial significance. At a time when throughout Western Europe capital punishment was being used on an enormous scale, and when its places of confinement inspired horror and loathing, exile appears as an undoubtedly progressive phenomenon in the area of penal policy, preserving thousands of lives, which, without it, would have been cut short on the scaffold, or slowly extinguished in those stinking, disease-ridden cesspits which constituted the prisons of the time.[12]

Rather than suffering grotesque forms of execution or a lingering death in a fetid dungeon or *oubliette*, in Siberia thousands of people were allowed, not only to continue their mortal existence, but also to make a positive contribution to the general good of the state. That, at any rate, was the theory.

In practice, the system was already plagued with the same myriad difficulties, problems and drawbacks which were to undermine the efficacy of the operation throughout its history. Apart from the physical obstacles of distance and climate, and logistical impediments of poor communications, inadequate supervision and supplies, there were four major factors which bedevilled the smoother and more efficient settlement of the area from the seventeenth to the early twentieth centuries. First was the problem of flight (*pobeg*). The high levels of escape and abscondence from the designated places of exile was a problem with which the inadequately manned police authorities were never able to cope. Flight led to the second problem – that of brigandage. By definition, the majority of the exiles were of a criminal disposition, and, once they had escaped, it was only natural for them to revert to their former activities of robbery and other forms of banditry in order to survive, with obviously deleterious effects on the free communities, including the native peoples. Third, despite the government's efforts to 'fit the man to the job', as discussed above, industry, diligence and enthusiasm were not among the most obvious characteristics of the average exile. On the contrary, idleness, intractability and incompetence perpetually undermined the objectives of compulsory colonization. As noted in Chapter Three, on the whole, murderers, rapists, arsonists, perverts and crooks do not make particularly wholesome or successful pioneering stock. Finally, and this was arguably the major problem, there was quite simply the shortage of women. The chronic disproportion between the sexes in both the exile and the free populations of Siberia not only militated against the establishment of stable family and community life, but also led, despite various government efforts to correct the imbalance, to a situation in which rape, abduction, incest and bestiality were rife. All these four associated problems will be returned to below.

The three major developments during the eighteenth century, as already discussed in Chapter Three, were the introduction of *katorga* (heavy, forced labour), the increased use of Siberia as a place of banishment for the regime's political opponents, and the granting to the serf-owning nobility the personal right to hand over their recalcitrant, unwanted peasants to the authorities in return for a military recruit quittance. Except for the political exile factor, the other two practices only served to exacerbate the problems referred to in the previous paragraph. At the turn of the eighteenth and nineteenth centuries, the whole exile operation was suffering from a state of such dreadful malad-ministration, human misery and sheer chaos, that the new Governor-General, Mikhail Speranskii, when he arrived in 1819, could not fail to turn his attention to its reform.

SSYLKA AND SPERANSKII

Speranskii tackled the exile situation with the same degree of urgency with which he had approached the 'native question' (see Chapter Five), and applied the same mixture of humanitarian compassion and bureaucratic, systems-management techniques in an attempt to resolve the problems. From his observations, however, he was not convinced by the proposition that exile could in any way contribute to the satisfactory settlement and development of the territory, nor had it in the past. In a letter to his daughter, the exiled Governor-General wrote:

> Do not allow yourself to think that Siberia has been populated by exiles and criminals. Their numbers are like a drop in the ocean; they are hardly to be seen, except on some public works ... Scarcely 2,000 arrive here each year, among whom there are rarely any women ... Generally speaking, exiles contribute very little to the population of Siberia. The majority die without any offspring, and consequently the idea that Siberia has been in the past, or can be in the future, significantly populated and settled by exiles is a totally baseless prejudgement.[13]

Despite his doubts about the efficacy of exile and compulsory settlement, Speranskii nevertheless sought to bring some kind of order out of the chaos with the publication of his Exile and Convoy Regulations (*Ustav o ssyl'nykh* and *Ustav ob etapakh*) in 1822. One of the deficiencies of the legislation is that it did not deal adequately with the question of *katorga*, and those sentenced to hard labour. What he did suggest was that *katorga* was to be either for life or a fixed term, 'lifers' in fact serving 20 years' hard labour, partly in confine-ment and partly in reformatory settlements near their factories or mines. After their release they were registered among the rest of the exile population. The exiles themselves were divided into six categories: factory workers (*zavodskie rabochie*); road workers (*dorozhnye rabochie*); artisans (*remeslenniki*); servants' guild (*tsekh slug*); settlers (*poselentsy*); and the unfit (*nesposobnye*). It is unnec-essary to go into more detail about the various rules and regulations pertain-ing to each category, as in almost every case the implementation of the new system of classification proved totally unworkable. Apart from the 'unfit', who were dispersed among rudimentary hospitals and charitable institutions, of the remainder only the settlement of exiled peasants on the land had any degree of success, and that only limited. As for the rest: such factories as existed were already overfilled with those undergoing *katorga*, and refused or were unable to take on any more workers; the 'road workers' in fact never existed, and this category was formally abolished in 1828; very few artisan's workshops were established and accounted for only a tiny percentage of all exiles (those few that did function for a while were all closed down by 1852); and the 'servants guild', composed of exiled 'household servants, Jews and others unfit for agricultural work', was really a non-starter, as most well-to-do folk in need of domestic servants understandably refused to employ individuals who were by definition convicted criminals. Therefore, of Speranskii's six categories of exile, the only really viable form of dealing with the exiles was to set them to agricultural labour, either in the villages of the free 'old inhabitants' (*starozhily*) or in purpose-built agrarian settlements.[14] But even this posed serious problems, which are discussed in the following section.

However, the chief reason why the 'Speranskii system' did not work was that he made a bad miscalculation as to the numbers likely to be involved. His regulations were based on an expected influx of around 3,000 exiles per year, which was about right for the first quarter of the nineteenth century. No sooner had his legislation come into effect, though, than the figures leapt alarmingly, seriously overloading the distribution and settlement network. Between 1824 and 1828, a yearly average of 11,000 people were exiled to Siberia, and throughout the 30-year reign of Nicholas I (ruled 1825–55), the yearly mean works out at around 7,500. In the mid-1870s, during the reign of the 'Tsar Liberator', Alexander II (ruled 1855–81), the annual total of exiles soared to as many as 19,000.[15] In these circumstances, it is not surprising that the organizational infrastructure designed by Speranskii for a much lower figure began to crumple under the sheer weight of numbers.

Various attempts later in the nineteenth century were made to review, alter, reduce or even abolish the Siberian exile system. But the enormous size of the operation, other government priorities in the aftermath of the emancipation of the serfs in 1861, the terrorist campaign of the late 1870s, the industrial revolution of the 1890s and other pressing concerns meant that the system continued to operate by default on much the same unsatisfactory lines until new legislation in 1900 introduced a few minor reforms, as will be seen. The dearth of alternative means of correction, such as prisons and workhouses, meant that several temporary measures like the reintroduction of the death penalty for crimes committed by convicts undergoing *katorga*, the use of alternative localities in the remoter provinces of European Russia, the establishment of chain-gangs and attempts to found new agricultural settlements hardly scratched the surface of the problem and were soon abandoned. Needless to say, the government itself was incapable of recognizing the obvious fact that the evils of the exile system were simply a reflection of the iniquitous social and political order of tsarist Russia as a whole – which still incorporated remnants of medieval feudalism – and that only a fundamental, qualitative change in that order would create conditions in which judicial and administrative exile would be rendered superfluous and wither away.

As with his legislation concerning the native peoples, so with Speranskii's 1822 regulations governing the operation of the exile system: the intention was a far cry from the reality. What *was* the reality of exile and convict life in Siberian exile as experienced by its victims?

THE EXILE OPERATION

In practice, there were six main categories of exile. First, and most severe, was still *katorga*. This sentence could only be pronounced by the courts and was either for a limited term or for life. The 1842 Code of Laws contained 82 articles specifying *katorga* for a wide range of offences, gradation in the severity of the punishment being determined both by the length of the sentence, the place where it was to be served and the type of labour prescribed.[16] For the first few years, prisoners were assigned to the so-called 'probationary' class (*ispituemye*) and kept in close confinement, and thereafter, depending on good behaviour, transferred to the 'reformatory' category (*ispravlyayushchiesya*), where living and working conditions were slightly less intolerable. Although now living outside the prison walls in what was called the 'free command' (*volnaya kommanda*), the *katorzhane* (hard labourers) still worked extremely long hours, and were subject to regular floggings, foul food, overcrowding and the constant wearing of heavy fetters (*kandaly*). In the mines and gold-fields many were perpetually chained to their wheelbarrows, even at night, and the disease and mortality rates were unsurprisingly high. Another rather odd problem was that, as the century wore on, there were fewer and fewer 'work opportunities' for those condemned to it. The gradual hiving off of state factories to private enterprise and the steady exhaustion of the imperial gold and silver mines in Transbaikal meant that there was a gradual reduction in demand for the increasingly larger numbers of convicts available. The government tried to respond to the problem by building a number of 'central convict labour prisons' (*tsentral'nye katorzhnye tyur'my*, or *tsentral'niki*), and also, from the late 1860s, by turning the island of Sakhalin into what amounted to a large isolation camp in which – despite the rather breezy observations of an English visitor, Harry de Windt – conditions were particularly vile.[17]

Next in order of severity was 'exile for settlement in Siberia' (*ssylka na pose-lenie v Sibiri*). Of Speranskii's six categories of exile detailed above, the only two that actually materialized were the 'settlers' and the 'unfit'. Of the latter, little need be said, despite their numbers – as much as 40 per cent of the exile population in some provinces. They therefore far outweighed the facilities available for their accommodation and maintenance, and existed in the most pitiful conditions. The fate of the exile settlers (*poselentsy*) was governed by a complex set of rules and procedures that defined their place of settlement, their fiscal obligations and concessions, their rights of marriage, property ownership and movement, as well as detailing the heavy corporal punishments to be inflicted if these regulations were breached. Also, as set out in the official 'Scale of Punishments' contained in the new Code of Laws of 1845, those condemned to *ssylka* were deported (in order of severity) either to 'the remotest places in Siberia' (*v otdalenneishikh mestakh Sibiri*), or to 'not so remote places in Siberia' (*v mestakh Sibiri ne stol' otdalënnykh*).[18] Whether in the most remote or not so remote locations, the *poselentsy* were either divided among the villages of the 'old inhabitants', or else directed to newly established agricultural settlements run on almost military lines. The practice of billeting exiles in the old inhabitants' villages was nearly always unsuccessful as the free peasants were reluctant to share their land with the newcomers – convicted criminals whom they treated with a mixture of suspicion, fear and open hostility.

No more successful were the purpose-built settlements. In 1827 the Siberian Committee of the State Council set aside nearly half a million rubles to establish a chain of such colonies in Yeniseisk province. Between 1830 and 1837, 22 villages were founded, but, despite all efforts to ensure their success, they were doomed to failure. The provision of land, accommodation, agricultural supplies and clumsy attempts to boost the female population did little to overcome the familiar obstacles of disinclination or inability to undertake hard agricultural graft, desertion, depopulation, vagabondage and violence. Many turned into virtual ghost towns, while the remainder fell into abject poverty. In 1842, those that did manage to maintain some sort of existence were redesignated as regular state-owned villages and details of their original status officially suppressed. It has been estimated that in some Siberian provinces as few as 10 per cent of those condemned to exile managed to settle successfully. The rest simply fled their appointed destinations and either sought employment elsewhere, forming a great, shifting lumpenproletariat of casual workers, or else remained permanently on the run, reverting to the same types of crime and brigandage which had brought many of them to Siberia in the first place, despite the savage battery of punishments that awaited them if recaught. The associated phenomena of flight and vagrancy will be returned to below.

A third category of 'exile for resettlement' (*ssylka na vodvorenie*) was established in 1853, specifically to deal with the problem of vagabondage and brigandage, under which recaptured criminals were relocated, sometimes to more distant places, from which, at an appropriate opportunity, they would once more take flight, only to be recaptured yet again. In order to break this vicious circle, after 1869 the dreaded Sakhalin, from which it was almost impossible to escape, became the authorities' most favoured place of relocation for serial fugitives – Russia's equivalent to Devil's Island of French Guiana.[19] In the inimitable words of John Stephan, between 1875 and 1905:

> the island stagnated as a vast penal colony, a monument to human misery. On Sakhalin, the guards were more criminal than the convicts … On Sakhalin, convict

women, rationed like precious commodities, were known to murder their designated spouses in hope of a better match ... On Sakhalin the aborigines enjoyed an open season on escapees with a bounty for each corpse ... On Sakhalin, peasants talked wistfully of that same Siberia that Muscovites dreaded ... Sakhalin infused its unfortunate residents with a special malady. Chekhov called it 'febris sachalinensis' and described it as sensations of dampness, shivering fits, severe headaches, rheumatic pains and a sinking feeling that one would never be able to leave the island. He added that 'if only those who liked Sakhalin lived there, the island would be uninhabited'.[20]

The remoteness of the island, its insalubrious climate, the draconian discipline and gratuitous violence endemic in the tense atmosphere of an overwhelmingly criminal society earned Sakhalin a deserved reputation as the final circle of the Siberian exile hell. Murder and suicide were commonplace, as well as such regular practices as flogging to death, gang rape, child prostitution and cannibalism (see Figs 4 and 5).

Another minor category was that of 'exile for residence' (*ssylka na zhit'ë*), which was introduced in 1845 for offenders from the privileged classes who were exempt from corporal punishment. This formed a miniscule proportion of the exile population as a whole. To take one random year, in 1883 out of a total number of 10,704 people exiled to Siberia, only 177 were deported *na zhit'ë*.[21] The circumstances of those so banished were not particularly onerous, and indeed many made a lucrative living for themselves in their new surroundings. (A further category, 'exile to the Trans-Caucasus', existed for religious offenders, which lies outside the geographical limits of this study.)

Finally, and most significantly in terms of numbers, came the category of 'administrative exile' (*ssylka v administrativnom poryadke*). This was such a peculiar and preponderant feature of the exile system that it deserves a separate section, or indeed chapter, to itself. Unfortunately, lack of space precludes, but a brief résumé is essential at this point to underline its importance.[22] Among Solzhenitsyn's many mistakes in his account of the tsarist exile system is his assertion that administrative exile 'took root' only towards the end of the nineteenth century.[23] On the contrary, the very origins of Siberian exile were the result of administrative rather than judicial practice. In the early years, this was the prerogative of the tsar (see above), but during the eighteenth and nineteenth centuries a whole gamut of government officials, bureaucratic agencies, social and professional organizations gradually acquired and regularly exercised the right to hand over, sentence or condemn to exile those individuals who were deemed to be, or indeed merely suspected of being, either politically subversive or in some way socially unacceptable to the rest of the community. This was in addition to the serf-owners' right to divest themselves of their unwanted serfs for exile to Siberia first granted by Empress Elizabeth (see Chapter Three). In the nineteenth century, administrative, as opposed to judicial, exile accounted for the majority of all people banished to Siberia, and comprised two distinct types. First was the practice of banishment by the state authorities of people whom they

Figure 4   Fitting convicts' fetters on Sakhalin, early 1890s. Note (centre-left) prisoner chained to his wheelbarrow, and (right) three carrying their shackles waiting to be fitted.

Source: de Windt. H., *The New Siberia* (London, 1896), p. 95.

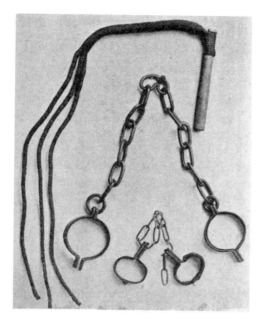

Figure 5   Instruments of flagellation and restraint used on exiles to Siberia: the three-thonged lash (*plet'*) and ankle- and wrist-fetters (*kandaly*).
Source: de Windt. H., *The New Siberia* (London, 1896), p. 93.

considered to be politically, ideologically or intellectually dangerous (even potentially) to national security – usually referred to as 'political exiles' or 'state criminals' (*gosudarstvennye prestupniki*). Next – and the numbers far outweighed all other categories of exile – was the right of serf-owners, and later peasant communes, and some urban organizations to hand over to the state authorities for administrative exile those of their members whose behaviour was judged by the landowner or by collective decision to be no longer acceptable to the community.

Again, this peculiar form of banishment was of two types. First was exile 'for depraved behaviour' (*za porochnoe povedenie*). Under this dispensation, communities had the right to expel people, who, while not being found guilty of any proven criminal activity, were nevertheless ostracized as being in some way socially undesirable, often for quite trivial misbehaviour. In this way, however reprehensible their individual conduct, the same severe punishment of exile to Siberia could be meted out to drunkards, wastrels, fornicators, tax-dodgers and hooligans as was passed by the higher judicial organs on murderers, robbers, rapists and other serious felons. Moreover, once sucked into the system, little or no distinction was made between them all by the exile authorities. Special conditions pertaining to *katorzhane* apart, all suffered from the same degrading treatment and the same horrendous conditions. As the government report of 1900 acknowledges, exiles of all descriptions – whether serial killer, petty thief or social misfit – were merged together into one huge 'indistinguishable mass' (*odna obshchaya odnoobraznaya massa*).[24]

The second type of non-political administrative exile resulted as a consequence of 'non acceptance' (*neprinyatie*) back into the commune of a convicted criminal who had already served some other sentence, such as a spell of imprisonment, imposed by the courts. On release, an ex-convict could find himself rejected by his home community and handed over for administrative banishment to Siberia, even though the original offence had not attracted that heavy penalty in the first place. This, of course, not only amounted to double jeopardy, and totally ignored the concepts of rehabilitation and reform, but also flouted the principle in law of *non bis in idem* (i.e. that a person should not be punished twice for the same offence).

After the emancipation of the serfs in 1861, continual debates took place as to whether the newly liberated communities of illiterate peasants should be allowed to wield such awesome power over their members – dispensing the same heavy penalties as were available to the highest courts of the land – or whether its continuing practice was a useful supplement to police responsibilities of maintaining law and order. At any rate, despite the debates and various attempts at reforming or tinkering around with the system, administrative exile to Siberia, either for bad behaviour or for non-acceptance (the latter accounting for a clear majority of cases), was retained until the exile reform law of 1900.

Table 6.1   Average yearly number of convicts passing through the exile administration's main forwarding prison at Tyumen, 1882–98.

Exiled to settlement	2,706
Exiled to re-settlement	1,273
Exiled to residence	189
Exiled by administrative process	4,417
Total	8,585

Table 6.2   Average yearly number of administrative exiles, according to type, passing through the main forwarding prison at Tyumen, 1882–98.

Exiled by government or police order	282
Banished by commune for misconduct	1,594
Exiled after non-acceptance by commune	2,541
Total	4,417[25]

The latter figure represents 51.4 per cent of the overall total, but if wives and children are included (yearly average 3,200) then the proportion goes up to 57 per cent of all of those exiled to Siberia during those years. It is obvious, therefore, that without the existence of administrative exile by the communes, numbers would have been drastically reduced; the whole system may have become a more manageable and effective operation, and, importantly, with less damaging effects on Siberia's feeble civil society.

Under the terms of the Exile Reform Law of 12 June 1900, powers of exile after non-acceptance were abolished and replaced with a system of police surveillance. Exile for 'bad behaviour' was removed from the power of urban communities, but retained in the case of peasant communes, although the latter were now required to contribute towards the maintenance of those so banished, and new rules were formulated to ensure that the continuing prerogatives were exercised with due restraint and circumspection. The police still retained its powers of administrative exile for actual or suspected political offences, and indeed the massively increased use of these powers against the background of increasing social and political unrest in the early years of the twentieth century just about offset the reduction in exile numbers caused by the Reform Law. In other words, recourse to administrative exile as a means of dealing with industrial strikes and rural uprisings meant that both workers and peasants continued to be transported to Siberia in large numbers, joining the ranks of 'political criminals', which had hitherto been almost the exclusive preserve of dissident nobles and the militant intelligentsia.

The fate of the political exiles in Siberia during the nineteenth century varied enormously, from conditions of relative tolerability to the downright horrific, driving many to the point of madness or suicide. The first large contingent of 'politicals' were the participants in the fatally unsuccessful 'Decembrist' uprising of 14 December 1825. This abortive military revolt against the autocracy was led by members of some of the most distinguished noble families in the land – fierce patriots who had fought against Napoleon and 'intellectuals in uniform' inspired variously by the ideas of constitutional government, the Enlightenment, the French Revolution, or opposition to autocracy and serfdom. They were hopelessly disorganized and disunited over aims and methods. As mentioned previously, their leaders, including Pavel Pestel, were hanged and over a hundred others – part of the cream of educated Russian society – were sentenced to various forms of *katorga* and exile in Siberia. There is a voluminous memoir and scholarly literature concerning the experience of the exiled Decembrists, all bearing witness to their resilience, fortitude and courage while serving out their sentences. Not without reason were the Decembrists regarded by later generations of radicals and political activists as outstanding martyrs in the revolutionary struggle against tsarist autocracy. No less admirable were the personal sacrifices made by many of the Decembrists' wives who chose to forsake their privileged positions in St Petersburg high society and voluntarily share their husbands' fate in the remotest depths of Siberia.

There is no space to give a full account of the Decembrists' experiences in exile, but after serving their sentences of hard labour, and even after an amnesty was granted to them in Emperor Alexander II's coronation manifesto in 1856, many of the survivors chose to remain in Siberia, where their post-custodial activities had already made a significant contribution to the intellectual, educational, cultural and scientific life of the country. The intellectual influence of the Decembrists and the exiled members of Mikhail Petrashevskii's socialist discussion group on the early Siberian regionalists (*oblastniki*) has already been mentioned in Chapter Four. The Decembrists were not strictly speaking 'administrative' exiles, in so far as their sentences had been handed down by a special, but dubiously constituted, judicial tribunal. However, with the growing incidence of political opposition and the increasingly revolutionary activity of the radical intelligentsia during the reign of Alexander II (ruled 1855–81), the use of political exile without trial became ever more prevalent, but much more so after the assassination of Alexander by populist terrorists in 1881.

In the panic following the regicide, and in the politically reactionary atmosphere under Alexander III (ruled 1881–94), the new tsar's secret security services (the *Okhrana*) exercised perhaps the greatest powers of surveillance, arrest, detention, interrogation and administrative disposal of their victims throughout their entire history, and there are myriad recorded instances of the arbitrariness, inhumanity and callousness with which they employed their authority against often totally innocent citizens. In the interests of tightening up internal security in the aftermath of the assassination, two new instruments were introduced that gave virtually unlimited powers of surveillance, arrest and administrative exile to police and government officials. The first, promulgated on 14 August 1881, was the 'Statute on Measures for the Preservation of Political Order and Social Tranquillity', which Lenin once described as the '*de facto* constitution of Russia'.[26] Although this was meant to be a temporary measure, its provisions were in fact reaffirmed every three years and remained in force right up to 1917. According to this legislation local officials were given the right to hand over to the military anyone in their locality suspected of being likely to be detrimental to the maintenance of law and order, a very vague and comprehensive ruling, which was given greater precision by a subsequent law of 12 March 1882, the 'Statute on Police Surveillance'. Hitherto, police powers of surveillance of those either under suspicion or already in exile were rather amorphous and depended on the whim or caprice of the local constabulary, as is still the case in many modern societies. The new legislation sought to standardize the dispersal, reception, imbursement and control of the exiles, and set out detailed instructions governing their behaviour, movement, correspondence, acquaintanceships, occupation and domestic circumstances.[27]

In some cases conditions were not terribly onerous – such as those in which Lenin, for instance, spent three relatively trouble-free years at Shushenskoe in southern Siberia – but many exiles suffered in conditions of intolerable hardship, privation and police brutality, stories of which abound illustrating the inanity, vindictiveness and sheer bloody-mindedness of the police and exile authorities, including cases of young women being flogged to death.[28] Although they comprised only a very tiny percentage of the total exile population (just over 1 per cent in fact),[29] right until the revolutions of 1917 succeeding generations of tsarism's political enemies and opponents – the Decembrists, the Petrashevtsy, countless revolutionary populists, terrorists, liberals, constitutionalists, regionalists, social democrats, socialist revolutionaries, anarchists, trade unionists, striking workers and peasant rebels, as well as their passive sympathizers, their relatives and the totally innocent – were swallowed up in the vast maw of Siberian exile by the state's continuing use of political exile by administrative process.

CONVOYS AND COMMUNES[30]

In some respects one of the grimmest parts of the ordeal for all Siberian exiles was the journey there. From all parts of European Russia, convicts were gathered in the collecting prison in Moscow, and thence dispatched via Nizhnii Novgorod, Kazan, Perm and Yekaterinburg to the main forwarding prison and headquarters of the Exile Bureau (*Prikaz o ssyl'nykh*) in Tyumen, Tobolsk province. Thus far, transport was by wagon, barge or, later, railway. At Tyumen the prisoners were registered and codified according to their personal details, type of crime, sentence and destination. They were then provided with uniform convict garb, some had their heads half-shaven, and all, except the extremely infirm, were shackled together in twos or threes with heavy iron ankle fetters (*kandaly*) and handcuffs linked together with a three-foot chain, before setting off in all weathers on their gruelling thousand-mile trek along the 'road of chains' *(kandalnaya doroga)*.

The exile convoys, usually between 200 and 300 strong, were marched under heavy guard in two-day stages between the wayside transit prisons known as *etapy* (sing. *etap*) set at about 64-kilometre (40-mile) intervals interspersed with half-way houses (*polu-etapy*) every 32 kilometres (20 miles). After two days on the road and one overnight stop at a half-way house the convoy would stop for 24 hours' rest (the *dnëvka*) at a regular *etap*, before starting off on its next three-day stint, two days on the march, one day off. If the purpose of the *dnëvka* was rest and recuperation, then so repugnantly filthy, overcrowded and insanitary were the majority of these roadside prisons that the effect of being incarcerated in them, however briefly, was as likely further to debilitate as to fortify them for the next leg of the journey. Men, women and children, hardened killers and innocent youths were packed together overnight in unventilated common cells (though segregated by sex) with no other furniture than the solid plank sleeping platforms (*nary*) and a large open tub for excrement. Some of the *etapy* had a small hospital wing (*lazaret*), but standards of medical care were abysmally inadequate to cope with the high incidence of sickness and disease which were rife among the prisoners, especially typhus, tuberculosis, scurvy and syphilis (see Fig. 6).

Figure 6   Cartoon depicting a Siberian exile convoy in the English magazine, *Judy*, 3 April 1880.

Equally as binding as the shackles they wore was the prisoners' loyalty to the collective organization of the 'convicts' commune' (*arestantskaya artel'*), which governed the lives and controlled the activities of the exiles even more closely and effectively than the regulations and agents of the exile administration itself. All criminal societies throughout the ages, from Robin Hood's outlaws to modern Mafia – what Eric Hobsbawm calls 'social bandits' – have operated on the basis of a shared body of principles, conventions, unwritten laws and an unshakeable group solidarity, transgression against which incurs the terrible collective vengeance of the organization.[31] To betray the collective, to break *omertà* (the code of silence), to conspire or act against the interests of the family is usually to sign one's own death warrant. However, in return for unswerving loyalty come protection, mutual benefit and corporate security from the unwanted attentions of the group's enemies, persecutors or vengeful victims. Among the Siberian exile convict community, the agonies of exile life would have been even more intolerable without the support and protection of the commune against officialdom, police, guards, executioners and the hostility of the Siberian peasants and natives. In the words of George Kennan, the prisoners' *artel'* was 'the body politic of the exile world; it fills in the life of the exile the same place that the *mir* or commune fills in the life of the free peasant'.[32] The *artel'* had its own elected officials, its own customs, institutions, commercial operations, central exchequer, argot and folklore, and a draconian code of discipline, retribution and reprisal.

The convicts' commune was not, of course, an official institution, but the exile administration recognized both its existence and its internal authority, turned a blind eye to some of its illegal practices and to a certain extent even depended on its goodwill and cooperation for the smooth running of the whole convoy operation. The first serious business of organizing the *artel'* took place at the very first stop for rest and refreshment (the *prival*) or at the first *polu-etap* after leaving the forwarding prison. Here the prisoners would elect their own leader or 'elder' (*starosta*) and other 'officials', and work out a binding set of arrangements which overlaid those made by the Exile Bureau. From now on the prisoners' life would be dominated by this new, self-generated, quasi-autonomous communal association until they arrived at their final destination. This is how one contemporary observer describes the convicts' devotion to their commune: 'The prisoners love their own *artel'*; without it the journey through the *etaps* and life in the prisons are impossible. The *artel'* is the source of life and joy to the prisoners' family – its solace and its peace.'[33]

Important financial and commercial arrangements were also made at the first opportunity. First a levy was made on every prisoner, which went into the communal fund (*artel'naya kassa*), safekeeping of which was the responsibility of the elder (*starosta*). Next came the crucial business of auctioning off the franchise to operate the commune's own co-operative store – the *maidan*, which was a cross between a travelling grocer's, tobacconist's, liquor store and gambling den. Whoever won control of its transactions was totally responsible for procuring the commodities and catering for the needs of the entire *artel'* in both officially permitted and illicit goods. In the larger convoys the *maidan* was often auctioned off in three separate lots: one controlling the sale of comestibles such as tea and sugar; one in charge of illegal alcohol and the tobacco trade; and one responsible for the supply of essential gambling materials such as playing cards, knuckle-bones, dominoes and dice. The revenue was divided in two, the smaller portion going to the *starosta* to use for communal needs, and the larger split equally among the commune members. The *maidanshchik* (*maidan*-keeper) was therefore a central figure in the social and economic life of the convicts' *artel'*. Among the most important purposes to which the community kitty was put was that of bribing the convoy officers or prison staff in order to secure various privileges, both on the road and off. While on the march, the three most crucial objectives of the collective bargaining were the receiving of permission to beg for alms in the villages along the way, the removal of the ankle-fetters, and the hiring of extra wagons to carry the sick and the elderly. On the whole the Siberian peasants were full of compassion for the wretched plight of the exiles while actually on their miserable journey (in contrast to the hostility displayed to them once they arrived at their destination), and in order to tap this reservoir of pity to the most profitable effect, bands of prisoners would, with the guards' permission, trudge around the villages dotted along the route, clanking their chains and keening to the melancholy rhythm of the exile dirge – the *miloserdnaya* – begging for charity as they went. The proceeds would go into the community chest or used to purchase extra victuals.

Removal of the hefty iron ankle-fetters while on the march, while strictly against the rules, was a much valued concession, only bought from the guards by a suitable bribe and – more importantly – the conclusion of a solemn communal pact with the convoy officers under the terms of which prisoners were allowed to shed their chains only on the strict condition that no one attempted to escape. Such contracts made by the *artel'* were absolutely binding on all the members, and anyone breaking the deal and making an individual dash for freedom would, on recapture, be severely punished, not only by the guards, but also by the *artel'*, whose collective oath had been violated. A.S. Maksimov tells of an incident that he personally witnessed when a would-be escaper, after being beaten by the guards on recapture, was then again flogged so mercilessly by the other prisoners as to make even the most hardened convoy officers blanch.[34] Even if the escape was successful, a posse of seasoned convicts would be given permission to scour the forests for some unfortunate runaway – not necessarily the right one – who would either be bribed or bullied into replacing the escaped fugitive so as to maintain the full complement of prisoners to hand over to the next relay of guards. The honour of the *artel'* was thereby upheld. The greasing of palms in order to obtain permission to hire or purchase extra wagons and horses, at the commune's expense, from the local peasantry was also a much valued concession that would have been virtually impossible to secure on an individual basis.

Prison guards in the *etapy*, the transit prisons, were also bribed for other clandestine purposes and added privileges. For instance, the guards could be suborned to permit more frequent access to the prison bath-house than regulations allowed; to smuggle in supplies of vodka, tobacco and other contraband; to allow the *maidanshchik* to operate his forbidden, candlelit casinos undisturbed throughout the night; and to turn a blind eye to secret nocturnal trysts between male and female prisoners in the sexually segregated cells. Prisoners sentenced to be flogged for some contravention of the regulations were provided with a small sum of cash from the common fund with which to bribe the executioner not lay on too heavily. This tip was known as the *rogozhka*.

Finally, an extremely important function of the *artel'* was that of confirming and guaranteeing contracts of one sort or another made between individual prisoners. These contracts could be of a purely financial or intensely personal nature – as in the practice of name-swapping. This was a curious, though common, phenomenon, inoperable without the corporate guarantee of the commune that the agreement, once made, would never be breached. What often happened was that a hard-bitten criminal condemned to, say, 20 years' *katorga* in the mines, would pay to exchange identities with someone with a much lighter sentence. It was amazingly easy for a wily old jailbird to take advantage of a weaker and less experienced fellow prisoner's craving for alcohol, tobacco or extra clothing in order to seduce him into selling away his identity in exchange for some temporary physical gratification. Despite the dreadful consequences of a harsher sentence for the weaker party, such deals were indissoluble and rigorously enforced by the iron rules of the *artel'*. Anyone seeking to renege on the arrangement would therefore be offending against the implacable collective jurisdiction of the commune, and be punished accordingly, even, in Kennan's words, 'condemned to death as traitors by this merciless Siberian Vehmgerichte'. Over the head of such turncoats, he continues, 'hung an invisible sword of Damocles, and sooner or later, in one place or another, it was bound to fall'.[35] Such was the awesome, ubiquitous and relentless nature of the authority of the *arestantskaya artel'*.

SEX, VIOLENCE AND 'GENERAL CUCKOO'S ARMY'

Everything that has been said about the internal organization and discipline of the exile marchers' commune extended throughout the length and breadth of Siberia. Escapes and flight from the convoys and *etapy* were not too common, but once the convicts had reached their destination, abscondment became a mass phenomenon, as every springtime thousands of convicted criminals and compulsory settlers deserted their places of registration or broke out of their cells to join the ranks of what was popularly known as 'General Cuckoo's army'. The quaint cuculine image derives from the fact that it was traditionally the call of the first cuckoo in spring that gave the signal for the annual vernal exodus 'to serve with General Cuckoo' (*sluzhit' u generala Kukushkina*). These escapers, the veteran vagabonds, were known as *brodyagi*, meaning literally 'vagrants' (from the Russian verb *brodit'* – 'to roam'), though some distinction was made in popular parlance between relatively harmless wandering beggars and hobos, called *zhigany*, and the more violent and dangerous gangs of bandits and brigands, known as *varnaki*.[36]

This huge itinerant criminal community was bound together in a vast network of cooperatives and *artel*'s referred to as the *brodyazheskaya obshchina*. The same kind of unshatterable group loyalty, laws of retribution, rituals, camaraderie, legends and belief systems pervaded the prisons, fortresses and the Siberian taiga where the *brodyagi* roamed and carried out their murderous attacks on the territory's townships and villages. Not even the larger towns escaped the attention of the criminal gangs, dozens of which would regularly camp on the outskirts of such centres as Tyumen, Mariinsk, Kainsk and others, creating a huge suburban bivouac of thieves, tramps and murderers who made lightning forays into the downtown areas, terrorizing the local population. Rates of violent crime were much higher in Siberia than in European Russia – which was obviously a direct consequence of the exile system itself.

Acts of bloodcurdling atrocity that would have caused a journalistic sensation in Moscow or St Petersburg hardly raised a collective eyebrow among Siberia's limited reading public and were simply reported under 'current events'. Just to give a few examples: the newspaper *Otechestvennye zapiski* ('Fatherland Notes') in July 1875 tells how one Siberian town was regularly attacked by gangs of youths who would gallop around the town in their troika, carousing and capturing unwary passers-by with lassos and boat-hooks. This must have been a common sport, for George Kennan was later to report similar disturbances in the major town of Tomsk: 'Even the city of Tomsk itself was terrorized in February 1886, while we were there, by a band of criminals who made a practice of riding through the city at night and catching belated wayfarers with sharp grappling hooks.'[37] Young girls would be routinely snatched, driven out of town, gang-raped and dumped back on the street. Another report describes how the large town of Krasnoyarsk in 1897 was in virtual state of siege as a result of brutal gangs of exiles plundering the townsfolk and often slaughtering whole families at a time. Even armed patrols of local vigilantes could do little or nothing to stop the carnage.[38] Elsewhere, not just whole families, but whole communities were wiped out. Anton Chekhov, for instance, tells of a massacre on the island of Sakhalin in which a gang of 16 fugitive criminal exiles raided an Ainu village, tortured and killed the men, raped all the women and hanged all the children.[39]

Despite the horrors to which the free citizens and villagers of Siberia were constantly exposed, turning the country, in Yadrintsev's words, in to a 'perpetual field of battle', there nevertheless remained a kind of grudging admiration for some of the brigand chiefs which sometimes bordered on hero-worship, and the Siberian folk memory retained the names of many of these who became a legend even in their own lifetime. Of these some of the most notorious were Gorkin, Korenev, Bykov, Chaikin and Kapustin – the Robin Hoods, Ned Kellys and Billy the Kids of the Siberian taiga whose audacious deeds are now little remembered beyond the scene of their former crimes.[40] But in the nineteenth century tales and legends were still told about their boldness, physical prowess, derring-do and even supernatural powers. Siberian children played in the woods not at cops and robbers or cowboys and Indians, but at 'brodyagi and soldiers', and peasant girls were often seduced into leaving their villages by fantasies of a life of excitement and glamour in the forest as a Siberian gangster's moll, though they sometimes met with a gruesome fate. Yadrintsev, for instance, relates the story of a young peasant woman who was either forced or persuaded to accompany a brodyaga on his travels. On the road they were joined by another itinerant rogue who wished to share the woman with the first. An argument ensued, but, rather than falling out over who should have her – thereby allowing a woman to break the brodyagi's fraternal bond – they decided to abandon her, but not without first gratuitously tormenting her for being the unwitting object of their dispute. Accordingly, they stripped her naked, raped her and left her hanging by her hair from a tree, where she was later discovered, not quite dead, her bloated body eaten alive by gadflies, midges and mosquitoes.[41]

In fact, the fate of women in general in Siberia was hardly a bed of forest flowers, and was one of the major causes of social distress in the region. The problems of vagrancy and banditry apart, the chronic, and historical, imbalance between the sexes in Siberia, among both the free and the exile population, not only undermined the establishment of settled communities and family life but also added to the incidence of violent and sex-related crime.[42] Such a gross disproportion between the genders created an environment in which rape, abduction of native females, prostitution, incest, child-abuse, homosexuality and intercourse with animals (skotolozhstvo) were commonplace. Without adducing any definite statistics, the government report of 1900 avers that, in the absence of women, the two most common outlets for male sexual urges were buggery and masturbation. These practices, the report maintains, were particularly widespread among brodyagi, who during the winter months, when they would surrender themselves to the relative comfort, warmth and companionship of a local jailhouse, passed on their habits to the rest of the prison population, thereby, we are told, 'undermining the last remnants of their strength'. Another debilitating consequence of the sexual mores of Siberian exile was the very high levels of venereal disease, especially syphilis, which was particularly rife among factory workers in Transbaikalia, often in its secondary and tertiary stages, which led to cases of elephantiasis caused by venereally induced failure of the body's lymphatic drainage system.[43]

Crime statistics throughout Siberia in the nineteenth century, analysed in great detail by E.N. Anuchin, reveal a significant correlation between the types of crime people were originally sentenced for – especially violent offences such a murder, rape and severe wounding – and the felonies they went on to commit while actually in Siberia, which earned the territory a deserved, though unenviable, reputation as the Russian Empire's 'principality of crime', with disastrous ramifications for the territory's free, largely law-abiding inhabitants.[44] Although it is possible to regard Siberia's criminal exiles as in some way victims of tsarist Russia's unjust social and political system, it is difficult to fit them into Hobsbawm's image of 'social bandits', robbing the rich to feed the poor and allegedly living by a code of honour which forbade molesting defenceless maidens, only attacking corrupt officials, wicked land-lords and fat abbots. They were, on the contrary, most of them *anti*-social bandits and a curse on the community. In the case of Siberia's brigands and *brodyagi*, it would be 'a mistake', in Hobsbawm's words, 'to think of bandits as mere children of nature roasting stags in the greenwood'.[45] To suggest otherwise would be to be living in 'cloud-cuckoo-land'.

SSYLKA: FOR AND AGAINST

Towards the end of the nineteenth century, the Russian government decided once more to subject the entire exile operation to detailed scrutiny and recon-sideration. The reasons for this were fivefold. First, the accumulation and extension of the system's fundamental drawbacks already discussed in this chapter; second, the huge influx of voluntary migrants who crossed the Urals to settle in Siberia in the early twentieth century (see Chapter Seven), thereby eliminating the need for enforced colonization and adding to the chorus of those clamouring for total abolition of the system; third, the enormous cost of the operation and the need to seek alternative methods of punishment and correction; fourth, the difficulties of finding sufficient work opportunities for exiled criminals;[46] and, fifth, the increasing pressure of criticism from Siberian society itself, from its enlightened opponents within the judicial and legal establishment, and not least from international opinion.

There was, in fact, a good deal of public debate at the turn of the century about the desirability and effectiveness of punitive exile both in Russia and elsewhere in the world. The arguments for and against exile can be briefly rehearsed as follows:

For Exile

1. Its flexibility; if simple removal from the criminal's native society loses its deterrent or exemplary effect, it can easily be supplemented or reinforced with further deprivations or added penalties: e.g. transfer to hard labour, removal to a harsher location, corporal punishment, etc.
2. The wide range of different types of exile used in Russia seems to support this argument.
3. It preserves the security of the metropolitan society both directly and indirectly, by preventing the possibility of further crimes committed there by the condemned criminal, and by removing his/her influence on others to commit crime.
4. It is an attractive and humanitarian alternative to capital punishment, thereby satisfying abolitionist sentiment and allowing rectification of possible miscarriages of justice.

5. It is also an attractive alternative to imprisonment for the most serious and incorrigible offenders as it removes them from metropolitan places of confinement, thereby facilitating prison reform.

6. Rehabilitation of the criminal is made easier in so far as he/she is isolated both from former partners-in-crime and from the disapproval of the general public. Furthermore, on completion of a fixed-term sentence of exile, transition to normal society is easier than from a custodial sentence.

7. It satisfies the demands of new territories for labour (when required and available), both during sentence and after release, and is therefore to the greater good of the state.

These arguments, sound as some of them may be, are almost all pitched at the theoretical or abstract level, whereas in practice certain obvious material difficulties render them less convincing.

Against Exile

1. There is the problem of finding suitable localities. The area *must* be underpopulated, and yet be suitable for habitation. If it is congenial to habitation, this will be more successfully achieved through the voluntary migration of those who actively wish to live and work there. If it is not congenial to habitation, then there is little point in populating it, unless to find the necessary manpower to exploit natural resources found in inhospitable locations.

2. The latter point assumes that only fit and able-bodied criminals, capable of carrying out the necessary labour, will be so exiled, which had never been the case, and hence a tacit admission that exile is not a suitable punishment for the elderly and feeble; there thus arises the problem of how to keep such people usefully occupied or adequately maintained. Further, if there are large numbers of exiles sentenced to hard labour, then industrial enterprises have to be artificially created, which is a costly and unprofitable undertaking in remote and inaccessible areas.

3. Even if suitable localities and employment are available, there still remains the problem of transportation. Shifting large numbers of prisoners is an expensive and unsatisfactory business. Even if conditions of travel are improved by the greater use of vehicles (as happened on the completion of the Trans-Siberian Railroad) the same problems of supervision, of living in a packed criminal environment, and the opportunities for mutual corruption, friction and violence etc. still continue to exist.

4. Supposing the exile has survived the journey in one piece, has arrived in a suitable locality and has been assigned some useful employment, there is still the biggest problem of all – that of satisfactory and successful settlement. Apart from the familiar impediments of character, indiscipline and insufficiency of women, there is also the added complication caused by the basic incompatibility between the aims of punishment and those

of colonization, the former involving deprivations of civil rights that are essential the achievement of the latter.

5. The fact that exile tends mostly to be for life militates against the arguments for flexibility and rehabilitation.

6. The existence of a penal colony not only obstructs the orderly cultural development of a chosen region, but also sets its often brutal stamp on the civil administration of the area, thus affecting the rights and expectations of the free inhabitants.

Therefore, out of all the allegedly desirable aims of punitive exile and enforced colonization, when put into practice we find that the exile system:

1. has little or no deterrent value – as witnessed by the high rates of recidivism;
2. runs contrary to the objectives of correction and reform;
3. fails to achieve the proper security of the metropolitan society;
4. is positively and demonstrably harmful to the interests of the exile territory's own society;
5. is extremely expensive to run; and
6. has built into it the very obstacles to the successful ekistic role it was partly developed to perform.

All in all, the long, sad and sorry history of the tsarist exile system in Siberia failed to live up to Napoleon Bonaparte's opinion that '*l'exil est le meilleur system à purger le monde ancien en peuplent un nouveau*' (exile is the best way of purging the old world while populating a new one). Ultimately, it failed in both respects, and is perhaps better described in the words of another famous Frenchman, Victor Hugo, a one-time exile himself, who referred to what for many was the living death of exile as '*la guillotine sèche*' (the dry guillotine) – though his place of exile, the island of Guernsey, was hardly comparable to the frigid wastes of Siberia.

7

The Last Tsar of Siberia:
Railroad, Revolution and Mass Migration

When Peter the Great assumed his new title of 'Emperor and Autocrat (*Imperator i Samoderzhets*) of All Russia' in 1721, there was added a long roll-call of honorifics to be used in his correspondence with foreign powers, including: '[Emperor] of Moscow, Kiev, Vladimir, Novgorod; tsar of Kazan, tsar of Astrakhan, *tsar of Siberia* [emphasis added]...' and many, many more.[1] These orotund titles, and the imperial possessions that they signified, were all inherited – indeed, added to – by his successors, including the last Romanov emperor, Nicholas II (ruled 1894–1917, died 1918). 'Bloody Nicholas', as he came to be called, is therefore literally *entitled* to be regarded as 'the last tsar of Siberia'. This in an odd way is fitting, as Siberia experienced a number of significant, dramatic events and developments during his spectacular and, from his own and his government's point of view, catastrophic reign that ended in the revolutions of 1917.

Among the most noteworthy of those events and developments that had a direct effect on Siberia were: the industrial revolution, of which the building of the great Trans-Siberian Railroad (hereafter usually referred to as the Trans-Sib) was the centrepiece; the Exile Reform Law of 12 June 1900, briefly discussed in the previous chapter; the Russo-Japanese war of 1904–5; the revolutionary situation and peasant wars of 1905–7; the agrarian reforms introduced by Prime Minister Pëtr Stolypin (1862–1911) in 1906, and the consequent flood of government-sponsored peasant migration across the Urals; the massacre of demonstrating goldminers in the Lena goldfields of north-east Siberia in 1912; the First World War; and the collapse of autocracy (and therefore the end of the tsar's rule over Siberia) in the February 1917 Revolution. The course of that revolution, the Bolsheviks' October Revolution and the subsequent Civil War in Siberia and the Far East are dealt with in Chapter Eight.

Before turning to the saga of the building of the Trans-Sib, some brief discussion is required regarding the general nature of the Siberian economy in the late nineteenth and early twentieth centuries.

THE SIBERIAN ECONOMY: MONOMORPH OR MOSAIC?

In one of the last articles he wrote before his death in 1999, the distinguished Siberian historian, Leonid Mikhailovich Goryushkin, criticized the manner in which a whole range of Russian, Soviet and Western scholars had sought to characterize the nature of the region's economy in the quarter-century or so before the 1917 revolutions, by pinioning it on to Procrustean beds of dogmatic interpretation or ideologically driven definitions. While being himself a convinced Marxist and an albeit maverick member of the Soviet Communist Party, Goryushkin typically challenged the unsatisfactory, even faulty, methodology and conclusions of many of these studies, accusing their authors of 'academic "opportunism" (konyunkturshchina) and over-dependence on ideological directives from above'.[2] Failing to take into account 'the totality and complexity of economic relationships', previous researchers, he continued, had 'distorted economic reality and painted an over-simplified, rather primitive picture'.[3] Anticipating the advent of Gorbachevian glasnost', the pre-perestroika publication of two important anthologies of essays on the history of the working class and peasantry of Siberia had facilitated a more dispassionate, objective analysis of the situation, underpinned by a wealth of statistical data on the condition of industry and agriculture in Siberia between the emancipation of the serfs in 1861 and the 1917 revolutions.[4] Three things clearly emerge from these studies: first is the fact that between 1861 and 1917, the phases of Siberia's economic development broadly coincided with those of Russia as a whole; second, during this period Siberia became the major region of colonization in the Russian Empire, taking in 80 per cent of all emigrants seeking to escape from the 'land hunger' of the central provinces; and third, as in Russia as a whole, and despite the diversity of economic formations in Siberia to which Goryushkin draws attention, the overwhelming trend was towards the development of capitalist relationships, in both small- and medium-scale industry and in agriculture. To those observations must be added: the fact that the region's economy remained based overwhelmingly on agricultural production, and its population predominantly peasant; and the fact that the vast majority of the Siberian population (which totalled 10.3 million on the eve of the First World War), its industrial enterprises and peasant farms were located in the south, along the route of the Trans-Siberian Railroad in the so-called 'basin of colonization'. By contrast, in the northern tundra and taiga zones, the population density – or sparsity – was about 1.5 persons per square kilometre.

Without doubt the most important factor which contributed to Siberia's economic development during this period was the Trans-Sib, the construction of which is discussed in the following section. Many of the changes which took place in the agricultural and industrial sectors, as indeed in the composition of Siberian society, can be either directly or indirectly attributed to the laying of this vital transportation and trade link between European Russia and the Pacific. The heavy demand for coal, iron, steel and, naturally, manpower, central to the mammoth engineering project, played a large role in the overall boom during the years of Russia's belated industrial revolution, masterminded by the energetic Minister of Finance, Sergei Witte (1849–1915), and, by opening up the territory for both domestic and foreign capital investment, had a major impact on the local economic situation. Equally, Siberia felt very keenly the effects of the slump during the countrywide economic crisis between 1901 and 1905. In fact, without going into detailed analysis of the various sectors of the economy, what emerges throughout the whole period is a fluctuating pattern of boom and bust, upsurge and decline, rising demand and falling production, take-off and recession in response to both internal and external factors (e.g. the completion of the Trans-Sib, social unrest in both factory and field, the war with Japan, international competition, soaring immigration, etc.). However, despite these vicissitudes – which were, of course, not peculiar to Siberia – a number of constants are clearly visible.

First was the startling, exponential increase in population. In the two decades between 1893 and 1913 the population of Siberia almost doubled from 5.8 million to 10.3 million, which was twice the growth rate in European Russia. The rapid increase was the result both of immigration (see below) and 'on the spot' natural procreation, whereas the siphoning off of young virile and fertile adults from the European provinces contributed to the lower birth-rate in that area. This, together with the more intense exploitation of Siberia's natural resources, formed the essential base for the development of the colony's productive forces.[5]

Second, the agricultural sector of the economy experienced a huge expansion of both arable, especially cereal-based, farming and animal husbandry – particularly cattle-rearing, in which the major role was played by dairy herds. This in its turn transformed Siberia into one of the main centres of the world's butter industry. The growth of the Siberian dairy industry was truly astonishing: for example, between the 1860s and the second decade of the twentieth century the number of cattle in Siberia almost doubled from around 5.7 million to 11.1 million head. Milk products rocketed with the introduction in the 1890s of the mechanical cream separator. In 1894 only two such factories equipped with these were in operation. By 1913 there were 4,092.[6] To quote Goryushkin yet again, the creameries 'sprang up like mushrooms after rain', not only private enterprises, but also co-operative ventures, which accounted for around half of total butter production. Over a dozen companies were involved in the export of Russian butter, 90 per cent of which came from Siberia. The major customer was Britain, where, according to Lenin, staying in London in 1907 for a Social-Democratic Party congress, his landlady had assured him that in England 'they all know Barabinsk butter and Chulym cheese'.[7] In terms of export revenue, in fact, the value of Siberia's 'creamery gold' at this time exceeded that of her 'solid gold'. In addition to cattle-rearing, gross figures for the total amount of all domesticated livestock in the territory, according to N. Poppe, rose between 1904 and 1916 from 11.5 to 38.5 million head. By his reckoning, or those of his sources: 'By 1913 Siberia had 53 horses, 63 head of cattle, 61 sheep and 13 pigs per hundred of the population. According to the records for 1916, Siberian farms possessed an average 20 farm animals as opposed to only 9 for the farms of European Russia.'[8] Poppe's figures, however impressive, overlook the tens of thousands of reindeer tended by the indigenous nomadic herders of the far north. Goats and camels are also conspicuous by their absence from his calculations.

The area of cultivated land in Siberia also increased remarkably during this period. Between 1905 and 1913 Tomsk district alone more than doubled its area of tilled and sown land from 1,455,000 desyatinas (one desyatina = 2.7 acres or 1.09 hectares) to 3,544,000; and of this total, figures for land given over entirely to wheat almost trebled from 641,000 to 1,851,000 desyatinas respectively.[9] The new immigrants brought into Siberia different techniques, different varieties of seed and fresh energy, but also learnt profitably from the time-developed methods of the starozhily (old inhabitants) who were, of course, more used to regional climatic, seasonal and pedological conditions. It was in every meaning of the term a process of mutually beneficial cross-fertilization between the old and the new Siberians. Between 1910 and 1914, the wheat harvest for the whole of Siberia averaged 3,247,200 tons and the rye harvest 828,576 tons, a considerable amount of which was exported either to European Russia or abroad.[10] Most experts on Siberia's agrarian economy in the first two decades of the twentieth century seem to agree – whatever other differences of opinion they may have – that the Siberian peasantry was generally more prosperous, owned more land, was better mechanized and enjoyed a much higher standard of living than its European Russian counterpart. Many more economic indicators could be presented to demonstrate that, without exaggeration, during the reign of the last tsar of Siberia the territory, in terms of agricultural output, became one of the most successful and productive in the entire realm.

Arable-farming and livestock-rearing apart, Goryushkin points out that a significant contribution to the diversity of the Siberian economy was made by the immigration of skilled workers, artisans and craftsmen who established a whole variety of enterprises, cottage industries and workshops, and developed many different trades in Siberia. Carpenters, tanners, blacksmiths, saddlers, potters, basket weavers, milliners, coopers and sundry other craftsmen and women who had learnt their trade in their home provinces now spread throughout Siberia, particularly in the more populated south, near major towns and along the route of the Trans-Sib, in many instances passing on their skills to the old inhabitants. At first, these workmen would undertake jobs for individual customers, but in many cases managed to accumulate sufficient capital to establish their own permanent workshops, smithies, mills, sewing shops, breweries and so on, even hiring their own labourers, apprentices and journeymen. Very few of these enterprises were of large proportions, and remained on the scale of cottage industries (kustarnye promysly), but the widespread small- and medium-sized centres of light peasant industry helped to transform Siberia into what Yadrintsev described as 'a huge peasant factory' (*ogromnaya muzhichyaya fabrika*), and added to the multifaceted nature of Siberia's economy.[11]

Although iron industries had been established in Siberia in the eighteenth century, as described in Chapter Three, large-scale manufacturing – in comparison to the metallurgical extractive industries – did not on the whole play a significant role in Siberia, and the territory generally relied on the importation of finished goods from factories in the industrial centres of European Russia. However, despite the absence of major industrial enterprises (at least not major in comparison with the huge plants in Moscow, St Petersburg and elsewhere), the economic infrastructure of capitalism had taken root, a good deal of it as the result of foreign investment in Siberia. American, British, German and Danish companies, banks and joint-stock conglomerates all ploughed capital into various sectors of Siberia's economy, ranging from creameries and agricultural machinery to gold-mining and profitable steamship lines on the Ob-Irtysh and Yenisei river systems. Even in small-time artisanal and agricultural enterprises, the general trend was clearly towards the capitalist direction of development. After weighing the evidence, and eschewing monomorphic templates, it is difficult to resist Goryushkin's conclusion that:

> While small-scale production units predominated in quantitative terms, capitalism in both its developed and more primitive forms was clearly the major mode of production. The Siberian economy at this time represented a mosaic of relationships and types of activity, most of it concentrated in the south, most of it of an agricultural nature, and its general level lagging behind that of European Russia.[12]

THE TRANS-SIBERIAN RAILROAD

The emancipation of the Russian serfs in 1861 finally marked the beginning of the country's unsteady transition from a feudal to a capitalist economy, and eventually to her belated industrial revolution. Although the terms of the emancipation settlement had built into it obstacles seemingly designed to frustrate that process, preventing primary capital accumulation and mobility of labour for instance, nevertheless during the 1860s, 1870s and 1880s the financial and institutional infrastructure began to be laid down which would facilitate the great industrial lurch forward under the stewardship of (later Count) Sergei Witte, Minister of Finance from 1892 to 1903, and protagonist behind the building of the Trans-Siberian Railroad, which was, as mentioned above, both the centrepiece and showpiece of Russia's industrial lift-off. The process of economic modernization had its uniquely Russian and indeed bizarre aspects, and was different from that of other European states. These included very large factories concentrated in only three or four major industrial centres employing thousands of workers packed into overcrowded and insanitary working and living conditions; state initiative and political, rather than purely economic, forces driving what came to be called the 'Witte system'; continued exploitation and over-taxation of the peasantry; and reliance on massive investment of foreign capital and managerial personnel.

There was also the added twist that the emperor who presided over this process of economic modernization was distinctly 'un-modern' in his personal, political and religious views. Nicholas II was steeped in the traditions of Muscovite medievalism, believing until the bitter end in the 'divine right of tsars', somewhat dim-witted, openly xenophobic and anti-Semitic, regarding himself as the 'little father' (tsar-batyushka) of his people – those very people who dubbed him 'Nicholas the Bloody' (Nikolai krovavyi), the first tsar to earn such a damning sobriquet since Ivan the Terrible. He was also pig-headedly impervious to the rising tide of nationwide social and political discontent and revolutionary rumblings that would eventually destroy him and his unhappy empire. It was, therefore, somewhat ironic that it was Nicholas, then still heir to the throne, who was chosen by his father, the reactionary, authoritarian Alexander III (ruled 1881–94), to conduct the ceremony in distant Vladivostok which initiated the building of the Trans-Sib in 1891.

The introduction and expansion of modern railway networks had come typically late to Russia, and there were those in government circles who still regarded them with some suspicion. However, despite continuing objections by both arch-conservatives and radical intellectuals, rapid progress was made – both state and privately financed – and between 1860 and 1890, the country's railway system increased from 1,400 kilometres (870 miles) of track to around 30,000 (18,600 miles).[13] (This expansion, and its social and economic consequences, are reflected in the Russian creative literature of the day: Nikolai Nekrasov's poignant poem 'The Railway' [Zheleznaya doroga, 1864] and the tragic fate of Tolstoi's Anna Karenina come to mind.)[14] Discussions about the desirability of connecting European Russia with the Far East had been going on in various ministries, government offices, in specialist journals and in business and military circles since at least the late 1850s. The pros and cons, based on economic, social, financial, geopolitical and strategic arguments, have been concisely summarized and analysed by David Collins, and the whole construction project from beginning to end expertly and entertainingly covered in Steven Marks's scholarly monograph, Road to Power, from which this section draws much of its information, though not necessarily its conclusions.[15]

From commencement to completion, the line was, in Mote's words, 'mired in controversy', both a technological marvel of its day and a 'monument to bungling'.[16] It was bedevilled from the outset, not only by bureaucratic wrangling over its precise original purpose, but by dreadful geophysical and climatic conditions, manpower and managerial problems, dangerous engineering deficiencies, bribery and corruption, incompetent officialdom, inadequate planning, lack of proper book-keeping, lethal accidents, sub-standard materials, sabotage and large-scale crime on the part of managers and workers alike. Given these obstacles, which were of Augean proportions and which required commensurately Herculean efforts to overcome, it is a wonder that the project was completed at all. The fact that it was finished was in very large measure due to the persistence, vision and ambition of its main driving force, Sergei Witte.

Witte and Pëtr Stolypin, whose policies on peasant migration are dealt with in a later section, were two of the most influential statesman of late imperial Russia. Both served at different times as prime minister, and both had an enormous impact on the country's economic development, Witte in the industrial sector, and Stolypin in the agrarian. Both were unswerving monarchists,[17] but both saw the absolute necessity of reform if the empire were to survive, and both in one way or another earned the displeasure and distrust of an emperor who was mentally incapable of fully appreciating their efforts on his and the regime's behalf. Witte, grandson and son of colonial officials in the Caucasus, and graduate (in mathematics) of Novorossiisk University, first came to government office as Minister of Transport in 1892, having spent his professional career until then in railway administration and development. In August of the same year he became Minister of Finance and thenceforth became the leading advocate of the building of the Trans-Sib which he saw, not simply as an economic enterprise, but as an essential element in the strengthening of Russian imperial power, and in reinforcing the bonds between the European and Asiatic parts of the empire. Beyond that, he believed that the Trans-Sib and its economic and strategic benefits would have the effect of enhancing Russia's power and prestige in the global perspective. He was also a shrewd political schemer, and it was on his suggestion that the young tsarevich, Nicholas Alexandrovich, was appointed chairman of the newly established Committee of the Siberian Railway, the government agency in supreme control of all aspects of the railway's subsequent development. Nicholas himself had been enthused with the Far East after visiting the territory on a grand tour in 1890–91, and Witte thereby assured himself of the future tsar's continued backing for his premier project. This was important because, as mentioned previously, the railway was not without its opponents.

So what were the arguments for and against the enterprise? These can be broadly divided into economic, political, military-strategic, colonial and imperialist arguments, and although they were all complex and hotly debated, they can for present purposes be reduced to fairly simple terms.[18] The economic case in favour of the Trans-Sib was that such a link between Europe and the Pacific would stimulate both trade and industry, bringing greater prosperity to the region and not only boost Siberia's industry and agriculture, but also benefit the country as a whole. It would create demand for more industrial goods, offer better commercial opportunities, both domestic and international, and also facilitate transportation – and hence expansion – of agricultural products. Opponents, who, until Witte's arrival, were located mainly in the Ministry of Finance, which traditionally took a rather curmudgeonly attitude to public expenditure, argued that the whole scheme was simply too expensive and that forecasts of economic benefits were wildly optimistic. Ministry officials were also sceptical about the possibility of raising the necessary funding from private sources, or from the Siberian population, and also very chary, in this case, of encouraging foreign investment, unlike in other sectors of industry.

At the political level, fans of the Trans-Sib urged that the building of the railroad would enhance the integration and greater unity of the Russian state. For instance, N.A. Voloshinov, a military officer who took part in surveys of Transbaikalia in the 1880s, impressed with the opportunities for developing gold-mining in the region, added the political to the economic argument by stating in rather effusive terms: 'The Siberian railroad will be the great culmination of [Y]ermak's work. It will be the real, final subjugation and incorporation of Siberia for the use and benefit of the Russian people and the Russian state.'[19] (The use of the word 'subjugation' [pokorenie] is significant in this context as an indication of the 'imperialist/colonialist' attitude of the central authorities towards its north-Asian possessions.) The emperor, Alexander III, was obviously sympathetic to this view, and, while avoiding historical allusions to the sixteenth-century cossak 'conqueror' of Siberia, stated that the region was 'an indivisible part of Russia', and that the final forging of a binding link uniting different parts of the empire would 'bring glory to our dear Fatherland'.[20] Such sentiments were anathema to the Siberian regionalists. Right at the heart of Siberian oblastnichestvo (regionalism) lay the concept, the aspiration and passion for the greater autonomy or even complete independence of Siberia from Russia, based on their belief in the unique circumstances and special qualities of the Siberian people, both indigenous and Slav. What they feared, as the public discussions and debates about the desirability of the railroad developed, was that, if the project went ahead, it would lead inevitably to an even greater degree of Russian dominance over their beloved homeland. In their view, articulated in scores of articles in the regionalist press, the chief beneficiaries of the new transport link would be not the ordinary people of Siberia, but the centralized Russian state. Support for the national state occupied a prominent place in the arsenal of the pro-railroaders. Equally, it was support for the Russian national state to which the oblastniki at first vehemently objected. It is fair to point out that these objections resulted not from a stubborn, irrational opposition to technological progress and improved transport and communications systems per se, but from an anxiety as to the uses to which these were likely to be put by the imperial Russian state.

The regionalists' objections, of course, cut no ice – as it were – with the railway's proponents, and their political case was augmented by arguments that the building of the new line would help to alleviate famine in the European part of Russia by facilitating the transportation of agricultural produce from Siberia to stricken areas, thereby reducing the threat of rural insurrections. Such views turned out to be ill-founded and over-optimistic, as in the event, although the railway was given the go-ahead and more or less completed by 1902, this did nothing to prevent the massive wave of violent peasant uprisings which swept through the country during the years of the 'Red Cockerel' between 1902 and 1907.[21]

In strategic terms, the debate revolved around the question of whether or not the proposed railway would reinforce Russia's military and defensive capabilities in the Far East. The lack of an adequate, rapid means of internal transport and communications system had been a significant contributing factor to Russia's humiliating defeat in the Crimean War (1853–6). Following the acquisition of the Amur and Ussuri regions and the consequent need to colonize them more purposefully, together with the perceived threat, or at least possibility, of some future military confrontation with China or Japan, not to mention apprehensions about American ambitions in the region, it was argued that the railway was essential, not only for the more intensive settlement of the region, but also for its defence. After all, Vladivostok was a lot further away from the metropolis than Sevastopol. Some of the more Cassandra-like warnings of war in the east may have seemed somewhat exaggerated at the time, but the fact is, of course, that in 1904 Russia *did* go to war with Japan, a war which she lost, notwithstanding the successful construction of the line that its military backers had asserted was so essential for the defence of St Petersburg's Far Eastern territories. It is tempting, therefore, to conclude that the Trans-Sib did little or nothing to enhance Russia's military preparedness or performance in that particular arena (see below).

However, Russia's defeat in 1905 only served to revive the old arguments about further construction plans. The problem was that, in 1896, the Committee of the Siberian Railway had taken the decision to build the link from Transbaikalia to Vladivostok, not through Russian territory along the northern bank of the Amur river, but by laying a track from Chita south-eastwards across Chinese-held Manchuria via Harbin to Vladivostok – the Chinese-Eastern Railway (CER). A southern spur (the South-Manchurian Railway, SMR) connected the CER to the Liaotung peninsula and the naval base at Port Arthur, for which Russia had wrung a lease from China in 1898, much to the annoyance of Japan (see Map 7). Accepting both the postwar reality of Japanese power in the east, and realizing the ineffectiveness of the CER during the conflict, the government, supported by the State Duma, took the decision to build a new section of the Trans-Sib – the Amur Railway – this time entirely on Russian sovereign territory, following the course of the Amur from a point near Stretensk to Khabarovsk, and thence due south alongside the Ussuri to Vladivostok.[22] Much debate took place, not about the actual route, but about the distance there should be between the river and the railroad. These debates, not surprisingly, involved the by-now familiar mixture of economic, strategic and colonial arguments surrounding the original Trans-Sib. Locating the line too close to the river would make it vulnerable to attack and interruption from potential enemies from the south, argued some; locating it a 160 kilometres (100 miles) or so further north, though strategically

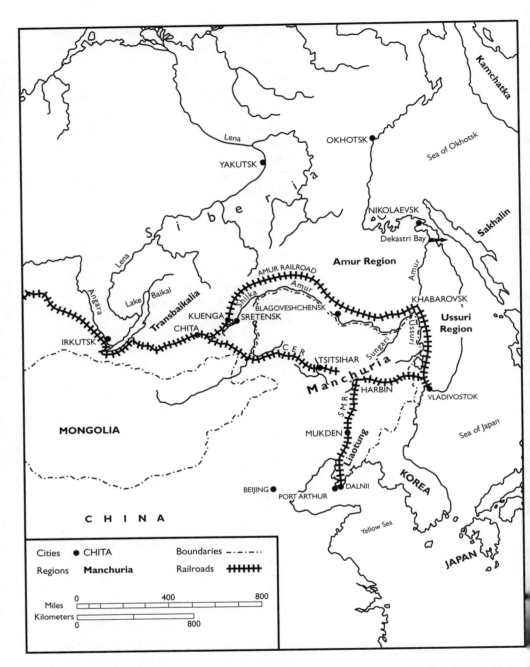

Map 7   The Far-Eastern section of the Trans-Siberian Railroad, showing the routes of the Amur, Chinese-Eastern and South-Manchurian Railways.

Source: Sibirica, The Journal of Siberian Studies, vol. 1, no. 1. (1993–4), (Amended).

more secure, would follow a route through uninhabited, difficult and barren territory, and therefore serve no useful purpose, objected others.[23]

Eventually, with the backing of the tsar and the Duma, both shrugging off the engineering problems, geophysical obstacles and financial ramifications of the project – many of the arguments based on appalling ignorance of the region's geomorphology – the decision was taken to follow the more southerly route, and construction began in 1907. Whatever the usual military and economic agenda items put forward by both sides, in the final analysis – as with the original debates over the Trans-Sib – it was once more support for the national state that was the clinching factor in favour. National pride, residual imperial ambitions, defence of Mother Russia, fear of the 'yellow peril', intense Russian chauvinism – all these irrational emotions eventually held sway over the more sober arguments both for and against, though of course this patriotic fervour favoured the 'ayes' rather than the 'nays'. Some even went so far as to assert that the building of the Amur Railway was essential to the very survival of the Russian Empire.

But the empire did *not* survive, and the last 'tsar of Siberia' was forced to abdicate in February 1917, only a few months after the opening of the Amur Railway Bridge at Khabarovsk in 1916, the last link in the track. To that extent, the imperial case for the building of the Trans-Sib seems to have been a chimera – defined in the *Oxford English Dictionary* (in its transferred rather than original mythological sense) as 'a bogy; thing of hybrid character; fanciful conception'. The construction of the Trans-Siberian Railroad had cost millions and millions of rubles (the equivalent of around US$1 billion in 1916) and claimed thousands of human lives, but its usefulness in terms of colonial settlement, economic benefit and national defence was at best questionable and at worst negligible. From one point of view, it was the concretization of all those chimerical fancies. It has also been described in black-and-white zoomorphic terms as both a 'white elephant' and a '*bête noire*'.

The railroad – around 7,500 kilometres (4,660 miles) in length from Chelyabinsk to Vladivostok, and covering several time zones – was built by a motley, ragtag army of Russian labourers, native navvies, convicts and Korean, Japanese and Chinese coolies across swamps, rivers, floodplains and permafrost, traversing the taiga, tunnelling through mountains and straddling fearsome terrain subject to subsidence, landslips and seismic shifts. Its overall cost, in both financial and human terms, was gargantuan by any contemporary yardstick. It could be argued – and indeed it was – that the vast resources that were sunk into that grandiose scheme would have been better spent on fostering the economic prosperity, educational opportunities, medical facilities, local government institutions and overall social welfare of, not just Siberia and the Far East, but the common people of the entire Russian Empire, and thereby go some way to prevent its implosion. This is to indulge in counterfactual historical speculation, and the causes of the 1917 revolutions are, of course, far more complex than this line of argument suggests, but it is a factor worth taking into consideration.

Short-term difficulties and drawbacks apart, in the longer historical perspective it can be argued that the Trans-Sib ultimately paid dividends on the initial investment, wager or sacrifice. Victor Mote, writing in 1998, sums it up as follows:

> During its construction, there can be no doubt that the Trans-Siberian Railroad was a serious drain on the tsarist economy, and later, the war effort. Despite the criticism, the Trans-Siberian more than paid for itself during the subsequent century. Indeed, it would be hard to imagine Greater Siberia without it. It has become the veritable symbol (and unifier) of the region.[24] (See Fig. 7.)

WAR AND REVOLUTION

During the first five years of the twentieth century the Russian Empire went through a period of massive social upheaval, class struggle, international war, domestic terror and political crisis which in 1905 threatened the very existence of the tsarist regime, but which it (temporarily) survived. The causes, course and consequences of the nationwide 1905 revolutionary situation are too complex to enter into at this point, but as far as Siberia is concerned, a number of significant developments took place that deserve some attention. First was the Russo-Japanese War of 1904–5. Against the domestic background of mounting social, political and industrial unrest – these were the years of the 'Red Cockerel', the emergence of revolutionary political parties like the Marxist Social Democrats and the neo-populist Socialist-Revolutionaries, terrorist assassinations and industrial strikes – the international situation in the Far East was getting more and more fraught, particularly as regards relations between Russia and Japan. In addition, China, Korea, the United States of America, Great Britain and, to a lesser extent, France and Germany, were all involved in the escalating far-eastern imbroglio.

This is not the place to delve into the convoluted diplomacy, imperial posturings, territorial ambitions and misplaced perceptions of the period, but it is not just with benefit of hindsight that one can see that Russia grossly overestimated its own military power and potential in the region, and at the same time fatally underestimated those of the Japanese, whom the tsar contemptuously and nippophobically dismissed as 'little apes' (makaki). Delusions of imagined Russian grandeur in the Far East, of which the building of the Trans-Sib was a part, allied to exaggerated expectations of commercial gain, led to a situation in which 'nebulous metaphysics ... allied with faulty economics'[25] eventually exploded into all-out war. Nicholas had foolishly accepted the equally foolish advice of his Minister of the Interior, Vyacheslav von Plehve (1846–1904), that a 'small, victorious war' would defuse and deflect public attention from the deteriorating domestic situation, and accordingly formally declared war on Japan in January 1904 immediately following Admiral Togo's sudden scuttling of the Russian Far Eastern fleet while still at anchor in the harbour of Port Arthur. Right at the outset of

Figure 7 Drawing entitled 'Building the Siberian Railroad' in *Velikii put'* ('The Great Way'), No. 1 (1899), Krasnoyarsk.

hostilities, therefore, St Petersburg paid the price for a Far Eastern policy which Florinsky describes as 'a near perfect example of shameless duplicity'.[26] Naval replacements from the Baltic fleet were long in coming (and then ending only in utter catastrophe in the Tsushima Strait), and the war for the time being was destined to be fought on land, which is where the Trans-Siberian Railroad's much vaunted strategic role on the far-eastern stage came into play. To continue the theatrical metaphor, that role turned out to be not only a tragic one, but the whole performance a total flop.

In the opinion of Michael Perrins, even as early as 1900, 'Russia's commercial and political expansion in Manchuria had outstripped the Russian army's capacity to defend itself.'[27] Notwithstanding the completion of the Trans-Sib, and despite the gung-ho attitudes of the central government, the logistical problems of defending territories and concessions thousands of kilometres from the main centres of population and industry in the metropolitan heartland were enormous. Perrins continues to argue that the Russian high command had not even seriously prepared for a war with Japan and that 'the mere suggestion that the Japanese were a power to equal the Russians in the Far East was considered by some senior officers to border on treason'.[28] Such overweening attitudes, together with institutional rivalries and personal disagreements and antagonisms within the military and political establishment, lack of proper plans for mobilization of Far Eastern units or for the transportation of troops from the European provinces, simple things like inadequacy of maps and, indeed, general unfamiliarity with the terrain, together with the shock of the Port Arthur naval disaster, all boded ill for the outcome of the war for Russia. Port Arthur itself capitulated in December 1904, but the decisive land engagement was the battle of Mukden in February 1905, a battle which raged for 20 days along a 160-kilometre (100-mile) front and which cost Russia over 90,000 men. However, despite their military victory, Japanese casualties were almost as high, and, '[A]lthough a staggering defeat for Russia, Mukden nevertheless was not a Waterloo or a Sedan ... The final blow ... was delivered on the high seas'.[29] The maritime *coup de grâce*, which led to the opening of peace negotiations on the intercession of the US president, Theodore Roosevelt, was the sinking of Russia's Baltic fleet that had sailed for six months round the world, only to be sent straight to the bottom in the battle of the Tsushima Strait in May 1905. A final peace and the Treaty of Portsmouth soon followed, one of the terms of which was Russia's surrendering of the whole southern half of Sakhalin to Japanese rule. It was not to regain control until Japan's defeat in the Second World War in 1945.

Russia's military and naval debacle in the Far East occurred against the background of nationwide civil unrest of revolutionary proportions following the slaughter of hundreds of innocent, unarmed demonstrating workers and their families in St Petersburg on Sunday 9 January 1905 – 'Bloody Sunday'.[30] The massacre was greeted with national – and international – horror and revulsion, soon turning to boiling anger, which rapidly spread from the working classes and peasantry to include almost the whole of

Russian society. It also spread equally swiftly from the capital to the provinces, including Siberia. Indeed, as Henry Reichman points out: 'In the Russian Revolution of 1905 conflict was often more intense at the empire's peripheries than in central Russia ... From Krasnoiarsk east, Siberia experienced the most extensive breakdown of authority, culminating in the *de facto* seizures of power by revolutionaries in several cities and towns.'[31]

One of the most noticeable aspects of the revolutionary situation in Siberia was the joining of forces of the militant workers, particularly railway workers, and mutinous soldiers. In European Russia, although the incidence of military mutinies was more widespread than is traditionally thought,[32] nevertheless, in the final analysis it was the loyalty, or obedience, of the armed forces which was instrumental in finally suppressing the civilian uprisings and ensuring the survival of the autocracy – or at least the postponement of its inevitable demise. In Siberia, however, it was the combination of proletarian, peasant and military rebellion that created such an explosive cocktail of revolutionary activity, a clear adumbration of the critical situation throughout the empire in 1917. Reichman identifies the 'newly opened Siberian Railroad as a special hotbed of labor unrest'.[33] It was here, all along the Trans-Sib and in the major towns on its route, where the dangerously combustible mixture of militant workers and rebellious soldiers, first on their way to, and then on their way back from the Far Eastern front, met in revolutionary solidarity. On 16 January 1905 the Krasnoyarsk committee of the Social Democratic Workers' Party issued an inflammatory leaflet entitled 'Revolution in Russia', calling for an all-out strike of workers along the Trans-Sib, and for soldiers to refuse to go the front. On the following day a further flyer addressed to the 'Workers of the Krasnoyarsk workshops and depots' carried the following slogan: 'Down with the war! Quit work today. March out of your workshops and depots with songs! Stop the trains and join in fraternity with the soldiers! Long live our strike!'[34]

The Siberian railway workers were a highly volatile and heterogeneous mixture of skilled and unskilled operatives, engine drivers, engineers and labourers, who, although earning considerably higher wages than their counterparts in European Russia, nevertheless had to contend with commensurately higher prices, harsh living conditions and the usual hardships of enduring the Siberian environment. Many of them had received at least a rudimentary education, and were also very susceptible to the agitation and propaganda of committed revolutionary activists from the Social Democratic Workers' Party, both Menshevik and Bolshevik. The ranks of these had, of course, been added to by the government's continued practice of exiling its political opponents to Siberia in large numbers. In this way the tsarist authorities themselves insouciantly connived at spreading the revolutionary virus throughout its distant north-eastern provinces. Unsurprisingly, the revolutionary ardour of the political deportees was not quenched while in exile, and there are many examples of their continuing militancy even before the outbreak of revolutionary events in January 1905. For example, in 1902, a protest of political exiles in the Aleksandrovskaya transit prison near Irkutsk, led by the Polish Bolshevik, Feliks Dzerzhinskii (future head of the Cheka – Lenin's political police), resulted in the brief establishment of the 'Prison Republic' (*tyuremnaya respublika*), the raising of the red flag over the prisoners' cells, and a demand that they be released from jail and allowed to proceed to their exile destination. Their demands were granted, but this was followed by the introduction of strict new laws and regulations by the Governor-General of Irkutsk, Count Kutaisov, which even more severely curtailed the movement and activities of political exiles throughout eastern Siberia. The exiles' response led in one notorious case to the so-called 'Yakutsk protest', or the '*Romanovtsy*' affair.

In February 1904, shortly after the opening of the war against Japan, 57 political exiles in the far north – consisting of Bolsheviks, Mensheviks, Jewish Bundists, three Socialist-Revolutionaries and a number of non-party peasant insurrectionists – gathered together in Yakutsk, armed themselves with a variety of guns and knives and barricaded themselves in a two-storey house belonging to a native Yakut by the name of – ironically – Romanov. The major demand of the protesters, who came to be known as the '*Romanovtsy*', was for the immediate abrogation of the 'Kutaisov laws'. After a three-week stand-off the house was attacked by armed police, one of the protesters killed, three wounded, and the rest sentenced to twelve years' *katorga*. Their sentence led to further widespread demonstrations against the tsarist regime, and ultimately the 'Kutaisov laws' were rescinded. International workers' day on 1 May 1904 was celebrated in Siberia with demonstrations led by the Union of Siberian Social Democrats (*Sibirskii sotsial-demokraticheskii soyuz*) under slogans calling for the eight-hour working day, an end to the tsarist war, an end to tsarist autocracy, peace between the peoples and, 'Long live Socialism!'[35]

On the wider industrial front, Reichman demonstrates that even before the outbreak of hostilities with Japan, the strike movement had been gaining in numbers and momentum, with 53 incidents of industrial action in such centres as Krasnoyarsk, Omsk, Ilansk, Irkutsk and Chita between 1898 and 1905. While most of these were for economic reasons, the movement took on a definitely more political complexion after news of the Bloody Sunday butchery reached Siberia. Lack of space prevents a detailed analysis of the intensity and extent of the revolutionary workers' and soldiers' activities in southern Siberia and the Far East during 1905. Suffice it to say that from 'Red Krasnoyarsk' through Irkutsk and Chita to Vladivostok, the incidence of anti-government activity, strikes, walk-outs, demonstrations, mass protest meetings, both spontaneous and led by Social Democratic agitators, the setting up of local soviets – all fuelled by grass-roots resentment against the corrupt tsarist regime and its disastrous military adventurism against Japan – proved Siberia to be one of the most inflammatory theatres of revolutionary protest and action during the nationwide turmoil of that year. The unrest in the east lasted until well after the promulgation of the 'October Manifesto' brought some measure of 'normality' to the rest of the empire.[36]

Following the bloody suppression of the December workers' uprising in the Presnya district of Moscow – almost the final act of the revolutionary tragedy west of the Urals – the government now turned its thoughts to mopping up the remnants of the discontent in Siberia and the Far East. In January 1906 punitive military expeditions (*karatel'nye ekspeditsii*) were dispatched simultaneously from Moscow in the west and Harbin in the east, which carried out ruthless acts of revenge in a savage campaign of arrests, summary executions of strikers and protesters and, finally, the imposition of martial law throughout Siberia. In the countryside, despite the relative material well-being of the Siberian peasants in comparison with their cousins in central European Russia, there was also a wave of agrarian uprisings. Although perhaps an expression of what Marxists describe as 'false consciousness', this was nevertheless another clear indication of the mass dissatisfaction of the entire Russian, and Siberian, people with a totally discredited regime and a by-now almost universally hated tsar. Curiously, it was to be a crazy Siberian peasant, one Grigorii Rasputin, who was to bring the last tsar of Siberia, and his tsarina, into even greater public disrepute during the last few years of his reign (see below).

But both before and after Rasputin made his indelible mark in the capital, hundreds of thousands of other Siberian peasants throughout the country demonstrated their disapproval of the regime in a series of rural disturbances to which Soviet historians have devoted a number of scholarly works meticulously documenting their often violent development, and debunking more traditional accounts that throughout the peasant wars of 1905–7, 'the Siberian countryside stayed silent'.[37] For instance, a volume of statistical information and essays, compiled by L.M. Goryushkin, Ye. I. Soloveva *et al.* in 1985, presents a detailed chronicle complete with tables, dates, locations and vivid graphs illustrating the scope and magnitude of what the editors refer to in the title as 'The Peasant Movement in Siberia'. The information reveals that between January 1905 and May 1907 there were in the provinces of western Siberia 643 recorded incidents of peasant uprisings against the local civil and ecclesiastical authorities, and in eastern Siberia 626 over the same period – a total of 1,269.[38] Peaking dramatically between October 1905 and March 1906, the peasant revolts investigated by the scholars in Novosibirsk provide an impressive display of both the breadth and depth of popular discontent during this period, which was not just confined to 'bolshie' railwaymen and awkward Russian squaddies. Nor did the agrarian reforms of Prime Minister Stolypin, introduced in 1906 and partly designed to encourage peasant migration to Siberia on a huge scale (discussed in the following section), do much to alleviate or diminish the level of peasant discontent. According to archival statistics gathered by the same team of scholars, from June 1907 to mid-1914 1,155 peasant villages in western Siberia and 806 in the eastern provinces were the scenes of further rural disturbances, despite the continued imposition of martial law.[39] When set against the huge geographical and demographical extent of Siberia, these may not seem to be enormous figures, but nor are they indicative of a general peasant peace within Siberia. The Siberian peasantry was clearly revolting.

The indigenous peoples of Siberia – like other national minorities elsewhere in the empire – also made their own contribution to the countrywide crisis of tsarism. However, their various protests, popular assemblies and dissident groups had no unified organization or agenda, each of the 'small peoples' pursuing its own interests according to both national and also social grievances and aspirations. The Yakut *toyons* (clan chieftains and in many cases government officials), for instance, had different objectives from Buryat peasants and Altai mineworkers, but many communities took advantage of the empire-wide collapse of public order in an attempt to snatch what they could from the flames of revolution.

The dramatic events of 1905, however, whatever their common designation, did not really add up to a 'revolution' in the proper sense of the term. They did not bring about the end of autocracy or real devolution of political power; there was no redistribution of wealth or property; society's hierarchical class system was not restructured, either in European Russian or Siberia; and the powers of the police, the military, the bureaucracy and the Church remained unaltered. But, reverting to the peasant question, it is clear that at both ends of the political spectrum, Vladimir Lenin, leader of the Bolshevik wing of the Russian Social Democratic Workers' Party on the extreme left, and Pëtr Stolypin, chairman of the tsar's Council of Ministers, each learned the same lesson from the troubles of 1905, though with obviously different conclusions and policies. Both political leaders realized that the paramount question to be addressed was that of the Russian peasantry, including those of Siberia, whose devastating force for opposition, rebellion and change had been demonstrated in the popular upsurge of that year, and after. In July 1905, Lenin wrote a new revolutionary pamphlet entitled *Two Tactics of Social Democracy in the Democratic Revolution*. In this he argued that what was necessary for the execution of the 'democratic revolution' was not an alliance between the workers with the bourgeoisie, but the establishment of what he described as the 'revolutionary-democratic dictatorship of the proletariat and the poor peasantry'.[40] Stolypin on the other hand drew the conclusion that what was needed was the creation of an independent, yeoman peasant class of private farmers, free from the shackles of the traditional village commune, and able to migrate freely and with government assistance to the fertile lands of southern Siberia. His subsequent programme of agrarian reforms led to what Donald Treadgold has described as *The Great Siberian Migration*.[41]

MIGRATION AND MASSACRE

The 'emancipation of the Russian serfs' in 1861 is something of a misnomer. To be sure, the Russian peasants were granted various legal liberties and freed from their servile position as mere human chattels of the their noble masters – what Aleksandr Herzen described as 'baptized property' – but they were still subject to many legal, fiscal, penal and social restrictions that marked them out as a separate 'caste' from the minority privileged estates of Russian society. Among those restrictions was the inability to depart without official permission from their village commune or local officials and seek an occupation or dwelling place elsewhere. Nevertheless, despite these controls at both local and national levels, there was some shift of population during the final decades of the nineteenth century. However, it was the popular fury unleashed during the years of the 'Red Cockerel' and through 1905 that frightened the government into realizing that a much more positive, energetic and financially supportive policy needed to be undertaken with the twin aims of alleviating peasant land-hunger in the European provinces and simultaneously boosting the population and agricultural potential of Siberia. The new Prime Minister, Stolypin, who already had a reputation for dealing severely with rebellious peasants as Governor of Saratov province between 1904 and 1906, while still remaining equally severe, brought in a wide tranche of agrarian reforms that it was hoped would finally solve the glaring inadequacies of the emancipation settlement of 1861. The two most important features of the complex and cumbersome legislation were the granting of the right of peasants to leave their traditional communes and possess their own private farms, and a massive increase in government subsidies to encourage migration from the central provinces and Ukraine to Siberia.

Stolypin's reforms, although ultimately unsuccessful in solving Russia's agrarian problems (as witnessed in 1917), together with the facilitation of west-east transport and movement via Witte's new Trans-Sib, resulted in a huge tide of peasant migration and settlement into Siberia, probably the largest shift of human population anywhere in the early twentieth century. In Treadgold's words: 'Stolypin coupled a policy of fostering the growth of individualization in land tenure and use with an effort to encourage migration on a broad scale. For several years this policy swept Russia like wildfire.'[42]

The igneous image obviously presents an exaggerated picture, but there is no doubt as to the consequences of the new policy. Overall figures vary in different sources, but on a rough calculation, one can extrapolate a number of something in the order of 3.5 million peasant migrants crossing the Urals between 1906 (the introduction of the legislation) and the end of 1913 (the eve of the First World War). Some of the figures include so-called 'scouts' (*khodiki*), i.e. people sent ahead to reconnoitre suitable localities for settlement and report back, and do not take account of 'returnees', those who were unable to settle and returned to European Russia. On the other hand, they fail to include both criminal and political exiles who remained and settled in the territory even after their sentences were complete.[43] In just eight years, therefore, the numbers of migrants settling in Siberia exceeded by more than 1 million the total of all immigrants coming into the territory, either voluntarily or involuntarily, during the whole century between 1801 and 1900.[44]

Stolypin's new migration policy must be understood in the context of the agrarian problem in Russia as a whole, and, following the turmoil of 1905, of the government's urgent need to pacify the overwhelming peasant majority of the population, without alienating or affecting the interests of the noble landowning class. Put simply:

> The basic purpose of the reform was to preserve the system of noble land-tenure (*pomeshchich'e zemlevladenie*) by means of creating a new base of rural support [i.e. for the government] in the shape of the rich peasantry (*kulachestvo*) which would lead to the plundering of the peasant commune, and through the emigration of the dissatisfied to the outlying territories.[45]

Accordingly, the emigration agencies flooded the villages with propaganda leaflets, urging the peasants to take advantage of the opportunities offered in Siberia and beguiling them with promises of abundant land, privileges and low-interest loans to encourage their resettlement. Lenin, typically, took a very cynical view of the campaign, which he regarded as an operation designed 'to get rid of the *restless* peasants to Siberia', a policy which pursued purely 'political aims, and took absolutely no account of the interests of either the migrants or the old inhabitants' of Siberia.[46] While Lenin – again typically – may be overstating the case, there is no doubt that there were many drawbacks and deficiencies in the organization of the trans-Urals exodus, and many did not find it to be the Promised Land flowing with milk and honey as the proponents of the scheme had prophesied. The loans were far lower than promised, travelling conditions on the Trans-Sib, often in cattle wagons, were squalid, insanitary and overcrowded. The bureaucratic agencies, both west and east of the Urals, were often unhelpful and inefficient, and the archives contain thousands of complaints from both native peoples and the old inhabitants (*starozhily*) about their own lands being sequestered by the state to allocate to the new settlers. Documents, including official reports, letters and petitions of the immigrants, contemporary memoirs and scholarly researches also contain a wealth of information concerning instances of the outrageous and arbitrary behaviour of officialdom, lack of adequate facilities, bribery, theft and corruption, incorrect payment of promised subsidies and loans, insufficient amenities, harassment, and painting overall 'a picture of terrifying chaos and confusion'.[47]

Despite these abuses, which Western commentators have often overlooked or ignored, the immigrants continued to flow in, although after a peak around 1908, numbers (albeit still in their hundreds of thousands) began to decline steadily while the number of 'returnees' seems to have increased, though the figures for these are less reliable.[48]

Overall, though obviously conditions varied from province to province, and depending on the industry, expertise, resilience and determination of the would-be new settlers, the 'Great Siberian Migration', facilitated by the building of the Trans-Sib, must finally be judged a success in terms of boosting the population of Siberia, adding to its agricultural development and production, and in general bringing about a greater level of integration between the European and Asiatic portions and populations of the Russian

Empire. However, although this part of the government's policy appears to have succeeded, where it noticeably failed was in its attempt to defuse popular discontent, which still continued to simmer during the suppression of one revolutionary situation in 1905 and the more critical outbreak of others in 1917. One such example of the continued confrontation between the discontented and exploited lower classes of Russian society and the tsarist authorities was what is usually referred to as the 'Lena Goldfields Massacre'.[49]

At the beginning of 1912, the Russian Empire, seven years after the revolutionary drama of 1905, gave the surface appearance to the outside world of relative tranquillity. Compared to the years of the 'Red Cockerel' and the strikes, mutinies and civil strife of 1905, the Russian people seemed to have lapsed into a state of temporary quiescent exhaustion. Elections had taken place, following the Prime Minister's unconstitutional alteration of the voting system disenfranchising much of the population, which, not surprisingly, returned a conservative, right-wing Duma. Stolypin's agrarian reforms were showing some progress (even though their author was assassinated in 1911). The economy was picking up after the slump years of 1902–5. On the cultural front, *belles lettres*, art and the intellectual community seemed to be experiencing something of a renaissance, not that the fancy symbolist poetry and abstruse quasi-religious philosophizing of the age affected the largely illiterate masses. The revolutionary parties themselves were in a state of disarray, riven by internal ideological squabblings and with most of their leaders either abroad or in exile. The superficial calm, however, was soon shattered, and the origin for the recrudescence of mass protest occurred far from the capital in the prosperous goldfields of north-east Siberia on the river Lena and its tributaries.

The discovery of the precious metal in the region during the early nineteenth century led to a 'gold-rush' that rapidly made many fortunes, originally for Siberian merchant entrepreneurs, who eventually sold out to powerful business companies with equally powerful political connections. The largest of these mining enterprises at the turn of the nineteenth and twentieth centuries was the giant Lena Gold-mining Company (*Lenzoto*) owning 423 mines in the basins of the Lena, Olekma, Vitim and Bodaibo rivers, and controlling over one-third of Siberia's gold production. The workers lived in filthy, freezing huts or barracks, wages were grotesquely low and often paid in coupons rather than cash, which could only be spent at the company stores, women were routinely abused, the average working day was 11.5 hours, labour contracts were almost impossible to terminate, the rate of industrial injuries, often fatal, was distressingly high, sanitation and medical provisions were crude and abysmally insufficient, and as recently as the late nineteenth century floggings for breaches of labour discipline were frequent. Lenzoto's workers already had a history of strikes before 1912, but the flashpoint for the infamous Lena shootings *(Lenskii rasstrel)* came in February 1912 at the Andreevskii mine.

The famous naval mutiny on the battleship *Potëmkin* during the 1905 revolution had been sparked off by the crew's complaints about the putrid, maggot-ridden condition of the ship's meat. Similarly, the serving of rotten horsemeat in the works' canteen, later identified as a stallion's putrescent penis, led to a protest and walk-out by the Andreevskii miners. They defied orders to return to work, and within days the strike had spread throughout the region from one minework to another and far into the taiga. The workers' demands had now gone well beyond complaints about a horse's pizzle, and called for a 30 per cent wage increase, an 8-hour working day, restrictions on female and child labour, lifting of fines, improved medical facilities, better housing, recognition of workers' committees and the removal of 27 members of the company's management. Some degree of cohesion and organization was given to the strike by workers who were members of the Bolshevik Party. After some days' stand-off, the management, in cahoots with local police and government officials, and in telegraphic touch with St Petersburg, arrested a number of the strike leaders. Armed troops were also ominously deployed, under the command of one Captain N.V. Treshchenkov, assistant police chief of Irkutsk, a man already notorious for his bloody suppression of strikes elsewhere and with an unsavoury reputation for his excessive drinking and sexual habits.

Incensed by the arrests and the high-handed action of the authorities, on the morning of 4 April a crowd of over 3,000 protesting, unarmed workers gathered to march on the headquarters of the Nadezhdinskii mine to hand in their individual handwritten petitions, as requested by the management. There have been suggestions that this was a ploy on the part of the authorities to get as many people together in one place at one time in order that any military action would be more effective. As the peaceful demonstrators approached the settlement, Treshchenkov's men were given the order to open fire. In the ensuing fusillades around 500 workers were killed or seriously wounded. Estimates of the precise number of the dead, as with the calculations following the 1905 slaughter on Bloody Sunday, vary from source to source, and the real figure will probably never be determined. The response to the massacre again recalled the aftermath of Bloody Sunday as a tide of indignation, sympathetic strikes and industrial unrest swept throughout Siberia and beyond. However, the remoteness of the tragedy's location meant that the repercussions were not quite as dramatic or earth-shaking as the shockwaves following Bloody Sunday. As the present author has written elsewhere: 'Hundreds of dead mine-workers in remote north-east Siberia, however many and however dead, just did not evoke quite the same public reaction as the sight of countless corpses bleeding in the snow on Palace Square in front of the royal residence. And there were not many foreign journalists on the lower Lena at the time.[50]

Nevertheless, the Lena goldfields massacre did signal the beginning of a marked upswing in labour unrest that was to rumble on throughout the country until the outbreak of the First World War in 1914. But before moving on to consider the impact on Siberia of the Great War, the revolutions of 1917 which partly resulted from it and the ensuing Civil War, it is worth saying a few words about the weird Siberian peasant, self-proclaimed holy man and malign presence in the royal household – the notorious Grigorii Rasputin (c.1864/5/9/72–1916).

THE SIBERIAN SVENGALI

Svengali is the name of a character in George Du Maurier's melodramatic 1894 novel, *Trilby*, set in the 'Bohemian' society of mid-nineteenth-century Paris. He, Svengali, is described by the author thus: '[He] would either fawn or bully ... both tawdry and dirty in his person ... greasily and mattedly unkempt ... seeking whom he might cheat, betray, exploit ... was about as bad as they make 'em'.[51] The name of this fictitious, plausible rogue soon passed into language and literature as a byword for an evil manipulator, conman and mesmeric predator on females. He was also a skilled practitioner of hypnotism. Du Maurier might well have been describing the real-life – indeed, one might say larger than life – figure of Grigorii Rasputin, whose scandalous activities and malignant personality became so intimately entwined in the final years of the last Romanov royal family.

Rasputin was not, as often erroneously described, a 'mad monk'. This is wrong on two counts. First, although bizarre in his behaviour, he was not mad in the clinical sense of having been medically certified as suffering from any kind of mental disability or morbid psychiatric condition. Second, he was not an ordained or inducted member of any officially recognized monastic order, nor did he possess any kind of ecclesiastical status. What he was, was a filthy, malodorous, lecherous, priapic Siberian peasant; a self-proclaimed 'holy man'; a charlatan, horse-thief and drunkard who, through trickery, fraud, magnetic personality and the extraordinary gullibility of those with whom he came into contact, progressed from his hovel in his native village of Pokrovskoe in Tobolsk province, west Siberia, to be lionized in the boudoirs, bedchambers and brothels of St Petersburg. He was also attached to an extreme schismatic sect of religious perverts and flagellants (the *khlysty*) who believed in the 'doctrine', and practice, of redemption through sin, especially sexual sin.

When he was not busy debauching the swooning, grateful ladies of the capital's high society, connections were made through which he was soon introduced into the royal household. The reason for this was that, among his other dubious accomplishments, Rasputin also had a reputation for clairvoyance, faith-healing and therapeutic hypnotism. The heir to the throne, the tsarevich Aleksei, suffered from haemophilia. His mother, the tsarina Alexandra, was a highly strung and emotional woman, inclined to mysticism, spiritualism and any kind of quackery that might act as a cure, or at least a palliative, for her son's suffering. Given the combined circumstances of the boy's illness, the empress' psychopathic emotional state and rumours of Rasputin's alleged miracle-working powers, it is hardly surprising that he was welcomed into the Winter Palace with such alacrity. There is some evidence

Figure 8 Postcard of 1917 depicting Rasputin and Empress Alexandra in a compromising pose. The Russian word under the picture, '*Samoderzhavie*', means '*Autocracy*', cognate with the verb '*derzhat*", meaning 'to hold'. The pun implying the hold of Rasputin on the wife of the autocrat is obvious.
Source: Houghton Library in Figes, O. and Kolonitskii, B., *Interpreting the Russian Revolution: The Language and Symbols of 1917* (New Haven, CT, 1999), facing p. 120.

that, under the spell of Rasputin's mesmeric gaze, the tsarevich's pain and occasional profuse bleeding were in some way actually assuaged. This seemingly miraculous ability naturally endeared the 'holy man' to the royal couple and he soon inveigled himself right into the heart of the family, not only as a healer, but also as political adviser and 'friend'. This was not without serious ramifications for the country's governance. On Rasputin's advice – usually in return for sexual favours and lavish gifts bestowed by ambitious politicians – a parade of ludicrously inept, senile and mentally suspect characters were promoted to a number of high ministerial positions during the heyday of Rasputin's influence at court. This was particularly dangerous at a time when Russia was already in the throes of a disastrous international war with Germany and Austria-Hungary. The toxic mixture of Rasputin's libidinous shenanigans, his scandalous rampages through the bars and bordellos of St Petersburg, his intimacy with the discredited royal family, his pernicious political influence and his suspected pro-German sympathies, led to something like a public outcry. There is, however, almost certainly no truth in the salacious innuendoes that the Siberian peasant enjoyed sexual relations with the tsarina or her daughters, a canard which was the ribald subject of scurrilous popular cartoons depicting the pair of them in indecent juxtaposition (see Fig. 8).

Rasputin, neither 'mad monk' nor even a genuinely holy man, but a weird, philandering confidence trickster stoically enduring chronic satyriasis was finally done to death in appropriately bizarre circumstances arranged by a member of the royal family and a bunch of extreme right-wing politicians in December 1916. Prince Felix Yusupov, husband of the tsar's favourite niece, the richest man in Russia and a practising homosexual, lured Rasputin to a late-night party at his palace, where he was poisoned with a stiff cocktail of best Madeira and potassium cyanide, shot three times, beaten about the head with a dumbbell and his body dumped beneath the ice of the frozen river Neva. Scarcely two months later, the empire collapsed, as Rasputin had prophesied it would if he were to be killed. But there is, of course, no causal connection between the two events, other than the indirect factor that it was the machinations and malevolent influence of the peasant pseudo-priest from Siberia that was partly instrumental in finally undermining any residual public loyalty that there might have been for 'Bloody Nicholas'. How the 'last tsar of Siberia' finally lost his throne, and the impact that the revolutions of 1917 had on Rasputin's homeland, is the subject of the following chapter.

8

Red Siberia: Revolution and Civil War

The repercussions of the Lena goldfields shootings in terms of strikes, walk-outs, demonstrations and subversive working-class activity, including proletariat-versus-police punch-ups, were building up to a potentially revolutionary climax in the first half of 1914.[1] More workers were on strike between January and July 1914 than throughout the entire crisis of 1905. However, Germany's declaration of war against Russia on 1 August led to a brief upsurge of jingoistic, bellicose chauvinism, which for a short period brought about a spurious sense of national solidarity and a brief pause in the industrial unrest. This apparent domestic unity, however, was soon shattered as Russia's armies suffered defeat after disastrous defeat on her western front. Despite some successes in early engagements with the forces of Austria-Hungary, the Russian army's battering at the battle of Tannenberg in August, which cost 300,000 men, really set the pattern for the empire's fortunes or misfortunes throughout the rest of the war. Like Tollund Man, her ill-equipped peasants in uniform were sucked into the deadly mire of the mud- and blood-baths of Russia's western marches. Included among the fallen were thousands of recruits and conscripts from Siberia and the Far East, who knew even less of the reasons for which they were forced to fight in the battlegrounds of eastern Europe – half a world away from their villages and homelands in northern Asia – than did European Russia's home-grown cannon fodder. Siberian regiments fought bravely at Tannenberg, Galicia, in the autumn of 1914, and on dozens of other local fronts. Their sacrifice was, of course, in vain.

Apart from its fighting and falling manpower, Siberia's main contribution to the war effort was – consequent to naval blockades in the Baltic, the Dardanelles and the White Sea harbours of Murmansk and Arkhangelsk – as a conduit for the supply of military materiel through the port of Vladivostok and on to the western front via the Trans-Sib. Not that all supplies arrived at their intended destination. The import of so many weapons from the Allies – guns, bullets, shells, grenades, etc. – far outstripped the railroad's capacity to move them westward. Thousands of tons of equipment remained literally bogged down in Siberia and the Far East, later to be captured and utilized by various contenders in the ensuing Civil War (see below).

The patriotic fervour that attended the outbreak of hostilities rapidly dissipated, and the government's bungling conduct of the war, now exacerbated by the tsar's ludicrous and disastrous decision to take over personal supreme operational command of his armies at the front, led to a political crisis in February 1917 in which Nicholas faced no realistic alternative but to throw in the blood-soaked royal towel and abdicate. This low-key enacted event, though of world-shaking proportions, took place on 2 March in the rather undramatic surroundings of a dismal railway siding in the town of Pskov, to where the emperor's train had been diverted by militant workers while on its way from military headquarters at Mogilëv to Petrograd (as St Petersburg – a Teutonic place name – had been renamed at the start of hostilities with Germany). In the capital a combination of street parades marking international Women's Day on 23 February, angry bread queues, citywide strikes, mutinies of the garrison troops, news of the virtual vote of no confidence in the commander-in-chief by the general staff, attacks on the police and the disaffection of Duma politicians led inexorably to the small-minded tsar almost nonchalantly shrugging off the leadership of the world's largest land-empire like water off a lame duck's back. From the telegrams and letters passed between the uxorious emperor and his deranged consort, it is clear that in the throes of the bloodiest war in his country's history, the Autocrat of All Russia was much more concerned with his children's measles than with the slaughter of thousands of his subjects at the front. So much for the benign image of the *tsar-batyushka* (little father), which, since 'Bloody Sunday' in 1905, had scant credibility in any case. However, the people's revolution of February 1917 succeeded in bringing to an ignominious end the three-century-old Romanov Empire, and with it the near three-and-a-half centuries' tsardom of Siberia, to where Citizen Romanov and his brood were soon to be dispatched, though spared the heavy fetters with which his own convicted exiles had been enchained.

Following Nicholas's abdication, two centres of political authority appeared in Petrograd: the unelected first Provisional Government, composed mainly of upper-class centre-right politicians from the now dispersed fourth Duma, and the popularly elected Petrograd Soviet (i.e. 'council') of Workers' and Soldiers' Deputies. This unique situation was described by Lenin as 'dual power' (*dvoevlastie*), which lasted until the final takeover of total political power by the Bolshevik-dominated Petrograd Soviet on the night of 25–6 October, the arrest of most members of the last Provisional Government and the formation of the world's first revolutionary socialist government – the Soviet of People's Commissars (*Sovnarkom*). Vladimir Lenin was its chairman, Lev Trotskii its Commissar for Foreign Affairs, and Josef Stalin, recently returned from Siberian exile via the Trans-Sib, its Commissar for Nationalities, i.e. the non-Russian peoples of the old empire, including, of course, those of Siberia. All three were veterans of the Siberian exile system, and all three were to play a dramatic role in the history of Russia, and the world.

The first two actions of the new government were to pass the Decree on Peace and the Decree on Land, the former promising an end to Russia's participation in the war, and the latter more or less rubber-stamping the peasants' spontaneous seizure and redistribution of privately owned estates, a grass-roots movement which had been, in Trotskii's phrase, 'the subsoil of the revolution'. Both the February and October revolutions began as essentially metropolitan affairs, but what happened on the streets of Petrograd in 1917 quickly reverberated throughout the stricken empire, affecting the most far-flung regions of the country.

Among the farthest flung were, of course, Siberia and the Russian Far East. The collapse of tsarism at the centre meant that all the props and institutions of autocracy throughout the land collapsed with it. Provincial governors, the courts, the hated police and gendarmerie, gentry-dominated local councils, and both the urban and rural bureaucracies no longer had any base of power or authority. The peasants justifiably grabbed the land, soldiers understandably fled from the human abattoir of eastern Europe ('voting with their feet', in Lenin's pedestrian phrase), local soviets and peasants' and workers' committees spontaneously took over the administration of their own regional affairs, and, in the old empire's borderlands, long-nursed ambitions for local or national independence from Russian imperial rule were given the opportunity for unrestrained expression – and action. Throughout the whole country a kaleidoscope of politically diverse groupings, independent institutions, assemblies, councils, soviets and self-styled regional governments sprang up like poppies in Flanders fields. Not all of them, however, were red.

In Siberia, at one point in 1918 there were at least 19 different 'governments' of varying political hues operating between Chelyabinsk and Vladivostok. Over the next four years, the only quality that these bodies shared was their ephemerality. The ruination of the Romanov regime and the crumbling of its agents' authority meant that for the first time since the sixteenth century Siberia was free from the direct rule of Moscow or St Petersburg. The occasion thus presented itself for the public assertion and implementation of political regional agenda. Apart from ultra-right-wingers and monarchists, the main contenders in the Siberian political arena were: the Constitutional Democrats (Kadets), a 'liberal' party of the centre-left;[2] the regionalists (*oblastniki*), many still intent on establishing some kind of independent Siberian republic, but with little popular support; the neo-populist Socialist-Revolutionary Party (SRP), which had gained a majority of the votes in the elections for a national Constituent Assembly in November-December 1917, a body unceremoniously dispersed by the new Soviet government on 6 January 1918; and the Marxist Social Democrats, both Bolshevik and Menshevik. In order properly to understand the nature and the course of the Revolution and Civil War in Siberia, these political groupings need closer examination.

LEFT, RIGHT: RED, WHITE

Support for the extreme right and those in favour of a restoration of the monarchy was initially negligible, only gaining some ground after the spring of 1918 during the so-called, misnamed 'democratic counter-revolution' (see below). The anti-Bolshevik, anti-Soviet nature of this movement was certainly counter-revolutionary, but democratic it emphatically was not. Its only support came from superannuated officials of the defunct tsarist establishment, rich business-men, dispossessed landowners and senior officers of the old imperial armed forces, with its main base in Omsk. Even at the peak of its uncertain ascendancy during the period of Admiral A.V. Kolchak's dictatorship (November 1918–February 1920, see below) it had no clear political programme, no organiza-tional homogeneity and no effective social or economic policies that could appeal to the bulk of the population. Essentially, its adherents and hangers-on were too closely identified with the dodo Romanov dynasty and its strutting aristocratic sycophants to stand any realistic chance of political victory over the forces of revolutionary change. This basic lack of popular support was a princi-pal cause of the 'White' movement's ultimate defeat in the Civil War, of which Siberia was the largest theatre.

The Kadets' limited backing came from sections of Siberia's tiny urban middle class, but that support was diluted by the attraction that many professional people and some members of the intelligentsia felt for the region-alists' programme, however amorphous (see below). But the Constitutional Democrats were suspicious of the *oblastniki*'s preoccupation with purely regional issues, whereas the professedly more 'worldly', Western-oriented (or occidented) Kadets dismissed what they regarded as this petty parochialism in favour of championing a centralized Great Russian state. But perhaps the largest white albatross around the Constitutional Democratic Party's neck was its former participation in the popularly despised Provisional Governments between February and October 1917. Although the Kadets in the fourth State Duma, led vociferously by Pavel Milyukov (1859–1943), had spearheaded anti-government feeling in the house, after the February Revolution they were tainted with the failure of all four Provisional Governments to deal effectively with the two most urgent problems of the day: land redistribution and Russia's participation in the war. After the October Revolution and the commencement of the Civil War, the Kadets in Siberia drifted further to the right of the political spectrum, even espousing the idea of a one-man dicta-torship. This is not the right place to discuss the philosophical, political and nationalist traditions of Russian 'liberalism', but it is quite clear that with the extreme polarization of revolutionary and counter-revolutionary politics during the Civil War in Siberia, indeed throughout Russia, the lily-livered policies of a putative centre party had as much chance of success as a Siberian snowball in the Sahara. There is no word in the Russian language for 'compromise' (apart from the Western lexical borrowing, *kompromiss*). As Aleksandr Herzen once remarked, Russia does not understand the concept of '*le juste milieu*'.

The Siberian *oblastniki* not surprisingly pressed their demands for greater autonomy for Siberia, with a regional administration acting independently *within* a Russian federation to promote the discrete interests of Siberia and its peoples as opposed to those of central government. However, following the February Revolution the whole territory was in such a state of disarray and administrative chaos that it is very difficult to draw a coherent picture of regionalist politics during this period. There were just so many conflicting views, interests, programmes and contending factions that any kind of clear vision or plan for Siberian autonomy, independence, separatism, nationhood, federalism or indeed of *oblastnichestvo* as a viable, realizable concept is shrouded in obscurity and confusion.[3] To repeat the mythological allusion used in the previous chapter in relation to the Trans-Sib, the whole notion of a separate Siberian state, or even an autonomous part of some kind of federal republic, was also a chimera.

Before the February 1917 Revolution, the Siberian regionalists' cause had been propagated mainly in intellectual circles, newspapers, scholarly publications and local associations. But from early 1917 until 1920, during the upheavals of the Revolution and Civil War, it became a real, immediate and practical issue for hard political struggle, and also for internal schism within the regionalist movement itself. Like all the other political parties or groupings, the *oblastniki* were riven with left, centre and right factions, personal rivalries and even inter-regional disputes. There was little talk of all-out separatism, but a large number of enthusiastic meetings, assemblies and congresses – even self-proclaimed temporary governments – were convened in hurly-burly circumstances throughout Siberia and the Far East. These adopted various regionalist slogans, called for greater regional autonomy or independence, raised the green and white regionalist flag (symbolizing the forests and snows of Siberia) and advocated elections to a Siberian Regional Duma. However, despite the progressive nature of the *oblastniki*'s rhetoric, it found little resonance among the mass of the Siberian people, and was to a large extent confined to the chattering classes in the university town of Tomsk, where various congresses and conferences took place mainly under the nominal chairmanship of Grigorii Potanin, who, after the death of Nikolai Yadrintsev in 1894, had become the undisputed doyen of Siberian regionalism, though by the time of the Revolution he was well into his dotage, still mentally alert but physically feeble and almost blind. In a sense, it could be argued that his debility and myopia were symbolic of the regionalists' general incapacity to act or see forward in any politically meaningful way, despite their best efforts. As it happened, a meeting of the self-styled 'All-Siberian Congress' attended by 169 delegates from all over the territory at the Tomsk Technological Institute in October 1917 was overtaken by more dramatic events in Petrograd – the Bolshevik Revolution, which was to alter the complexion of Siberia's development for the rest of the century.

The political party that won most support from the Siberian peasantry, including old inhabitants and recent settlers, which together accounted for around 90 per cent of the population, was the Socialist-Revolutionary Party (SRP). This is hardly surprising, given that the vast majority of Siberia's population was composed of peasants, and that the SRP based its political programme on the inalienable right of the peasants to their own land. Also, on the eve of the February Revolution, there were over 600 Socialist-Revolutionary political exiles in Siberia, scattered through the towns of Irkutsk, Krasnoyarsk, Novonikolaevsk, Tomsk and others, organized into 15 Socialist-Revolutionary organizations and political groups. It is therefore reasonable to assume that they exercised a not inconsiderable influence on the peasant population of Siberia.[4] In the all-Russian elections to the Constituent Assembly in November to December 1917, the Socialist-Revolutionaries received 50 per cent of the Siberian vote (compared to the Bolsheviks' 10 per cent). However, the SRP, far from forming a solid, unified bloc, presented a patchwork of contending allegiances, factions and splinter groups with no common leadership, and no coherent programme of action. Right from the foundation of the party back in 1901, it had had its 'right' and 'left' fractions, its maximalists and its minimalists, even a terrorist wing with its 'fighting detachments', responsible for scores of political assassinations in the tradition of the mid-nineteenth-century populist parties.

In Siberia, after the February Revolution, and more so after the October Revolution, the split within party ranks became even more polarized, with the 'right' Socialist-Revolutionaries gravitating towards the Kadets and some regionalists, and the 'left' Socialist-Revolutionaries, some of whom, though eschewing Marxist ideology and theories of the class struggle, even briefly made common cause with the Bolsheviks. Those who did not were, of course, condemned by the new Soviet government as 'counter-revolutionary', and most Soviet Marxist commentators have traditionally insisted that the SRP essentially represented the interest of the petit-bourgeois class, with no roots in the proletariat or the 'poor' (i.e. non-kulak) peasantry. However, that assessment seems to be contradicted by the results of the elections to the Constituent Assembly. This is one of the reasons why Lenin dissolved it, and also brings us to a consideration of the position of the Russian Social-Democratic Workers' Party (*Rossiiskaya Sotsial-demokraticheskaya rabochaya partiya*, RSDRP) in Siberia.

This is not the place to rehearse in detail the origins of Russian Marxism, the creation of the RSDRP or the organizational and ideological polemics that led to the split of the party in 1903 into the two opposed factions, which came to be known as the Bolsheviks and the Mensheviks.[5] Without oversimplification, the Bolsheviks are traditionally described as the 'hard-liners', Lenin believing in organizational centralization and discipline (what he called 'democratic centralism'), unswerving devotion to the party programme and the leading role of the party as the 'avant-garde' of the proletariat in the revolutionary struggle against the twin enemies of Russian tsarism and international capitalism. The Mensheviks, initially led by Yulii Martov (1873–1923), took a less authoritarian line, advocating a broader membership of the party and active co-operation with, rather than opposition to, other anti-government organizations. Much of these arguments and inner-party feuds may sound rather arcane, and in any case were largely confined to the activists and propagandists in the party leadership. Many of the political nuances and semantic intricacies of the Bolshevik/Menshevik dispute were entirely lost on the ordinary workers at factory-floor level, even those who were party members.

If this were the case in European Russia, it was even more so in Siberia, where Bolsheviks and Mensheviks – already thin on the ground – regularly co-operated at both rank-and-file and local leadership levels. (The 'Yakutsk protest', described in the previous chapter, is a case in point.) Quite a large number of senior members of the Bolshevik Party, including Stalin, were in Siberia as political exiles at the time of the February Revolution, but used this occasion to return to the epicentre of events in Petrograd and Moscow, which was where, for a while, most of the political action was played out. Social-Democratic Party discipline and leadership in Siberia were therefore quite weak, though their strength fluctuated from town to town, and from urban centres to the countryside. In the villages, the major source of Bolshevik support came from peasant soldiers returning from the battlefields of Russia's western front, known therefore as *frontoviki*. These were mainly young, battle-hardened, embittered and politically radicalized ex-conscripts who were attracted to the Bolsheviks, rather than the Mensheviks, by the formers' slogans and revolutionary programme of 'Peace and Land' and 'All Power to the Soviets' – i.e. the elected representative organs of the common people. A combination of still-armed *frontoviki* and new settlers, many of whom had not yet acquired a fully legal right to their land under the old regime, was chiefly responsible for the great surge of spontaneous peasant uprisings and land seizures that swept through the countryside, on both sides of the Urals, in the summer and early autumn of 1917. In this way, the mainly urban-based Social-Democrats attracted – for a while – rural support. Why that support swiftly evaporated is explained below. Of the towns themselves, the most militant and pro-Bolshevik was Krasnoyarsk on the river Yenisei. The town thereby revived its reputation for left-wing militancy, which it had already earned during the revolutionary events of 1905, and in August 1917 an assembly of 5,000 Bolshevik supporters convened and founded the 'Central Siberian Regional Bureau' to direct party activities and secure control of all workers', soldiers' and peasant soviets in the territory.

After the October Revolution the Bolsheviks succeeded in giving substance to Lenin's slogan of 'All Power to the Soviets' by establishing 'Soviet power' in most of the major towns in Siberia with astonishing speed. The reason why it was astonishing was the numerical weakness of the industrial working class in Siberia, which is where the party's major support lay, rather than in the peasantry, which leaned overwhelming to the SRP, and also the relative loose-ness of party organization and leadership. But two factors facilitated the Bolsheviks' early success. These were the support and involvement of the radicalized *frontoviki* mentioned above, and the opportunistic use of the Trans-Sib, staffed by militant railroad workers, which acted as a fast conduit for the rapid spread of revolutionary activity through the towns, stations and depots along its track. Soviet power was declared in 'Red Krasnoyarsk' by the end of

October, only a few days after the Bolshevik coup in Petrograd, quickly followed by Omsk, Tomsk, Irkutsk, Chita, Khabarovsk and Vladivostok. The west-east crimson tide was not, of course, without opposition. There were plenty of counter-revolutionary groynes, dykes and dams in its path, but the anti-Bolshevik protests, demonstrations and occasional mutinies suffered from lack of coordination and political cohesion, which together contributed considerably to the initial advance of Soviet – i.e. Bolshevik – power. In the Far East, the most ferocious expression of anti-Bolshevism was the so-called *atamanshchina* – a blood-curdling campaign of inhuman atrocities led by wild cossak atamans (chieftains) and warlords whose savageries will be returned to below.

At the end of January 1918, the Central Executive Committee of Siberian Soviets (*Tsentrosibir'*) ordered the dispersal of the Siberian Regional Duma, recently established at Tomsk, thereby repeating the precedent of abolishing elected bodies regarded as counter-revolutionary already established with Lenin's dissolution of the Constituent Assembly in Petrograd a few weeks earlier. However, despite the sudden appearance of urban and rural soviets in large areas of southern Siberia in the first months of the revolution, the consolidation of Soviet power throughout the region was a formidable task, bedevilled by remoteness from the political centre in Moscow (to where the capital of the new Russian Soviet Federative Socialist Republic [RSFSR] had been transferred from Petrograd in March 1918), lack of strong local leadership, conflicts of interests among different party organizations and the now growing confidence of anti-Bolshevik opposition groupings. Another big problem for the Soviet regime – one of the principal causes of its unpopularity among the majority peasantry – was the introduction of its economic policy of what was called 'War Communism'. Without going into all the details and history of this much resented programme, one of its most unpopular, and fiercely opposed, features was that of *prodrazvërstka*, meaning something like 'redistribution of produce', a euphemism for the forcible requisitioning of grain and other agricultural produce from the peasantry by armed squads of Red Amy soldiers, officers and Communist Party officials in order to feed the towns and army units. In 1917 the Bolsheviks had promised 'Peace and Land', and now, in mid-1918, they were in effect conducting a war on the peasantry, by sequestering at gunpoint the fruit of their recently acquired land.[6] Not unsurprisingly, the peasants throughout Russia and Siberia regarded this as a reactivation of tsarist-style high-handedness and cupidity.

By the late spring of 1918, the Bolshevik/Soviet grip on Siberia had already begun to weaken. However, two unforeseen events were to cause it to break: the landing of Japanese interventionist military forces at Vladivostok in April, and the revolt of the 'Czech Legion' in May. The Civil War in Siberia had now started in earnest.

THE 'DEMOCRATIC COUNTER-REVOLUTION'

Japan took advantage of the Russian central government's weakness in the Far East to press its own territorial ambitions in that region. In April 1918 a Japanese expeditionary force, with hesitant US backing, retaliated against Russian assaults on Japanese citizens stationed in Blagoveshchensk and Vladivostok by disembarking at Vladivostok, closely followed by military contingents of other foreign powers. This was the thin end of the interventionist wedge. Over the next few months thousands of troops from many nations – Japan, China, America, Britain, France, Canada and more – poured into the Russian Far East ostensibly to support the rebellious Czech Legion (see below) and to protect their own national interests and assets in the region, but without any shared political or military agenda, other than a vague anti-Bolshevism. American forces, for instance, were ordered not to take sides in Russia's internal struggle, although in practice all their considerable material assistance went to the Whites. This powerful foreign backing for the counter-revolutionaries was one of the triggers for the reorganizing and re-energizing of the various anti-Red forces throughout Siberia in the early summer of 1918.

The other was the revolt of the Czech Legion. The so-called 'Legion' (*korpus*) originally consisted of a combination of Russian-born Czechs and both Czech and Slovak prisoners-of-war in Russian hands who were organized into regiments that fought alongside Russian troops on their western front. After the Bolshevik Revolution, Thomas Masaryk, leader of the Czechoslovak National Council in Paris, negotiated with the new Soviet government to have the legionaries evacuated from Russia in order that they could join the war against the Central Powers on Europe's western front. To this the Bolshevik government agreed, but only after the signing of the Treaty of Brest-Litovsk in March 1918, which unilaterally withdrew Russia from the war. The original plan was to evacuate the Czech forces via Murmansk and Arkhangelsk in the north, but logistical and strategic factors forced a change of route and it was decided to dispatch them along the Trans-Siberian Railroad to Vladivostok, then under Soviet control, whence they would embark on a voyage across the Pacific, through the Panama Canal and across the Atlantic to join the struggle on the European front.

The first armoured train-load of men and munitions (in Russian, *eshelon*) set off in mid-March. These men were no ragtag-and-bobtail army, nor even simply 'peasants in uniform', but well-disciplined, highly organized, properly educated, fully armed and eager to rejoin the fray, fired by the knowledge that the defeat of the Austria-Hungarian Empire would lead to the formation of an independent Czechoslovak state. In view of the highly volatile, indeed anarchical, nature of the territory through which they were to pass, under the terms of the evacuation the Czechs were allowed to retain their weapons for self defence. In numbers (up to 40,000 men), determination and discipline, the well-armed Czech soldiers were undoubtedly the most effective fighting force in the whole of Siberia at the time – as was soon to be proven. They were also – initially – strictly neutral in their attitude to the various contending left and right, Red and White forces during the birth pangs of the Russians' Civil War, though the majority of them probably leaned towards the socialists', if not the Bolsheviks', cause.[7] Their only objective was to get out of Russia back to the main battlefront in Europe, even if it meant almost circumnavigating the globe to reach it. It is an indication of their determination to add their strength to the anti-German, anti-Habsburg struggle that they were prepared to undertake a many thousand-mile train- and ocean-voyage across the world when initially they were positioned in an almost eye-ball-to-eye-ball confrontation with the soldiers of the Central Powers in the trenches of eastern Europe (see Fig. 9).

However, given the confused current political situation in Siberia, especially in the major towns through which the Legion's journey took them, it was practically impossible not to get involved in local disputes and antagonisms. At first there were a few minor confrontations with town soviets and pro-Bolshevik forces (including Hungarian 'internationalists' who wished the Czechs to 'join the revolution'), but in May the situation changed and the Czech Legion soon became a major factor in the Civil War in Siberia and a serious force of opposition to the Bolsheviks. The reason for this dramatic volte-face in the attitude of the Legion was that, following a sudden shoot-out between Czechs and pro-Bolshevik Hungarians at the station in Chelyabinsk, Trotskii, the new Commissar for War, sent out an ill-considered order for the total disarmament of the Czech Legion and called a halt to its onward journey to Vladivostok. His instructions read: 'All Soviets along the railroad are ordered, under heavy responsibility, to disarm the Czechs. Any Czech along the railroad found carrying a weapon is to be executed on the spot. Any train containing a *single* armed Czech is to be emptied and all passengers confined in a prisoner-of-war camp.'[8]

Trotskii's order was not only unenforceable, but also politically disastrous for recently established Soviet 'power' in Siberia. The Czechs, not surprisingly, rejected Trotskii's command, and informed him that, while they sympathized with the aims of the October Revolution, they nevertheless were not convinced that the Soviet government could guarantee their safe passage to Vladivostok. In these circumstances, the legionaries refused to surrender their arms and determined to proceed to the Far East, if necessary to fight their way there. At the time of Trotskii's ultimatum, 12,000 to 14,000 Czechs had already arrived in Vladivostok, while more than 20,000 straggled along the entire railroad, which they rapidly and easily seized, together with the major towns and depots along its route. In a very short space of time they had taken Novonikolaevsk (present-day Novosibirsk, a major junction on the river Ob), Chelyabinsk, Tomsk, Omsk, Irkutsk and pretty well all stations east from the Urals to the Pacific, leading to the disintegration of the local soviets, and an opportunity for the forces of the White counter-revolution – both military and political – to regroup and reassert themselves. The Czechs themselves made no attempt to govern or set up any kind of political authority in the centres they had taken over, but they had starkly revealed the impotence of 'Soviet power' in Siberia. The American historian, Richard Pipes, has argued that it was the revolt of the Czech Legion that provided the main impetus for the recruitment and formation of the ultimately triumphant Red Army in the spring of 1918.[9] While his argument is superficially plausible, it also clear that there were many other urgent reasons and imperatives for the conscription and organization of the Red Army in response to the raising of counter-revolutionary White military battalions elsewhere.

Figure 9   Armoured train of the Czech Legion in Siberia during the Civil War, 1918.
Source: Imperial War Museum, London.

The Czechoslovaks' easy victories persuaded the Allies to raise the level of their support for anti-Bolshevik forces, which, with enhanced foreign encouragement, now profited from the Siberian soviets' debacle by creating a number of new government authorities and institutions. In June the Czechs had taken over the town of Samara on the river Volga, and it was here that a number of the elected members of the national Constituent Assembly, dispersed on Lenin's orders in January 1918, reassembled and established a quasi-government, dominated by Socialist-Revolutionaries and calling itself the Committee of Members of the Constituent Assembly (*Komitet uchreditel'nogo sobraniya*), familiarly known by its acronym *Komuch*. In western Siberia, Komuch's main rival (Bolsheviks apart) was the self-styled Provisional Siberian Government (PSG) which formed itself in the vacuum created by the Omsk soviet's collapse, and became the virtual headquarters of the 'democratic counter-revolution'.

As mentioned earlier, 'counter-revolutionary' (i.e. anti-Bolshevik) these bodies certainly were, but there was very little about their flimsy mandate or their vacuous policies to qualify them for the label 'democratic'. While Komuch adopted a moderate socialist stance (after all, most of the members were Socialist-Revolutionaries), even raised the red flag and recruited a modest 'People's Army', the PSG was politically much further to the right, enjoying the support of the Kadet party – which despite its liberal protestations, had always been a party representing the interests of the wealthy middle classes – and the officer corps, introducing anti-trade union measures and returning property expropriated by the rebellious peasantry back to private landowners, as well as entertaining themselves by casually hanging or shooting a large number of uppity peasants. Many of the increasingly restless and influential army officers who gave their nominal support to the PSG, while at the same time disporting themselves in the clubs, bars and brothels of Omsk, scarcely distinguished between the Socialist-Revolutionaries and the Bolsheviks. Fine political thinking was hardly their forte. Not even widespread peasant resistance to Moscow's hated campaign of *prodrazvërstka* (requisitioning of agricultural produce from the peasantry), nor occasional outbreaks of working-class opposition to the Bolsheviks could unite the Samara-based Komuch and the Omsk PSG on a common platform. The White forces' pathetic inability to form a united front against the new revolutionary regime in Moscow was one of the principal factors that led to their ultimate defeat and the reinstatement of Soviet power in 1921. The White generals, admirals and officers in Siberia and on all other fronts were frankly inept, uncoordinated, arrogant and superciliously quite out of synch with the revolutionary ethos of the time – dinosaurs doomed to extinction.

Atrocious Atamans

Lack of unity in the White camp was not confined to the Samara/Omsk rivalry. At the other end of the old empire, in Transbaikalia and the Amur and Maritime provinces, some of the most bloody and horrific episodes of the Civil

War in the Far East were being enacted amid scenes of gut-churning, sickening savagery. The three most prominent psychopathic villains and self-styled atamans responsible for the macabre, tragic drama of the *atamanshchina* being played out beyond Baikal were Grigorii Semënov, 'Baron' Roman Ungern-Sternberg and Ivan Kalmykov. Between them, it is no exaggeration to say that they unleashed a reign of absolute, unmitigated terror in which mass murder, rape, torture and systematic slaughter of men, women and children – Russians, native Siberians and foreigners alike – were quotidian activities, part of the daily routine. Nothing on the scale of their remorseless, sadistic cruelties had occurred in Russia since the holocaust ignited by Ivan the Terrible in the sixteenth century.

Semënov, son of a cossak father and a Buryat mother, and junior officer in the Russian army, had raised a regiment of Buryat warriors originally intended to fight on the western front, but after the Bolshevik Revolution used them to create a military fiefdom under his own command in Transbaikalia with his headquarters at Chita, from where, aged only 27, he launched a brutal campaign ostensibly aimed against the Bolsheviks, but in reality destroying anyone or anything that stood in the way of his murderous and rapacious ambitions. Those ambitions were hardly political in the proper sense of the word. He was in reality simply a bloodthirsty and evil-minded bandit-king. In 1919, with lavish financial support from the Japanese, who had an interest in the continuing political instability of the region and whose gold and munitions enhanced the loot of Semënov's own armed robberies and extortions, he declared himself 'Ataman of the Transbaikal Cossak Host', and continued his fearsome depredations until the Red Army regained control and re-established Soviet power and a semblance of peace in the Far East in 1920–21. His wretched victims can be counted in their thousands, subject to mass shootings, hangings, mutilation, decapitation, burning alive and disembowelling. According to one commentator, Semënov bragged that he could not sleep peacefully at night unless he had killed at least one person during the day.[10] The number of those who daily perished at his hands must have induced a state of deep somnolence to rival that of the legendary Rip Van Winkle. It was certainly a drastic prophylactic against insomnia.

Ataman Semënov was aided and abetted in his criminal activities by one of the most loathsome creatures in the rogues' gallery of the Civil War, indeed one might even say in the annals of Siberia's entire history: Baron Roman Fëdorovich Ungern-Sternberg. Tracing his career or reading his biography is like delving into the deepest depths of human – or inhuman – wickedness, viciousness and pathological depravity.[11] Born into the Estonian nobility in 1885, Ungern-Sternberg saw military action as a young officer in the Far East during the Russo-Japanese War of 1904–5, and while there developed a taste for oriental mysticism and Buddhism. This was not, however, the benign, pacific Buddhism of the Western imagination, all joss-sticks, tinkling bells, transcendental meditation and navel-gazing, but of fierce warrior gods at whose feet the bloody Baron kowtowed in the temples of Urga in Mongolia on the eve of the First World War. According to James Palmer, it was the porno-graphic effigies in the Mongol temple of copulating deities, severed heads, naked, tortured sinners and mangled bodies 'speared by pendulous-breasted demonesses, frozen in icy lakes, consumed by scorpions' that served to 'tantalise his sadism'.[12] These grotesque images were not that too far removed from the real-life, real-death barbarities in which Ungern-Sternberg indulged his psychopathic lusts as self-proclaimed ruler of Dauria on the Mongolian-Manchurian frontier and later as virtual dictator of Mongolia. In 1921 his troops invaded the pro-Moscow Far Eastern Republic (see below) but were routed by the resurgent Red Army and their leader captured and sentenced to death by a Bolshevik military tribunal in Novonikolaevsk in 1921. His swift execution was a good deal more merciful than the agonizing torments that he and his brutal myrmidons had inflicted on their own victims during his grue-some reign of horror. A whole grotesque gamut of daily torture and agonizing execution methods had been a standard feature of Ungern-Sternberg's hellish regime (see Fig. 10).

All that has been said about the murderous, almost genocidal activities of Semënov and his psychotic acolyte, Ungern-Sternberg, could be repeated in relation to another notorious Far Eastern cossak warlord, Ivan Kalmykov. It would, however, be gratuitous to rehearse all the grisly details of his dreadful campaigns, save to say that this reptilian torturer, sadist and hands-on killer,

Figure 10   Ataman 'Baron' Ungern-Sternberg, one of the most cruel and sadistic Far Eastern atamans during the Civil War in Siberia.
Source: Photographer unknown.

operating as ataman of the Ussuri cossaks from his headquarters in Khabarovsk was, to quote W. Bruce Lincoln, 'complicit in every sort of murder, rape and robbery [and] violated the laws of nature, man and God in Siberia's Far East during the dark and bloody days of 1918 and 1919'.[13] Such was the extent of his legendary cruelty (though himself not yet 30 years of age) that his regime was commemorated by his own surname as the *Kalmykovshchina*.[14]

For all its barbarities, indeed, because of them, the *atamanshchina*, far from destroying Bolshevism, created so much suffering, popular loathing and fear that the great majority of the population was prepared to welcome, or at least give passive support to, the Red Army's and the Soviet government's successes in the closing months of the Civil War. Ultimately, the new Communist regime benefited both politically and militarily from the atamans' atrocities with which the White counter-revolutionary cause was bloodily and indelibly stained. What the atrocious atamans had sown in their campaign of indiscriminate slaughter was finally reaped in the political victory of the Soviet commissars. Before that victory, however, the course of the Civil War in Siberia was to take a number of dramatic turns.

The End of the Tsarism

Until their resurgence, the Bolsheviks continued to suffer a number of further reverses, being forced in July to August to abandon Simbirsk (Lenin's birthplace) and Kazan, the repository of the imperial gold reserves worth around 750 million rubles. These were now sequestered by the Whites and transported to Omsk, though to where they ultimately disappeared in the vortex of the Civil War is a question that has still to be properly answered. The whole financial and monetary situation in Siberia was a total mess. Among the various bizarre currencies in circulation were ex-tsarist rubles, 'Kerenskii coupons',[15] PSG bonds, printed notes known popularly as 'sibirki' and even cigarette packet labels. Jonathan Smele, in his excellent analysis of the financial farce in Civil War Siberia tells us that the PSG and afterwards the Kolchak government together:

> may have put into circulation by the end of 1919 some 150,000,000,000 roubles' worth of what were variously known as Omsk, Kolchak or Siberian Roubles, 'yellow money', or, familiarly, *sibirki*. As the presses rolled day in and day out at Omsk, in the words of a contemporary economist, 'the value of the Siberian Rouble multiplied and inflated until it approached the point at which begins complete nullification'.[16]

In other words the currency was not even worth the value of the paper it was printed on. Meanwhile, despite the economic chaos and the political impasse dividing Omsk and Samara, the Siberian Bolsheviks were still in disarray. But a notable casualty of the Reds' retreat was the execution of Nicholas Aleksandrovich Romanov, the last tsar of Siberia.

After his abdication in March 1917, the ex-tsar, his wife and children were placed under house arrest in the comfortable surroundings of their former palace at Tsarskoe Selo on the outskirts of Petrograd. Following the October Revolution, they and their entourage were transferred to confinement in Tobolsk in western Siberia, close to the home village of their murdered mentor, Rasputin. As the Civil War in Siberia and elsewhere gained pace, the Soviet government, fearing that the Romanovs would act as a rallying-point for right-wing, pro-monarchist, restorationist White tendencies, moved them westwards and incarcerated them in the town of Yekaterinburg in the Urals at the sequestered house of a retired merchant named Nikolai Ipatev, which came to be known as 'the house of special purpose'. The 'special purpose' was to be their execution. In the early hours of 17 July 1918, as Czech and White troops threatened to take the town, the family, their personal doctor and a couple of servants were woken from their sleep and ordered down into the cellar, where they were arranged, seated and standing as if for a group photograph, and gunned down by their Bolshevik guards. Despite various fanciful legends and rumours of the survival of the tsarevna Anastasia and the tsarevich Aleksei, there is today plenty of forensic evidence, following the discovery and exhumation of their acid-disfigured remains in the mid-1990s, that the entire royal family was exterminated. Also, recently released archival data seem to confirm information already committed by Trotskii to his personal diary that the execution order came directly from Lenin, the man whose elder brother, Aleksandr Ulyanov, had been hanged by Nicholas's father, Alexander III, in 1886. In terms of revolutionary justice, death by firing squad may have been a fitting end for Nicholas the Bloody, but hardly so for his innocent children, though tens of thousands of other children along with their parents had been killed in Nicholas's own campaigns of military and police suppression of civil protest, senseless international wars and brutal pogroms.

The rediscovered bones of the Romanov family were eventually interred in a specially prepared side-chapel of the Saints Peter and Paul Cathedral in the renamed St Petersburg, and Nicholas canonized by the Orthodox Church as St Nicholas the Passion Sufferer (*strastoterpets*). Among those attending the funeral was the then Russian President, Boris Yeltsin, himself a Siberian by origin, and the same man who years before, as Communist Party boss of Sverdlovsk (the old Yekaterinburg), had ordered the demolition of the still-standing Ipatev house. As the present author has written elsewhere: 'the obsequious obsequies which marked the internment of his and his family's relics can never disguise the fact that in life he was known by his own suffering subjects as Nicholas the Bloody – a fitting, sanguinary sobriquet for the last ruler of the blood-stained Romanov Empire'.[17]

The death of Nicholas in 1918 did not, of course, immediately save the Bolsheviks' fortunes, but the urgency of the situation in Siberia, as on other fronts, impelled the central government to inaugurate a vigorous campaign of military recruitment into the Red Army and reinforce its deployment over the Urals under the new command of the Latvian General I.I. Vatsetis in September, and later M.V. Frunze, one of the brightest luminaries of the Red

Army and a military theorist who had previously been twice sentenced to death and served hard labour in Siberia for his revolutionary activity. He was later to succeed Trotskii in 1925 as Soviet Commissar for War.

As Norman Pereira has correctly pointed out, had it not been for the anti-Bolshevik intervention of foreign powers it is very unlikely that the divided, mutually antagonistic and bickering White forces in Siberia could have held out as long as they did against the Reds. Komuch in Samara and the PSG in Omsk were still at each other's throats rather than combining their strength against the Communist enemy. In the late summer of 1918 Lenin identified Siberia as the 'main and critical theatre of the Civil War', and the successive appointments of Vatsetis and Frunze, in addition to massive eastwards disposition of troops from European Russia, 'turned the military tide back in favour of the soviets in Siberia'.[18] In the face of this gradual sea-change, the Allies, including the Czechs, applied fresh pressure on the feuding Whites to settle their differences and establish a concerted, united military and political front to halt the Red advance. Urgency was given to their appeals with the Bolsheviks' recapture of Kazan in September, just as the various White factions were assembling at Ufa in an attempt to reach an agreed course of action. The result was the formation on 23 September of the All-Russian Provisional Government (ARPG) with a five-man 'Directory', which included in the quincumvirate two Samara Socialist Revolutionaries and was headed by N.D. Avksentev, who had been Minister of the Interior in Kerenskii's last Provisional Government. In October the new 'government' shifted its seat to Omsk, and established – with no elections and therefore absolutely no democratic mandate – a Council of Ministers which included the recently arrived Admiral A.V. Kolchak (1874–1920) as Minister of War and Navy. Within six weeks, Kolchak, a man with no political experience, a maritime officer and Arctic explorer now thousands of kilometres from the nearest coastline, and a known drug addict, was catapulted from his new post to the position of military dictator, grandiloquently styled 'Supreme Ruler of the Russian State' (*Verkhovnyi pravitel' rossiiskogo gosudarstva*). A new phase in the conduct of the Civil war in Siberia had begun – the *Kolchakovshchina*.

KOLCHAKOVSHCHINA, NOVEMBER 1918–FEBRUARY 1920

Among the bizarre pageant of grand princes, tsars, emperors and other 'supreme rulers' of Russia, Admiral Aleksandr Vasilevich Kolchak must rank among the most unlikely, though there are plenty of other contenders for that description. Since the days of Kievan Russia in the early middle ages, the country has been cursed by a motley parade of incompetent, illiterate, venomously cruel, promiscuously sybaritic and plain stupid leaders, most of them placed where they were by accidents of birth, arranged marriage, conspiracy, assassination, palace coup and whatever is the opposite of serendipity – i.e. 'the making of happy discoveries'.[19] Certainly, Admiral Kolchak was not a happy choice as Russia's new 'Supreme Ruler'. His early career as a naval officer had a few distinguished passages, including service in the Russo-Japanese War (though he did spend time as a Japanese prisoner-of-war) and with the Black Sea fleet in the First World War. He had also taken part in a few voyages of exploration on the Arctic, and published some minor scientific works on hydrology. However, nothing in his training, naval service, intellect, political acumen or knowledge of land-warfare prepared or equipped him for the daunting role into which the Russian and Siberian counter-revolution had now thrust him.

It is not necessary to compile a full psychological profile of Kolchak for the purposes of this chapter, but it is worth quoting some of the comments made by Jonathan Smele in what is arguably the most thorough recent western study of the egregious, febrile and unstable tar-cum-quasi-tsar. Smele, citing members of Kolchak's equally dodgy entourage – 'pygmies ... not to be trusted to manage a whelk stall' – describes the admiral as follows:

> He was quite plainly a sick man ... 'certainly a neurasthenic' ... sunk in a world of political chicanery ... in 1919 Kolchak's frustration at his own inability to control events would ever more frequently become manifested in outbursts of raging, ungovernable temper. Kolchak was, in other words, quite simply unfit – in terms of his physical and mental health and of his education and experience – to perform the Herculean tasks placed before him as Supreme Ruler.[20]

As the tide of the Civil War turned against the irascible admiral and his moronic minions, he became increasingly subject to 'gloomy, mistrustful and suspicious moods', alternating with 'uncontrollable fits of anger' and 'pained hysterical yelling', smashing objects and slashing about him with a knife.[21] Of course, whoever else might have been placed in Kolchak's position would have been faced with similar daunting tasks, though probably not with the same temperamental and psychotic reactions, but in his case his bizarre behaviour and his tragi-farcical antics and tactics were to end in his defeat and death. Kolchak's title as 'Supreme Ruler of Russia' was, of course, a conceit from the start. Central European Russia, with its First World War arsenals and the hub of the nationwide railway system, was always firmly under Moscow's control, and at the other end of the country Transbaikalia remained the virtual fiefdom of the ruthless independent atamans, bankrolled by the Japanese who had not yet abandoned their own expansionist aims on the mainland. Reactions to Kolchak's elevation were as to be expected: the right (including now the Kadets) were enthusiastic; the left were appalled; and the Allies were cautious – though the head of the British Military Mission to Siberia, Major General Alfred Knox, informed his government that 'there is no doubt that Kolchak is the best Russian for our purposes in the Far East'.[22] It is also clear that, unlike the Bolshevik government, which was a totally *Russian* phenomenon, the Whites, without the political and military support of overseas powers, could not have survived as long as they did. As Smele so felicitously puts it: 'although the admiral's patriotic credentials were unimpeachable, the Omsk government ... relied *ab initio* on foreign alms and foreign arms'.[23] To the majority of the

Siberian peasants, who had obviously never heard of Kolchak, and to the Siberian native peoples, his appointment was a matter of utter indifference and unconcern. For most of these ordinary folk, one Russian ruler – from Yermak to Yeltsin – was as bad as another.

Despite some early military successes that placed Kolchak's forces within striking distance of Simbirsk, Samara and Kazan, his 'reign' was fraught with obstacles and difficulties to the military victory that was so essential to his political triumph. For example, he was geographically separated by hundreds of kilometres from the armies of other White generals, such as Anton Denikin and Pëtr Wrangel in southern Russia and Ukraine, and Nikolai Yudenich in the north-west. There was therefore little chance of a strategic or tactical link-up, encirclement or combined invasion of the Bolshevik heartland, not that the other White generals would have accepted the Omsk-based admiral's authority and his ridiculous title. After the 11 November 1918 armistice in Europe, the purported original military justification for the Allied intervention in Russia (i.e. to get the country back into the war after the Treaty of Brest-Litovsk) disappeared and support was gradually withdrawn, further exacerbating Kolchak's vulnerability. Such military materiel that did continue to be supplied by the Japanese and Americans via the Far East were regularly plundered and purloined by the mad atamans for their own nefarious purposes. Thousands of American guns, for instance, destined for remaining anti-Soviet forces in central Siberia, were extorted from the conveyors by the local warlords as a kind of tariff for the remainder of the munitions' onward transportation. The Czech Legion too, after the end of the war in Europe and the founding of the newly independent Czechoslovak state, wished to disengage from involvement in Russia's internal troubles and simply return as soon as possible to their liberated homeland, thus removing another anti-Bolshevik factor in the polynomial political equation in Siberia. Furthermore, Kolchak and his subordinates controlled only about 800 kilometres (500 miles) of the 6,500-kilometre (4,000-mile) Trans-Sib as far as Omsk. He was, therefore, desperately isolated.

As indicated above, he was also temperamentally and mentally unsuited to his role. He had no experience of government, economic planning, diplomacy or international statesmanship. He was apparently addicted to alcohol and narcotics (but then so have been many other public figures, soldiers and politicians: Lavrentii Beria, Boris Yeltsin, Franklin D. Roosevelt and Winston Churchill spring to mind). His administration, too, was unwittingly sabotaged by incompetent and venal underlings, and even his inept military commands were often ignored. Most seriously, he enjoyed no mass support or popular loyalty. The economy, with its confetti currencies, was in ruins, despite his stewardship of the imperial gold reserves, and, with the loss of the Urals, he had no industrial base. His conscript troops were unreliable in battle at the front, and in the rear a constant thorn in his flesh was the unrelenting guerrilla warfare of hundreds of peasant partisan bands fighting for their own interests in the face of Kolchak's own contradictory land policies. These 'green guerrillas' were also distrustful of Bolshevik intentions, particularly with regard to the hated policy of enforced requisitioning (*prodrazvërstka*), but at the bottom line their sympathies lay more with the Reds than the Whites who were still identified with a possible return to the discredited pre-revolutionary order. These instincts were reinforced by the Kolchak regime's use of terroristic methods to apply its policies, including public floggings, pitiless pogroms (Kolchak was an overt anti-Semite) and mass executions.

By November 1919 a combination of all these problems and failures, aggravated by the reinvigorated Red Army's inexorable eastwards thrust across the Urals, panicked Kolchak and his government ministers into abandoning their HQ in Omsk and scuttling like frightened rabbits with their scuts between their legs via the Trans-Sib eastwards to Irkutsk. The supreme non-ruler's train was impeded by unsympathetic, hostile railway workers, delayed by disgruntled Czechs, harried by hordes of partisans and encumbered by the heavy burden of the former imperial gold reserve's ingots. Meanwhile, the Red Army, under its forceful new commander, M.V. Frunze, was also forging east and rapidly catching up with Kolchak. The latter was finally halted literally on his tracks at Nizhneudinsk, just short of Irkutsk, which was then in the hands of a new left-leaning government calling itself the Irkutsk Political Centre (IPC). The end of Kolchak's world was nigh. On 15 January 1920, he was handed over by Czech legionaries to the IPC, which shortly surrendered its own authority – and Kolchak – to the local Bolsheviks. A special commission appointed to investigate his activities interrogated Kolchak for several days and finally on 7 February – as White forces mounted a forlorn last-ditch attempt to rescue him – Kolchak and his last Prime Minister, V.N. Pepelyaev, were executed by firing squad and their bodies shoved beneath the ice of the river Ushakovka, a tributary of the Angara. The former admiral had finally found his watery grave (see Fig. 11).

The Bolsheviks and the Red Army now once more controlled Siberia from the Ural Mountains to Lake Baikal. But it was to take another two-and-a-half years to regain the Far East and reach the Pacific Ocean.

FAR EASTERN FINALE: FEBRUARY 1920–OCTOBER 1922

With Kolchak disposed of, the resurgent Bolsheviks were now faced with the urgent task of pacifying and sovietizing the most highly volatile area of conflict in the Civil War. In the west, Denikin and his ilk had been more or less dealt with, but the whole region from Baikal to Vladivostok was still chaotically administered by a constantly shifting variety of political and military factions, the battleground of mutually hostile local Reds, Whites, Greens, Socialist-Revolutionaries, residual Kolchakovites, peasant partisans, Czechs, Japanese, Americans and marauding cossaks led by their awful atamans. In the short term, Lenin, back in the Moscow Kremlin, chose temporarily to surrender Far Eastern space in order to gain time to settle more urgent problems by again redeploying Red Army units to mopping-up operations on his

The bourgeois, the fat-bellied priest
And the rich kulak
From beyond the far-off mountains
Convey in friendship Kolchak.

Joy to the sated, joy to the drunk,
The knout for the workers and landsmen,
Stirring the dust in their frenzy,
The troika drags on its hangman.

Figure 11 Bolshevik political poster depicting Admiral Kolchak, 1919. He is drawn in his war chariot by a fat capitalist, a paunchy priest and a rich farmer. The slogan above Kolchak's crowned head reads 'The land and factories – to the landlords and capitalists', and on the gallows is the warning: 'To the workers and peasants – the rope'.
Source: Created by V.N. Deni, 1919.

European fronts. However, still conscious of the vital nature of the Far East to the integrity of the new Soviet state, and unwilling to sacrifice Russia's provinces in the region to the surviving Whites and the Japanese, Moscow sanctioned the setting up of a new, nominally independent state in Transbaikalia called the Far Eastern Republic (FER), which would act as a kind of buffer regime between Soviet Siberia and Japan. Founded exactly two months after Kolchak's death, its capital was originally located at Verkhneudinsk, from where it shifted to Chita after ataman Semënov was forced to abandon the headquarters there of his short-lived Buryat-Mongol Republic. After a brief sojourn in Dauria, he was again compelled to decamp, this time to Manchuria. The *atamanshchina*, which had brought so much mayhem to the Far East was soon to be mercifully at an end.

Not everyone was happy with the new moderate socialist FER, and it was not until the end of 1920 that most of the large urban centres grudgingly recognized its authority, and even then bitter hostilities were to rage throughout the territory over the next 18 months, often scarred with terrifying atrocities. For instance, in January 1920, Red partisans slaughtered almost an entire Japanese garrison at Nikolaevsk-na-Amure, only to be visited by reprisals in other Far Eastern towns, during which nearly 3,000 suspected Bolshevik sympathizers were killed. Four thousand more Russians were later massacred by the partisans in Nikolaevsk itself as Japanese troops attacked the town. Similar horrors continued to be perpetrated on all sides. A murderous deadlock seemed to have set in. It was not to be broken until renewed international pressure finally persuaded Tokyo to announce that it would evacuate its troops from the Siberian mainland by the end of October 1922. Now bereft of sustained financial, military and political support from abroad, the remaining shattered anti-Soviet forces finally disintegrated.

However, before the final Bolshevik victory in the Far East, one last desperate throw by two Vladivostok businessmen, the brothers S.D. and N.D. Merkulov, took place during the early summer of 1921. Having by various ruses managed to overthrow the Vladivostok agents of the Far Eastern Republic, they and their supporters declared the formation of a new 'Provisional Priamurskii Government'. (It is curious that so many transient political institutions that were set up in Russia after the February 1917 Revolution described themselves as 'Provisional', as if aware of their own built-in evanescence.) Now faced with the promise of the impending Japanese withdrawal, it was compelled to give way to the imposition of a brief period of martial law under the command of a former officer of the Czech Legion, M.K. Dietrichs. This in its turned collapsed – such being the fragile nature of political power in the region – and on 25 October FER and Red Army troops entered Vladivostok under the fresh leadership of I.P. Uborevich, parading in triumph through the city as the last Japanese vessels steamed out of the Golden Horn. Following the Red victory, thousands of Russians fled abroad as émigrés, littering the capitals of the world with the detritus of the old tsarist empire, while remaining counter-revolutionaries in Transbaikalia were swept up by the security forces of the FER. The purported independence of the latter had been a sham from the start, and on 15 November 1922 it yielded what little bogus sovereignty it had, and was formally incorporated into the Russian Soviet Federative Socialist Republic. Despite some sporadic anti-Soviet resistance in the far north-east and the continuance of Japanese occupation of northern Sakhalin (which did not end until 1925), to all intents and purposes the Revolution, counter-revolution and Civil War in Siberia and the Far East, as elsewhere in Russia, were over.

Many of the traditional explanations given by both Russian and Western historians for the Communist victory beyond the Urals require re-examination. Among the objective factors to be considered are: Siberia's geographical remoteness from the centre and the awesomeness of its climate and terrain; the superior military experience of the White armies' officer class; the traditions of suspicion and hostility on the part of many Siberians towards metropolitan Russia; and the impact and extent of the foreign intervention in supporting those sworn to overthrow Lenin's government. Given all these apparently adverse circumstances and impediments to Red victory, when all the odds seemed to be against it, it is ironic that the anti-Bolshevik 'Whites' and the peasant partisan 'Greens' — both colours traditionally symbolic of Siberia's snows and forests — should have been finally superseded by the crimson colour of Soviet Communism.

For the next 70 years the red flag of the USSR with its potent symbol of the hammer and sickle — representing proletarian and peasant power — was to fly over Siberia, and it is to the tumultuous events of those seven decades that the next two chapters are devoted.

9

Siberia under Stalin:
Growth, GULag and the Great Patriotic War

The years 1921 and 1922 were almost as crucial a turning point in the history of Russia as 1917. The Civil War was all but over, the Red Army and the Communist government were now in control of most of the territory of the old empire and the Union of Soviet Socialist Republics (USSR) established in December 1922. In response to the manifest public opposition to the policy of War Communism, which, as its name suggests, had been a mixture of wartime exigency and ideological commitment to destroy capitalism, Lenin took the decision to abandon it, chiefly to appease the still hostile peasantry, and in its place introduced the New Economic Policy (NEP), which to some extent was a compromise with capitalism, a retreat from all-out socialism, and a bold experiment in what later came to be called a 'mixed economy'.

NEP's main features, very briefly, were the abolition of the detested food-requisitioning campaign and its replacement with a tax-in-kind on agricultural produce (*prodnalog*). There was also a return to a limited market economy whereby peasants and farmers were able to retail their surplus goods on local market stalls. One of the Communist Party's leading economic theorists and ideologists, Nikolai Bukharin (1888–1938), frankly urged the peasants to 'enrich yourselves', a slogan which did not endear him to those on the left-wing of the party during the 'great debate' over industrialization in the mid-1920s. Many small industrial enterprises were denationalized and in some cases returned to their previous owners, though there was still a restriction on the number of workers who could be employed, and, obviously, a tax on profits made. To those of his critics who reckoned that NEP was a betrayal of revolutionary socialist principles (the 'New Exploitation of the Proletariat', as one leading Party official put it), Lenin retorted that it was only a brief, tactical retreat in order to buy time to consolidate the new Communist regime after seven years of international, revolutionary and civil war – a kind of economic Brest-Litovsk. How it worked in practice, with particular reference to Siberia, will be discussed below. So long as the state held on to what Lenin called the 'commanding heights' of the economy – heavy industry, mining, fuel, electricity, transport, foreign trade, banking, etc. – the future of socialism was secure.

On the other hand, NEP certainly favoured the economic interests of the better-off peasantry, who were more plentiful in Siberia than in European Russia, and also provided a lucrative opportunity for the shady activities of a new sub-class of small-time (in some cases big-time) entrepreneurs, fixers, dealers, black-marketeers, fences and spivs – the so-called NEPmen – who to a large extent kept the cogs and wheels of the new mixed economy lubricated.

Other significant events took place in 1921 and 1922. Nineteen twenty-one was the year of the Xth Congress of the renamed (in 1918) 'Russian Communist Party (Bolsheviks)'. At this crucial meeting, the most significant item on the agenda was Lenin's 'Resolution on Party Unity', which, without going into the fine print, banned organized factions within the party and insisted on all members toeing the central party-line on threat of expulsion. Other socialist parties such as the Mensheviks and Socialist-Revolutionaries were practically banned, many of their members arrested, and the brave new world of Soviet Russia became in effect a one-party state. It was not yet, however, the monolithic, totalitarian dictatorship it was to become under Josef Stalin. It was in 1922 that the Georgian Bolshevik was appointed to the newly created post of General Secretary of the Communist Party, mainly because no one else wanted what was seen to be a humdrum office job. Rather than humdrum, Stalin was to turn it into the most powerful political position in the country, which it continued to be until 1991. Before his death in 1924, Lenin warned the Party Central Committee that, because of his 'rudeness' and other political and personal defects, Stalin was unfit for the job and should be removed from office.[1] However, Stalin – by virtue of the enormous powers of bureaucratic patronage that were built into his role as General Secretary – ultimately outmanoeuvred his rivals in the Politburo and established one of the most death-dealing dictatorships in the history of the twentieth century, personally authorizing the arrests, show trials and execution of his former comrades. Apart from those who received the routine bullet through the back of the neck in the cellars of the Lubyanka, it was amid the icy wastes and labour camps of Siberia, the Arctic north and the Far East to which most of his victims were trucked and there worked, froze and starved to death in their millions. These camps were the islands of misery and suffering in the vast land-ocean of Siberia that Alexander Solzhenitsyn was later to describe as the 'GULag archipelago', the operations of which will be returned to below. But before analyzing that murky and horrific episode of Russia's history, it is necessary to examine the effects of the end of the Civil War and War Communism, and the onset of NEP in Siberia and the Far East during the 1920s – an enigmatic, contradictory and tantalizing period in the country's history.

The reason for its paradoxical nature is that, in contrast to the political monolithism of the 1930s and 1940s, and in spite of the inception and growth of the one-party state, NEP Russia still managed to maintain a degree of social, economic and cultural pluralism. Despite Lenin's Resolution on Party Unity, there was nevertheless a good deal of open political and ideological debate, opposing economic arguments were publicly aired, and there was a whole plethora of contending and experimental movements in the arts, literature, architecture, film, music and theatre, unlike the compulsory 'socialist-realist' conformism of the oppressive, sterile 1930s. Progressive educational systems were introduced, the laws on marriage, cohabitation, divorce and women's' rights were totally revamped, and a vigorous drive to improve literacy levels – including the creation of new alphabets and writing systems, at first in the Roman and later in the Cyrillic script, for some of the Siberian native peoples who till then had no written language – was set in motion.[2] The fledgling Soviet Union was still pulsatingly in the avant-garde of postwar European culture, and many foreign politicians, writers, intellectuals and 'fellow travellers' visited the crucible of socialism, imbued with a heady mixture of curiosity, enthusiasm, camaraderie and naivety. So how did all this activity specifically affect Siberia and its peoples?

SIBERIA AND NEP

Both during and after the Civil War, in European Russia and in Siberia the major problem (apart from military operations and their demographic aftermath) facing the Soviet government was that of the peasantry, and, more precisely, relations between the party and the peasants – and, even more precisely, the 'rich' peasants, the 'kulaks'.[3] After the Red Army's victory and the re-establishment of Soviet power in Siberia and the Far East as described in the previous chapter, Moscow's hold over the vast territory was nevertheless fairly tenuous. While the peasants had to be placated, at the same time all traces of regional autonomism needed to be expunged and Siberia brought firmly under the Kremlin's heel. Residual regionalists were arrested and placed on trial as counter-revolutionaries, but in defiance of the persecutions, there still existed a spirit of proud individualism and traditional anti-Moscow sentiment among much of Siberia's population, especially the peasants. Moscow was therefore presented with a 'double-whammy' – that of continuing peasant hostility to centrally imposed policies and that of the legacy of instinctively felt Siberian regional consciousness. A third problem was that of the relative scarcity of party activists in Siberia following the various massacres of local Bolsheviks carried out by vindictive Whites, feral atamans and foreign interventionists during the Civil War.

The compulsory grain procurements – *prodrazvёrstka* – under War Communism had hit the relatively wealthy Siberian peasants particularly hard. James Hughes reckons that in the period 1920–22, government agents extracted over one-quarter of the Russian Soviet Federative Socialist Republic's entire grain requisitions from Siberia,[4] which was not unnaturally seen yet again by the population of the province as an extension or continuation of metropolitan Russia's exploitation of 'Siberia as a colony' – the concept put forward by Yadrintsev in the previous century in his seminal study (see Chapter Four). Agricultural production in Siberia, as in other areas of Russia, had suffered from the military campaigns and social chaos of the Civil War, aggravated by the ravages and extortions of War Communism. Not that the peasants had taken this lying down. Just to give one example, in 1920 and in the first few weeks of 1921 thousands of peasant insurgents rose up against the Bolsheviks in Tobolsk province, capturing the city itself in February. The Red Army retaliated and retook Tobolsk in April, but only 'at the cost of countless thousands killed and wounded on both sides, including an esti-mated 5,000 Siberian communists and local soviet officials'.[5] Large sections of industry had been shattered, and the transport and distribution network, including tracts of the Trans-Sib, were in many cases practically inoperative and in a state of disrepair.

On the surface, NEP offered an opportunity for a resurgence of agricultural production and the prosperity that much of the Siberian peasantry had enjoyed prior to the uncertainties and hardships of the Revolution and Civil War, during which, rather than producing for the market, the peasants scaled down to subsistence farming. However, there was initially some resistance to NEP in the Siberian countryside. Why? Firstly because it was a policy inaugurated by the Moscow Kremlin, and therefore was met with knee-jerk suspicion and non-compliance, and secondly because prices for agricultural produce remained artificially low, persuading the peasants either to hoard their grain, withhold it from the market, feed it to their animals or turn it into vodka, in anticipation of increased selling prices in the future.

However, the financial incentives offered by NEP meant that by 1926, the year which many economic historians deem to be the zenith of its success, not only had output of Siberian agriculture recovered, but it far superseded the levels of 1920. According to Hughes, in 1926 over a third of Soviet grain (mainly wheat) exports originated in Siberia, thereby making a major contri-bution to foreign currency earnings that could be 'ploughed' back into financing national industrial development. He continues: 'When one adds butter shipments, it is clear that Siberia had once again become an important source of food and hard currency earnings for the state at the crucial juncture when Bolshevik industrialisation plans were becoming more ambitious and their successful realisation increasingly dependent on guaranteed deliveries of cheap agricultural produce.'[6]

The chief Communist Party official in Siberia, S.I. Syrtsov (1893–1937) – an ardent Bukharinist supporter of NEP – did all he could to promote Siberian grain production, seeing it as the basis of the Siberian economy, which would ultimately create the revenue to stimulate industrial development to the ben-efit of the entire USSR and to the building of socialism. In the eighteenth century the great polymath scholar, Mikhail Lomonosov, had stated: 'Through Siberia ... shall the might of Russia grow' (see Chapter One). In the post-revolutionary 1920s it was almost as if his prophesy was being adapted to something like: 'Through Siberia shall socialism be constructed', though this was patently not the immediate or cherished ambition of the Siberian kulaks. And it was this particular socio-economic stratum, or class, that over the next few years was to bear the brunt of Stalin's zeal, wrath or vengeance for what he perceived to be their sabotage of the Soviet economy.

The agrarian successes of 1926 were not replicated in the national harvest of 1927, largely because of crop failures in Ukraine and the Caucasus. Siberia still managed some spectacular yields, though the produce did not always reach the market, and grain production was down nationally by a half, a situation which is usually referred to as the 'grain crisis'. Although there are many natural factors that account for this in part, Stalin, whose personal monopoly of political power was increasing with his defeat of the so-called 'left opposition' (Trotskii, Evgenii Preobrazhenskii and co.), became increasingly convinced that the main culprits were the Siberian kulaks. Suspicious and paranoid by nature, Stalin decided to undertake a personal investigation of the problem and embarked on a two-week tour of the Siberian province (then known in administrative terms as *Sibkrai*) in order to assess the situation for himself. What he discovered there appalled and shocked him in two major respects. First was what he regarded as the treacherous collaboration of Siberian party officials with the 'self-enriching' local kulaks, and, second, by the sight of huge piles of useable agricultural produce lying around, sometimes rotting, in peasant villages when it could be gathered to feed the towns or, through exports, continue to generate the revenue to boost industrial development. This was a pivotal moment. Stalin inaugurated a purge of the Siberian Communist Party leadership, re-introduced the strong-arm grain requisitioning policies reminiscent of the worst excesses of War Communism – what came to be called the 'Urals-Siberian method' – and was the sticking point at which Stalin determined to introduce the full-scale, enforced collectivization of the peasantry, not just in Siberia, but throughout the USSR, and, finally, 'to liquidate the kulaks as a class'. It is James Hughes' firm opinion that it was crucially Stalin's experience in Siberia that created the great economic, agrarian, industrial and also social transformation of the Soviet Union between 1928 and 1933, and indeed beyond. In his own words:

> Stalin extrapolated from these distinct Siberian conditions and concluded that the degeneracy of the party and the existence of a powerful kulak stratum were endemic in the country as a whole. The only solution ... was immediate large-scale purging of the party and a rapid advance to collectivisation ... [The] Siberian expedition saw a significant radicalisation of Stalin's views against the policy of conciliation of the peasantry enshrined in NEP. This point marked the juncture where the Soviet Union began the descent into the cataclysm of the 'second revolution'.[7]

If one follows Hughes' persuasive reasoning in this instance, then, once more, one cannot escape the conclusion that, whereas metropolitan Russia obviously had, and since the mid-sixteenth century had always had, a dramatic impact on the history and development of the lands east of the Urals, equally, Siberia and its peoples had a profound, reciprocal influence on the history and development of the whole of Russia and the Soviet Union. The 'Urals-Siberian method' and Stalin's virtual war on the Siberian peasantry in 1928 was in effect a dress rehearsal for the mass collectivization of the agrarian economy throughout the USSR during the years of the first and second five-year plans for the rapid industrialization of the country in the late1920s and the 1930s – the basis of the Soviet 'command economy' for over the next half-century. The phases of Siberia's economic development during that period, because of the centralized planning mechanism, more or less kept pace with that of the rest of the country – collectivization, industrialization, the five-year plans, special wartime policies, relocation of factories, postwar reconstruction, etc. – but nevertheless Siberia still had its own idiosyncratic role to play. But two more special cases in terms of the effects of NEP need to be considered before moving on from the tempestuous 1920s to the traumatic 1930s. Those are the fate of the Russian Far East – i.e. from Lake Baikal to the Pacific, including the vast territory of Yakutia in the north – and the experience of Siberia's aboriginal peoples.

NEP, THE FAR EAST AND THE SIBERIAN NATIVE PEOPLES

The Russian Far East (RFE), an area which then included Transbaikalia, the Maritime region (Primor'e), the Amur district and parts of the Sea of Okhotsk littoral, had not been technically part of Soviet Russia for five years (1917–22), and had managed to retain its own peculiar local identity despite the ravages of the Civil War caused by the Red-White conflict, the ferocious *ataman-shchina* and the foreign intervention. The fighting and destruction of the Civil War had led to a dramatic decrease in agricultural production in the region, a decline in the number of prosperous peasant and cossak farmsteads, a reduction in the area of cultivated land and a severe loss of livestock. On the other hand, the territory had escaped the forcible expropriations of War Communism, and also, in the face of the violence and marauding activities of the various factions and phalanges in the Civil War, its economic infrastructure had managed to survive in variegated formations, which included private enterprises, co-operatives, foreign investment and a flourishing commercial trade with neighbouring countries, in particular China and Korea. To some extent, therefore, it is fair to say that in the Russian Far East, unlike the rest of the Russian Soviet Federative Socialist Republic, the New Economic Policy was not so much *new* as a continuation of the situation that already existed.

Partly because of their remoteness from Moscow, and partly because of their own distinctive history, the Far Easterners, perhaps even more so than the inhabitants of western, central and eastern Siberia, maintained a strong sense of regional identity (still very evident today)[8] and of being a part of the Asian-Pacific international community. For instance, in 1923 almost 58 per cent of all industrial enterprises in the Russian Far East – including fishing, forestry, food-processing and construction – were owned by foreign business concerns, including, predominantly, Japan and the United States of America.

Foreign capital was also paramount in the financial services sector, and in total around 60 per cent of the Russian Far East's economic turnover was in the hands of private capitalist enterprises, both Russian and foreign.[9]

The special nature of the Russian Far East was not simply a result of economic circumstances. As John Stephan has put it: 'The Far East was traditionally a haven as well as a receptacle for mavericks: convicts and exiles, escaped serfs, hunters and trappers, and gold prospectors. Cossacks and sectarians made up fiercely independent communities … Political dissidents and misfits continued to flow into the Far East [even] after the establishment of Soviet rule.'[10] The remoteness from the country's political capital and central government agencies meant that, rather like Siberia's voracious *voevody* and greedy governors of an earlier epoch, the local military and political leaders in the Far East during the 1920s, and even well into the 1930s, were able to act with a good deal of autonomy and caprice which would not have been tolerated closer to the centre of power.

Whereas Stalin had been much perturbed by what he had witnessed in western Siberia in January 1928, he had far more urgent concerns closer to home, as it were, than the semi-independent activities of local officials and businessmen in distant Vladivostok and the Far East, which Victor Mote describes as 'the periphery on the periphery'.[11] While there was no direct, overt opposition to Moscow's rule, John Stephan tells us in his precise prose: 'Central Committee decrees that impinged upon the interests of provincial cliques were imaginatively emasculated amid gestures of sedulous compliance.'[12] Leaving delicately aside the eye-watering concept of 'imaginative emasculation', beneath the fig-leaf of 'sedulous compliance' a whole cohort of rough-hewn, tough-minded and inherently anti-bureaucratic Far Eastern Party leaders and military men carved out for themselves a virtually autonomous fiefdom without manifestly flouting Moscow's authority. People like Vasilii Blücher (1890–1938, Red Army Civil War hero and former Minister of War in the Far Eastern Republic) and the Ukrainian Yan Gamarnik (1894–1937, chairman of the Far Eastern Revolutionary Committee [Dal'revkom] between 1923 and 1928) built up a network of similarly focused local activists and introduced independent policies – social, economic, cultural, commercial and educational – that were specifically designed to enhance the prosperity, security and prestige of the Far Eastern province. Trade links were developed with China and Japan. Transport and communication lines were improved. New agricultural projects – particularly rice-production – were introduced. A fresh wave of immigration from European Russia was implemented (around 30,000 new settlers arrived in 1926 alone). A small merchant fleet was created, and the port at Vladivostok was refurbished and expanded.

Also, a vigorous educational programme to improve literacy rates among the local population, both Russian and aboriginal, under the slogan of 'liquidating illiteracy', was pursued.[13] However, while the latter campaign was well intended and semi-successful, the strictly Marxist-Leninist content of much of the newly available pedagogical literature (remember, for all their independent-mindedness, both Blücher and Gamarnik were dedicated, unswerving Communists) found little resonance among the 'little peoples' of the north and Far East. It is, after all, a bit tricky to translate such things as the 'labour theory of surplus value', 'dialectical materialism', the 'bourgeois-democratic revolution' and the 'dictatorship of the proletariat' into a language whose native speakers have no understanding of, or vocabulary for, such economic and ideological constructs. Indeed, many of the Siberian native languages did not even contain the word 'work'. In the West, as also in Russia, the concepts of 'going to work' (as opposed to being at home), the 'workplace', the 'working class' etc. are familiar, but for the Siberian peoples there was no distinct set of activities that were separate from the daily tasks of herding, hunting, fishing and engaging in traditional handicrafts. There was no 'working class' as a distinctive, identifiable part of the whole community. Nor, of course, was there a 'bourgeoisie'. To Arctic and eastern hunters, reindeer-herdsmen and fisher-folk, the mysteries and mythology of shamanism and the bear-festival were perfectly understandable, but not so the alien intricacies of the philosophical, political and economic theories of Karl Marx, Friedrich Engels and Vladimir Ilyich Lenin, based on an analysis of west European industrial capitalism and the class struggle.

It cannot be gainsaid, however, that the new Soviet regime did what it could – given its other urgent proprieties – to improve (in its own way) the lives of the Siberian native peoples, as opposed to the neglect, persecution and sometimes genocidal policies of the Romanov tsars. This was only possible, though, once the endemic and continuing violence in the north-east and Far East had come to an end. Siberia has sometimes been described, by analogy with America's 'Wild West' – 'a rough, tough frontierland roamed by outlaws, gunslingers, gold-diggers, bounty-hunters, and pesky Indians' – as Russia's 'Wild East'.[14] If this was true of Siberia as a whole, then the areas of Yakutia, the Chukotka peninsula and from Baikal to the Pacific were not only the territory's easternmost areas, but also its wildest. Although it was the southern regions of the Far East – Transbaikalia and the Maritime region – which suffered most from the savagery of the Civil War, as described in the previous chapter, the more remote regions of the far north also felt the knock-on effects of the fighting in the south. Interruption of vital supplies and the virtual collapse of the crucial fur trade reduced many of the hunting and trading communities to near destitution, as did the slaughter of their animal herds by marauding gangs of soldiers, bandits and warmongers on all political sides during the Civil War. For instance in Yakutia, in a single year between 1921 and 1922, the number of cattle fell from around 465,000 head to 371,000, and horses from 137,000 to 92,400. The area of sown land was drastically reduced, and such industrial enterprises as there were in the territory – producing lead, salt, gold, timber, etc. – had more than halved output between 1917 and 1921.[15]

It was essential for the central government to reconstitute Yakutia's economy as soon as it was practical to do so. Initially, the local Bolshevik authorities still practised some of the strong-arm methods of War Communism, but after fierce local resistance, from 1924 – following the founding of the Yakut Autonomous Soviet Socialist Republic in 1922 – there began a more conciliatory and supportive policy by introducing substantial cash grants from the state budget, and supplying large quantities of equipment, textiles, hunting gear, building materials and grain. Rates of taxation were slashed, and some of the furthest outlying peoples, e.g. the Evenks, Evens, Yukagirs and Chukchi, were totally exempt from payment. The transition to NEP in Yakutia would have been impossible without central state assistance, but even that was greatly impeded by the fluctuating fortunes of continuing military activity in the region. However, in 1923, two circumstances facilitated its economic recovery. First was the final defeat of anti-Soviet forces, and second, the discovery of large, valuable gold deposits in the region of Aldan, which obviously provided a major stimulus to the Yakut economy. In the late 1920s the Yakut goldfields were producing between 20 and 30 per cent of the USSR's total output, and employing up to 17,000 workers. The existence of this large labour force, as well as the needs of the mines' infrastructure, also provided a boost to the region's economy as a market for the supply of provisions for the mining settlements, including fodder for the draft horses, maintaining the transport network, building accommodation, and other sundry services which created work and income for the local population.[16]

In 1924, against the background of a more stable economic situation throughout the USSR, the government was able to pay more attention to the political organization, economic, social, cultural, judicial and educational needs of Siberia and the far north. To this end in 1924 there was created an organization called the Committee of the North, on which, as James Forsyth points out, the political influence of Communist Party officials was to some extent offset by the inclusion among its members of distinguished ethnographers and other scholars such as B.M. Zhitkov (1872–1943), V.G. Bogoraz (1865–1936) and L. Ya. Shternberg (1861–1927), all of whom had extensive personal knowledge of the area, including – in the case of Bogoraz and Shternberg – years spent as political exiles in the Far East for their revolutionary activities in Russia in the late nineteenth century. As members of the Committee of the North, these men did what they could to make sure that the indigenous cultures and lifestyles of the Siberian peoples should be preserved as much as possible against the ideological and political ambitions of the centre.[17]

Apart from the far north, central Soviet government policy towards all the Siberian indigenous peoples, the *inorodtsy*, was driven by a combination of ideology and philanthropy. On the one hand they – the government – wished to introduce, if necessary impose, administrative institutions such as local soviets that conformed to the national model, while at the same time allowing the continued existence of traditional structures of self-administration based on tribal or clan organizations. The government also inaugurated a whole range of genuinely well-meant policies designed to increase the physical and cultural welfare of the native population. Throughout Siberia vigorous educational, social and medical programmes and institutions were introduced, including schools, clinics, veterinary services, emporia and a complex of other social utilities in remote areas, which were called 'cultural bases' (*kul'tbazy*). Academic departments and faculties dedicated to the study of the Siberian peoples were set up in the major Siberian cities, and in 1925 the 'Workers' Department' of Leningrad State University established a special unit called the 'Northern Department', which in 1930 was upgraded to the status of the 'Institute of Northern Peoples' with an intake of over 350 students of 24 different Siberian and Far Eastern nationalities.[18] There is no doubt that the Committee of the North did much to enhance the welfare, health and education of the 'little peoples' of Siberia, but its activities were sadly brought to an end in 1935, just before the promulgation of the new 1936 Constitution of the USSR, which blandly declared that under conditions of the construction of socialism, all ethnic problems in the USSR had been resolved. The now defunct committee's responsibilities were thereafter transferred inexplicably to an organization rejoicing in the grotesquely clumsy acronym of *Glavsevmorputi* (Northern Sea Route Directorate), a sub-branch of which took over duties for the development of the 'small peoples' of the north. It was not until 1957 that the Council of Ministers of the USSR recognized that the abolition of the Committee of the North in 1935 had been 'untimely', and set up new commissions to deal specifically with ethnic, cultural and economic problems in the region.

On the industrial front, Siberian enterprises recovered rapidly under NEP after the end of the Civil War, and some major new enterprises were developed, particularly in gold and coal production, which made a significant contribution to the Soviet economy. One specific, but little known, enclave of industrial and international initiative in mid-1920s Siberia was what has been described as 'Project Kuzbas'. In 1921, a team of American Communists, led by William ('Big Bill') Haywood, a convicted labour activist in the United States under threat of imprisonment, met with Lenin in the Kremlin and reached an agreement for the setting up of a 'colony' of American miners and engineers in Kemerovo, heart of the Kuzbass coal-mining region. Between 1922 and 1926 over 600 American citizens travelled to southern Siberia and, motivated by a mixture of ideology and idealism, made a significant contribution to the infant socialist republic's industrial development. Monuments, museum pieces and mementos to their activities are still on display in present-day Kemerovo.[19] The 'great leap forward' in the intensive industrialization of the Soviet economy, as well as the campaign for the enforced collectivization of the peasantry, based on the 'Urals-Siberian method' was launched in 1928–9 along with the implementation of the first 'five-year plan'.

COLLECTIVIZATION AND INDUSTRIALIZATION

As mentioned above, it was above all the grain crisis of 1927–8, observed personally by Stalin in Siberia, which was the immediate trigger for the abandonment of the policy of conciliating the peasantry, which was at the heart of NEP,

and a reversion to something reminiscent of War Communism, leading ultimately to mass collectivization and dekulakization.[20] The collectivization of
Russian peasant agriculture was one of the most unnecessarily tragic episodes
in the history of the USSR, and remained a blight on the Soviet economy for
several decades. 'Radio Armenia', a fictitious radio station that used to operate
as a phantom medium for the dissemination of political jokes in the Soviet
Union, was once asked: 'What is the definition of a catastrophe?' Answer: 'I'm
sorry, we don't answer questions on Soviet agriculture.' Between 1928 and
1933, the vast majority of the Russian peasantry, and those of other nationalities, including the nomadic herdsmen of Siberia, had been cajoled, forced or
coerced – often on threat of exile or execution – to merge their privately or
communally held farmsteads, together with their livestock and equipment,
into huge state-organized collective farms (*kolkhozy*) or state farms (*sovkhozy*).
On paper, there was some superficial economic sense in the enterprise, but in
human and productive terms the whole policy (as implicitly acknowledged by
'Radio Armenia' in the joke) was catastrophic, in some cases leading to famine
of almost genocidal proportions.[21] The *Practical Dictionary of Siberia and the
North* rather jerkily describes collectivization as follows:

> one of the major political actions of the Communist Party in the 1920s – early 1930s,
> that radically changed economic basis of agricultural production … class structure
> of rural population and way of life of the countryside … With industrialization just
> starting, the problems of food supplies to growing urban population was solved [*sic!*]
> by maximum cooperation of small manufacturing and expropriation of property of
> the most well-off rural population … [The] grain shortage in 1928 had developed
> into a radical policy of liquidating the so-called kulaks; this caused fierce resistance –
> to the point of armed revolt – by a significant part of the peasantry.[22]

This major recent reference work goes on to give detailed statistics, based on
archival sources and documents, of the horrific scale of the dispossessions,
slaughter of livestock, arrests, deportations of euphemistically designated
'special settlers' (*spetsposelentsy*) in the far north and far east, and also summary executions: 'Directions for area public prosecutors of N. Terr[itories] as
of Jan. 8, 1930 stressed the necessity of intensifying repressions "to the point
of shooting kulaks and other counter-revolutionaries dead."'[23]

The scale of the massacre and violent peasant protest reached such a pitch,
not just in Siberia, but throughout the USSR, that on 2 March 1930 Stalin published an article in the Communist Party newspaper, *Pravda*, entitled 'Dizzy
with Success', in which he implicitly exonerated himself from the excesses of
the collectivization campaign by blaming the overzealous, 'anti-Leninist'
enthusiasm of local party officials both in ignoring the intended '*voluntary
character* of the collective farm movement', and in not '*taking into account the
diversity of conditions* in various regions of the U.S.S.R.'[24] (In the text there is
explicit reference to the 'northern areas' of the country – including, one
assumes, parts of Siberia – where 'conditions for the immediate organization of

collective farms are comparatively less favourable'.)[25] The article is, of course, an exemplary manifestation of the duplicitous hypocrisy in which Stalin was well practised. It was, after all, he who had inaugurated the whole disastrous process after witnessing what he regarded as the connivance of unassiduous party officials with Siberian kulaks in 1928. On the other hand, Stalin could not have implemented the collectivization campaign without the connivance and co-operation of thousands of grass-roots party workers and also, importantly, the peasants – particularly the poorer peasants – themselves. Hughes argues that Stalin was able to use the economic stratification of the peasants – poor, middle and rich (*bednyak, serednyak, kulak*) – the traditional institution of the village assembly (*skhod* – from which, in this case the kulaks were excluded) and 'the mobilization of the "rural proletariat" ... in the application of the new policy [which] gave it a semblance of democratic legitimacy'.[26] To put it bluntly, and without oversimplifying, what Stalin did was to utilize the traditional economic diversification within the ancient Russian peasant commune (the *obshchina* or *mir*) – which had widened as a result of Stolypin's agrarian reforms and the incentives of NEP – in order to rekindle a kind of class struggle within the rural community, pitting the poor peasants against the rich. In this confrontation, in which were embedded old, atavistic rivalries, envies and resentments, exacerbated by recent ideological calculations, the lower socio-economic strata became, as it were, unwittingly enlisted as agencies of the state and party authorities without appearing to be so. To quote Hughes once more:

> The Stalinist strategy organized small groups of poor and middle peasant actifs as caucuses to wrest the *skhod* from kulak hegemony and then use its legitimacy as the governing peasant institution to vote approval for party policies. Participation was secured by the provision of selective material incentives... for poor peasants who supported the state... All of these factors were significant inducements for peasant participation.[27]

In other words, the collectivization campaign, based on the 'Urals-Siberian method', was not simply a matter of the state versus the peasants, but of the state utilizing traditional peasant rivalries and fissiparous tendencies within the agrarian communities to achieve what Hughes calls 'the capturing of the peasantry'.

Ultimately, of course, it was not just the kulaks, but the entire Russian peasantry that suffered in a campaign whose victims numbered around 100 million people, all in the name of industrialization, economic modernization and the construction of Communism. In terms of the focus of this book, it is significant, and also sadly ironic, that this nationwide economic and human tragedy of collectivization was sparked off by Stalin's perception of the role of the prosperous peasant class in Siberia, thousands of whom had seen the lands beyond the Urals, and been encouraged to settle there, as a place of freedom, opportunity and potential wealth.

That wealth, derived from agricultural production, was intended to finance the ambitious plans for the rapid industrialization of the Soviet economy through the implementation of the first – and subsequent – 'five-year plans'. In this grandiose project, Siberia was also to play a significant part. After Stalin's experience of 1928, Siberia was to receive 'special' attention during the following quarter century of the dictator's rule. While continuing its role as an invaluable resource frontier, it also resumed – in even greater proportions – its pre-revolutionary status as Russia's 'vast roofless prison' for the political and common criminal effluent of Stalin's purges. To a large extent the exploitation of the territory's natural wealth and the building of her new giant industrial plants were carried out by the persecution of its convicted exiles and forced labourers. *Ssylka* and *katorga* were back with a vengeance (see below). The region also underwent a series of political-administrative internal boundary changes introduced to bring it more tightly under Moscow's central control.

The first two five-year plans (1928–32 and 1933–7) were designed with the purpose of forcing the USSR to undertake a 'great leap forward' towards becoming a major industrial power, to catch up in ten years with what it had taken the West a century or more to achieve. In this process Siberia and the Far East were crucial, not only as a source of raw materials, but also as producers of industrial goods, including military materiel. The centrepiece of this massive enterprise was the creation of the Urals-Kuznetsk Combine (UKK), which linked the vastly expanded coalfields of the Kuznetsk Basin (Kuzbass) via a 1,900-kilometre (1,200-mile) railroad to the huge new metallurgical-industrial complex based at the Urals town of Magnitogorsk (Magnetic Mountain), an area that had long been known for its ferrous and non-ferrous metal deposits, but never before exploited on such a titanic scale. A sister metallurgical plant was also constructed in the Kuzbass at the town of Stalinsk (later renamed Novokuznetsk). During the 1930s the Siberian UKK, the Kuzbass coalmines and the iron- and steelworks became in a sense the iconic symbol of the 'construction of socialism' in the USSR while the capitalist West languished in a slough of economic depression, financial ruin and mass unemployment. Struggling in what were still appalling living and working conditions, in the space of one decade Magnitogorsk's workforce, consisting of volunteers, immigrants, idealistic foreigners and conscript labourers – and their plants fuelled by Kuzbass coking coal – transformed the town into the world's largest producer of iron and steel. Statistics vary according to different sources but on any reckoning the industrial upsurge east of the Urals was of gargantuan proportions, and one cannot help wondering what the outcome of the Second World War, Russia's second 'Great Patriotic War', might have been if this huge industrial and manufacturing base had not been created in the relative strategic safety of Siberia in advance of the Nazi invasion, occupation and devastation of European Russia in 1941 (see below).

On the matter of statistics (and bearing in mind the aphorism popularized by Mark Twain that: 'There are three kinds of lies – lies, damned lies and statistics'), it is worth quoting just a few. Victor Mote reckons that by 1938, Magnitogorsk and Stalinsk were producing almost a quarter of total Soviet steel output; coal production rocketed by 270 per cent from 1928 to 1932, and a further 250 per cent between 1933 and 1938. Coal-fuelled electrical power-stations in Siberia accounted for no less than a 1,000 per cent increase in electrical energy output during the first and second five-year plans. In terms of the extractive industries, he continues: 'By 1940, Greater Siberia was contributing the lion's share of the USSR's gold, 95 per cent of its tin, 80 per cent of its tungsten, 70 per cent of its molybdenum, and almost all of its flu-orspar and mica.'[28] The demands of the construction industry (new factories and towns, etc.) and the expansion of the railway network also stimulated production of cement for building purposes and timber for railroad sleepers.

Using more fanciful comparative imagery, Harmon Tupper, quoted by W. Bruce Lincoln, produced the following figures:

> Estimated to hold at least half a billion metric tons of some of the highest-grade iron ore in the world, [the] Magnetic Mountain ... could provide enough steel to build the skeletal structures of 7,938 Empire State Buildings, or 3,969,140 diesel locomotives. Using local ore in combination with Kuzbass coking coal, Magnitogorsk was to become the largest steel mill in Eurasia and the western anchor of Stalin's huge Urals-Kuznets combine.[29]

Although one might add a fourth category to Twain's profile of lies by including 'Soviet government statistics', it is nevertheless worthwhile to record some of the figures for the economic achievements of the first two five-year plans produced by respectable Soviet scholars, which, even if taken with a soupçon of scepticism, are still pretty impressive. Stripped of the inevitable party rhetoric in which they are often couched, some of the calculations of the contributors to the Academy of Sciences' authoritative five-volume *History of Siberia* are as follows. During the first five-year plan:

1. More than 4,000 million rubles were invested in the Siberian economy, of which the majority went into the expansion and development of heavy industry, especially the coal, chemical and metallurgical sectors.
2. While industrial output throughout the whole of the USSR doubled, in Siberia it quintupled.
3. In comparison with 1913 figures, the value of gross industrial production was 4.7 times higher; in comparison with 1928, more than 3 times. In western Siberia the corresponding figures are 8.3 and 3.5 respectively.
4. Despite the non-achievement of targets in some sectors of the economy, due to environmental factors, inadequate use of new technology and shortage of sufficiently qualified personnel, nevertheless the period of the first five-year plan saw the rapid transformation of the Siberian economy from an overwhelmingly agrarian one to making the territory one of the most important industrial regions in the country. Whereas in 1928, heavy industry

in Siberia accounted for 22.5 per cent of gross production in the region's economy, by 1932 in western Siberia it accounted for 54.1 per cent, and in eastern Siberia almost 61 per cent.

5. One of the obvious knock-on effects of Siberia's industrial boom was a rapid growth in the urban population, the construction of new towns such as Novokuznetsk, Igarka, Belovo and Prokopevsk, and the development of new educational, medical, social insurance and cultural facilities.

The picture during the next five years very much repeats the achievements of the first. Again, the bare statistics tell the tale: during these years, gross industrial production throughout the USSR grew by 2.2 times, in Siberia the figure was 2.8, an achievement which was based on the building of new enterprises and the technological upgrading of old ones, and confirmed Siberia's new role as one of the country's key industrial regions. Heavy industry was particularly successful, accounting for 64.1 per cent of total production in western Siberia, 65.5 per cent in Krasnoyarsk district and 55 per cent in Siberia as a whole. In 1937 alone Siberia produced 2,000 million kilowatt-hours of electrical energy, 28.4 million tons of coal, 1471.3 thousand tons of iron ore and 1631.6 thousand tons of steel.[30] Another feature of the development of Siberia during the second plan period, which replicated the first, was the growth of new towns and settlements, including Komsomolsk-na-Amure, Sovetskaya Gavan, Magadan and Norilsk, the latter two gaining notoriety as major centres of forced labour.

Although many Western commentators have taken some of these figures with a large pinch of Siberian salt, it cannot be denied that Siberia and the Far East made an enormous contribution to the spectacular industrial expansion of the Soviet Union during the 1930s, an expansion without which, as mentioned above, the country would have been worse equipped to withstand the devastating shock of Nazi Germany's invasion of the USSR in 1941. But before examining Siberia's role in the Great Patriotic War, it is necessary to turn to the distressing subject of Stalin's purges, the 'Great Terror' and the operation of the forced labour camp system – the GULag.

GULAG

'GULag' looks, sounds and is an ugly word, signifying an ugly reality. If the 1930s are marked by the remarkable economic achievements of the five-year plans, then they are also branded and eternally scarred by what has become known as Stalin's 'Great Terror'. What that amounted to was a nationwide campaign of eradication and elimination of all forms of political, ideological and personal opposition to Stalin's regime and its policies by a deadly process of denunciation, accusation, arrest, imprisonment, interrogation, torture, show trials, administrative sentences without benefit of judicial procedure, mass exile, forced labour and execution of those who were deemed to be 'enemies of the people'. The murder of the popular Leningrad Communist Party boss, Sergei Kirov (1886–1934), in 1934 is generally regarded by historians as the catalyst for the countless, inexorable arrests, exiles and executions that reduced the population of the Soviet Union to a state of mutual, communal suspicion (even family members denounced one another), cowed obedience and sheer terror. This is not the place to examine the causes, course and consequences of what are euphemistically referred to in Russian as Stalin's 'repressions'. The literature on the subject is immense.[31] Suffice it to say here that in the deadly trawl between 1934 and 1939, literally millions of Soviet citizens were snatched by the agents of the NKVD (*Narodnyi komissariat vnutrennikh del* or People's Commissariat for Internal Affairs – in effect a sinister political police force similar to Hitler's Gestapo), mainly on trumped-up charges, and arbitrarily dealt with by the officers and operatives of the Main Camp Administration, the GULag – or, to give it its full title, *Glavnoe upravlenie ispravitel'no-trudovikh lagerei, trudovykh poselenii i mest zaklyuchenii* ('The Main Administration for Corrective Labour Camps, Labour Settlements and Places of Imprisonment'). It was formed in 1934 at the same time as the NKVD, and the two organizations were jointly the chief instruments of Stalin's machinery of oppression. The word GULag has passed into popular and literary usage as a kind of synonym for the whole system of exile and imprisonment during Stalin's dictatorship, though in the West it is often erroneously used to mean simply 'a camp'. (References in journalistic and even historical literature, for example, to someone being 'sent to a gulag', or, 'she spent 15 years in a Siberian gulag' are simply misinformed and inaccurate.)

What can accurately be said is that Siberia, the far north and the Far East were, as they had been under the tsarist exile system (see Chapter Six), the main location for the nefarious operation of the GULag network of works camps, settlements and other islands of misery, torment and death on what, as mentioned above, Solzhenitsyn immortalized as the 'Gulag Archipelago', in his book of that title.[32] (Indeed, it is chiefly through Solzhenitsyn's 'experiment in literary investigation', as he called it, that the word 'gulag' became familiar in the West.) It is, however, impossible in the present book to give a thorough description and analysis of the Soviet camp system. Reasons of space allow only a brief indication and impression of the scale, workings and sheer inhumanity of the operation. For a full, scholarly treatment of the subject, readers are referred to Anne Applebaum's *Gulag: A History of the Soviet Labour Camps*.[33] Two important points that Applebaum makes clear are that, first, unlike the Nazi death camps such as Auschwitz, Sobibor, Treblinka and elsewhere, the Soviet versions were built not with the *specific* objective of deliberately exterminating their victims; and, second, their primary purpose was *economic*, but economic in the same sense that slavery is an economic institution. True, millions did die in the camps from starvation, from diseases such as scurvy, tuberculosis and pellagra, and from hypothermia, frostbite and sheer physical exhaustion. Tens of thousands more were beaten to death, savaged by dogs, or arbitrarily shot dead by the camp guards. But that was not the GULag's central purpose. The end result of both systems may have been similar, i.e. mass annihilation, but the means and the motives were distinct – not that that mattered to the victims. One writer summed up the situation by describing the Soviet camps as 'Auschwitz without the ovens'.[34]

The camps were not, of course, confined to Siberia but existed in every republic and region of the USSR. In Lincoln's words: 'Like a cancer of the most deadly sort, the network of Gulag forced-labour camps metastasized across the Soviet Union.'[35] But given its size and its huge depository of precious resources, which needed an equally huge labour force to mine and extract them, it is not surprising that the majority of labour camps and settlements were located in Siberia. Although the exact figures will never be known, Mote quotes Solzhenitsyn's estimates, which indicate that of the 225 'camp regions' throughout the USSR, 120 were in Siberia, 50 in western Siberia, and 70 further east. Each of these 'camp regions' contained dozens, scores or over a hundred individual camps, each one containing hundreds of forced labourers.[36] After their arrest and after their sentence had been decided, the prisoners, from all over the Soviet Union, were loaded into railway cattle-wagons, as many as 80 to each box-car, packed together like frozen fish, given hardly any food and water and forced – if they were able to get there in time – to elbow their way through the crush in order to use the latrine, which consisted simply of a small hole in the wagon floor. Not surprisingly in these horrendous conditions, the incidence of illness, disease, contagion and death was deplorably high. Those bound for the gold mines on the Kolyma in the far north were, on arrival at Vladivostok after over a month's train journey in the hellish wagons, transferred to irregular tramp steamers on which conditions were, if anything, even more ghastly, and where the prisoners suffered the sadistic cruelty of the ships' crews. These vessels were the twentieth-century equivalent of the eighteenth-century slavers carrying their wretched human cargoes from Africa to the Americas, or British ships transporting thousands of exiled criminals to Australia and Tasmania in the nineteenth century.

The hard labour to which the prisoners were put, irrespective of their physical condition, ranged from lumbering and logging, to gold-mining, tunnelling, railroad-laying, construction, nickel extraction and sundry other forms of gruelling graft in sub-zero temperatures in the long winters and midge-, gnat- and mosquito-infested brief summers. On arrival at their destination they were stripped naked, medically inspected, and had their head and pubic hair (both men and women) shaved with blunt, unsterilized knives and razors in order to eradicate nits and lice – a sensible precaution, but a further humiliating practice. Morbidity and mortality rates were astronomical. Camp diet was lower than bare subsistence level. People scrabbled for inedible scraps of rotten bits in the garbage piles. Dead rats were a tasty treat. Medical facilities were minimal. In order to relieve themselves, prisoners squatted together on the filthy rim of a wooden tub – the *parashnaya bochka* – in which the excreted contents of their bowels and bladders stank and putrefied until emptied at the early morning wake-up clang.

The camp guards were casually brutal. Sometimes, prisoners were 'promoted' to the status of guard, and they became even more brutal than those who formerly abused them. In the words of an old maxim that occurs in many cultures, in the Siberian camps, 'Man was wolf to man'. As for the women prisoners, they were routinely and repeatedly raped, or else desperately driven to surrender their undernourished, emaciated bodies in return for meagre extra rations. The memoir literature written by some of those who did survive is replete with horror stories of the cruelty, humiliation, heartbreaking misery and torture of the GULag's agonized victims, crucified on the icy cross of the Siberian camps.[37] Particularly excruciating were the conditions of work and half-life at the camps around Magadan, Vorkuta and Norilsk in the far north-east, the operations of which were under the control, in co-operation with the GULag – though the two were technically separate organizations – of an outfit called *Dal'stroi* (The Far East State Construction Trust), which, under the command of its first director, E.P. Berzin, was responsible for the total economic output, social and penal institutions and administration of what in effect became a kind of state within a state (see Fig. 12).

Within his north-eastern quasi-tsardom, Berzin earned himself something of a reputation as a kind of benevolent dictator, in so far as he regarded his convict labourers as an economic resource that needed to be properly fed, clothed, sheltered and given adequate rest periods from their labours in order that they would be healthy and robust enough to fulfil their quotas. Needless to say, the top brass at the NKVD regarded this as unnecessary 'coddling' of enemies of the people, and in 1938 he was recalled to Moscow on a false pretext, arrested and shot.

Meanwhile, the number of the GULag's victims continued to escalate. Perhaps surprisingly, the numbers of the camp inmates was much greater after the end of the Second World War than at the height of the purges in the late 1930s. This was partly the result of the transportation of large numbers of ex-prisoners-of-war, both foreign and Russian, and members of ethnic minority groups suspected of pro-German sympathies. Anne Applebaum, while introducing many caveats about the reliability of the now published NKVD archives, gives the following figures (as at 1 January in each year):

Table 9.1 No. of GULag camp inmates, 1930–53

1930:	179,000
1935:	965,742
1937:	1,196, 369
1941:	1,929,729
1946:	1,703, 095
1950:	2,561, 351
1953:	2,468,5243[38]

'Corrective-labour camp' ... It doesn't sound too bad. But behind those words is hidden such a deadly indifference towards people that is more fearful than hatred.

All the wisdom accumulated by mankind was used by the slave-owners of the mid-twentieth century in order to employ the system to turn human beings into beasts.

It is shameful to watch how six or ten healthy young men with guns and dogs guard a dozen or so half-dead, half-alive emaciated women! All the more shameful that somewhere at the battle-front young soldiers are defending the motherland with their own breasts.

The construction of the Egyptian pyramids employed more technology ... But why use machinery when there are thousands and tens of thousands of slaves to do the same job?

Figure 12 Sketches and notes from the prison-camp diary of Yevfrosinia Kersnovskaya.
Source: Ogonëk, no. 4, January (1990).

The macabre mathematics of the camp operation's victims, as indeed of those who died or disappeared in Stalin's Great Terror as a whole, has been the subject of much academic debate and almost Jesuitical juggling of numbers.[39] Some of the figures reproduced above are too precise to warrant any credibility. The camp population was constantly shifting: new arrivals, deaths (both recorded and unrecorded), the rare escapes, promotions of prisoners into camp staff, conscription of inmates into the armed forces, nameless igloo graves of those who dropped dead on the job, births of babies to what were called 'camp wives', legitimate post-sentence-served releases, sloppy accounting methods, fiddled files, etc., all contribute to a wholly unsatisfactory and not in any way accurate enumeration of the millions of those who ultimately became the martyred victims of Soviet economic modernization, and the ghosts of the GULag who still haunt Siberia's and the Russian Far East's frozen wastes.[40] (See Figs 13 and 14.)

WAR AND RECONSTRUCTION

It is a sad reflection on the historiography and popular conceptions in the West that the role of the USSR in the victory over Nazi Germany in 1945 is only rarely given full appreciation. The Soviet Union suffered more casualties, both military and civilian, than any other of the belligerent countries in the conflict – around 27 million dead by recent estimates. And it is virtually indisputable that the battle of Stalingrad was the crucial turning point in Hitler's and the Wehrmacht's ultimate defeat. In that defiant and dauntless Soviet war effort, Siberia and the Russian Far East once again had a specific and vital role to play. Not only had a solid industrial base been laid on its home soil or permafrost during the 1930s, but it was also the recipient and new site of hundreds of factories from the occupied or threatened areas of European Russia, which were literally dismantled, packed up – often brick by brick, bolt by bolt – loaded and transported across the Urals and there reassembled, screwed down and jump-started into new operation and production. Altogether, in the space of only 5 months – July to November, and in the face of the murderous German *Blitzkrieg* – over 1,500 factories were transported across the Urals, relocated and brought back into full production.

With most of Soviet Europe under military occupation and its working population decimated, the Siberian industrial base became both the major arsenal and, in a sense, the headquarters of the Soviet resistance and fight-back against Germany and its allies. Siberia was, in Lincoln's words, the stage setting for 'a battle of war production that would pit the mills and mines of Magnitogorsk, the Kuzbass and Urals against the might of the Nazi Ruhr'.[41] In 1812, then faced with Napoleon's invading *Grande Armée*, the Governor General of Moscow, Count Rostopchin, wrote to Tsar Alexander I that: 'The empire has two powerful defenders in its vastness and its climate. The emperor of Russia will always be formidable in Moscow, terrible in Kazan, and invincible in Tobolsk.'[42] That prescient statement was equally true of the

Figure 13 Open gold-mining site in the Kolyma region.

Figure 14   Main entrance to a forced labour camp at Vorkuta. The legend over the gates reads, 'Work in the USSR is a matter of Honour, Glory and Pride', somewhat similar to the notorious inscription at the gates of the Auschwitz extermination camp – '*Arbeit macht Frei*' ('Work will make you free').

Second, as of the First, Great Patriotic War. In effect, Stalin, who had turned Siberia not only into an industrial giant, but also into a torture chamber and charnel house, was saved from military defeat by Siberia's resources and its people. While European Russia and its towns and villages were crushed, bombed and burned, and their populations massacred as what Hitler had fanatically condemned as *Untermenschen* (subhumans), Siberia and the Far East continued to flex its newly created economic and industrial muscle, and to recruit its human resources to sustain the entire nation during its four-year ordeal. *Pace* Adolf, and to his cost, the Russian and Siberian peoples, when faced with an inhuman foe, turned out to be not subhuman, but almost superhuman.

Since the 1917 Revolution and the end of the Civil War, Siberia and the Russian Far East had been what the late John Erickson described as both a military 'outpost and bastion'.[43] Throughout the 1920s and 1930s, Stalin, the Soviet government and the Red Army's high command had been acutely aware of both the strategic importance and also the vulnerability of its eastern provinces. It is generally forgotten in the West that ever since the time of the ferocious Mongol invasion of Russia in the thirteenth century, the country had experienced what has been called a 'siege mentality', conscious of simultaneous military threats and invasion from both east and west. After the misguided and mishandled war against Japan in 1904–5, Russia's relations with her Asiatic neighbour had been fraught with the possibility of further conflict. Alert to the prospect of a Japanese attack on Russia's Far East, between 1931 and 1938, according to estimates by Saburo Hayashi, Soviet military strength in the Transbaikal region had quadrupled, with around 20 rifle divisions, 4 cavalry units, 1,200 aircraft under the command of a newly established Far Eastern Air Force and 1,200 tanks.[44]

In 1938 and 1939, while Hitler was busy invading and occupying eastern and western Europe, Russia and Japan were once more engaged together in warfare at the battles of Lake Khasan (July–August 1938) and Khalkin Gol (July 1939), the latter conflict ending in the resounding defeat of the Japanese by Soviet troops under the command of a then little-known officer (later Marshal) Georgii Zhukov (1896–1974), soon to be the hero of the battle of Stalingrad, the lifting of the siege of Leningrad, the capture of Berlin and other vital, or deadly, operations leading to the end of the Second World War. At the beginning of that war, however, the threat of invasion in the east still loomed, which is why, in the autumn of 1941, while German tanks, troops and aircraft rolled, marched and flew relentlessly across the steppes and plains of European Russia, destroying almost everything in their path, thousands of kilometres to the east '15–30 per cent of the Red Army's total combat capability [were] at various times kept back from the deadly struggle in the west'. One million troops, up to 16,000 guns, 2,000 tanks, nearly 4,000 airplanes and 100 warships were deployed and locked down in eastern Siberia and on the Pacific littoral in anticipation of a Nippon-style *Blitzkreig*.[45]

When it became clear, however, that the Japanese government had decided against an invasion of Siberia, preferring instead to take on the United States by bombing Pearl Harbor in December 1941, winter-hardened soldiers from the Far East were rapidly transferred westwards – with white-camouflaged, hooded, ski-borne Siberian shooters taking a leading part in the Red Army's counter-attack in defence of Moscow. According to Erickson, citing Soviet figures on troop movements:

> In all, the Far East and Trans-Baikal sent more than 400,000 men, 5,000 guns and in excess of 3,300 tanks – in total, 3 field armies, 39 divisions ... 21 brigades and 10 independent regiments. Overhead, US aircraft were also ferried from Alaska to Yakutsk and Krasnoyarsk, with a peak traffic of 300 planes per month, most of which then went westwards to the Soviet-German front.[46]

Within half a decade, Hitler had conquered almost all of Europe. He then turned east, and that, of course, caused his eventual ruin. It was a far different matter from annexing Austria, taking over the Sudetenland, invading Poland, ploughing through France, Belgium and elsewhere, to facing the twin terrors of the Russian winter and the hard-bitten battalions from Siberia and the Far Eastern front.

Three months after the 'war in the west' was won and Europe carved up into 'zones of influence' among the Allied leaders at the conferences of Tehran, Yalta and Potsdam, the USSR declared a state of war against Japan and launched a massive 5,000-kilometre (3,100-mile) front – the so-called 'August storm' – at the same time as the United States dropped its atomic bomb on the city of Nagasaki. The gratuitous bombing of both Hiroshima and Nagasaki were politically directed more at Moscow than Tokyo in the opening stages of the Cold War. The war in the east was now over, as it had been in the west. But in that combined victory over the Japanese Empire and the Third Reich, Siberia and the Russian Far East had played a tremendous, heroic and honourable role – one that is still little known about, understood or acknowledged in the West.

Between the end of hostilities in 1945 and Stalin's death in 1953, the whole of the Soviet Union, Siberia included, had to face the mammoth task of reconstructing the country's flattened economy and decimated society. Apart from the millions of deaths, thousands of towns and villages had been all but obliterated, transport and communication networks destroyed, bridges blown up, and industrial and agricultural regions devastated. Many of the factories relocated – to good effect – over the Urals in 1941 were now transported back to their original sites in reoccupied Soviet Europe. The huge landmass from the Urals to the Pacific had been spared the ravages and ruination of the Nazi invasion, but both during the war and in the period of postwar reconstruction Siberia played an essential role, and was destined to play an even more crucial part in the development of the USSR, and in the new Cold War with the West, until the Soviet political system itself finally collapsed in 1991. In the following, final chapter, the story of how Siberia contributed to the process of economic expansion, exciting visions, social change, de-Stalinization, foreign relations – particularly in the Asian-Pacific region – and eventual political debacle will be examined. However, the penultimate words in this chapter go to Victor Mote, whose damning conclusion on Siberia under Stalin reads: 'Never before in human history had a geographic region been used so effectively as an instrument of oppression and execution. By 1953, the periphery and its residents, including its native minorities, were absolutely subordinate to Moscow.'[47]

But then, Siberia had been under Moscow's heel and its people and resources exploited as a colony ever since the reign of Ivan the Terrible in the sixteenth century, and continued to be so after his equally terrible successor's death.

10

Siberia since Stalin, 1953–91: Boom, BAM and Beyond

Josef Vissarionovich Stalin died on 5 March 1953. Three years later, towards the end of February 1956, Nikita Sergeevich Khrushchev (1894–1971), his eventual successor as party leader, delivered his notorious 'secret speech' to a closed session of the XXth Congress of the Communist Party of the Soviet Union. In that speech he revealed to a shocked, but also disingenuous, audience the extent of the late dictator's crimes, his creation of the 'cult of personality', his destruction of the old, revolutionary Bolshevik Party leadership, his deviation from 'Leninist norms' and multiple violations of 'socialist legality'.[1] The four-hour diatribe was a bombshell, the reverberations of which soon echoed around, not just the Soviet Union, but the whole world. It was a damning indictment of a man whom all of the assembled delegates from every Soviet republic had until that day regarded as something of a demi-god. Otherwise, they wouldn't have been there. However, Khrushchev, despite his portly bulk, had to perform some nimble footwork in order to exonerate, or at least give a superficial gloss on, his own role and that of his politburo comrades in his dead master's dastardly deeds.

Even before Khrushchev's speech, the publicly unacknowledged process of what came to be called 'de-Stalinization' was already under way. From 1953 there had been something of a literary, artistic and intellectual 'thaw'. There were a range of economic reforms and the introduction of more personal freedoms for collective farm workers. The NKVD lost some of its powers. Thousands of the GULag's miraculously surviving victims were amnestied, rehabilitated and released to something resembling a free life. Although the Cold War still continued to poison international relations, new overtures to the Western powers were made and Soviet politicians went on diplomatic jaunts to Europe and the United States. The whole of the USSR, including, of course, Siberia and the Far East, had entered a new phase in its history, with a radically changed leadership. But let there be no mistake: all of these top party and government figures – Khrushchev, Beria, Malenkov, Molotov, Kaganovich, Brezhnev, Voroshilov, Suslov *et al.* – were Stalin's creatures. The country was still a one-party state, and the official ideology of Stalin's crooked version of Marxism-Leninism, though somewhat attenuated, was still de rigueur. However, the essential difference from the recent past was that there was no longer just one supreme, individual potentate. The members of the new so-called 'collective leadership' had to jockey with each other for positions and power, and though there continued to be a good deal of rivalry, personal jealousies, bickering and attempted 'Kremlin coups', recalling Muscovy's medieval past and the palace plots of the eighteenth century, the murders, the mayhem and the massacres of the mid-twentieth century seemed to be over. As far as we know, Lavrentii Beria (1881–1953), the odious head of Stalin's political police since 1938, was the last senior Soviet politician to be arrested, tried and shot, shortly after Stalin's death. It is against this fresh, though flawed, political backdrop that the next stage in the development of Siberia needs to be examined in order to understand how 'the thaw' affected Russia's 'frozen frontier'.[2]

'THE THAW'

Under Stalin, everything was dictated from the centre, indeed by Stalin him-self. After his death there was a limited amount of slack in the system. Rivulets of semi-independent thought began to trickle across the melting permafrost of Stalinism and the new leadership was able to take stock of the novel situation in which it found itself. Among the many daunting issues facing them was that of regional development, i.e. whether to invest more resources and allow greater local initiative in the non-Russian republics and outlying regions of the country, or to continue the command economy's total, centralized control. In the event, something of a compromise was reached – a rare thing in Russia's history – by which, while the men in the Kremlin remained firmly in the driv-ing seat, various segments of Soviet society and the economy, and various interest groups including the regions, were granted a certain amount of space to put forward and pursue their own particular agenda. In the case of Siberia, it was clear, even to the most dogmatic, die-hard centralist, that a new course needed to be taken. One of the most pressing problems to be tackled was that of the GULag system.

Although it was not openly admitted, it was obvious to many senior politi-cians and officials that the forced-labour camp network – which had contributed much to the industrial effort in the USSR, including Siberia, in the 1930s – was no longer cost-effective or economically efficient. Part of the problem was the great expense, not only of transporting and provisioning the prison-ers, but also the relatively high wages paid to the camp guards and adminis-trative personnel. In short, the whole of 'GULag & Dal'stroi Co. Ltd' was no longer in profit, and, on the contrary, a drain on the nation's economy. Moreover, it was also known that the vast majority of the inmates, of whom there were in excess of 2.5 million in 1953, were innocent of the alleged crimes for which they had originally been charged and committed. The announcement of the death of Stalin had already triggered rumbling rumours of anticipated changes throughout the camp population itself. Urgent action was clearly needed. Surprisingly, the lead in the relaxation of the camp regime was taken by Lavrentii Beria, Minister of Internal Affairs, the monster who for the last decade-and-a-half was more responsible than any for dispatching most of the convicted there in the first place. Only one week after Stalin's death, he cancelled over 20 of the GULag's major construction projects, and shortly after that recommended to the Party Central Committee the immediate amnesty and release of various categories of camp inmates. These included the sick and elderly, pregnant women, women with children, juveniles under the age of 18 and those serving a sentence of less than 5 years (most of whom were common criminals, rather than 'politicals'). The reasons for Beria's initiative remain unclear – he was hardly distinguished by his compassion, philanthropy or humanitarianism – but the directive went into immediate effect, and even after his disgrace and execution there was little that the rest of the party leadership could do to reverse the policy. 'The clock was now ticking: the Gulag's era was coming to an end.'[3]

However, despite the amnesties and the easing up of the draconian daily regime in some camps, hundreds of thousands still remained in others where there was little change in their punitive working and living conditions. When news of Beria's 'liberalizing' measures spread throughout the other 'special' camps, where long-sentence *zeks* (Russian slang for prisoners) still stayed encaged, an astounding and almost unprecedented phenomenon occurred. 'Almost' unprecedented, because isolated instances of insubordination and protest had already taken place and been put down in the late 1940s. But what happened after Stalin's demise was the development of a determined strike movement, organized opposition to the camp authorities, the stealthy but systematic murder of informers (*stukachi*) and stool-pigeons, petitions to the GULag administration, intimidation of the guards, circulation of clandestine handwritten newspapers and, in sum, what Applebaum describes as the '*Zeks'* Revolution'.[4]

The protests, demonstrations and strikes were fairly widespread, but the three main flashpoints were camp complexes at Norilsk, Kolyma and Vorkuta in the Arctic north. The response of the state authorities was varied. On the one hand some concessions were granted, such as allowing food parcels and money to be received on a more regular basis, more frequent family visits, removal of the hated identification number tags from camp clothing, less severe punishments for insubordination and easing of workloads for female inmates. Also, in some cases emissaries were sent from Moscow to conduct negotiations with protesters, something unimaginable only a few weeks before. At the other extreme, armed troops and even tanks were sometimes used to crush the rebellions and the rebels themselves, with consequent loss of life.

One of the longest and ultimately violently suppressed stand-offs took place, not in Siberia itself, but in what was called *Steplag* (Steppe Camp Complex), near Kengir in Kazakhstan. After weeks of recalcitrance and stubborn opposition on the part of the thousands of inmates, Moscow finally ran out of patience and sent in the heavy brigade. On 26 June 1954 nearly 2,000 soldiers, 100 dogs and 5 T-34 tanks stormed the camp and began a relentless, remorseless attack on the prisoners. Groups of silently demonstrating inmates were flattened beneath the caterpillar treads of the tanks, literally ground into the ground, while scores of others were gunned down on the spot. Official figures put the number of dead at 40 plus. Survivors' later accounts put it at nearer 500, with hundreds more seriously wounded.[5] Other prisoners, not only at Kengir but elsewhere throughout the GULag empire, were rounded up and transported to different camps in an attempt to contain the disturbances. However, this policy only boomeranged on the government, as the dispersal of the more militant agitators simply served to spread the virus of revolt even more widely. The problem therefore came winging back to them with even more force and purpose.

Confronted with the obdurate, now fearless, resistance of mutinous inmates of such key centres of the GULag operation as Vorkuta, Norilsk and Kolyma, the regime was finally forced into a position of conditional capitulation. Although the prison camp system was not fully dismantled for many years, at least a process of more widespread release and rehabilitation took place during the period of collective leadership, and the horrors of the GULag archipelago were now a matter of public knowledge. The party and police *apparatchiki* (officials) could no longer hide behind the barbed-wire barrier of official dumbness and denial. The execution of Beria in December 1953, the publication of Ehrenburg's novel, *The Thaw* – attacking despotic bureaucratism – in 1954, Khrushchev's 'secret speech' denouncing Stalin in 1956, the appearance in the pages of Russia's leading literary journal, *Novyi mir*, of Solzhenitsyn's long short story, 'One Day in the Life of Ivan Denisovich' in 1962, describing the appalling conditions in a typical 'corrective labour' camp,[6] the continuing amnesties and releases, the posthumous rehabilitation of Stalin's prominent victims like Nikolai Bukharin – all of this was symptomatic of the inexorable process of de-Stalinization. So how, apart from the gradual depopulation of the camps, was Siberia affected by this process?

A chronic problem was the mismatch between her enormous size and rich resources on the one hand, and the paucity of her population on the other. With the camps being slowly emptied, but with the USSR still desperately in need of Siberia's exploitable mineral wealth, a new plan to attract armies of voluntary workers, both skilled and non-skilled, to settle east of the Urals needed to be worked out. What occurred (to continue the military metaphor) was the opening of a new front or, rather, three combined fronts – agrarian, industrial and academic – each of which met with varying degrees of strategic success. On the agrarian front, the so-called 'Virgin Lands' campaign was ultimately a 'Radio Armenia'-style catastrophe (see Chapter Nine). On the linked industrial/academic fronts, the funding and building of new scientific research institutes and the consequent discovery of huge reservoirs of oil and natural gas in north-western Siberia and the Far East, and the building of gigantic hydroelectric stations on the country's eastern river systems once again emphasized the crucial role of the territory for the whole of the nation's economy, energy needs and power.

The Virgin Lands campaign was what was later to be derided by Nikita Khrushchev's detractors as one of his 'hare-brained' schemes. Between 1954 and 1961, tens of thousands of young volunteers quit their homes, jobs and universities to join in a massive, highly publicized assault on the undeveloped virgin soil: millions of hectares of untilled land in south-western Siberia and northern Kazakhstan. In Kazakhstan alone, the area to be put under the plough was more than three times the size of the United Kingdom. At first the scheme met with some success and substantial agricultural yields seemed to vindicate the bold initiative. Bumper harvests in 1956 and 1958 turned the Virgin Lands (officially so named in 1960 – the *Tselinnyi krai*) into what Violet Conolly described as the Soviet Union's 'second "bread-basket" with a record production of 23,823,000 tons of grain in 1956 … [and] in 1958, 21,991,000 tons'.[7] But the result was ultimately a near-disaster. A number of factors combined to turn the initially promising enterprise into an agro-fiasco. Aridity, soil erosion, lack of fertilizers, shortage of machine maintenance, undersupply of skilled personnel and the terrible social infrastructure (inadequate housing, schools, hospitals, etc. to cater for the 'patriot volunteers') – all contributed to the pulverization of Khrushchev's grand design, which was a major factor leading to his political ouster in 1964. To mix metaphors, far from continuing to be a bread-basket, the Virgin Lands had turned into a dust-bowl.

The project was not, however, entirely abandoned. The 'dust-bowl' managed to put forth some fresh green shoots, and under the guidance of agrarian scientists at specialized institutes in Akademgorodok (see below), north Kazakhstan and the fecund arable- and lush pasture-lands of the Altai managed to make a significant contribution to the country's total agricultural output, though not sufficient to avoid the embarrassing purchase and import of large quantities of cereals from the West during the mid-1960s. Apart from helping the Virgin Lands to limp along, teams of eager young scholars and researchers at Akademgorodok, sometimes translated as 'Science City', were to play a leading role in the 'third discovery' of Siberia.

SIBERIA'S 'NEW ATLANTIS'

In the late 1950s and early 1960s, much to the chagrin of the West, Soviet science and technology were on a spectacular upswing. The USSR was already a nuclear power. The world's first man-made space satellite, the *Sputnik*, was launched and circled the planet in 1957. Shortly afterwards the first animal in the cosmos, a dog called 'Laika' (actually the name of a Siberian breed, similar to the husky), was blasted up into the stratosphere. It, too, circled the earth, but never came back. The first human being in space, Yurii Gagarin (1934–68), sped around the planet in 1961 in his space capsule, symbolically named *Vostok* ('The East'). He *did* come back, a hero of the Soviet Union, only to die in an aircraft test-flight accident in 1968.

Meanwhile, back down on terra firma the Soviet government and the highest echelons of the academic establishment were seriously involved in planning a new scientific project deep in the heart of Siberia. In 1956, the redoubtable mathematician and member of the Soviet Academy of Sciences, Mikhail Alekseevich Lavrentev (1900–80), persuaded Nikita Khrushchev to fund and give the government's backing for the foundation and construction of a new town a few kilometres beyond the major Siberian industrial city of Novosibirsk, which would become the intellectual power-house of a scientific revolution and make a spectacular contribution to the whole nation's economy. This was Akademgorodok, future headquarters of the newly founded Siberian Branch of the Soviet Academy of Sciences (SO AN SSSR).

Between 1957 and 1961 a massive building development programme took place in the middle of the Siberian taiga. Most of the new research institutes were dedicated to the pure and applied sciences and technological disciplines such as physics, geology, cybernetics, hydrodynamics, mathematics, organic and inorganic chemistry, chemical kinetics and combustion, cytology and genetics, theoretical and applied mechanics, computer studies, biology and botany, soil science and many more. The social sciences and humanities were not neglected, with the opening of the Institute of History, Philology and Philosophy under the directorship of Academician Aleksei Pavlovich Okladnikov (1908–81), a native Russian Siberian (*sibiryak*) born in Irkutsk province. Also established was the prestigious Institute of Economics and the Organization of Industrial Production, which included on its staff such luminaries as Abel Gezevich Aganbegyan, a key figure in the economic reforms of the 1980s, and the formidable sociologist, Tatyana Ivanovna Zaslavskaya, who opened up hitherto unexplored avenues of sociological research.[8] In the early 1960s the multimillion-volume State Public Scientific-Technological Library (GPNTB) was opened in the centre of Novosibirsk, as well as Novosibirsk State University, located in Akademgorodok itself, which attracted brilliant young students from all over the USSR, taught and supervised by senior Academicians.[9]

As well as the building of the research and teaching institutes themselves, obviously the new town needed plenty of accommodation, apartment blocks, shops, restaurants, meeting halls, bath-houses, concert and artistic venues – including the 'House of Scholars' (*Dom uchënykh*) – and even the creation of an artificial beach with thousands of tons of imported sand spread on the shore of a great man-made reservoir formed on the banks of the river Ob. All of this activity resulted in the formation of the fledgling Siberian 'Atlantis' (the analogy is with Francis Bacon's seventeenth-century allegorical vision of a scientific utopia, *The New Atlantis*, written in 1608), which became both a symbol and a centre for the classic Marxist synthesis of theory and praxis in the study and exploitation of Siberia's invaluable natural resources. Akademgorodok swiftly became not only one of the USSR's most prestigious learning and research institutions – with 'filials' throughout Siberia and the Far East, in Tyumen, Omsk, Tomsk, Barnaul, Kemerovo Krasnoyarsk, Kyzyl, Irkutsk, Ulan-Ude, Chita, Yakutsk and Vladivostok – but also a political battlefield in the struggle between intellectual independence and ideological constraint.

Far from the stifling bureaucratic bumbledom of Moscow and Leningrad, Akademgorodok's pioneering scholars had been seduced from their more traditional, ultimately Stalinist, institutions by the prospect of openly pursuing, discovering or rediscovering areas of knowledge that had previously been limited, muzzled, persecuted or anathematized by the Soviet political establishment. In the late 1950s and early 1960s, with the blessing of the post-Stalin Kremlin leadership, Lavrentev and his colleagues laid the intellectual and concrete foundations of the new science city. Paradoxically, perhaps, Siberia's harsh and inhospitable climate provided an enormous cold-frame in which the seeds of exciting new scientific ventures could germinate, flourish and thrive. Eventually, however, the free-thinking, free-wheeling nuclear physicists, cyberneticists, mathematicians, economists and their colleagues fell foul of the heavy-handed Brezhnevite 'era of stagnation' in response to their outspoken support of Soviet intellectual and literary dissidents, and the Czechoslovak reform movement of 1968. The American scholar, Paul Josephson, provides a thoroughly researched and impressively well-informed history of the conception, birth, teething troubles and precocious development of this uniquely Russian brain-child.[10] Apart from the essential science involved, Josephson gives a fascinating account of the often fraught interplay of politics, ideology, personalities and the pursuit of pure and applied learning across the whole range of disciplines represented at Akademgorodok, united, for the most part, by the employment of mathematical techniques, and inspired by the Lavrentevan triangle of interdisciplinary primary research, linkage of theoretical analysis with economic and industrial production, and the training of fresh scientific cadres.

It is impossible to study not only the intellectual development, but also the social, economic and environmental history of modern Siberia without understanding the role played in the territory's 'third discovery' by Akademgorodok's scientific personnel. Remarkable characters like Lavrentev himself; the iconoclastic nuclear physicist, Gersh Budker; battling biologists such as Dmitri Beliaev and Grigorii Galazii; precursors of Gorbachev's *perestroika* like economist Aganbegyan and sociologist Zaslavskaya, and their fellows, strove to place the Siberian Branch of the Soviet Academy of Sciences firmly in the world's premier league of scholarly institutions. They were supported by hundreds of zealous young research assistants, candidates of science, student *Wunderkinder* at Novosibirsk University, and other comrade *cognoscenti* who gathered not only in the laboratories and seminar rooms, but also in the coffee clubs, cultural societies, saunas, shopping queues and private apartments in the unique democratic/elitist, relaxed/intensive atmosphere of this technopolis in the taiga (see Fig. 15). The present author, after several research visits to Akademgorodok, can give personal testimony to the vibrant intellectual atmosphere of the place, and also to the kindness, care, hospitality and both official and domestic generosity of the local scholars and their families. In the depths of Siberia's wildwoods, one experienced the exhilaration of living and learning in a truly civilized and cultured community, lavishly lubricated with a sagacious blend of lore and liquor.

The struggle of the geneticists against the stultifying legacy of Lysenkoism;[11] the battle to preserve the purity of the pellucid waters of Lake Baikal; the clash between what came to be called 'engineers of nature' and genuine Siberian environmentalists – i.e. those who sought to alter and exploit, and those who wished to preserve and nurture, the region's ecosystem; the planning and building of the Baikal-Amur Mainline (BAM, see below); the futuristic schemes to divert the water of Siberia's great north-flowing rivers to irrigate the arid lands of the Central Asian republics; systematic study of the social attitudes and grievances of Siberian peasants and blue-collar workers – all of this and much more demonstrates that Siberia and its capital academic city played a major role in the economic, scientific and industrial development of the entire country. This was formally acknowledged in a resolution of the Communist Party of the Soviet Union (CPSU) Central Committee in February 1977, which stated:

> The Siberian Division of the USSR Academy of Sciences, its institutes, filials and pilot-production subdivisions have become a major science centre, making a substantial contribution to the resolution of the most important problems of communist construction. It has accomplished serious fundamental and applied research work, which has enhanced the country's scientific, technological and industrial potential and added to the prestige of Soviet science.[12]

However, within a decade of this accolade, the Soviet Union itself had embarked on a process of radical, but ambivalent, institutional and economic change that led finally to its implosion in 1991. Although it is beyond the chronological limits of this book, it is pertinent to note that although Akademgorodok did not die along with the USSR in 1991, the devastating political, social and economic changes which attended its collapse have had their repercussions on the academic community. Maverick market forces, incompetent capitalism, Mafia-like pillaging of academic resources, continuing social problems, environmentally reckless industrial projects and what may be described as the cerebral haemorrhage of both old and new scientific talent heading for more lucrative metropolitan or foreign centres might suggest that Siberia's brave new Atlantis has found it as difficult to keep its head above the waters of political and economic uncertainty as did the vanished mythical island of Plato's imagination.[13]

Figure 15   Akademgorodok, headquarters of Siberia's 'Science City'.

Source: Sibirskoe odelenie Akademii nauk SSSR (Moscow, 1982).

Although the years of Leonid Brezhnev's General-Secretaryship of the CPSU (1966–82) are often somewhat disparagingly referred to as the 'era of stagnation' (*zastoi*) – presumably in comparison with the frenetic horrors of Stalinism and the volatility and vicissitudes of Khrushchev's mercurial incumbency – they could also equally be described as a period of consolidation, and in certain areas even of 'boom', new construction and productive investment. On the economic front, as far as Siberia is concerned, these were the years of tremendous expansion in the oil and natural gas industries, and of the laying down of the ambitious new railroad project in East Siberia and the Far East, the BAM, both of which form the subject matter of the following section.

BOOM AND BAM

The Oil and Gas Rush

As mentioned in Chapter One, Siberia and the Russian Far East contain the mammoth's share of the Soviet Union's, and still now the Russian Federation's, deposits and reservoirs of hydrocarbon fuels. In global economic terms, oil and gas are the most valuable of these, and are the country's biggest export revenue earner. For centuries the remote north-west of Siberia, around the lower reaches of the river Ob, had remained relatively neglected while the bulk of Russian invaders, traders and explorers gravitated to more southerly routes across the continent in the quest for territory, fur and plunder. Meanwhile, the indigenous peoples of the area, then called Voguls and Ostyaks, continued to follow their reindeer herds across the northern landscape, and also to follow their traditional way of life. It was not until the late 1950s that Russian geologists were able to demonstrate what a treasure trove of natural wealth was hidden beneath the swamps, ice and tundra of the far north, and even then the Soviet government took little heed of their discoveries, or at least was rather sceptical of the scientists' claims about the oleiferous and gaseous riches that were there waiting to be drilled down to, tapped, piped and exploited from under some of the harshest and most inhospitable terrain – either boggy or frozen – on the planet.

Ultimately, however, under the persistent pressure of such eminent scientists and scholars as Lavrentev, Aganbegyan, the outstanding geologist, A.A. Trofimuk and other members of the feisty 'Siberian lobby', and with more and more proof of the jumbo subterranean oil and gas sumps coming to light, the politicians were unable to ignore the advice and prognostications of the expert geologists and mineralogists. Most importantly, in political terms, the new General Secretary of the Communist Party, Leonid Brezhnev (1906–82), was finally persuaded that the government and the economic planning organizations should begin to provide the financial, technological and human resources necessary to break through the permafrost, lay down the infrastructure and embark on yet another round of robbing Siberia of its hidden riches. In earlier centuries, the object of Moscow's and St Petersburg's rapacity had been fur, land, gold, diamonds, nickel, even butter, but now it was oil and gas, and still for the benefit of the Russian central economy. A new stage had been reached in Siberia's history as a resource frontier, or, more bluntly, as a colony. Without reiterating the data contained in Chapter One, it is worth underlining the fact that Siberia still remains the world's largest producer and exporter of both oil and natural gas. Despite the horrendous difficulties of working in either swamp-soaked or ice-locked terrain, and the struggle for human survival in those regions, nevertheless north-west Siberia has over the last half-century been turned into the major generator of the country's most important and lucrative revenue earnings. The same is also to some extent true of the Russian Far East where oil and gas fields have recently been developed both inland and off the Pacific coast around the island of Sakhalin.

Towards the end of the twentieth century Siberia accounted for more than 80 per cent of the USSR's proven oil resources and 90 per cent of its gas. Other reservoirs are known to exist in the far north and the Far East. After the gigantic Samotlor oilfield was discovered in 1968, with an estimated 3,500 million tons of proved and probable reserves, the west Siberian oil and gas region developed at an astonishing rate in the last two decades of the Soviet Union's existence. The figures reproduced in the following table give ample evidence of the vigorous rate of expansion.

Table 10.1   Oil Production in the USSR, 1970–90 (millions of tons)

	1970	1975	1980	1983	1984	1985	1990[a]
Siberia	34	151	317	372	380	376	458–68
rest of USSR	319	340	286	244	233	219	172
Total USSR	353	491	603	616	613	595	630–640

[a] Five-year plan target.
Source: Wilson, D., 'The Siberian Oil and Gas Industry', in Wood, A. (ed.), Siberia: Problems and Prospects for Regional Development (London, 1987), p. 98 (amended).

Table 10.2   Gas Production in the USSR, 1970–90 (billions of cubic metres)[a]

	1970	1975	1980	1983	1984	1985	1990
SIBERIA	11	40	158	284	329	373	N/A
rest of USSR	187	249	277	252	258	267	N/A
Total USSR	198	289	435	536	587	640	830–50

[a] One billion = 1,000 million
Source: Wilson, D., 'The Siberian Oil and Gas Industry', in Wood, A. (ed.), Siberia: Problems and Prospects for Regional Development (London, 1987), p. 98 (amended).

The majority of this tremendous output came from the West Siberian Basin on the river Ob, mainly in Tyumen province, but also stretching south-eastwards to the Tomsk, Novosibirsk and Krasnoyarsk regions and northwards into the Yamal Peninsula and the Kara Sea. According to David Wilson, by 1980, close on 300 oil and gas deposits had been discovered and were already being exploited, including the world's largest gasfield at Urengoi, with estimated reserves of over 10,000 billion cubic metres (353,000 billion cubic feet).[14] Despite some jaundiced prognostications by a few American pundits about the unsustainability of Siberian oil and gas output, and despite the still daunting problems involved in developing new towns, building roads and railroads through the fearsome terrain, drilling through the permafrost and laying thousands of kilometres of pipelines, Siberia's hydrocarbon industry still remains in a vigorous, productive and profitable state. In 1985, Academician A.A. Trofimuk, one of the world's leading geologists who was among those who had first pointed out the sub-glacial riches of north-west Siberia, predicted without reservation that 'not only in the twentieth century but also at the beginning of the twenty-first century, [oil and gas] extraction will increase thanks to what lies beneath the West Siberian Plain'.[15] Twenty-five years on, his projections and prophesies still appear to be vindicated.

Throughout the 1970s, 1980s and 1990s the discovery, verification and extraction of northern Russia's huge hydrocarbon deposits increased exponentially, and still continue to do so. Trofimuk's calculation, made in 1985, about the expected oil and gas wealth of Siberia is backed up by recent statistics. Across the whole continent from the Khanty-Mansi and the Yamal-Nentsy autonomous areas of the north-west, further east in the Krasnoyarsk and Irkutsk districts, in Evenkia, Yakutia (Sakha), Magadan region, Chukotka, Sakhalin province and elsewhere in Siberia and the Russian Far East, the production figures are astounding. Without overburdening the text with too many figures, a few examples of output rates will serve to illustrate the situation. In 2002, the northern regions of the Russian Federation accounted for 282.4 million tons – 74 per cent – of the whole country's oil and gas-condensate production (and remember, Russia is the world's largest single producer). In the same year the Khanty-Mansi and the Yamal-Nentsy autonomous areas extracted 253 million tons of hydrocarbon fuel. Also in 2002, East Siberia's prospected oil and gas reserves were 1,190 million tons. In the Far East, total production of both fuels combined was 3.25 million tons. In Sakhalin province, mainly on the Sakhalin Shelf, around 340 million tons of hydrocarbon fuels have been discovered. In the Sakha Republic, almost 420,000 tons of oil were extracted in 2002.

The figures for natural gas on their own are equally impressive. In 2002 the northern regions of Russia accounted for 94 per cent (560.2 billion cubic metres/19,783.3 cubic feet) of gas, and it has been estimated that by the year 2020, this figure will increase to between 600 and 700 billion cubic metres (21,188 to 24,720 cubic feet). Again, it is the three administrative areas of West and East Siberia and the Far East (as defined in Chapter One) that provide the overwhelming majority of contributions to this bonanza.[16] Nothing seen by the present author suggests that the situation will alter significantly, in economic terms, in the near future.

What has altered, and will continue to alter, are the effects of this new exploitation of Siberia on the natural environment. Apart from the severe damage caused to landscape, flora and fauna by the drilling rigs and pipelines, the rushed jerry-building of new settlements and towns like Surgut and Urengoi for the Russian roughnecks attracted to Siberia by the large wage increments has brought with it a host of problems. There were poor sanitation, abandoned junk, unmetalled roads, earth and ice surfaces gouged out and churned up by heavy-duty vehicles that were not designed for the delicate terrain across which they juggernauted their reckless way, destroying large areas of fragile Arctic plant life that will take centuries to regenerate. Surface oil seepage, unnatural meltwater, broken pipelines, risky bleeders, filthy oleaginous mires, human detritus and severe pollution of local rivers and lakes (with consequent loss of edible fish), disruption of traditional migration routes of the reindeer herds – these and other hazards have created, in the name of economic gain, a potentially lethal concoction which may result in a verdict by some later historical coroner's court as 'death by ecocide'.[17] W. Bruce Lincoln sums up the dangers as follows: 'Exploited for the benefit of others, drained of its wealth, and poisoned to a point beyond which complete recovery may no longer be possible, Siberia may bear the burden of that terrible verdict most heavily of all.'[18] (Not that Russia and Siberia are the only guilty parties contributing to the despoliation of the world's natural environment in pursuit of subterranean or submarine energy sources – there are plenty of examples of man-made ecological disasters created by western companies, most recently the blow-out of the BP operated oil-rig in the Gulf of Mexico in April 2010.)

Hydroelectric Power

Although it still remains the case that oil and gas are the main source of Russia's energy resources, another major contributor to the country's power-grid is what has been described as the 'cascade' of huge hydroelectric stations (in Russian known by their acronym GES) in East Siberia built in the 1950s, 1960s and 1970s. The most widely trumpeted of those at the time was the mighty Bratsk GES. In the early 1920s Lenin coined the rather silly slogan that 'Communism is Soviet power plus the electrification of the whole country'. Despite the banality of the propaganda jargon, electricity was in fact connected to thousands of homes and industrial enterprises throughout the USSR (not that that had anything to do with building Communism). In the late 1950s Khrushchev seemed to throw his not inconsiderable weight behind Lenin's 'trans-mission statement' by commissioning the construction of a great chain of hydroelectric dams and stations along East Siberia's rivers and powerful waterfalls, of which the most publicized project was the Bratsk GES. The now thriving (though atmospherically polluted) town of Bratsk, with a population of *c*.280,000, was originally a small cossak settlement on the river Angara, almost 500 kilometres (311 miles) north of Irkutsk. (It was here that the exiled rebel Archpriest Avvakum was imprisoned in a freezing wooden keep in the mid-seventeenth century – see Chapter Two).

In the mid-1950s, when construction of the dam began – at about the same time as the Virgin Lands campaign in West Siberia – thousands of workers, technicians, builders, navvies and engineers lived in makeshift accommodation in sub-zero temperatures during the long winters and were attacked by dense swarms of pestiferous insects in the short, hot summers. At the time, by any standards the construction of the Bratsk GES was a gargantuan undertaking and resulted in the creation of what was then the world's most powerful hydroelectric station with an output, when it came online, of 4,050 megawatt (MW) of energy. It was soon to be accompanied, and in some cases superseded, by new dams and stations at Irkutsk (662 MW), Krasnoyarsk (6,000 MW), Sayangorsk (6,400 MW), Ust-Ilimsk (4,320 MW) and other GES facilities at Vilyuisk, Khantayka, Zeya and elsewhere. All of the electricity produced by this torrential Siberian 'cascade' not only supplied local industries and towns in such heavy consumption centres as Irkutsk, Novosibirsk, Bratsk and Krasnoyarsk, but was also fed into the USSR's national grid, with millions of kilowatts of distant Siberian hydroelectric energy fuelling, illuminating and powering the cities, population centres and factories of European Russia. This was yet another example of Siberia's role as a resource frontier for the benefit of the metropolitan centre. And it cannot be overlooked that, as in other cases of the exploitation of Siberia's riches, both the environment and the indigenous people suffered. The creation of huge artificial water reservoirs, the flooding of valleys, the much-resented relocation of whole population groups, the drowning of their villages, woodlands, pasture-lands and hunting grounds, the destruction of wild-life habitats, etc., has had a damaging, deleterious and detrimental effect on the preservation and sustainability of Siberia's natural ecological system (see Fig. 16).

The BAM

Equally damaging and detrimental to the environment was the construction of what at the time was extravagantly hailed in Soviet sources as 'the most grandiose building project of the twentieth century ... that has no equal anywhere in the world'.[19] This is the *c*.4,300 kilometre (2,672 miles) Baikal-Amur Mainline railway (*Baikalo-Amurskaya magistral'*), usually referred to as the BAM, stretching from Taishet through Bratsk, Ust-Kut, Nizhneangarsk, Tynda, Zeya, Urgal, Komsomolsk-na-Amure and terminating at the port of Sovetskaya Gavan on the Pacific coast. This 'grandiose project' had been planned from as early as the 1920s, and in fact sporadic preliminary work had been carried out, unconnected lengths of track were laid and a rudimentary infrastructure was developed during succeeding decades. However, it was never fully linked

Figure 16 Bratsk hydroelectric station and dam.
Source: Pristavkin, A., *Bratsk* (Moscow, 1974).

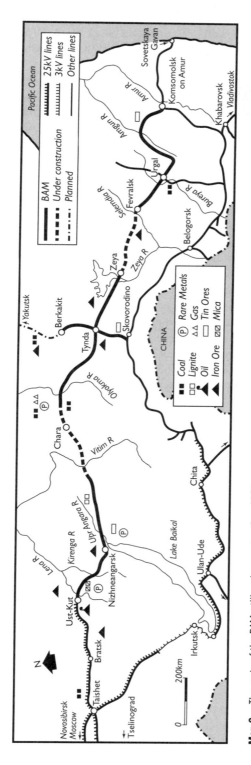

Map 8 The route of the BAM, still under construction, 1983.

Source: Railway Gazette International, July 1983.

up until vigorous, purposeful construction work with strong government backing resumed in earnest in the mid-1970s. Since the early twentieth century the main artery for human and freight transport across Russia's eastern expanses had been the Trans-Sib (see Chapter Seven). In addition to the main west-east track, in western Siberia a modest network of north- and south-running branch lines had been laid down, and in eastern Siberia and the Far East spasmodic attempts had been made to construct a line roughly parallel to, but hundreds of kilometres north of, the original Trans-Sib. But there was no totally operational, continuous, 'joined-up' railroad through the territory, which contained much of the USSR's most precious mineral deposits — 'the whole of Mendeleev's table of elements', in the words of Academician Aganbegyan.[20] It was, in fact, Aganbegyan who was one of the most vociferous and pertinacious advocates of the completion of the BAM. The lobbying from Aganbegyan and his fellow enthusiasts' lobbying was finally rewarded in 1974 by Brezhnev's public endorsement and announcement at a Komsomol (Young Communist League) conference at Alma-Ata that work on the 'project of the century' had commenced, and exhorted the youth of the country to join in the grand enterprise, rather as Khrushchev had urged participation on the Virgin Lands campaign 20 years earlier.

Unquestionably, military and strategic considerations had influenced the General Secretary's support as much as economic factors. In 1969 the USSR and the Chinese People's Republic had engaged in open armed conflict along the tense, sensitive border of the river Amur, which had exposed the vulnerability of the Trans-Sib.[21] A more northerly route from the top end of Lake Baikal to the Tatar Strait would obviously provide this vital communication link with much greater security. In Victor Mote's words: 'It [the BAM] was more secure from Yellow Peril than was the Trans-Siberian.' He also suggests that the 1973 Arab oil embargo, creating an international energy crisis, may also have affected Brezhnev's decision in favour of the BAM.[22]

The tasks that lay ahead of the railroad builders, the so-called *Bamovtsy*, during the next decade of construction work were awesome. The route of the new railway runs through some of the world's toughest and roughest terrain. The BAM crosses several mountain ranges, requiring sophisticated engineering and tunnelling technology to bore through geological strata characterized by a mixture of sedimentary, metamorphic and igneous rocks, and subject to earthquakes, landslides, avalanches, flash floods and other dangerous phenomena, including widespread incidence of karst (i.e. a region with subterranean drainage and great cavities caused by disintegration and dissolution of the rock base). The route also crosses ten large rivers including the Lena, the Angara, the Olëkma, the Zeya and the Amur. Seismic activity is extremely high, with as many as 1,000 quakes occurring in any one year with a measure of anything from 6 to 9 on the Richter scale.[23] During the eight-month long winters, temperatures average around −40°C, and in the more mountainous region can drop to as much, or as little, as −60°C. According to the then Deputy Director of the USSR Ministry of Transport's research institute for railway information, V.A. Shemanayev, so terrible were the problems posed by geological difficulties, including permafrost, which in places could plummet to a depth of 300 metres (984 feet), that about 1,200 kilometres (745 miles) of the proposed route were classified as 'unfavourable for construction'. In response: 'Surveying teams sought to avoid the worst locations such as narrow river gorges, thermal karsts, ice mounds, avalanche zones, large areas of talus, ground affected by heave and saturated areas known as "mar".'[24]

Between 1974 and 1984, nearly 400 million cubic metres (14,125 cubic feet) of rock and soil were mechanically or explosively excavated, of which half was hard rock or permafrozen ground, blasting the way for the construction of nine tunnels with an overall length of 32 kilometres (20 miles). One hundred and thirty-eight large bridges and viaducts were built, supplemented by 3,762 smaller bridges and culverts. By far the major obstacle was tunnelling, where the engineers had to tackle myriad geological problems caused by underground fissures, fractures and permafrost and the ever-present danger of submontain cave-ins. In order to meet the final connection deadline of 1984 – the so-called 'golden link' – those tunnels that were obviously not going to be completed on time were circumvented by building temporary loop-lines, often with steep gradients, such as the 26-kilometre (16-mile) bypass around the North Muya tunnel. During its decade of construction (if not total completion) the Soviet population was daily bombarded with literally thousands of newspaper and magazine articles, books, pamphlets, radio and television coverage, and all other forms of propaganda which made out the BAM to be something like the eighth wonder of the world – 'part pyramid and part colossus of Rhodes'.[25] Songs were composed, poems written – such as Aleksandr Tvardovskii's 'Space beyond Space' and Evgenii Yevtushenko's 'The Forest Cutting'[26] – parades were organized, lapel badges were coined, and 170,000 medals were awarded for 'BAM Construction'. Public posters abounded, some of them aimed at persuading young women to flock to the BAM region in order to offset the sexual imbalance among the working population there, and also, implicitly to copulate, marry and breed – not invariably in that order. The present author has one of those posters with the face of a pretty girl superimposed over a group of hard-hatted male BAM workers with the slogan *Kakaya stroika bez devchat?!* ('What sort of construction is it without young lasses?!') Many of the propaganda publications carry photographs, not only of the harsh yet spectacular landscape, construction work and jubilant engineers, but also of happy young brides and grooms celebrating their nuptial festivities in the snow.[27]

The 'BAM zone', covering an area of some 1.5 million square kilometres (0.6 million square miles), contains huge mineral deposits, which was one of the principal reasons for the building of the railroad in the first place. Copper, iron ore, new coalfields at Neryungri, asbestos deposits in Buryatia, more gold, silver, nickel, graphite and apatite resources, as well as a cornucopia of other mineral riches were there to be prospected, evaluated and exploited. The brouhaha surrounding the original construction of the BAM has now died down and is certainly no longer top of the Russian government's priorities, but the mainline still continues to be an important conduit for both human and freight traffic in the Far East. Over the last two to three decades, millions of people and millions of tons of goods have been ferried along the BAM, and through the 'Territorial Production Complexes' surrounding the route. Although the economic difficulties that both preceded and superseded the collapse of the USSR led to a huge reduction of investment in the BAM region, and also to an exodus of population, the railroad is still deemed by transport specialists to be 'a springboard for further economic development of the North, taking into account the social and economic interests of the numerically small peoples living in the BAM area and the possible industrial load on the environment'.[28] The 'golden link' was made in 1985, and the first through-journey made by a bunch of scientists and officials in the same year, but it was not until 2003 that the last construction project on the BAM was completed with the opening of the 15-kilometre (9.3-mile) North Muya tunnel, the longest in Russia, after 27 years of work by more than 30,000 labourers (see Fig. 17).[29]

Figure 17   A railway construction worker on the BAM.
Source: Sobelev, I. (ed.), *The Great Baikal-Amur Railway* (Moscow, 1977).

It remains now to describe the social, cultural and ethnic situation in post-Stalin Siberia, the continuing, if difficult-to-define, phenomenon of a special, specifically Siberian and Far Eastern identity, and the role of Siberia and the Russian Far East in today's world.

SIBERIAN REGIONALISM: PAST, PRESENT AND FUTURE[30]

In Chapter Four of this book the history and intellectual development of the Siberian regionalist movement (*oblastnichestvo*) in the late nineteenth and early twentieth centuries was described and analysed. Those regionalist tendencies were almost totally expunged after the end of the Civil War and during the period of Stalin's dictatorship, though they did hang on for a while in the Far East, as described in Chapters Eight and Nine. However, in the final decades of the twentieth century, as the Soviet Union underwent a period of internal crisis that led to its ultimate self-demolition, various ethnic, nationalist and regionalist movements began to reassert themselves. Most of these centre-periphery disputes were located in the non-Russian republics of the USSR, such as Ukraine, Georgia, the Baltic republics and Central Asia. Less well publicized was the resurgence of an identifiable, if rather amorphous, Siberian regional consciousness. Like its nineteenth-century predecessor, the more recent movement seldom went so far as to advocate complete Siberian autonomy or independence from mother Russia, but what it did express were the special needs and the peculiar problems of the territory and its peoples, of all ethnic groups.

It will be remembered that the five major concerns of the nineteenth-century Siberian *oblastniki* were:

- the high incidence of violent crime in the region as a direct result of the exile system, and its effects on Siberian society;
- the economic exploitation of Siberia and the pillaging of its natural resources purely for the benefit of the central government and exchequer;
- lack of adequate educational and cultural facilities;
- the need for a properly thought-out policy and programme of in-migration and settlement;
- the plight and rights of the Siberian indigenous peoples.

In the late 1980s, Gorbachevian *glasnost'* and political *perestroika* provided the opportunity for the reappearance of distinct trends, movements and events, which, while not replicating the experiences of the nineteenth century, did to some extent bear intimations of the re-emergence of a form of latter-day Siberian *oblastnichestvo*. Just as nineteenth-century Siberian regionalism sprang out of the reformist and incipient revolutionary atmosphere of the 1860s and 1870s, so did late twentieth-century manifestations of provincial self-awareness in Siberia emerge against the background of the 'restructuring' process and post-Gorbachev reforms. One of the recurring themes of recent academic conferences on Siberian development has been that of regional autonomy in both its historical and more modern manifestations. To take just one example, in February 1990 a two-day symposium took place in Novosibirsk on the theme of 'Problems of Self-Government in Siberian History'. Alongside the historical papers were ones with an obviously more contemporary application, with titles such as 'Current Problems of Siberian Economic Autonomy', and 'Contemporary Problems of Urban Self-Government in Siberia'.[31] Many of the papers on historical topics also had a clear relevance to more recent times, demonstrating that Siberian scholars and specialists were thinking very seriously about the same kind of issues, using similar arguments and similar vocabulary to those of their nineteenth-century predecessors. However, apart from the theoretical academic debates among Siberia's modern-day intelligentsia, more practical indicators of regional self-awareness and provincial particularism can be discerned which allow one to draw serious parallels with the past. It is possible to categorize these under much the same five-point programme of nineteenth-century Siberian *oblastnichestvo* outlined above.

Exile and Crime

It is clear that the phenomenon of *mass* criminal and political exile and forced labour no longer operates as it did in tsarist and Stalinist times. Nevertheless there is evidence of a good deal of public resentment at the continuing penal policy of banishing to and/or imprisoning often violent criminals in Siberia from other areas of Russia. On completing their sentences, many of these people – including murderers, rapists and robbers – choose to remain in the locality and revert to their former criminal activities, thus adding to the already high crime rate in the territory.[32] Before the collapse of the Soviet Union, reports in Russian newspapers suggested that in some areas of Siberia and the Far East as many as one in five of the local population was a released criminal. The figures are now somewhat out of date, but during the period covered in this book, taking just one example, an official of the Irkutsk province's Internal Affairs Administration was quoted in the government newspaper, *Izvestiya*, in 1989 as saying that in the East Siberian Angara district alone, around 17,000 convicts and alcoholics were released annually from the region's 36 penal labour colonies, of whom only 3,000 returned to their place of origin. The rest, unable to find work or permanent residence, stayed in the area and reverted to crime, over 50 per cent of which in the area is perpetrated by recidivist ex-prisoners.[33]

This is not to suggest that the prison and exile problem is as urgent and enfeebling to the community as it was in the past, but merely to point out that Siberia's old reputation as Russia's 'Wild East' has a certain resonance in more recent times, and is still a source of worry for the regional authorities, as well as the local population. Recent published research has also demonstrated that the alarmingly high rates of alcoholism, suicide and homicide in all the administrative territories of Siberia are much greater than elsewhere in

Russia and the former Soviet republics. Between 1980 and 1997, throughout the 22 regions of Siberia studied, the mean annual suicide rate was 50.5 per 100,000 of the population, and the homicide rate 38. By contrast, in the United States the corresponding figures for 1997 were 11.4 and 7.3 respectively, and in the UK 7.0 and 0.7.[34]

There has also recently been published a considerable amount of scholarly literature, both in Russia and the West, concerning the phenomenal growth of large-scale organized crime networks, particularly in the Far East. Rival gangs, Mafia-like turf wars, regular brutal murders, rampant corruption (often involving government officials), protection rackets and similar criminal activities are the stuff of everyday life in places like Komsomolsk-na-Amure and Vladivostok. According to one researcher, these incidents are 'normal features of the daily landscape, of conversation, of humour and of popular culture'.[35] One is reminded of a similar public insouciance that attended the reporting of violent crime, gang-rape and homicide in the mid-nineteenth-century Siberian press (see Chapter Six). But the author of the article who used the quotation referred to above is wrong, or at least historically myopic, in describing modern Russia, Siberia and the Far East's covert criminal culture and overt banditry as 'a product of the Soviet penal system' and 'a peculiar criminal structure during the Soviet period, sharply contrasting with other forms of organized crime'.[36] All, or most, of the features and practices of what he describes as 'the Thieves' organization' (*vory v zakone*) – things like group loyalty, strict internal rules, fierce discipline, a communal kitty (*obshchaya kassa*), a peculiar common language or argot, folklore, family and community networks, draconian punishments, *omertà*, etc. – go right back to the very origins of the Siberian exile system and the Russian criminal underworld. They are also common to many other criminal organizations elsewhere in the world, though arguably enforced with a peculiar degree of ruthless *savoir faire* and savagery.

However, the recrudescence, or rather prolongation, of such lawless and lethal activities in Siberia and the Far East indicate a continuing social, economic and humanitarian problem for the region and those most concerned for its future.

Economic Exploitation and Environmental Problems

As indicated in an earlier section, in the late 1980s the production of Siberian coal, oil and natural gas accounted for around 50 per cent of the USSR's total foreign currency earnings, and is still a major factor today. However, most of the revenue was used, not for the direct benefit of the energy-producing regions, but went straight to the central exchequer. The same applies to other sectors of Siberia's economic activity and natural wealth. In other words, Siberia was, and still is, being used as a 'resource frontier'.[37] At the same time, living conditions, housing standards, social and cultural facilities in Siberia's oil, gas and coal towns were very poor, even by comparison with the situation in other provincial urban centres. Chapter One contains evidence of the high levels, too, of atmospheric and environmental pollution. These problems provoked industrial unrest among colliers in the Kuzbass and roustabouts in north-west Siberia in 1989, demanding redress of economic, social and political grievances. After decades of censorship and oppression, Gorbachev's new, no doubt well-intentioned policy of *glasnost'* (openness, freedom of speech) let the genie of protest out of the bottle all over the Soviet Union, and it proved impossible to put it back. By the end of July 1989, thousands of Kuzbass mineworkers were on strike, and scores of pits and open-cast workings were brought to a halt in open revolt against both corrupt local officials and their masters in Moscow. Their demands were not just economic. The miners were, after all, among the highest-paid workers in the country. What they were seeking was greater control over their own enterprises and local affairs, more regional autonomy and less interference from the centre, democratic, multi-candidate elections and a clean-up of the environment. Pollution had resulted in high morbidity rates, still births, short life expectancy and lethally toxic water supplies caused by seepage into the rivers of poisonous waste and byproducts of both the mine-workings and the effluent of local heavy industries.

Not only workers, but also Siberian intellectuals, writers, local politicians and native leaders began to voice appeals for greater control over their economic resources and to express increased concern over the environmental damage caused by ever more intensive and extensive industrial exploitation of the territory. Campaigns to protect Lake Baikal from industrial pollution, and another which succeeded in causing the abandonment of plans for the construction of a hydroelectric station on the Lower Tunguska river in the Evenki Autonomous Region, which would have had disastrous repercussions for the local population, demonstrate a close connection between ecological and regional political issues.

During the last years of Gorbachev's administration, and continuing into Boris Yeltsin's presidency, core-periphery tensions increased with the appearance of ever more self-assertive pressure groups and institutions in the Siberian regions. An expanding number of territorial-administrative units – Sakha-Yakutia, for instance – declared themselves to be independent republics, and a range of provincial economic coalitions and organizations were established such as the 'Far Eastern Association', the 'Association of Siberian Towns' and the so-called 'Siberian Agreement', the signatories of which pledged themselves in autumn 1990 to cooperate inter-regionally in industrial and agricultural production, improvement in consumer goods output, and an acceleration of housing programmes.[38] None of these organizations was in favour of Siberian separatism (though a few fringe parties canvassed this notion), but lobbied the government in defence of Siberian interests to ensure that more of the wealth derived from the territory stayed there, and that the regions had a greater say in their own affairs.[39]

During the 1980s a number of 'Free Economic Zones' were set up in East Siberia and the Far East, designed by means of tax incentives to encourage foreign investment in Siberia, completely bypassing Moscow. Bilateral trading relationships were established between Siberian enterprises and foreign businesses ('joint ventures'), and local commercial banks, and even joint stock and commodity exchanges, were established, for example in Vladivostok, Chita, Ulan-Ude, Novosibirsk and Kemerovo. Over a hundred of these joint ventures, as of January 1991, with details of their location, names of the Soviet and foreign partners, their capital in rubles and their main commercial activity are listed in Michael Bradshaw's analysis of opportunities for foreign investment, published by the 'Economist Intelligence Unit'.[40] To give just one rather unusual example, Bradshaw's list includes details of a joint Anglo-Russian enterprise called 'Plembreed', located at Barnaul in the Altai. The Soviet partners are Barnaul Agricultural Breeding (39.4 per cent) and Rosplem Production Association (11.6 per cent); the UK partner (presumably holding the remaining 49 per cent share) is an outfit with the rather bulldoggish name of 'Britbreed'. With a combined capital of a modest 43,000 rubles (in 1991), its activity was the production of livestock embryos and semen, and breeding pedigree animals.[41]

Bradshaw's list, however, represents only the tip of the iceberg, or permafrost. Figures collated by Victor Mote indicate that by early 1993, no fewer than 6,000 joint ventures were registered in the Russian Federation, over half of them in Siberia and the Far East. In the latter region, hundreds of multilateral business links were established with partners in the countries of the Pacific Rim, including China, Japan, South Korea, the United States and Australia.[42] In addition to the territory's near-monopoly of many priceless resources, therefore, the financial and institutional infrastructure underpinning Siberia's case for greater economic independence was already becoming well established by the time of the collapse of the Soviet Union. This may well have been one of the factors contributing to that collapse.

Educational and Cultural Provision

The dearth of educational and cultural facilities in nineteenth-century Siberia was a constant source of concern for the early regionalists. In the twentieth century the problem had been very much alleviated. Apart from the campaign to eradicate illiteracy and the establishment of 'cultural bases' (*kul'tbazy*) for the indigenous peoples in the 1920s, the jewel in the crown of scientific and cultural development was, of course, the foundation of the Siberian Branch of the Soviet Academy of Sciences and the construction of its nerve-centre at Akademgorodok in the 1950s, discussed in an earlier section. Most of the other large Siberian cities – Omsk, Tomsk, Krasnoyarsk, Irkutsk, Barnaul, Kemerovo, Yakutsk and Vladivostok – all boast their own university, and, in addition, there are a dozen or so polytechnics and scores of specialized scientific, medical, technical and artistic institutes in all the major urban centres, and in other special locations, such as the Limnological Research Institute and the Baikal Ecological Museum on the shores of Lake Baikal.[43] As indicated above, Novosibirsk's Akademgorodok became a magnet attracting some of the country's most brilliant minds. There were fears that this trend had gone into reverse as a result of acute financial difficulties, and leakage of scientific personnel, lured by greater opportunities in private or foreign research centres. For example, according to a report written shortly after the disintegration of the Soviet Union and the shattering of Russia's economy, 40 members of Akademgorodok's prestigious Institute of Cytology and Genetics emigrated to work in Brazil. Near-bankruptcy, failure to pay academic salaries, crime and corruption, including the surreptitious selling off of irreplaceable archive materials to overseas bidders, and other distressing factors caused seriously damaging blight on the hitherto blossoming scientific enterprise.[44]

On the other hand, during the same period, there was a proliferation of independent newspapers, presses, radio programmes and television stations that expressed the particular concerns of various regions and to some extent replicated the *oblastniki*'s journalistic activities in the nineteenth century. In particular, *Sibirskaya gazeta*, founded in early 1990 as the organ of the newly formed Association of Siberian Towns, became something of a flagship for the public expression of regionalist views and sentiments, often, at least in its early issues, in total defiance of local government and Communist Party authorities, who accused the newspaper of 'populism, nihilism and vulgar commercialism'. On 7 April 1990 the Novosibirsk Regional Committee of the Communist Party threatened to withdraw printing facilities from the paper, giving it three months to 'reform itself' (*ispravitsya*).[45] The editor, V. Yukevich, was inundated with letters of support from readers, and, refusing to bow to party pressure or alter his editorial line, continued publication. (Interestingly, the paper's name was deliberately taken from that of a radical regionalist newspaper published in Tomsk during the 1880s, on which several well-known political exiles worked, and which was regularly denounced by the more conformist, conservative press at the time.)[46]

Also, from the 1960s a vigorous 'school' of Siberian creative writers emerged, which was vociferous in promoting the region's interests and identity. Among the best known authors are Valentin Rasputin, Viktor Astafev, Evgenii Popov, Leonid Borodin and Sergei Zalygin. There is no space here to engage in a literary analysis of their works, but they are all more or less united by a common theme, summed up by David Gillespie as follows: 'The writings in particular of Rasputin and Astaf'ev reflect not only the well-known oppositions of town and village, industry and nature, childhood innocence and adult corruption, idyllic past and disoriented present, but a more fundamental separation of Siberia and its spiritual and moral identity from that of European Russia.'[47]

Despite these manifestations of robust journalistic and literary activity, a chronic problem in Siberia is still the continuing lack, outside the major towns and cities, of adequate popular cultural facilities – theatres, libraries, cinemas, concert halls, circuses, etc. – particularly in the far north. This remains the subject of constant complaint and concern, and a further cause of discontent and dissatisfaction

Immigration and Labour Policy

A whole monograph on its own is needed to examine working patterns, inward migration, outward migration, labour turnover and wages policy in Siberia since the death of Stalin and the dismantling of the GULag's forced labour system. Again, lack of space precludes this. Suffice it to say that when the supply of convict labour gradually dried up, the government introduced a policy of financial and other incentives to attract the workforce required to exploit Siberia's riches and join in the massive construction projects in remote, inhospitable areas in the north and Far East. It would be more accurate to say 'reintroduced', as such monetary inducements to lure people to Siberia and encourage voluntary migration and settlement had been implemented in the early 1930s, in addition to the use of convict labour and the operations of Dal'stroi discussed in the previous chapter. However, despite the significantly higher and finely calibrated differential wage rates – the so called 'northern increment' (*severnaya nadbavka*) – the whole territory still experienced, and continues to experience, problems of high labour turnover and 'outward migration', which is due not only to adverse climatic and environmental factors, but also to socio-cultural inadequacies. Desperately poor housing provisions, hazardous working conditions, shortage of comestibles and consumer goods, lack of social amenities, serious health risks caused by atmospheric pollution and so on – all of these and other related difficulties still cause serious hindrance to Siberia's social and economic development, and act as a definite disincentive to continuing, sustainable and permanent settlement.

Even senior government and party leaders recognized this inescapable fact. For instance at the XXVIth Congress of the CPSU in 1981 General Secretary Leonid Brezhnev stated: 'Increments must be made, of course. But this alone will not solve the problem. More often than not a person leaves Siberia not because the climate is not suitable or the pay is small, but because it is harder to get housing there and put a child in a kindergarten, and cultural centres are few and far between.'[48] Similar sentiments were expressed by Mikhail Gorbachev during a visit to West Siberia in September 1985:

Over the past four years, the population of the Russian Republic's Eastern regions has grown through an influx of workers and specialists from other parts of the country. But one also cannot fail to see something else: large numbers of people have left the region. Hence, we shall have to continue to step up housing construction in Siberia and the Far East, improve the supply of food and consumer goods to the population, and develop the service sphere, public health and education.[49]

There was, therefore, a continuing mismatch between Siberia's paramount role in the country's national economy and the social, educational and domestic provision available for its key workers.[50]

Indigenous Peoples

During the period of the USSR's drawn-out death throes, there emerged an organized demand for greater regional sovereignty and an emphatic assertion of the national identity among the non-Russian peoples of Siberia. In 1990 the immense north-eastern republic of Yakutia declared its autonomy under the new name of Sakha (the Yakut name of the region); and the Yamal-Nentsy district of north-west Siberia unilaterally upgraded its status in the political administrative structure, as did other regions and national minority groups such as the Chukchi, the Koryaks and the Buryats. All of this was symptomatic of renewed national self-awareness, which, while not necessarily betokening a wider movement of Siberian independence, nevertheless provided evidence for continuing core-periphery antagonisms and tensions. Indeed, Mikhail Gorbachev even encouraged this embryonic movement in the belief that such fissiparous tendencies might undermine the authority of his political rival, the Russian Republic's President Yeltsin. All over Siberia associations were created which campaigned for the preservation or survival of attenuated native cultures and languages, and for the greater protection of the specific rights (e.g. to traditional lands) of their own peoples against the encroachment of central government agencies and non-aboriginal immigrants. Over the decades of Soviet power, at least from the end of the 1920s, a number of misconceived policies and practices had combined to cause the erosion, in some cases devastation, of ancient cultures, traditional lifestyles and even the fading of 'ethnic consciousness'. These practices included Stalin's collectivization drive of the 1930s and ensuing policies of sedentarization, de-nomadization, persecution of shamans, separation of native children from their families in urban boarding schools (the *internat*) and compulsory teaching of Russian at the expense of native languages, leading to the degradation of traditional hunting, fishing and herding skills among the younger generation. The disastrous consequences of the central government's policies toward Siberia's indigenes was, and is, therefore seen as not only the result of a disregard, but also as almost a sacrifice of the interests of the native peoples in favour of those of the national economy – which is run by politicians and 'planners' in Moscow.

One example of the response of the 'small peoples' to this situation was the setting up in March 1990 of a new organization with the rather prolix title of the Association of Indigenous Numerically Small Peoples of the North, Siberia and the Far East (AKMNS). Its first conference was held in the Moscow Kremlin, attended by representatives of around 30 registered local associations, academics and senior politicians, and was addressed by Mikhail Gorbachev himself. Among its stated aims were to deal with: 'urgent issues of the socio-economic situation of the small ethnic communities inhabiting the Soviet northern regions, Siberia and the Far East, of improvement of the ecological state of their permanent habitats, and the creation of necessary conditions for the preservation of their national and cultural heritage and traditional crafts'.[51]

The Association elected the Nivkh writer and scholar, Vladimir Mikhailovich Sangi (b.1935) as its first president (1990–94), and established an organizational structure consisting of 29 geographical divisions with a membership of 190,000 representatives. In 1993 it adopted a charter setting out its aims and practical objectives. AKMNS also participates in international fora, including the United Nations, the Arctic Council, the Inuit Circumpolar Conference and other organizations, for example in Canada and Denmark.[52]

The creation of AKMNS was more than merely symbolic of the renewed attention being paid to the pressing needs and problems of the indigenous peoples, though the uncertainties, economic chaos and political instability caused by the disintegration of the Soviet Union to some extent served to exacerbate, rather than ameliorate, still less solve, the issues it was founded to tackle. What is clear, though, as mentioned above, is that many of the concerns of the original nineteenth-century *oblastniki* still find a clear echo in the preoccupations of those who have begun to advance the cause of Siberia's aboriginal peoples in the late twentieth and early twenty-first centuries.

THE SPECTRE OF SEPARATISM

The opening sentence of the introduction to Marx and Engels' *Communist Manifesto* of 1848 states: 'A spectre is haunting Europe – the spectre of Communism.' Almost a century-and-a-half later on, one could reasonably speculate that the spectre of separatism was hovering in the gelid atmosphere of Siberia like a wisp of quivering political ectoplasm. Certainly the modern-day regionalists are committed to the cause of 'life on the other side' – of the Urals, that is. As noted in Chapter Four, the nineteenth-century Siberian regionalist movement uttered only very few, isolated calls for the absolute political separation of the country from Russia. It was only in the immediate aftermath of the 1917 Revolution and during the Civil War that Siberia became temporarily detached from the direct political control of Moscow (see Chapter Eight), thus providing an opportunity for the establishment of ephemeral regional assemblies, councils and committees, even self-declared independent states or governments, all of which ultimately failed to achieve any degree of political coherence or, indeed, to attract much popular, democratic support for their programmes and activities. After the establishment of Soviet power from the Urals to the Pacific those pretensions gradually disappeared. However, in the 1980s and early 1990s, a few straws in the wind suggested that there were those, albeit only a few, who wished to go beyond appeals for more local control, boldly calling for the political separation of Siberia from Moscow under the slogan of *Sibir' sibiryakam!* ('Siberia for the Siberians!').[53]

In the Far East, knowledge about the earlier, brief existence of the nominally independent Far Eastern Republic (1920–22), increasing revelations about the extent of Stalin's terror in the region and a fierce spirit of sustained local identity led to the emergence of various pressure groups voicing demands for something more than simply greater participation in the running of their own affairs. At its most extreme, the determination to achieve the region's total sovereignty expressed itself in the founding, in September 1990, of the Far Eastern Republic Freedom Party. This was a rather eccentric organization with very few members, a fanatical leader (A.A. Zabolotnikov) and a programme that envisaged in a future independent republic complete denationalization of state-sector industry, priority of individual citizens' rights over those of society (including the right to carry guns), and freedom of enterprise and initiative. It also promised, on coming to power, to shoot all Communists.[54]

Far less extreme in its aims, but nonetheless evidence of the exponential nature of traditional core-periphery antagonisms in Siberia was the First Congress of People's Deputies of the Territories of Siberia, held in Krasnoyarsk in March 1992. The congress was attended by 136 out of 155 elected delegates representing 8 Siberian administrative territories, and the language of the delegates' adopted resolutions and demands was uncompromising in their assertion of the Siberian regions' urgent need for enhanced legal, economic and social rights. Specific proposals for greater jurisdictional powers, more independence in the running of economic, constitutional and agrarian matters were passed, to be forwarded to the Russian Supreme Soviet. Speeches contained emotional attacks on Moscow's continuing colonial exploitation of Siberia's resources, the tone of which was echoed in the meeting's formal resolutions, which were redolent of the old *oblastniki*, as illustrated in the preamble to Congress's formal published report:

Congress notes that:

- For many years the central powers have pursued policies towards Siberia that have led to the economic ruin and ecological devastation of her territories, and to the social and spiritual impoverishment of her people … In a time of radical economic reform throughout Russia, the situation has even deteriorated.
- Congress condemns the policies of the federal organs of State power and the conduct of its economic reforms without regard for the specific, concrete conditions of existence for the populations of the various regions of our enormous country. This has reduced Siberia – the country's fundamental source of raw materials and energy – to the position of a supplicant begging for social and humanitarian aid. Congress considers that at the present day there can be no economic or moral justification for the continuation of the [government's] colonial policies towards Siberia.[55]

Nowhere in the Congress documents is there any specific mention of separatism as such, but there is a detectable subtext permeating their contents and proposals, which suggests that such an eventuality is not beyond question. The only direct call for an immediate declaration of independence came from one Boris Perov, leader of the tiny Party of Siberian Independence, whose fanciful calls for a takeover of all industries and enterprises in Siberia, a ban on foreign investment, and the expropriation of the armed forces and security services were dismissed by the Congress chairman, V.A. Novikov, as 'very stupid'.[56] However the prospect of an independent, sovereign Siberia was also entertained by some economic managers, as well as politicians. For instance, in 1992 the director of a huge oilfield in north-west Siberia told a reporter on *Moscow News* that if the central government continued to interfere in bilateral financial arrangements made between Siberian undertakings and foreign customers, this would: 'bring about a still bigger fall in oil production and oilmen's living standards. This will provide local politicians ... with additional trump cards in order to create something like a Kuwait on the soil of Tyumen. The result will be an impetuous roll-over to an independent Siberian state.'[57]

So, with the spectre of Siberian separatism not entirely exorcized, it is nevertheless difficult to imagine anything like a struggle for independence on the lines of the recent bloody conflicts between Moscow and the would-be breakaway state of Chechnya. The Muslim insurgents or freedom-fighters – or, in the Kremlin's view, terrorists – in southern Russia are much more belligerent, organized, well-armed and, some might say, fanatical in their objectives than anything that could be remotely contemplated in Siberia and the Far East. The murderous wars in Chechnya are indeed a frightening indication of the lengths to which the Russian government will go in order to preserve the Federation's territorial and political integrity. That is not to say that the various 'autonomous' territorial-administrative areas in Siberia may not extend the scope of their own self-governance (*samoupravlenie*) and greater economic independence (*samostoyatel'nost'*) from the centre. It should, however, be remembered that Siberia, including the Far East, is really too huge and heterogeneous a territory to unite or co-ordinate its political, economic and national interests in any coherent way that would make more sense than the system or the arrangements it has experienced so far. It would be a nice indulgence to speculate on the future formation of a fully independent 'United States of Siberia and the Far East', free from the centuries-long thraldom to Moscow or St Petersburg, but this is not realistically on the agenda. Despite the central exchequer's reliance on the continued supply of Siberia's priceless, and seemingly inexhaustible, natural resources, which it may be thought could be used by the trans-Uralian territories as a political lever on Moscow, there are too many inter-regional, inter-ethnic and inter-sectoral conflicts of interest for any kind of joined-up programme for total Siberian independence to work successfully in the immediate or, indeed, long-term future.

While in futuristic mode, it is worth pointing out the there is also danger that in any putative independent Siberia, the old colonialism of Moscow could be replaced by a new economic imperialism, as the country's resources fall prey to greedy international and multinational business conglomerates in the global capitalist market. In the rush to exploit huge new investment opportunities, the conglomerates may be no more solicitous of Siberia's own interests than they have shown themselves to be elsewhere in the developing world, where fat profits are made at the expense of the rape of the natural environment and the survival of indigenous populations.

For the present, and no doubt for many decades to come, it seems that in terms of realpolitik and real economics the fundamental relationship between the Russian Federation's European core and the territories of its Asian periphery will remain very much as it has been for the last nearly four-and-a-half centuries since Yermak's cossaks' original incursion. It will still remain Russia's own 'frozen frontier', and the lands beyond the Urals will continue to be regarded and treated as what the great regionalist scholar and publicist, Nikolai Mikhailovich Yadrintsev, famously described in the nineteenth century as *Siberia as a Colony*.[58]

Afterword

Two decades have elapsed between the political disappearance of the Union of Soviet Socialist Republics in 1991 and the appearance of this book. In the preceding pages I have attempted to offer a narrative analysis of the complex history of the relationship between succeeding Muscovite, Imperial and Soviet Russian governments and the peoples of their enormous empire of Siberia, which straddles such a gigantic swathe of the earth's land surface, and has often played a crucial role in the whole country's economic, cultural, military, social and political history. The magnitude of Siberia's contribution to that history is widely either misunderstood or unknown among the general public, and also, indeed, in highly educated and sophisticated circles, not just in the West, but within Russia itself. Many of my academic colleagues, family members and friends, both here and 'over there', have been bemused and baffled by my fascination with the place. I hope that this book will help to dispel some of the misconceptions, myths and ignorance with which the 'lands beyond the Rock' are still suffused.

Despite the loss of the USSR's super-power status and the end of the Cold War, Russia still remains the world's biggest country and a key player on the international stage, a nuclear-armed power and a permanent member of the United Nations' Security Council. It is the world's largest producer of oil and natural gas (most of it from Siberia), and an active participant in trade and commerce with many parts of the world, including the countries of the European Union and the nations of the Asian-Pacific Rim. It has an ambiguous relationship with the former Soviet republics (what Russians call 'the near abroad'), but still retains a certain amount of clout there, as witnessed by the recent spat between Russia and Ukraine over the price of energy supplies from Siberia. Since 1991 the Russian Federation, and with it Siberia and the Far East, has undergone many vicissitudes, the story of which requires a separate volume to recount and examine in adequate detail. It has experienced political dismemberment, ethnic unrest, military conflict in Chechnya and with Georgia, economic meltdown, rocketing rates of organized and violent crime, terrorist attacks, rigged elections, the almost routine assassination of awkward investigative journalists and broadcasters, imposition of government control over most of the national media outlets, rewritten 'constitutions', an attempted coup and the abandonment of elected provincial governors in favour of centrally appointed ones. Its economy has also undergone denationalization, privatization and then renewed state control of the major industries, during the process of which huge fortunes were made by parvenu entrepreneurs who scooped up billions of dollars out of the economic chaos and reckless selling off of national assets during the 1990s. Of these financial high-flyers – the so-called 'oligarchs' – some of whom now languish in Siberian jails or luxuriate in foreign exile, probably the best-known to UK readers is Roman Abramovich, precocious multimillionaire playboy businessman, close buddy of ex-President Vladimir Putin, appointed governor of the far north-eastern province of Chukotka, and also owner of the English Premier League's Chelsea football club (also reputed to be the second richest person in the UK, with the Queen struggling to make ends meet in 254th position, according to the *Guardian*, 26 April 2010). Other prominent sons of Siberia, both natural and adopted, permanent or tempo-rary, either born there, migrated there, worked there or sent there – many of whom appear in these pages – include Archpriest Avvakum, Radishchev, Speranskii, the Decembrists, Dostoevskii, populist revolutionaries, Lenin, Trotskii, Stalin, Rasputin, hundreds of the tsarist and Soviet artistic, literary and scientific intelligentsia, Marshall Zhukov, the 'Virgin Landers', Lavrentev, the *Bamovtsy*, Chernenko, Yeltsin and countless intrepid explorers, brilliant scientists, administrators, geologists, engineers, sailors, as well as the millions of anonymous peasants and workers, and also ardent writers and scholars who over the centuries have chronicled the saga of Siberia's unique, dramatic, often tragic, but also epic, past. Despite the tentative conclusion and caveats contained in the last chapter of this book, Siberia's future is, of course, impossible accurately to predict, and I hesitate to do so. However, what can confidently be said is that Russia's frozen frontier will undoubtedly continue to play a vital, if probably under-appreciated, economic and strategic role in that country's and the world's destiny.

As they say in the advertising business: 'Watch this space'. In the case of Siberia and the Russian Far East, there is plenty of space to watch.

Figure 18   The author with dog-sleigh on the frozen Lower Tunguska river, Evenkia National District, April 1992.

Suggestions for Further Reading

This is simply a select list of English-language books (one part-French and part-Russian) – placed in alphabetical order of the surname of author or editor – on the history, culture, ethnography, memoir literature, economy, geography, penal system, etc. of Siberia and the Russian Far East, most of them published in the late nineteenth, twentieth and early twenty-first centuries. More detailed data and references to articles in academic journals, publications in Russian, archive collections and other sources consulted in the research for and preparation of this book are contained in the notes to the individual chapters. The list is by no means exhaustive, and interested readers are invited to consult the bibliographies contained in the volumes recommended in the following list. Especially valuable is David Collins' annotated bibliographical compilation indicated below, updated in recent issues of the journal *Sibirica*. The book also contains a section of references to other bibliographical guides.

Amalrik, A., *Involuntary Journey to Siberia* (San Diego, New York and London, 1970).

Applebaum, A., *GULAG: A History of the Soviet Camps* (London, 2003).

Armstrong, T. (ed.), *Yermak's Campaign in Siberia: A selection of documents translated from the Russian by Tatiana Minorsky and David Wileman* (London, 1975).

Atkinson, T.W., *Oriental and Western Siberia: Seven Years' Explorations and Adventures* (London, 1858, reprint 1970).

Balzer, M.M. (ed.), *Shamanism: Soviet Studies of Traditional Religion in Siberia and Central Asia* (New York and London, 1990).

Bardach, J. and Gleeson, K., *Man is Wolf to Man: Surviving Stalin's Gulag* (California, 1988; reprint London, 2003).

Barratt, G., *Voices in Exile: The Decembrist Memoirs* (Montreal and London, 1974).

Bassin, M., *Imperial Visions: Nationalist Imagination and Geographical Expansion in the Russian Far East, 1840–1865* (Cambridge, 1999).

Bobrick, B., *East of the Sun: The Conquest and Settlement of Siberia* (London, 1992).

Bradshaw, M.J., *Siberia at a Time of Change: New Vistas for Western Investment* (London, 1992).

Chernyshova, N.S. (ed.), *Siberia: Photo Album* (Moscow, 1984).

Chichlo, B. (ed.), *Sibérie II: Questions sibériennes: Histoire. Cultures. Littérature* (Paris, 1999).

Collins, D., *Siberia and the Soviet Far East*, World Bibliographical Series (Oxford, 1991) (Updates published in *Sibirica*, vol. 2, no. 1 [2002], *Sibirica*, vol. 2, no. 3 [2002] and *Sibirica*, vol. 3, no. 1 [2003]).

Connaughton, R., *The Republic of the Ushakovka: Admiral Kolchak and the Allied Intervention in Siberia 1918–20* (London and New York, 1990).

Conolly, V., *Beyond the Urals: Economic Developments in Soviet Asia* (London, New York and Toronto, 1967).

Connolly, V., *Siberia: Today and Tomorrow* (London and Glasgow, 1975).

Dallin, D.J. and Nikolaevsky, B.I., *Forced Labour in Soviet Russia* (London, 1947).

de Souza, P., *Territorial Production Complexes in the Soviet Union – with special focus on Siberia* (Gothenburg, 1989).

Deutsch, L., *Sixteen Years in Siberia: Some Experiences of a Russian Revolutionist* (London, 1903).

de Windt, H., *Siberia as It Is* (London, 1892).

de Windt, H., *The New Siberia* (London, 1896).

Dibb, P., *Siberia and the Pacific: A Case Study of Economic Development and Trade Prospects* (New York, 1972).

Diment, G. and Slezkine, Yu. (eds), *Between Heaven and Hell: The Myth of Siberia in Russian Culture* (New York, 1993).

Diószegi, V., *Tracing Shamans in Siberia* (Oosterhaut, 1968).

Dmytryshyn, B., Crownhart-Vaughan, E.A.P. and Vaughan, T. (eds), *To Siberia and Russian America: Three Centuries of Russian Expansion: A Documentary Record*, vol.1, *The Conquest of Siberia, 1558–1700* (Portland, 1985).

Dmytryshyn, B., Crownhart-Vaughan, E.A.P. and Vaughan, T. (eds), *To Siberia and Russian America: Three Centuries of Russian Expansion: A Documentary Record*, vol. 2, *Russian Penetration of the North Pacific Ocean, 1700–1797* (Portland, 1988).

Dmytryshyn, B., Crownhart-Vaughan, E.A.P. and Vaughan, T. (eds), *To Siberia and Russian America: Three Centuries of Russian Expansion: A Documentary Record*, vol. 3, *The Russian American Colonies, 1798–1867* (Portland, 1989).

Dostoyevsky, F., *The House of the Dead*, trans. McDuff, D. (Harmondsworth, 1985).

Dotsenko, P., *The Struggle for a Democracy in Siberia, 1917–1920: Eyewitness Account of a Contemporary* (Stanford, 1983).

Fisher, R.H., *The Russian Fur Trade, 1550–1700* (Berkeley, 1943).

Fisher, R.H. (ed.), *The Voyage of Semen Dezhnev in 1648: Bering's Precursor. With Selected Documents* (London, 1981).

Fitzhugh, W.W. and Crowell, A. (eds), *Crossroads of Continents: Cultures of Siberia and Alaska* (Washington, DC, 1988).

Forsyth, J., *A History of the Peoples of Siberia: Russia's North Asian Colony, 1581–1990* (Cambridge and New York, 1992).

Fraser, J.F., *The Real Siberia: Together with an Account of a Dash through Manchuria* (London and New York, 1911).

Gentes, A.A., *Exile to Siberia, 1590–1822* (New York, 2008).

Golubchikova, V.D. and Khvtisiashvili, Z.I. (eds), *Practical Dictionary of Siberia and the North* (Moscow, 2005).

Gregory, P.R. and Lazarev, V. (eds), *The Economics of Forced Labour: The Soviet Gulag* (Stanford, 2003).

Hill, F. and Gaddy, C., *The Siberian Curse: How Communist Planners Left Russia out in the Cold* (Washington, DC, 2003).

Hill, S.S., *Travels in Siberia* (London, 1854; reprint, New York, 1970).

Hughes, J., *Stalin, Siberia and the Crisis of the New Economic Policy* (Cambridge, 1991).

Hughes, J., *Stalinism in a Russian Province: Collectivization and Dekulakization in Siberia* (Basingstoke, 1996).

Humphrey, C., *Karl Marx Collective: Economy, Society and Religion in a Siberian Collective Farm* (Cambridge, 1983).

Hutton, R., *Shamans: Siberian Spirituality and the Western Imagination* (London and New York, 2001).

Josephson, P.R., *New Atlantis Revisited: Akademgorodok, the Siberian City of Science* (Princeton, 1997).

Kennan, G., *Siberia and the Exile System*, 2 vols (New York, 1891).

Khisamutdinov, A., *The Russian Far East: Historical Essays* (Honolulu, 1993).

Krasheninnikov, S.P., *Explorations of Kamchatka, 1735–1741*, ed. and trans. Crownhart-Vaughan, E.A.P. (Portland, 1972).

Landsell, H., *Through Siberia*, 2 vols (London, 1882).

Lantzeff, G.V., *Siberia in the Seventeenth Century: A Study of Colonial Administration* (Berkeley, 1943; reprint, New York, 1972).

Lantzeff, G.V. and Pierce, R.A., *Eastwards to Empire: Exploration and Conquest on the Russian Open Frontier to 1750* (Montreal and London, 1973).

Lengyel, E., *Secret Siberia* (London, 1947).

Lincoln, W.B., *The Conquest of a Continent: Siberia and the Russians* (London, 1994).

Marks, S.G., *Road to Power: The Trans-Siberian Railroad and the Colonization of Asian Russia, 1850–1917* (London, 1991).

Marsden, K., *On Sledge and Horseback to Outcast Siberian Lepers* (London, 1892).

Martin, J., *Treasure of the Land of Darkness: The Fur Trade and its Significance for Medieval Russia* (Cambridge, 1986).

Massey Stewart, J. and Wood, A., *Siberia: Two Historical Perspectives* (London, 1984).

Melancon, M., *The Lena Goldfields Massacre and the Crisis of the Late Tsarist State* (College Station, 2006).

Morray, J.P., *Project Kuzbas: American Workers in Siberia (1921–1926)* (New York 1983).

Mote, V.L., *Siberia: Worlds Apart* (Boulder, 1998).

Suggestions for Further Reading

Nansen, F., *Through Siberia: The Land of the Future* (New York, 1914; reprint, 1972).

Norton, H.K., *The Far Eastern Republic of Siberia* (London, 1923).

Oakes, J. and Riewe, R., *Spirit of Siberia: Traditional Native Life, Clothing and Footwear* (Washington, DC, 1998).

Palmer, J., *The Bloody White Baron* (London, 2008).

Pereira, N.G.O., *White Siberia: The Politics of Civil War* (Montreal and London, 1996).

Portisch, H., *I Saw Siberia* (London, 1972).

Raeff, M., *Siberia and the Reforms of 1822* (Seattle, 1956).

Raeff, M., *Michael Speransky: Statesman of Imperial Russia, 1772–1839* (The Hague, 1957).

Roeder, B., *Katorga: An Aspect of Modern Slavery* (London and Toronto, 1958).

St George, G., *Siberia: The New Frontier* (London, 1969).

Sano, I.P., *One Thousand Days in Siberia: The Odyssey of a Japanese-American POW* (Nebraska, Lincoln and London, 1997).

Scholmer, J., *Vorkuta: The Story of a Slave City in the Soviet Arctic* (London, 1954).

Semyonov, Yu., *The Conquest of Siberia: An Epic of Human Passions* (London, 1944).

Shabad, T. and Mote, V.L., *Gateway to Siberian Resources: the BAM* (New York and London, 1977).

Shifrin, A., *The First Guidebook to Prisons and Camps in the Soviet Union* (Toronto, New York and London, 1982).

Smele, J.D., *Civil War in Siberia: The anti-Bolshevik Government of Admiral Kolchak, 1918–1920* (Cambridge, 1996).

Solzhenitsyn, A., *The Gulag Archipelago, 1918–1956: An Experiment in Literary Analysis,* 3 vols (London, 1974–78).

Štajner, K., *7000 Days in Siberia* (London, 1989).

Starr, S.F. (ed.), *Russia's American Colony* (Durham, 1987).

Stephan, J.J., *Sakhalin: A History* (Oxford, 1971).

Stephan, J.J., *The Russian Far East: A History* (Stanford, 1994).

Stephan, J.J. and Chichkanov, V.P. (eds), *Soviet-American Horizons on the Pacific* (Honolulu, 1986).

Swearingen, R. (ed.), *Siberia and the Soviet Far East: Strategic Dimensions in Multinational Perspective* (Stanford, 1987).

Treadgold, D.W., *The Great Siberian Migration: Government and Peasant Resettlement from Emancipation to the First World War* (Princeton, 1957).

Von Mohrenschildt, D., *Toward a United States of Russia: Plans and Projects of Federal Reconstruction of Russia in the Nineteenth Century* (London and Toronto, 1981).

Witzenrath, C., *Cossacks and the Russian Empire, 1598–1725: Manipulation, Rebellion and Expansion into Siberia* (London, 2007).

Wood, A. (ed.), *Siberia: Problems and Prospects for Regional Development* (London, New York and Sydney, 1987).

Wood, A. (ed.) *The History of Siberia: From Russian Conquest to Revolution* (London, 1991).

Wood, A., *The Romanov Empire 1613–1917: Autocracy and Opposition* (London, 2007).

Wood, A. and French, R.A. (eds), *The Development of Siberia: People and Resources* (London, 1989).

Notes

Preface

1. Kirby, S., 'Siberia: heartland and framework', *Asian Perspective*, vol. 9, no. 2 (1985), p. 274.
2. Marx, K. and Engels, F., *Manifesto of the Communist Party*, translation and reprint (Moscow, 1965), p. 39.

Chapter 1   The Environment: Ice-Box and El Dorado

1. Fraser, J.F., *The Real Siberia: Together with an Account of a Dash through Manchuria* (London and New York, 1911), p. 4.
2. Lomonosov, M.V., *Polnoe sobranie sochinenii* (Moscow/Leningrad, 1951), vol. VI, pp. 448, 498.
3. On Akademgorodok, see Josephson, Paul R., *New Atlantis Revisited: Akademgorodok, the Siberian City of Science* (Princeton, 1997).
4. Okladnikov, A.P., *Otkrytie Sibiri* (Moscow, 1979), pp. 211–22.
5. See Hill, F. and Gaddy, C., *The Siberian Curse: How Soviet Planners Left Russia Out in the Cold* (Washington, DC, 2003).
6. Kolesnik, S.V. *et al.* (eds), *Sovetskii Soyuz: Geograficheskoe opisanie v 22 tomakh. Vostochnaya Sibir'* (Moscow, 1969); Kolesnik, S.V. *et al.* (eds), *Sovetskii Soyuz: Geograficheskoe opisanie v 22 tomakh. Zapadnaya Sibir'* (Moscow, 1971); Kolesnik, S.V. *et al.* (eds), *Sovetskii Soyuz: Geograficheskoe opisanie v 22 tomakh. Dal'nii Vostok* (Moscow, 1971).
7. In 1983 the present author had to wait for two days beyond schedule for his train to arrive at Novosibirsk.
8. Resnick, A., *Siberia and the Soviet Far East: Endless Frontiers* (Moscow, 1983), p. 40.
9. Climatic data are from Baranov, A.N. (ed.), *Atlas SSSR*, 2nd ed. (Moscow, 1969); Lydolph, Paul E., *Climates of the Soviet Union: World Survey of Climatology*, vol. 7 (Amsterdam, 1977); and Shaw, Denis, 'Geographical Background', in Wood, A. (ed.), *Siberia: Problems and Prospects for Regional Development* (London, New York and Sydney, 1987), pp. 23–9.
10. Hill and Gaddy, *The Siberian Curse*, pp. 28–35.
11. Hosseini, K., *A Thousand Splendid Suns* (London, 2007), p. 142.
12. Kozhenkova, S., 'How Tourism Development in Primorskii Krai can Influence Marine Ecosystems: The Example of Vostok Bay', paper presented at the 25th Jubilee Conference of the British Universities Siberian Studies Seminar, Vladivostok, September 2006.
13. The *Lenin* was laid down at the Admiralty Yard, Leningrad, in 1956, launched in 1959 and commissioned on 3 December 1959. Powered by three nuclear reactors it was capable of maintaining a speed of 2.4 knots across a 2.5 metre-thick ice field. It was deactivated in 1989, and now rests at anchor in the port of Murmansk, where it is being transformed into a museum.
14. Information from Marks, S.G., *Road to Power: The Trans-Siberian Railroad and the Colonization of Asian Russia, 1850–1917* (London, 1991), pp. 202–03.
15. Mote, V.L., *Siberia: Worlds Apart* (Boulder, 1998), p. 23.
16. Mote, V.L., 'Environmental Constraints to the Economic Development of Siberia', in Jensen, R.G., Shabad, T. and Wright, A. (eds), *Soviet Natural Resources in the World Economy* (Chicago, 1983), p. 22.
17. Solzhenitsyn, A., *One Day in the Life of Ivan Denisovich*, trans. H.T. Willetts (London, 1991).
18. On the concept and application of the TPC index , see Hill and Gaddy, *The Siberian Curse*, pp. 35–40, 217–20.
19. N.N. Urvantsev survived the camps, was formally rehabilitated in 1955 after Stalin's death, declared an 'honorary citizen' of Norilsk and awarded the Gold Medal of the Russian Geographical Society in 1959. He died in Leningrad in 1985, aged 92.

Notes

20. 'Hell on Earth', *Guardian* (2003), 18 April.
21. 'The World's Most Polluted Places 2007', Blacksmith Institute, CNN report (September 2007), retrieved 14 September 2007. Quoted in http://en.wikipedia.org/wiki/Norilsk [accessed 16 November 2010].
22. Report by Latyshev, Y., *Novye Izvestiya* (2001), 28 April.
23. Sergeev, M., *Baikal* (Moscow, 1990), p. 46.
24. Gudzii, N.K., *Zhitie protopopa Avvakuma: im samym napisannoe* (Moscow, 1960), p. 326.
25. On the Buryats' economic and social life see: Humphrey, C., *Karl Marx Collective: Economy, Society and Religion in a Siberian Collective Farm* (Cambridge, 1983).
26. '"Pearl of Kamchatka" geysers lost under mudslide lake', *Guardian* (2007), 5 June.
27. Yadrintsev, N.M., *Sibir' kak koloniya. K yubileyu trekhsotletiya. Sovremennoe polozhenie Sibiri. Yeya nuzhdy i potrebnosti. Yeya proshloe i budushchee* (St Petersburg, 1882).
28. Statistics in this section are taken from Golubchikova, V.D. and Khvtisiashvili, Z.I. (eds), *Practical Dictionary of Siberia and the North* (Moscow, 2005).
29. In the 1980s a British expert on Siberian fuel production who publicly challenged American official predictions was refused an entry visa to the United States to attend a conference on the subject.
30. http://www.forest.ru/eng/publications/wildeast/02.htm [accessed 16 November 2010].
31. Bando, E.G. (ed.), *Bratskii leso-promyshlennyi kompleks* (Bratsk, 1978).

Chapter 2   The Russian Conquest: Invasion and Assimilation

1. Much of the material in this chapter is a rewritten and expanded version of the present author's contribution entitled 'The Historical Dimension', in Wood, A. (ed.), *Siberia: Problems and Prospects for Regional Development* (London, New York and Sydney, 1987), pp. 36–44.
2. See for instance Okladnikov, A.P. et al. (eds), *Istoriya Sibiri s drevneishikh vremen do nashikh dnei*, vol. 1, *Drevnyaya Sibir'* (Leningrad, 1968); Rudenko, S.I., *Frozen Tombs of Siberia: the Pazyryk Burials of Iron Age Horsemen* (London, 1970); Derev'anko, A.P. et al. (eds), *The Paleolithic of Siberia: New Discoveries and Interpretations* (Urbana and Chicago, 1998).
3. Okladnikov, A.P., *Otkrytie Sibiri* (Moscow, 1979), pp. 18–22.
4. For a brief discussion of the impact of the 'Tatar yoke' on Russia, see Wood, A., *The Romanov Empire, 1613–1917: Autocracy and Opposition* (London, 2007), pp. 36–43.
5. The best recent biography of Ivan IV is de Madariaga, I., *Ivan the Terrible* (New Haven, 2006).
6. For a discussion of the merits of the various chronicles and an edited English translation, see Armstrong, T. (ed.), *Yermak's Campaign in Siberia: A selection of documents translated from the Russian by Tatiana Minorsky and David Wileman* (London, 1975).
7. Skrynnikov, R.G., 'Ermak's Siberian Expedition', *Russian History/Histoire Russe*, vol. 13, no. 1, Spring (1986), pp. 1–39.
8. Skrynnikov, 'Ermak's Siberian Expedition', p. 23. The use of the word 'rifles' here is an obvious mistranslation of Skrynnikov's original Russian. Rifled firearms, i.e. with spiral grooves inside the barrel, were not developed until the mid-nineteenth century.
9. Skrynnikov, 'Ermak's Siberian Expedition', p. 37. On the Yermak legend, see Harrison, W., 'Yermak as folk-hero', in Armstrong, T. (ed.), *Yermak's Campaign in Siberia: A selection of documents translated from the Russian by Tatiana Minorsky and David Wileman* (London, 1975), pp. 13–18.
10. Skrynnikov, 'Ermak's Siberian Expedition', p. 18.
11. Okladnikov, A.P. et al. (eds), *Istoriya Sibiri s drevneishikh vremen do nashikh dnei*, vol. 2, *Sibir' v sostave feodal'noi Rossii* (Leningrad, 1968), p. 172.
12. Vernadsky, G., *The Mongols and Russia* (New Haven and London, 1953), p. 389.
13. The knout (*knut*) was the most wicked and favoured instrument of flagellation in mediaeval and early modern Russia. A heavy leather scourge, soaked in glue and embedded with pieces of metal, it was capable of breaking the spine and causing death with a single blow. Its use was abolished by Emperor Nicholas I in 1848 and, in a humanitarian gesture, replaced by the three-thonged whip.
14. All quotations from Dmytryshyn, B., Crownhart-Vaughan, E.A.P. and Vaughan, T. (eds), *Russia's Conquest of Siberia: A Documentary Record, 1558–1700* (Portland, 1958), pp. 55–61.

15. Rezun, D. Ya., 'K istorii "postanavleniya" gorodov i ostrogov v Sibiri', in Vilkov, O.N. (ed.), *Sibirskie goroda XVII-nachala XX veka* (Novosibirsk, 1981), pp. 35–57.

16. Fisher, R.H., *The Russian Fur Trade, 1550–1700* (Berkeley, 1943), p. 29.

17. Fisher, *The Russian Fur Trade*, pp. 118–22.

18. Martin, J., *Treasure of the Land of Darkness: The fur trade and its significance for medieval Russia* (Cambridge, 1986).

19. Sable and other pelts were bundled together in batches of 40, which was a standard computing measurement in the fur trade. The Russian word *sorok*, '40', is thought by some philologists to be cognate with the word *sorochka*, meaning a shirt, and in old Russian also a bag. The term for a bag containing 40 pelts has therefore survived in modern Russian as the regular numeral. In all other Slavonic languages, '40' is rendered as a variant of 'four tens'. This obviously underlines the central importance of the fur traffic in old Russian accounting methods. In the passage quoted, '61 forties and 31 sables' would therefore add up to 2,471 skins, a fabulously valuable haul, given the figures quoted by Fisher above.

20. For the full translated text of Beketov's report, see Dmytryshyn *et al.*, *Russia's Conquest of Siberia*, pp. 136–48.

21. Dmytryshyn *et al.*, *Russia's Conquest of Siberia*, pp. 202–05 (abridged).

22. Quoted in Okladnikov, *Istoriya Sibiri*, vol. 2, p. 40.

23. Yepifanov, P.P., 'K istorii osvoeniya Sibiri i Dal'nego Vostoka v XVII veke', *Istoriya SSSR*, no. 4 (1981), pp. 71–2; Safronov, F.G., 'Solevarennye promysly Okhotska v XVIII-pervoi polovine XIX v.', in Vilkov, O.N. (ed.), *Sibirskie goroda XVII-nachala XX veka* (Novosibirsk, 1981), pp. 144–54.

24. The most recent study in English of the early Siberian cossaks is Witzenrath, C., *Cossacks and the Russian Empire, 1589–1725: Manipulation, Rebellion and Expansion into Siberia* (London, 2007).

25. Armstrong, T., *Russian Settlement in the North* (Cambridge, 1965); Coquin, F.-X., *La Sibérie: Peuplement et immigration paysanne au XIX siècle* (Paris, 1969); Treadgold, D.W., *The Great Siberian Migration: Government and Peasant Resettlement from Emancipation to the First World War* (Princeton, 1957). For a discussion of the Soviet historiography, see Collins, D., 'Russia's Conquest of Siberia: Evolving Russian and Soviet Interpretations', *European Studies Review*, vol. 12, no. 1 (1982), pp. 17–43.

26. Collins, 'Russia's Conquest of Siberia', pp. 27–37.

27. *Muzhik* was a common Russian term to describe a male peasant.

28. Ustyugov, V., 'Osnovnye cherty russkoi kolonizatsii Yuzhnogo Zaural'ya v XVIII v.', in Shunkov, V.I. *et al.* (eds), *Voprosy istorii Sibiri i Dal'nego Vostoka* (Novosibirsk, 1961), pp. 67–8.

29. On the social consequences of the shortage of females in Siberia, see Wood, A., 'Sex and Violence in Siberia: Aspects of the Tsarist Exile System', in Massey Stuart, J. and Wood, A., *Siberia: Two Historical Perspectives* (London, 1984), pp. 23–42, and Gentes, A.A., '"Licentious girls" and frontier domesticators: women and Siberian exile from the late 16th to the early 19th centuries', *Sibirica: Journal of Siberian Studies*, vol. 3, no. 1, April (2003), pp. 3–20.

30. See Chapter One. For more detail on Avvakum's involuntary journey through Siberia, see Wood, A., 'Avvakum's Siberian Exile, 1653–64', in Wood, A. and French, R.A. (eds), *The Development of Siberia: People and Resources* (Basingstoke, 1989), pp. 11–34.

31. Still the most authoritative scholarly account of Avvakum's life and the origins of the Schism is Pascal, P., *Avvakum et les débuts du Raskol: La crise religieuse au XVIIe siècle en Russie* (Paris, 1938).

32. The quotation is, of course, a reference to King Henry II of England's famous plea for someone to dispose of his 'criminous cleric', Thomas à Becket, finally murdered in 1170.

Chapter 3   The Eighteenth Century: Exploration and Exploitation

1. The best modern account of the reign of Peter the Great is unquestionably Hughes, L., *Russia in the Age of Peter the Great* (New Haven and London, 1998). For an excellent concise introduction, see Swift, J., *Peter the Great* (London, 2000).

2. The most accessible scholarly analysis of the documents pertaining to Dezhnëv's voyage, and the historical controversy surrounding it, is Fisher, R.H., *The Voyage of Semen Dezhnev in 1648: Bering's Precursor. With Selected Documents* (London, 1981).

3. *Polnoe sobranie zakonov rossiiskoi imperii (PSZRI)*, first series (St Petersburg, 1830), vol. V, p. 607.

4. *Polnoe sobranie zakonov rossiiskoi imperii (PSZRI)*, vol. VII, p. 413.

Notes

5. Krasheninnikov, S.P., *Explorations of Kamchatka, 1735–1741*, translated with introduction and notes by E.A.P. Crownhart-Vaughan (Portland, 1972).
6. Krasheninnikov, *Explorations of Kamchatka*, pp. 267–8.
7. Svet, Ya. M. and Fedorova, S.G., 'Captain James Cook and the Russians', *Pacific Studies*, vol. 2, no. 1 (1982), pp. 1–19.
8. See, for example, Fisher, R.H., *Bering's Voyages: Whither and Why* (Seattle, 1977).
9. Lincoln, W.B., *The Conquest of a Continent: Siberia and the Russians* (London, 1994), p. 116.
10. Black, J.L., 'J.-G. Gmelin and G.-F. Müller in Siberia, 1733–43: A Comparison of their Reports', in Wood, A. and French, R.A. (eds), *The Development of Siberia: People and Resources* (Basingstoke, 1989), p. 38.
11. Black, 'J.-G. Gmelin and G.-F. Müller in Siberia, 1733–43', p. 39.
12. Gmelin, J.-G., *Reise durch Sibirien von dem Jahr1733 bis–1743* (Göttingen, 1751–2).
13. Müller, J.-G., *Istoriya Sibiri*, 3 vols, reprint (Moscow, 1999–2001); see also, Buse, D.K. and Black, J.L. (trans and eds), *G.-F. Müller in Siberia* (Kingston, Ontario, 1988).
14. Black, 'J.-G. Gmelin and G.-F. Müller in Siberia', p. 42.
15. Black, J.L., 'Opening up Siberia: Russia's "window on the East"', in Wood, A. (ed.), *The History of Siberia: From Russian Conquest to Revolution* (London and New York, 1991), pp. 64–5.
16. Black, J.L., 'Rediscovering Siberia in the Eighteenth Century: G.-F. Müller and the *Monthly Compositions*, 1755–1764', *Siberica*, vol. 1, no. 2, Winter (1990–91), pp. 112–26.
17. Mote, V.L., *Siberia: Worlds Apart* (Boulder, 1998), p. 58.
18. Figures taken from *Otechestvennaya istoriya: Istoriya Rossii s drevneishikh vremen do 1917 goda, Entsiklopediya*, vol. 2 (Moscow, 1996), pp. 14–15.
19. Most of the information in this section on eastern Siberia is taken from Komogortsev, I. I., 'Iz istorii chërnoi metallurgii Vostochnoi Sibiri v XVII–XVIII vv.', in Shunkov, V.I. (ed.), *Sibir' XVII–XVIII vv.* (Novosibirsk, 1962), pp. 97–120.
20. Komogortsev, 'Iz istorii chërnoi metallurgii Vostochnoi Sibiri v XVII–XVIII vv.', p. 109.
21. Komogortsev, 'Iz istorii chërnoi metallurgii Vostochnoi Sibiri v XVII–XVIII vv.', p. 111.
22. Komogortsev, 'Iz istorii chërnoi metallurgii Vostochnoi Sibiri v XVII–XVIII vv.', p. 119.
23. Quoted in Komogortsev, 'Iz istorii chërnoi metallurgii Vostochnoi Sibiri v XVII–XVIII vv.', p. 119.
24. *Aziatskaya Rossiya*, vol. 2 (St Petersburg, 1914), p. 187.
25. Danilevskii, V.V., *Russkoe zoloto: Istoriya otkrytiya i dobychi do serediny XIX v.* (Moscow, 1959).
26. Lincoln, *The Conquest of a Continent*, p. 184.
27. Lincoln, *The Conquest of a Continent*, p. 184.
28. The following section is a brief résumé of the present author's article, Wood, A., 'Siberian Exile in the Eighteenth Century', *Siberica*, vol. 1. no. 1, Summer (1990), pp. 38–63, in which much more information may be found.
29. Safronov, F.G., *Ssylka v Vostochnuyu Sibir' v XVII veke* (Yakutsk, 1967), p. 13.
30. Safronov, *Ssylka v Vostochnuyu Sibir' v XVII veke*, p. 20.
31. *Polnoe sobranie zakonov rossiiskoi imperii* (*PSZRI*), no. 1732, 24 November (1699).
32. Wood, 'Siberian Exile in the Eighteenth Century'.
33. 'Menshikov at Berëzov' is the subject of the famous painting of Menshikov surrounded by his children by V.I. Surikov (1883), which hangs in the State Tretyakov Gallery in Moscow.
34. Pushkin's unfinished tale of his ancestor (*Arap Petra Velikogo*, 1827) is to be found in English translation in Pushkin, A., *The Queen of Spades and Other Stories*, trans. Rosemary Edmonds (Harmondsworth, 1962), pp. 15–57.
35. Quoted in Safronov, F.G., 'Zapiski Genrikha Fika o yakutakh i tungusakh pervoi poloviny XVIII v.', in Pokrovskii, N.M. and Romodanovskaya, E.K. (eds), *Istochnikovedenie i arkheologiya Sibiri* (Novosibirsk, 1977), p. 244.
36. Kolesnikov, A.D., 'Ssylka i naselenie Sibiri', in Goryushkin, L.M. (ed.), *Ssylka i katorga v Sibiri (XVIII–nachalo XX v.)* (Novosibirsk, 1975), p. 51.

Chapter 4   The Nineteenth Century: Russian America, Reform and Regionalism

1. Klyuchevskii, V.O., *Kurs russkoi istorii*, 5 vols. (Moscow, 1937), vol. 1, pp. 20, 21.
2. Yadrintsev, N.M., *Sibir' kak koloniya. K yubileyu trekhsotletiya. Sovremennoe polozhenie Sibiri. Yeya nuzhdy i potrebnosti. Yeya proshloe i budushchee* (St Petersburg, 1882).

3. Gibson, J.R., 'Russian Expansion in Siberia and America: Critical Contrasts', in Starr, S.F. (ed.), *Russia's American Colony* (Durham, 1987), p. 37.

4. Pierce, R.A. (ed.), *Documents on the History of the Russian-American Company* (Kingston, 1976), p. 38.

5. Gibson, 'Russian Expansion in Siberia and America', p. 34.

6. Polevoi, B.P., 'The Discovery of Russian America', in Starr, S.F. (ed.), *Russia's American Colony* (Durham, 1987), p. 24.

7. Polevoi, 'The Discovery of Russian America', p. 25 and footnote 84.

8. Dmytryshyn, B., 'Introduction', in Dmytryshyn, B., Crownhart-Vaughan, E.A.P. and Vaughan, T. (eds), *Russia's Conquest of Siberia: A Documentary Record, 1558–1700* (Portland, 1958), p. xxx; Radishchev as quoted in Goluchikova, V.D. and Khvitsiashvili, Z.I. (eds), *Practical Dictionary of Siberia and the North* (Moscow, 2005), pp. 845–6.

9. Dmytryshyn, 'Introduction', p. xlv.

10. For a short discussion of the historical and historiographical debate, see Wood, A., *The Romanov Empire, 1613–1917: Autocracy and Opposition* (London, 2007), pp. 272–6.

11. Wood, *The Romanov Empire*, pp. 254–65.

12. Most of the facts and figures in this section are taken from Gibson, J. R., 'The Sale of Russian America to the United States', in Starr, S.F. (ed.), *Russia's American Colony* (Durham, 1987), pp. 271–94.

13. Still the most erudite and informative English-language treatment of Speranskii's life and achievements is Raeff, M., *Michael Speransky: Statesman of Imperial Russia, 1772–1839* (The Hague, 1957); see also, Raeff, M., *Siberia and the Reforms of 1822* (Seattle, 1956).

14. For a full discussion of Speranskii's disgrace and exile, see Raeff, *Michael Speransky*, pp. 170–203.

15. Raeff, *Michael Speransky*, p. 172.

16. Raeff, *Michael Speransky*, p. 22.

17. Raeff, *Michael Speransky*, p. 170.

18. Letter from Alexander I to Speranskii, 22 March 1819, quoted in Raeff, *Michael Speransky*, pp. 252–3.

19. On the inanity of the Romanov tsars, see Wood, *The Romanov Empire*.

20. See Raeff, *Michael Speransky*, and Raeff, *Siberia and the Reforms of 1822*.

21. Raeff, *Michael Speransky*, pp. 266–7.

22. Raeff, *Michael Speransky*, p. 259.

23. Von Mohrenschildt quotes Alexander I's Minister of the Interior, O.P. Kozodavlev, as saying: 'The history of Siberia will henceforth be divided into two epochs: from Ermak to Speransky, and From Speransky to X.' Von Mohrenschildt, D., *Toward a United States of Russia: Plans and Projects of Federal Reconstruction of Russia in the Nineteenth Century* (London and Toronto, 1981), p. 89. How the good minister could have come to this conclusion regarding the impact of Speranskii's 1822 reforms is rather puzzling. Kozodavlev died in 1819.

24. Dostoevskii, F.M., *Zapiski iz mërtvogo doma* (Moscow, 1861–2); for the most recent English translation, see Dostoyevsky, F., *The House of the Dead*, translated by D. McDuff (Harmondsworth, 1985).

25. Lampert, E., *Studies in Rebellion* (London, 1957), p. 12.

26. Quoted by Luchinskii, G.A., 'A.P. Shchapov: Biograficheskii ocherk', in Shchapov, A.P., *Sochineniya*, 3 vols (St Petersburg, 1906–08), vol. 1, p. XXXI.

27. Kabanov, P.I., *Obshchestvenno-politicheskie i istoricheskie vzglyady A. P. Shchapova* (Moscow, 1954), p. 85.

28. Mirzoev, V.G., *Istoriografiya Sibiri (Domarksistskii period)* (Moscow, 1970), p. 284.

29. Yadrintsev, *Sibir' kak koloniya*, pp. 223–96.

30. Yadrintsev, *Sibir' kak koloniya*, p. 378.

31. Joseph Lancaster (1778–1838) was an English Quaker and educational innovator. His 'method', popular in the United States in the early nineteenth century, involved the passing on of instruction from one successful pupil to another, now sometimes referred to as 'peer tutoring'.

32. Yadrintsev, *Sibir' kak koloniya*, pp. 379–80.

33. Mirzoev, *Istoriografiya Sibiri*, p. 298.

34. Mirzoev, *Istoriografiya Sibiri*, p. 308.

35. Yadrintsev, N.M., *Sibirskie inorodtsy. Ikh byt i sovremennoe polozhenie* (St Petersburg, 1891).

36. Mirzoev, *Istoriografiya Sibiri*, pp. 314–15.
37. Mirzoev, *Istoriografiya Sibiri*, p. 300.
38. See Wood, A., 'Chernyshevskii, Siberian Exile and *Oblastnichestvo'*, in Bartlett. R. (ed.), *Russian Thought and Society: Essays in Honour of Eugene Lampert* (Keele, 1984), pp. 42–66.
39. Venturi, F., *Roots of Revolution. A History of the Populist and Socialist Movements in Nineteenth Century Russia* (New York, 1966), p. 1.
40. Quoted in Koval', S.F., 'Kharakter obshchestvennogo dvizheniya 60-kh godov v Sibiri', in *Obshchestvenno-politicheskoe dvizhenie v Sibiri v 1861-1917gg. Materialy po istorii Sibiri: Sibir' perioda kapitalizma*, Part 3 (Novosibirsk, 1967), p. 39.
41. Koval', 'Kharakter obshchestvennogo dvizheniya 60-kh godov v Sibiri'.
42. A detailed analysis of the relationship between Chernyshevskii in exile, *oblastnichestvo* and the Polish uprising is in Wood, 'Chernyshevskii, Siberian Exile and *Oblastnichestvo'*, pp. 42–66.
43. For a discussion of the position taken by various scholars, see Sesyunina, M.G., *G.N. Potanin i N.M. Yadrintsev – Ideologi sibirskogo oblastnichestva: (K voprosu o klassovoi sushchnosti sibirskogo oblastnichestva vtoroi poloviny XIX v.* (Tomsk, 1974), pp. 8–16.
44. Von Mohrenschildt, *Toward a United States of Russia*, p. 103.
45. The most scholarly, exhaustive analysis of the 'Amur episode' in English is to be found in: Bassin, M., *Imperial Visions: Nationalist Imagination and Geographical Expansion in the Russian Far East, 1840–1865* (Cambridge, 1999). For a much briefer but equally erudite treatment see: Stephan, J.J., *The Russian Far East: A History* (Stanford, 1994), pp. 20–70.
46. Stephan, *The Russian Far East*, p. 46.
47. See Bassin, M., 'Dreams of a Siberian Mississippi', Chapter 5 of Bassin, *Imperial Visions*, pp. 143–73.

Chapter 5   The Native Peoples: Vanquished and Victims

1. Mirzoev, V.G., *Istoriografiya Sibiri (Domarksistskii period)* (Moscow, 1970), p. 308.
2. Okladnikov, A.P., *Otkrytie Sibiri* (Moscow, 1979), pp. 16–23; Okladnikov, A.P. *et al.* (eds), *Istoriya Sibiri s drevneishikh vremen do nashikh dnei*, vol. 1, *Drevnyaya Sibir'* (Leningrad, 1968).
3. The literature on the ethnography, history, culture, economy and languages of the aboriginal, non-European peoples of Siberia and the Russian Far East – both in Russian and in English – is enormous. Lack of space does not allow full reference to or annotation of all the materials in this book. Most of the information in the present chapter is based on data contained in the following sources: Yadrintsev, N.M., *Sibir' kak koloniya. K yubileyu trekhsotletiya. Sovremennoe polozhenie Sibiri. Yeya nuzhdy i potrebnosti. Yeya proshloe i budushchee* (St Petersburg, 1882), pp. 86–125; Yadrintsev, N.M., *Sibirskie inorodtsy. Ikh byt i sovremennoe polozhenie* (St Petersburg, 1891); Poddubnyi, I.P., 'Naselenie Aziatskoi Rossii: Ethograficheskii ocherk', in *Aziatskaya Rossiya*, vol. 1 (St Petersburg, 1914), pp. 93–178; Okladnikov, A.P. *et al.* (eds), *Istoriya Sibiri s drevneishikh vremen do nashikh dnei*, vol. 2, *Sibir' v sostave feodal'noi Rossii* (Leningrad, 1968), pp. 93–108; Forsyth, J., *A History of the Peoples of Siberia: Russia's North Asian Colony, 1581–1990* (Cambridge, 1992); Slezkine, Y., *Arctic Mirrors: Russia and the Small Peoples of the North* (Ithaca and London, 1994); Golubchikova, V.D. and Vkhtisiashvili, Z.I. (eds), *Practical Dictionary of Siberia and the North* (Moscow, 2005). References to further specialist publications are to be found in the notes and bibliographies contained in these works. The interdisciplinary academic journal, *Sibirica*, founded by the present author in 1981, has also, following a change of editorship, recently contained a large number of scholarly articles of a mainly ethnographical and anthropological nature. For further information, consult sibirica@abdn.ac.uk.
4. Readers interested in pursuing this topic are referred to Forsyth, *A History of the Peoples of Siberia*, and for a shorter, though superficial, discussion in Hutton, R., *Shamans: Siberian Spirituality and the Western Imagination* (London and New York, 2001), pp. 9–14.
5. Dolgikh, B.O., *Rodovoi i plemennoi sostav narodov Sibiri v XVII v.* (Moscow, 1960).
6. Okladnikov, *Istoriya Sibiri*, vol. 2, attachment.
7. *Aziatskaya Rossiya*, vol. 1, p. 81.
8. See the discussion (and table) by Forsyth, J., 'The Siberian native peoples before and after the Russian conquest', in Wood, A. (ed.), *The History of Siberia: From Russian Conquest to Revolution* (London and New York, 1991), pp. 69–91.
9. Okladnikov, *Istoriya Sibiri*, vol. 2, p. 100.

10. Forsyth, 'The Siberian native peoples before and after the Russian conquest', p. 74.
11. Quoted in Okladnikov, *Istoriya Sibiri*, vol. 2, p. 99.
12. Okladnikov, *Istoriya Sibiri*, vol. 2, p. 95.
13. Golubchikova and Khvtisiashvili, *Practical Dictionary of Siberia and the North*, p. 1062.
14. The 1897 census recorded only 948 native Yukagirs (as opposed to *c*.5,000 in the seventeenth century), falling to 700 in the early twentieth century. In 1989 those figures had risen to 1,142, of whom 726 lived in Sakha (Yakutiya) rather than their traditional homelands, Golubchikova and Khvtisiashvili, *Practical Dictionary of Siberia and the North*. N.B. some of these demographic reductions and fluctuations may be the result of assimilation rather than extermination, though the outcome in linguistic and cultural terms was the same.
15. Okladnikov, *Istoriya Sibiri*, vol. 2, p. 103.
16. Quoted in Taksami, C.M., *Nivkhi: (Sovremennoe khozyaistvo, kul'tura i byt)* (Leningrad, 1967), p. 9.
17. Golubchikova and Khvtisiashvili, *Practical Dictionary of Siberia and the North*, p. 14.
18. Golubchikova and Khvtisiashvili, *Practical Dictionary of Siberia and the North*, p. 14.
19. Hilger, M.I., 'Japan's "Sky People": the Vanishing Ainu', *National Geographic* (February, 1967), pp. 268–96.
20. Collins, D., 'Colonialism and Siberian Development: A Case-Study of the Orthodox Mission to the Altay', in Wood, A. and French, R.A. (eds), *The Development of Siberia: People and Resources* (Basingstoke, 1989), pp. 50–71.
21. See Dawkins, R., *The God Delusion* (London, 2006) and Hitchens, C., *God is not Great* (London, 2007).
22. Okladnikov, *Istoriya Sibiri*, vol. 2, p. 96.
23. Golubchikova and Khvtisiashvili, *Practical Dictionary of Siberia and the North*, p. 82.
24. Gudzii, N.K., *Zhitie protopopa Avvakuma: im samym napisannoe* (Moscow, 1960), p. 80 (translation by the current author).
25. Interview with Rupert Issacson, 'Midweek', BBC Radio 4, 4 March (2009). See also Isaacson, R., *The Horse Boy: A Father's Miraculous Journey to Save His Son* (London, 2009), pp. 84–5.
26. Golubchikova and Khvtisiashvili, *Practical Dictionary of Siberia and the North*, p. 844.
27. Diószegi, V., *Popular Beliefs and Folklore Traditions in Siberia* (Bloomington, 1968).
28. Raeff, M., *Michael Speransky: Statesman of Imperial Russia, 1772–1839* (The Hague, 1957), p. 272.
29. Forsyth, *A History of the Peoples of Siberia*, p. 157.
30. Yadrintsev, N.M., *Russkaya obshchina v tyur'me i ssylke* (St Petersburg, 1872).
31. Yadrintsev, N.M., *Sibirskie inorodtsy. Ikh byt i sovremennoe polozhenie* (St Petersburg, 1891).
32. Yadrintsev, N.M., *Sibir' kak koloniya. K yubileyu trekhsotletiya. Sovremennoe polozhenie Sibiri. Yeya nuzhdy i potrebnosti. Yeya proshloe i budushchee* (St Petersburg, 1882).
33. Yadrintsev, *Sibir' kak koloniya*, p. 87.
34. Yadrintsev, *Sibir' kak koloniya*, pp. 88–91.
35. Yadrintsev, *Sibir' kak koloniya*, pp. 91–2.
36. See Marsden, K., *On Sledge and Horseback to Outcast Siberian Lepers* (London, 1892).
37. Yadrintsev, *Sibir' kak koloniya*, p. 102.
38. Yepifanov, P.P., 'K istorii osvoeniya Sibiri i Dal'nego Vostoka v XVII veke', *Istoriya SSSR*, no. 4 (1981), p. 70.
39. Raeff, M., *Siberia and the Reforms of 1822* (Seattle, 1956), p. 112.

Chapter 6   'Fetters in the Snow': The Siberian Exile System

1. Fraser, J.F., *The Real Siberia: Together with an Account of a Dash through Manchuria* (London and New York, 1911), p. 4.
2. Though this statement may contain some truth, in several other respects Solzhenitsyn's views on the tsarist exile system are full of historical, statistical and chronological errors, too numerous to go into at this point. See Solzhenitsyn, A., *Arkhipelag GULag* (Paris, 1975), pp. 351–6; and for a brief critique, Wood, A., 'Solzhenitsyn and the Tsarist Exile System: A Historical Comment', *Journal of Russian Studies*, no. 42 (1981), pp. 39–43.
3. Genesis, chapter III, verse 23.
4. Genesis, chapter IV, verse 12.
5. On transportation to Australia, see Hughes, R., *The Fatal Shore: A History of the Transportation of Convicts to Australia, 1787–1868* (London, 1987). Nothing chronicling the entire

Notes

history of the Siberian exile system, on the sweeping scale of Hughes' book, so far exists, though a start has been made in Gentes, A.A., *Exile to Siberia, 1590–1822* (New York, 2008).

6. Brokgauz, F.A. and Yefron, I.A., *Entsiklopedicheskii slovar'* (St Petersburg, 1890–1907), vol. 61, p. 372.
7. Foinitskii, I.Ya., *Uchenie o nakazanii v svyazi s tyur'movedeniem* (St Petersburg, 1889), p. 260.
8. Fel'dshtein, G., *Ssylka: Ocherki eya genezisa, znacheniya, istorii i sovremennago sostoyaniya* (Moscow, 1893), pp. 2–3.
9. Foinitskii, *Uchenie o nakazanii v svyazi s tyur'movedeniem*, p. 158.
10. Maksimov, S.V., *Sibir' i katorga* (St Petersburg, 1900), p. 369.
11. Sofronenko, K.A. (ed.), *Pamyatniki russkogo prava, vi, Sobornoe ulozhenie tsarya Alekseya Mikhailovicha 1649 goda* (Moscow, 1957), articles x. 129, 198; xix. 13; xxi. 9, 10, 11, 15, 16; xxv. 3, 16. The direct reference to Siberia occurs in xix. 13, where it states that certain law-breakers should be flogged and 'exiled to the river Lena in Siberia'; otherwise only general directions are given, such as, 'to be sent to remote towns, wherever the sovereign orders'.
12. *Ssylka v Sibir': Ocherk yeya istorii i sovremennago polozheniya* (St Petersburg, 1900), p. 7.
13. Quoted in *Ssylka v Sibir'*, p. 17.
14. *Ssylka v Sibir'*, pp. 18–19.
15. All statistics taken from *Ssylka v Sibir'*, appendix 1, pp. 1–2.
16. Foinitskii, *Uchenie o nakazanii v svyazi s tyur'movedeniem*, pp. 283–4.
17. de Windt, H., *The New Siberia* (London, 1896).
18. 'Lestnitsa nakazanii', in Brokgauz and Yefron, *Entsiklopedicheskii slovar'*, vol. 35, pp. 177–8.
19. On Devil's Island, see Belbenoit, R., *Dry Guillotine: Fifteen Years among the Living Dead* (London and Toronto, 1938).
20. Stephan, J.J., *Sakhalin: A History* (Oxford, 1971), p. 65.
21. *Ssylka v Sibir'*, appendix 2, p. 4.
22. For a much fuller discussion see Wood, A., 'The Use and Abuse of Administrative Exile to Siberia', *Irish Slavonic Studies*, no. 6 (1985), pp. 65–81.
23. Solzhenitsyn, *Arkhipelag GULag*, p. 352.
24. *Ssylka v Sibir'*, p. 109.
25. Calculations based on statistical information in *Ssylka v Sibir'*, appendix 3, pp. 3–13.
26. Quoted in Roshchevskaya, L.P., 'Zapadnosibirskaya politicheskaya ssylka v period reaktsii 80-x godov XIX veka', in Goryushkin, L.M. (ed.), *Ssylka i obshchestvenno-politicheskaya zhizn' v Sibiri XVIII- nachalo XIX v* (Novosibirsk, 1978), p. 141.
27. Roshchevskaya, 'Zapadnosibirskaya politicheskaya ssylka', pp. 141–59.
28. Many examples and accounts of such barbaric treatment are to be found in Kennan, G., *Siberia and the Exile System*, 2 vols (New York, 1891), vol. 2, pp. 29–59, 507–9.
29. Margolis, A.D., 'O chislennosti i razmeshchenii ssyln'nykh v Sibir' v kontse XIX v', in Goryushkin, L.M. (ed.), *Ssylka i katorga v Sibiri (XVII–nachalo XX v.)* (Novosibirsk, 1975), pp. 232–3.
30. This and the following sections are a modified and abridged version of the present author's chapters entitled 'Administrative Exile and the Criminals' Commune in Siberia', in Bartlett, R. (ed.), *Land Commune and Peasant Community in Russia: Communal Forms in Imperial and Early Soviet Society* (Basingstoke, 1990), pp. 395–414, and 'Russia's "Wild East": exile, vagrancy and crime in nineteenth-century Siberia', in Wood, A. (ed.), *The History of Siberia: From Russian Conquest to Revolution* (London and New York, 1991), pp. 117–37.
31. Hobsbawm, E., *Social Bandits* (London, 1972).
32. Kennan, *Siberia and the Exile System*, vol. 1, p. 391.
33. Maksimov, *Sibir' i katorga*, p. 14.
34. Maksimov, *Sibir' i katorga*, pp. 17–18.
35. Kennan, *Siberia and the Exile System*, vol. 1, pp. 391–2.
36. Kennan notes that the word *varnak* has its origins in the old practice of branding highwaymen with the letters V.R.N.K., the initial letters in Russian for *vor, razboinik, nakazannyi knutom* (robber, brigand, flogged with the knout). 'By adding two "a's" to these letters, the word *varnak* was formed'. Kennan, *Siberia and the Exile System*, vol. 2, p. 463, footnote 5.
37. Kennan, *Siberia and the Exile System*, vol. 2, p. 462.
38. *Ssylka v Sibir'*, p. 207–8.

39. Chekhov, A.P., *Ostrov Sakhalin*, in Chekhov, A.P., *Polnoe sobranie sochinenii i pisem v tridtsati tomakh* (Moscow, 1978), vol. 14–15, pp. 328–9.

40. Maksimov, *Sibir' i katorga*, pp. 171–95, 237–47; Ptytsin, V., 'Iz proshlago: Zabaikalskie razboiniki', *Istoricheskii vestnik*, no. 40 (1890), pp. 237–9.

41. Yadrintsev, N.M., *Russkaya obshchina v tyur'me i ssylke* (St Petersburg, 1872), pp. 403–12, 424–5. This particularly horrific incident is described on p. 411.

42. On the role of women in Siberia see Wood, A., 'Sex and Violence in Siberia: Aspects of the Tsarist Exile System', in Massey Stuart, J. and Wood, A., *Siberia: Two Historical Perspectives* (London, 1984), pp. 23–42; also, Gentes, A.A., '"Licentious girls" and frontier domesticators: women and Siberian exile from the late 16th to the early 19th centuries', *Sibirica: Journal of Siberian Studies*, vol. 3, no. 1, April (2003), pp. 3–20.

43. Wood, 'Sex and Violence in Siberia', p. 41.

44. Anuchin, Y.N., *Izsledovaniya o protsente soslannykh v Sibir' v period 1827–1846 godov: Materialy dlya ugolovnoi statistiki Rossii* (St Petersburg, 1873).

45. Hobsbawm, *Social Bandits*, p. 85.

46. On job-related problems for exiles, see Badcock, S., '"Taming the Wild Taiga": Work in Siberian exile during the last years of Tsarism'. Unpublished paper presented at a conference of the British Association for Slavonic and East European Studies, University of Cambridge, March 2009 (referred to here with permission).

Chapter 7   The Last Tsar of Siberia: Railroad, Revolution and Mass Migration

1. Decree of 11 November 1721. Full text translated in Vernadsky, G., *A Source Book for Russian History from Early Times to 1917*, 3 vols (New Haven and London, 1972), vol. 2, p. 342.

2. Goryushkin, L.M., 'The economic development of Siberia in the late nineteenth and early twentieth centuries', *Sibirica: Journal of Siberian Studies*, vol. 2, no. 1 (2002), pp. 12–20. For an obituary and appreciation of Goryushkin's life and work, see Wood. A., 'Leonid Mikhailovich Goryushkin (1927–1999)', in *Sibirica: Journal of Siberian Studies*, vol. 2, no. 1 (2002), pp. 8–11.

3. Goryushkin, 'The economic development of Siberia', p. 13.

4. Okladnikov, A.P. (ed.), *Rabochii klass Sibiri v dooktyabrskii period* (Novosibirsk, 1982), and Okladnikov, A.P. (ed.), *Krest'yanstvo Sibiri v epokhu kapitalizma* (Novosibirsk, 1983).

5. Goryushkin, 'The economic development of Siberia', p. 14.

6. Goryushkin, L.M., 'Migration, settlement and the rural economy of Siberia, 1861–1914', in Wood, A. (ed.), *The History of Siberia: From Russian Conquest to Revolution* (London and New York, 1991), pp. 140–57.

7. Quoted in Goryushkin, 'Migration, settlement and the rural economy of Siberia', p. 149. Barabinsk and Chulym are regions of western Siberia.

8. Poppe, N., 'The economic and cultural development of Siberia', in Katkov, G. *et al.* (eds), *Russia Enters the Twentieth Century, 1894–1917* (London, 1973), p. 146.

9. Okladnikov, A.P. *et al.* (eds), *Istoriya Sibiri s drevneishikh vremen do nashikh dnei*, vol. 3 (Leningrad, 1968), p. 312.

10. Poppe, 'The economic and cultural development of Siberia', p. 146.

11. Quoted by Goryushkin, 'Migration, settlement and the rural economy of Siberia', p. 154.

12. Goryushkin, 'The economic development of Siberia', p. 19.

13. For table, detailed statistics and source, see Wood, A., *The Romanov Empire, 1613–1917: Autocracy and Opposition* (London, 2007), pp. 303–04.

14. Nekrasov, N.A., *Stikhotvoreniya* (Moscow, 1965), pp. 104–8; Tolstoi, L.N., *Anna Karenina* (Moscow, 1877).

15. Collins, D.N., 'Plans for Railway Development in Siberia, 1857–1890, and Tsarist Colonialism', *Siberica: A Journal of North Pacific Studies*, vol. 1, no. 2, Winter, (1991–2), pp. 128–50; Marks, S.G., *Road to Power: The Trans-Siberian Railroad and the Colonization of Asian Russia, 1850–1917* (London, 1991). See also Okladnikov, *Istoriya Sibiri*, vol. 3, pp. 175–80.

16. Mote, V.L., *Siberia: Worlds Apart* (Boulder, 1998), p. 50; Marks, *Road to Power*, p. 170–95.

17. It is often overlooked that Witte's own devotion to the principle of autocracy was demonstrated by his leading role in the formation of the so-called 'Sacred Host' (*Svyashchënnaya druzhina*), an

Notes

extreme right-wing, pro-monarchist, proto-fascist, militant Christian organization of nobles set up during the 1880s in response to increasing revolutionary activity in the country.

18. For more extensive and detailed analysis of the debate, see Collins, 'Plans for Railway Development in Siberia', and Marks, *Road to Power*.

19. Quoted in Collins, 'Plans for Railway Development in Siberia', p. 135.

20. Quoted in Marks, *Road to Power*, p. 54.

21. The metaphor of the 'Red Cockerel' derives from the image of wealthy landowners' manor houses torched and burning against the night sky, the flames resembling a cock's red comb – a common sight during this period.

22. See Marks, S.G., 'The Burden of the Far East: The Amur Railroad Question in Russia, 1906–1916', *Sibirica: The Journal of Siberian Studies*, vol. 1, no. 1 (1993–4), pp. 9–28.

23. Interestingly, the more northerly west-east plan more or less followed the route of the Baikal-Amur Mainline (BAM) constructed during the 1970s and 1980s – see Chapter Ten.

24. Mote, *Siberia: Worlds Apart*, p. 51.

25. Florinsky, M.T., *Russia: A History and an Interpretation*, vol. 2 (New York, 1966), p. 1262.

26. Florinsky, *Russia: A History and an Interpretation*, p. 1267.

27. Perrins, M., 'Russian Military Policy in the Far East and the 1905 Revolution in the Russian Army', *European Studies Review*, vol. 9 (1979), pp. 331–49 (quotation, p. 333).

28. Perrins, 'Russian Military Policy in the Far East', pp. 333–4.

29. Florinsky, *Russia: A History and an Interpretation*, p. 1275.

30. See Sablinsky, W., *The Road to Bloody Sunday: Father Gapon and the St Petersburg Massacre of 1905* (Princeton, 1976).

31. Reichman, H., 'The 1905 Revolution on the Siberian Railroad', *Russian Review*, vol. 47 (1988), pp. 25–48 (quotation, p. 25).

32. See Bushnell, J., *Mutiny amid Repression: Russian Soldiers in the Revolution of 1905–1906* (Bloomington, 1985).

33. Reichman, 'The 1905 Revolution on the Siberian Railroad'.

34. Okladnikov, *Istoriya Sibiri*, vol. 3, p. 253.

35. Okladnikov, *Istoriya Sibiri*, vol. 3, pp. 248–9.

36. The Imperial Manifesto of 17 October 1917, drafted by Witte in an attempt to take the revolutionary wind out of the people's sails, legalized political parties, even those of the extreme left, and promised the promulgation of a constitution of sorts and elections to a national quasi-parliamentary assembly called the State Duma. On the spread of the revolutionary movement in Siberia between 1905 and 1907, see Okladnikov, *Istoriya Sibiri*, vol. 3, pp. 251–98.

37. Okladnikov, *Istoriya Sibiri*, vol. 3, p. 252.

38. Goryushkin, L.M. *et al.* (eds), *Krest'yanskoe dvizhenie v Sibiri, 1861–1917: Khronika i istoriografiya* (Novosibirsk, 1985), appendices, pp. 310–26.

39. Goryushkin, L.M. *et al.* (eds), *Krest'yanskoe dvizhenie v Sibiri, 1907–1914: Khronika i istoriografiya* (Novosibirsk, 1986), appendices, pp. 206–7.

40. Lenin, V.I., *Two Tactics of Social-Democracy in the Democratic Revolution*, in Lenin, V.I., *Lenin: Selected Works*, 2 vols (London, 1947), vol. 1, pp. 343–435 (quotation, p. 373).

41. Treadgold, D.W., *The Great Siberian Migration: Government and Peasant Resettlement from Emancipation to the First World War* (Princeton, 1957).

42. Treadgold, *The Great Siberian Migration*, p. 156.

43. Based on figures compiled from a variety of sources by Treadgold, *The Great Siberian Migration*, Table 3, p. 34.

44. Treadgold, *The Great Siberian Migration*, p. 33.

45. Okladnikov, *Istoriya Sibiri*, vol. 3, p. 301.

46. Okladnikov, *Istoriya Sibiri*, vol. 3, p. 301.

47. Okladnikov, *Istoriya Sibiri*, vol. 3, pp. 302–3.

48. Treadgold, *The Great Siberian Migration*, Table 3, p. 34.

49. This is the title of the most recent western monograph on the subject: Melancon, M., *The Lena Goldfields Massacre and the Crisis of the Late Tsarist State* (Texas 2006).

50. Wood, *The Romanov Empire*, p. 340.

51. Du Maurier, G., *Trilby* (London, 1894); quote from 1994 reprint, pp. 46–7.

Chapter 8   Red Siberia: Revolution and Civil War

1. This chapter is an expanded and reworked version of Wood, A., 'The Revolution and Civil War in Siberia' in Acton, E. *et al.* (eds), *Critical Companion to the Russian Revolution, 1914–1921* (London, 1997), pp. 706–18, where more references can be found.
2. The term 'Kadet' is derived from the initial Cyrillic letters 'Ka' and 'De', designating Constitutional Democratic Party. Its original name was the Party of Popular Freedom, and its programme was initially based on the principles of Western-style parliamentary democracy and constitutional monarchy.
3. For a clear and detailed analysis of the Siberian regionalists' activities during the Revolution and Civil War see Pereira, N.G.O., 'Regional Consciousness in Siberia before and after October 1917', *Canadian Slavonic Papers*, vol. XXX, no. 1, March (1988), pp. 112–33, and Allison, A.P., 'Siberian Regionalism in Revolution and Civil War, 1917–1920', *Siberica*, vol. 1, no. 1, Summer (1990), pp. 78–97.
4. Goryushkin, L.M., 'Esery v Sibirskoi ssylke v gody pervoi mirovoi voiny', in Bochanova, G.A. *et al.* (eds), *Politicheskaya ssylka i revolyutsionnoe dvizhenie v Rossii, konets XIX – nachalo XX v.* (Novosibirsk, 1988), pp. 107–25.
5. The literature on the subject is enormous, but for a very brief summation and further bibliographical references see Wood, A., *The Origins of the Russian Revolution, 1861–1917*, 3rd edn (London, 2003), and Wood, A., *The Romanov Empire, 1613–1917: Autocracy and Opposition* (London, 2007), pp. 309–15.
6. On War Communism, see Nove, A., *An Economic History of the USSR* (Harmondsworth, 1986), pp. 46–82.
7. Melgunov, S.P., *Tragediya Admirala Kolchaka* (Begrade, 1930), p. 133.
8. Quoted in Pipes, R., *The Russian Revolution, 1899–1919* (London, 1992), p. 627 (with amendments).
9. Pipes, *The Russian Revolution*, p. 629.
10. Alioshin, D., *Asian Odyssey* (London, 1941), p. 48.
11. A recent pop-biography of Ungern-Sternberg, sensationalized and not very scholarly, but conveying a flavour of the man's bestiality, is Palmer, J., *Bloody White Baron* (London, 2008).
12. Palmer, J., *Bloody White Baron*, p. 67.
13. Lincoln, W.B., *The Conquest of a Continent: Siberia and the Russians* (London, 1994), p. 301–2.
14. In Russian historical terminology, the suffix '-shchina' is often attached to the name of an individual who has lent his name to a particularly notorious, usually violent, passage of events: e.g. the *Pugachëvshchina*, after Emelyan Pugachëv, leader of a huge cossak rebellion during the reign of Catherine the Great, and the *Yezhovshchina*, after Nikolai Yezhov, head of Stalin's NKVD and orchestrator of the 'Great Terror' and purges of the late 1930s (see Chapter Nine).
15. Named after Aleksandr Kerenskii (1881–1970), leader of the last Provisional Government in 1917.
16. Smele, J., *Civil War in Siberia: The Anti-Bolshevik Government of Admiral Kolchak, 1918–1920* (Cambridge, 1996), pp. 401–2.
17. Wood, *The Romanov Empire*, p. 372.
18. Pereira, N.G.O., *White Siberia: The Politics of Civil War* (Montreal, Kingston and London, 1996), pp. 91–7.
19. *Concise Oxford English Dictionary*, 6th edn (Oxford, 1976). For a recent critical history of the Romanov dynasty, see Wood, *The Romanov Empire*.
20. Smele, *Civil War in Siberia*, pp. 131–2.
21. Smele, *Civil War in Siberia*, pp. 427–3.
22. Memorandum from Knox to the War Office, August 1918, quoted in Smele, J.D., 'The White Movement in Siberia: Economic and Other Aspects of Kolchak's Failure', unpublished paper presented to the Soviet Industrialization Project Series, University of Birmingham, February, 1997, p. 3.
23. Smele, 'The White Movement in Siberia', p. 6.

Chapter 9   Siberia under Stalin: Growth, GULag and the Great Patriotic War

1. Lewin, M., *Lenin's Last Struggle* (London, 1969 and 1973), pp. 77–103.
2. On language and literacy policy, see Forsyth, J., *A History of the Peoples of Siberia: Russia's North Asian Colony, 1581–1990* (Cambridge, 1992), pp. 283–7.

Notes

3. The word *kulak* in Russian literally means a fist. It began to be used in late nineteenth-century Russia as a pejorative term to designate members of the most wealthy stratum of the peasant class who benefited from the post-emancipation settlement to become more prosperous at the expense of the 'middle' and 'poor' peasantry. The term was extremely imprecise and elastic in its definition and was later to be used indiscriminately by Stalin against those in agrarian society whom he considered were opposing or 'sabotaging' his own economic policies in the countryside.

4. Hughes, J., *Stalin, Siberia and the Crisis of the New Economic Policy* (Cambridge, 1991), p. 22.

5. Hughes, *Stalin, Siberia and the Crisis of the New Economic Policy*, p. 22.

6. Hughes, *Stalin, Siberia and the Crisis of the New Economic Policy*, pp. 23–4.

7. Hughes, *Stalin, Siberia and the Crisis of the New Economic Policy*, p. 4.

8. During a recent visit to Vladivostok, the present author overheard a local Inturist guide explaining proudly and emphatically to her group of Western tourists who had just visited Novosibirsk and Irkutsk: 'You are no longer in Siberia; you are now in the Far East.'

9. Golubchikova, V.D. and Khvitisiashvili, Z.I. (eds), *Practical Dictionary of Siberia and the North* (Moscow, 2005), pp. 614–15.

10. Stephan, J.J., *The Russian Far East: A History* (Stanford, 1994), p. 174.

11. Mote, V.L., *Siberia: Worlds Apart* (Boulder, 1998), p. 89.

12. Stephan, *The Russian Far East*, pp. 174–5.

13. Stephan, *The Russian Far East*, pp. 177–8.

14. For example, see Wood, A., 'Russia's "Wild East": exile, vagrancy and crime in nineteenth-century Siberia', in Wood, A. (ed.), *The History of Siberia: From Russian Conquest to Revolution* (London and New York, 1991), pp. 117–37.

15. Statistics from Golubchikova and Khvtisiashvili, *Practical Dictionary of Siberia and the North*, p. 613.

16. Golubchikova and Khvtisiashvili, *Practical Dictionary of Siberia and the North*, pp. 613–14.

17. Forsyth, *A History of the Peoples of Siberia*, pp. 244–5.

18. Golubchikova and Khvtisiashvili, *Practical Dictionary of Siberia and the North*, p. 373.

19. Morray, J.P., *Project Kuzbas: American Workers in Siberia (1921–1926)* (New York, 1983).

20. The best modern account of the collectivization of the peasantry in Siberia is the innovative Hughes, J., *Stalinism in a Russian Province: Collectivization and Dekulakization in Siberia* (Basingstoke, 1996), from which this section derives much of its material.

21. There is a large literature on the Soviet collectivization drive in general, but see in particular Lewin, M., *Russian Peasants and Soviet Power: A Study of Collectivization* (London, 1968); and Nove, A., *An Economic History of the USSR* (Harmondsworth, 1986), pp. 136–87.

22. Golubchikova and Khvtisiashvili, *Practical Dictionary of Siberia and the North*, p. 176.

23. Golubchikova and Khvtisiashvili, *Practical Dictionary of Siberia and the North*, p. 177.

24. Full translation in Stalin, J., *Works*, vol. 12 (Moscow, 1955), pp. 197–205.

25. Stalin, *Works*, p. 200.

26. Hughes, *Stalinism in a Russian Province*, p. 206.

27. Hughes, *Stalinism in a Russian Province*, p. 209.

28. Mote, *Siberia: Worlds Apart*, p. 91.

29. Lincoln, W.B., *The Conquest of a Continent: Siberia and the Russians* (London, 1994), p. 322.

30. All figures taken from Okladnikov, A.P. *et al.* (eds), *Istoriya Sibiri s drevneishikh vremen do nashikh dnei*, vol. 4 (Leningrad, 1968), pp. 352–6, 391–4.

31. See for example: Conquest, R., *The Great Terror* (Harmondsworth, 1971); Pohl, J.O., *The Stalinist Penal System: A Statistical History of Soviet Repression and Terror, 1930–1953* (Jefferson and London, 1997); Medvedev, R., *Let History Judge* (New York, 1971); Carrère d' Encausse, H., *Stalin: Order through Terror* (London and New York, 1981); Thurston, R.W., *Life and Terror in Stalin's Russia, 1934–1941* (New Haven and London, 1996); Rayfield, D., *Stalin and his Hangmen* (London, 2004).

32. Solzhenitsyn, A., *The Gulag Archipelago* (London 1987).

33. Applebaum, A., *Gulag. A History of the Soviet Labour Camps* (London, 2003).

34. *Grani*, no. 62 (1966), quoted in Wood, A. 'The Resurgent Russian Intelligentsia', in Parekh, B. (ed.), *Dissent and Disorder: Essays in Social Theory* (Toronto, 1971), p. 91.

35. Lincoln, *The Conquest of a Continent*, p. 335.

36. Mote, *Siberia: Worlds Apart*, p. 94. See also Shifrin, A., *The First Guidebook to the Prisons and Concentration Camps of the Soviet Union* (Toronto, London and New York, 1982). It is also important to put on record that, despite the lionization of Solzhenitsyn in the West, he was essentially

an egocentric *litterateur*, a writer of fiction, rather than an objective historian, whose figures and 'facts' must be treated with some caution.

37. The following few titles represent a mere handful of the abundant GULag memoir literature available in English: Ginzburg, E.S., *Into the Whirlwind* (Harmondsworth, 1967); Petrov, V., *It Happens in Russia: Seven Years Forced Labour in the Siberian Goldfields* (London, 1951); Štajner, K., *7000 Days in Siberia* (London, 1989); Bardach, J. and Gleeson, K., *Man is Wolf to Man: Surviving Stalin's Gulag* (London, 2003); Panin, D., *The Notebooks of Sologdin* (London, 1976); Shalamov, V., *Kolyma Tales* (London, 1994). See also Dallin, D.J. and Nicolaevsky, B.I., *Forced Labour in Soviet Russia* (London, 1948); Roerder, B., *Katorga: An Aspect of Modern Slavery* (London, 1958); Scholmer, J., *Vorkuta: The story of a slave city in the Soviet Arctic* (London, 1954); Pohl, *The Stalinist Penal System*; Gregory, P.R. and Lazarev, V. (eds), *The Economics of Forced Labour: The Soviet Gulag* (Stanford, 2003).

38. Applebaum, *Gulag. A History of the Soviet Labour Camps*, pp. 515–16.

39. See for instance: Applebaum, *Gulag. A History of the Soviet Labour Camps*, pp. 515–22; Pohl, *The Stalinist Penal System*, pp. 10–11; Nove, A., 'Victims of Stalinism: How Many?', in Getty, J.A. and Manning, R.T. (eds), *Stalinist Terror: New Perspectives* (Cambridge, 1993), pp. 261–74; and Wheatcroft, S.G., 'More light on the scale of repression and excess mortality in the Soviet Union in the 1930s', in Getty, J.A. and Manning, R.T. (eds), *Stalinist Terror: New Perspectives* (Cambridge, 1993), 275–90.

40. On Stalin's purge of the Far Eastern cadres, see Stephan, J.J., '"Cleansing" the Soviet Far East, 1937–1938', *Acta Slavica Iaponica*, Tomus X (1992), pp. 43–64; Khisamutdinov, A., 'Death on the Outskirts of Red Russia: The Mechanism and the Personnel', in Khisamutdinov, A. (ed.), *The Russian Far East: Historical Essays* (Honolulu, 1993), pp. 103–29.

41. Lincoln, *The Conquest of a Continent*, p. 359.

42. Quoted in Florinsky, M.T., *Russia: A History and an Interpretation*, vol. 2 (New York, 1966), p. 675, footnote.

43. Erickson, J., 'Military and Strategic Factors', in Wood, A. (ed.), *Siberia: Problems and Prospects for Regional Development* (London, New York and Sydney, 1987), pp. 171–92.

44. Figures quoted in Erickson, 'Military and Strategic Factors', p. 178.

45. Erickson, 'Military and Strategic Factors', p. 180.

46. Erickson, 'Military and Strategic Factors', p. 181. Much of the intelligence on Japan's military intentions and plans in the Far East and the Pacific was provided by the brilliant Soviet spy based in Tokyo, Richard Sorge. See Deakin, F.W. and Storry, G.R., *The Case of Richard Sorge* (London, 1966).

47. Mote, *Siberia: Worlds Apart*, p. 101.

Chapter 10   Siberia since Stalin, 1953–91: Boom, BAM and Beyond

1. Khrushchev, N.S., *Doklad na zakrytom zasedanii XX s"ezda KPSS: "O kul'te lichnosti i ego posledstviyakh"* (Moscow, 1959); English translation in Khrushchev, N.S., *The Dethronement of Stalin* (Manchester, 1956).

2. The concept of 'thaw' as a symbol of post-Stalin relaxation and reform is derived from the title of the novel by Ehrenburg, I., *Ottepel'* ('The Thaw') (Moscow, 1954).

3. Applebaum, A., *Gulag: A History of the Soviet Camps* (London, 2003), pp. 430–2.

4. Applebaum, *Gulag*, pp. 435–53.

5. Applebaum, *Gulag*, p. 451–3.

6. Solzhenitsyn, A., 'Odin den' Ivana Denisovicha', *Novyi mir*, no. 11 (1962), pp. 8–74.

7. Conolly, V., *Beyond the Urals: Economic Developments in Soviet Asia* (London, 1967), p. 222.

8. See, for a brief example, Zaslavskaya, T.I. *et al.*, 'Social Development of Siberia: Problems and Possible Solutions', in Wood, A. and French, R.A. (eds), *The Development of Siberia: People and Resources* (Basingstoke, 1989), pp. 177–87.

9. *Sibirskoe otdelenie Akademii nauk SSSR* (Moscow, 1982), pp. 7–9.

10. Josephson, Paul R., *New Atlantis Revisited: Akademgorodok, the Siberian City of Science* (Princeton, 1997).

11. Trofim Denisovich Lysenko (1898–1976) was a charlatan 'geneticist' and pseudo-agronomist whose bogus, unscientific theories, based on falsified data, on acquired characteristics being

Notes

hereditable – which found favour with the political establishment – both dominated and retarded the development of genetic science in Russia for over a generation. Not until 1965 were his grotesque theories officially repudiated. See Medvedev, R., *The Rise and Fall of T.D. Lysenko* (New York, 1969).

12. Quoted in *Sibirskoe otdelenie Akademii nauk SSSR*, p. i.

13. Hughes, J., 'For sale – Russia's best brains', *Guardian*, 15 September (1992); Gentleman, A., 'Town where a Soviet dream turned sour', *Guardian*, 24 July, (2000); Gentleman, A., 'Russia's best brains for sale', *Guardian*, 25 July (2000). The struggle between academic freedom in Akademgorodok and the political establishment still apparently continues in post-Soviet Russia. Recent censorship and professional sanctions against the eminent historians, Professors V.L. Soskin and S.A. Krasylnikov, at Akademgorodok's Institute of History have recently come to light and have been widely condemned by the international academic community. For more detailed information, visit http://socialist.memo.ru/forum/index.php? [accessed 22 November 2010].

14. Wilson, D., 'The Siberian Oil and Gas Industry', in Wood, A. (ed.), *Siberia: Problems and Prospects for Regional Development* (London, New York and Sydney, 1987), pp. 100, 111. Wilson's article contains many more detailed data on Siberian oil and gas development and production figures during the 1970s and 1980s.

15. Wilson, 'The Siberian Oil and Gas Industry', p. 127.

16. All figures taken from Golubchikova, V.D. and Khvtisiashvili, Z.I. (eds), *Practical Dictionary of Siberia and the North* (Moscow, 2005), pp. 303–4 and 664–5.

17. Quoted in Lincoln, W.B., *The Conquest of a Continent: Siberia and the Russians* (London, 1994), p. 399.

18. Lincoln, *The Conquest of a Continent*. See also *Sibirica* (Special issue on the Oil and Gas Industry, Communities and the State), vol. 5, no. 2, Autumn (2006).

19. Mokhortov, K., 'The Road into Tomorrow', in Sobelev, I. (ed.), *The Great Baikal-Amur Railway* (Moscow, 1977), p. 7.

20. Quoted by Conolly, V., 'The Baikal-Amur Railway (The Bam)', in Wood, A. (ed.), *Siberia: Problems and Prospects for Regional Development* (London, New York and Sydney, 1987), p. 167.

21. See Salisbury, H.E., *The Coming War between Russian and China* (London, 1969). Salisbury's prescient analysis of the border tensions between the two Communist powers exploded into reality in March 1969: see 'Shest' tochek zreniya na vopros o sovetsko-kitaiskom voennom konflikte', in *Politicheskii dnevnik, 1964–1970* (Amsterdam, 1972), pp. 630–38.

22. Mote, V.L., *Siberia: Worlds Apart* (Boulder, 1998), pp. 119–23.

23. For instance between 1980 and 1983, the high point of the construction programme, *c.*4,000 earthquakes on that level were registered in the BAM zone: Shemanayev, V.A., 'BAM Conquers Siberia', *Railway Gazette International*, July (1983), p. 524.

24. Shemanayev, 'BAM Conquers Siberia'.

25. Mote, *Siberia: Worlds Apart*, p. 122.

26. Translated excerpts in Sobelev, I. (ed.), *The Great Baikal-Amur Railway* (Moscow, 1977), pp. 12–13 and 105–7.

27. See, for example, *BAM – Stroika veka: vo'smoi vypusk* (Moscow, 1984), pp. 338–41.

28. Golubchikova and Khvtisiashvili, *Practical Dictionary of Siberia and the North*, p. 76.

29. Golubchikova and Khvtisiashvili, *Practical Dictionary of Siberia and the North*, p. 76.

30. This final section is based on a paper delivered by the present author to a conference in Moscow in September 1993 on 'Democracy and Minorities in Post-totalitarian Societies', later published as 'Sibirskii regionalizm: Proshloe, nastoyashchee, budushchee', in Tishkov, V.A., Savoskul, S.S. *et al.* (eds), *Rasy i narody: Yezhegodnik*, no. 24, (Moscow, 1997), pp. 203–17.

31. Granberg, A.G., 'Sovremennye problemy ekonomicheskoi samostoiatel'nosti Sibiri', and Brodkin, F.M. and Pushkarev, V.M., 'Sovremennye problemy samoupravleniya gorodov Sibiri': papers presented at a symposium on 'self-government in Siberia', Novosibirsk, 6–7 February 1990.

32. Dienes, L., 'Crime and Punishment in the USSR: New Information on Distribution', *Soviet Geography*, vol. 29, no. 9, November (1988), pp. 793–808.

33. *Izvestiya*, 11 May (1989).

34. Lester, D. and Kondrichin, S., 'Research note: Suicide and homicide in Siberia', *Sibirica: Journal of Siberian Studies*, vol. 3, no. 1 (2003), pp. 103–07.

35. Ries, N., quoted in Holzlehner, T., '"The Harder the Rain, the Tighter the Roof": Evolution of Organized Crime Networks in the Russian Far East', *Sibirica*, vol. 6, no. 2, Autumn (2007), pp. 51–86.

36. Holzlehner, T., '"The Harder the Rain, the Tighter the Roof"', pp. 53–4.

37. Bradshaw, M.J., *Siberia at a Time of Change: New Vistas for Western Investment*, Economist Intelligence Unit, Special Report No. 127 (London, 1992), pp. 12–32.

38. Hughes, J., 'Regionalism in Russia: The Rise and Fall of Siberian Agreement', *Europe-Asia Studies*, vol. XLVI, no. 7 (1994) pp. 1133–61.

39. Duncan, P.J.S., 'The Politics of Siberia in Russia', *Sibirica: The Journal of Siberian Studies*, vol. 1, no. 2 (1994–5), pp. 13–23.

40. Bradshaw, *Siberia at a Time of Change*, Appendix 2, pp. 116–36; see also pp. 92–103.

41. Bradshaw, *Siberia at a Time of Change*, p. 117.

42. But see also Kirkow, P., 'Russia's Gateway to Pacific Asia', *Sibirica: The Journal of Siberian Studies*, vol. 1, no. 2, (1994–5), pp. 51–9.

43. For details of these and other research institutes dedicated to the study of Baikal, see Galazii, G.I., *Baikal v voprosakh i otvetakh*, 3rd edn (Moscow, 1988), p. 17.

44. Information obtained by the present author on personal visits to Novosibirsk, corroborated in Hughes, 'For sale – Russia's best brains'.

45. *Sibirskaya gazeta*, April (1990).

46. Vinogradov, F.G., 'Rabochaya pechat' v Sibiri: Istoricheskii ocherk', in *Iz proshlogo Sibiri* (Omsk, 1927), pp. 10–12.

47. Gillespie, D., 'A Paradise Lost? Siberia and its writers, 1960 to 1990', in Diment, G. and Slezkine, Y., *Between Heaven and Hell: The Myth of Siberia in Russian Culture* (New York, 1993), pp. 255–73. Quote, p. 256.

48. Quoted by Sallnow, J., 'Siberia's Demand for Labour: Incentive Policies and Migration, 1960–85', in Wood, A. and French, R.A. (eds), *The Development of Siberia: People and Resources* (Basingstoke, 1989), pp. 188–207, quote p. 202.

49. *Pravda*, 7 September (1985), quoted in Sallnow, 'Siberia's Demand for Labour'.

50. In addition to Sallnow, 'Siberia's Demand for Labour', see also Zaslavskaya *et al.*, 'Social Development of Siberia', and Bradshaw, *Siberia at a Time of Change*, pp. 33–42.

51. *Izvestiya*, 1 April (1990).

52. Golubchikova and Khvtisiashvili, *Practical Dictionary of Siberia and the North*, p. 67.

53. Kiselev, L., 'Sibir' ustavshaya', *Krasnoyarskii rabochii*, 24 April (1992).

54. *Krasnaya zvezda*, 22 September (1990) and 25 November (1990), quoted in *SUPAR Report*, no. 10, January (1991), p. 201. For brief biographical information on Zabolotnikov, see *SUPAR Report*, no. 10, p. 19.

55. *Rezolyutsiya I-go s"ezda narodnykh deputatov Sibiri po voprosu: O pravovom, ekonomicheskom i sotsial'nom polozhenii territorii Sibiri*, First Congress of People's Deputies of the Territories of Siberia, Final Report (Krasnoyarsk, 1992).

56. Quoted in *SUPAR Report*, no. 13, July (1992), p. 134.

57. 'We are no thieves: we fight against the government', *Moscow News*, no. 38, 20–27 September (1992), p. 11.

58. See Chapter Four.

Index

Index

Index